Schultz

Gordon Craig

GORDON CRAIG

CRAIG

The Story of His Life

by Edward Craig

Alfred·A·Knopf·New York·1968

ACKNOWLEDGEMENTS

The author and publishers would like to thank those who have graciously given permission to quote from copyright material: to Mrs. Eva Reichmann for the use of extracts from the works of the late Sir Max Beerbohm; to Mr. D'Arcy Hart, of Gilbert Samuel and Company, for permission to use extracts from Ellen Terry's unpublished letters; to Mr. Kerrison Preston for permission to quote from the late W. Graham Robertson's preface to The Art of the Theatre; *to Lord Howard de Walden for permission to quote from his late father's correspondence; to C. Walter Hodges, F.S.I.A., Laurence Irving, O.B.E., and David Magarshack, B.A., for permission to quote from their works and correspondence; and to Mr. Howard C. Rice of Princeton University, for permission to quote from the M.S. of the late Sylvia Beach.*

Passages from My Life in Art *by Constantin Stanislavski, translated by J. J. Robbins, Copyright 1924 by Elizabeth Reynolds Hapgood for the Stanislavski Estate, are reprinted with the permission of the publishers, Theatre Arts Books, New York, and Geoffrey Bles, London. Thanks are also due to Charles Scribner's Sons of New York, to quote from James Huneker's* Iconoclasts.

Dedicated to the memory of my father

What we believe in waits latent forever through all the continents,
Invites no one, promises nothing, sits in calmness and light, is positive and
composed, knows no discouragement,
Waiting patiently, waiting its time.
—Walt Whitman

Contents

Illustrations

line drawings

Introductory Notes and Acknowledgements

SEVERAL BOOKS have been written about Gordon Craig, but most of them suffer from a lack of information, including his own *Index to the Story of My Days*, which only covers the years up to 1907 and therefore excludes a large and important segment of his life. Some years ago, my father suggested that I should complete this work for him, but such a task seemed beyond me, for I could scarcely hope to emulate his delightfully individual style. Nevertheless, I began to organize the material that I had with a view to preparing it for use in a biography later.

For many years I was my father's assistant, so I knew the significance of all the documents in my collection. I knew the various codes that he enjoyed using (for he revelled in a bit of mystery), and I also knew the identities concealed by the strange names that he applied to friends and enemies alike, and the many initials, some inverted, which he used when making overcritical remarks about certain people in his correspondence and day-books. Above all, I knew and understood the workings of his mind.

I think we were very close; he seemed to think so too, for an entry in one of his diaries reads:

In any case Teddy and I were so much, so *well* in touch, that at long distance we knew each's thoughts and acted often as one—

and in a long letter to me years later, he wrote:

Come fine shine, dark death, stay firm about me—because there never were two who were so one as we were—and spite of my faults —and yours, we will remain so—

These, I suppose, could be my credentials.

As a boy, I was always fascinated by the stories of the lives of my parents and grandparents; this probably pleased them, for they seemed to enjoy telling me more and more, and often took me to the places associated with family history. Once, as a Christmas treat, my grand-mother, Ellen Terry, took me, together with my mother and sister, on a pilgrimage, visiting all the places where she had spent her early days with Edward Godwin. From our inn at St. Albans, we drove out each day to some house or landmark where she would recount every episode in detail, and as she was welcome wherever she went, we were able to go over the rooms in "The Red Cottage," "Fallows Green," and many other places in the neighbourhood. Later, we visited "The Audrey Arms" at Uxbridge and "Vine Cottage" at Putney, and in London, 20 Taviton Street and 22 Barkston Gardens, also the stage-doors of the Princess's Theatre and the Queen's Theatre, Long Acre, and many other places that have now disappeared for good. She told us endless stories of home life with her parents, Ben and Sarah, and these we asked for time and time again. Her picture of her parents differed slightly from that depicted by Marguerite Steen in *A Pride of Terrys*, for she seemed to remember her father's courage and whimsical turn of mind with greater relish than her mother's rather dour approach to life.

Ellen was very fond of my mother, who acted as her companion in the war years of 1914–17. She confided in her a great deal, particularly about her early life with Watts, Godwin, and Kelly. To her, Elena's romance with her son was in many ways a repetition of her own romance with Godwin, and my sister and I became, once again, her own little Teddy and Edy.

I remember my thrill on realizing that fate or chance had once brought my father's mother and my mother's father together, long before my own parents were born! They often talked of those distant days when she was young Mrs Watts and, with her husband, visited Mr Burne-Jones in his studio where, he, young Signor Gaetano Meo, was working as his assistant!

In Heidelberg, Berlin, and Weimar my father took me to all the haunts of his youth, and I grew up in Florence and Rapallo, where so much of his most important work took place.

I have noticed that as people grow older, the storehouse of their memories becomes so crowded that past names and dates get disordered or lost as they try to make room for the new arrivals; worse still, as the past recedes, their attitude towards it sometimes changes.

When my father wrote of his early days in his book *Woodcuts and Some Words*, he was only fifty-two, and he was gay about the past. He wrote *Index to the Story of My Days* between the ages of eighty-one and eighty-five, when he could not be bothered to verify details and had become bitter in his memories of certain friends, even people whom he had once loved—hence the unfair comments about his first wife, May, and about Jess, to whom he refers as "ABC"; at the same time he over-romanticized the description of his first meeting with Isadora Duncan, and, it would seem, did not refer to his note-books made at the time of their association, which are full of delightful accounts and many interesting perceptions.

In order to avoid similar pitfalls I feel that it is essential for me to compile this account before I am too old myself! I make no pretence at being a writer, but as a research worker I know the value of putting on record what information I have acquired from a study of my documents, what I have learned from personal knowledge and what I found out from other sources, so that those who can weave patterns with words will at least have a correct outline to follow.

Although many have attempted to write about Gordon Craig's work, no one has been able to write about his life—Gordon Craig, the man, has always remained hidden.

My father's character was so complex that students still find it difficult to understand him. His whimsical moments were intermingled with periods of vision and enlightenment, his caprices with his serious work; his sixty or seventy pseudonyms were the clever but infuriating masks that concealed his identity while he acclaimed or ridiculed friends, attacked enemies, and praised unknowns.

It is interesting to note that he never used his father's name. From birth he was known as "The Feather of England" and "Master Teddy"; Edward Wardell was the first name that he adopted and the one he used at school; Gordon Craig was the name he chose for the stage; his first pseudonym was Oliver Bath, and after that his invention knew no bounds.

He was lazy in his youth and learned very little, but as he grew older, nature endowed him with extraordinary powers of perception, and when he encountered an artist or craftsman doing this or that, or a poet or sage saying something profound, it all came to him as a revelation—

a discovery—*his* discovery—and the way in which he adapted or moulded each discovery so that he could use it in the theatre, his sole preoccupation, was quite astoundingly inventive.

If one or another person exhilarated him to the extent that it helped him with an idea, he would consume that person, then discard their shattered and disillusioned remains—in the same way that other creative artists consume spirits and toss the empty bottle into the dustbin. And in this respect he was particularly ruthless with women.

Inwardly, he lacked self-assurance, and, like his father, was always looking for some boost to his ego—hence his tremendous outpouring of letters and the almost feverish concern with which he awaited the replies. He particularly liked writing amorous letters to women; they generally succumbed easily to his charm, so he was certain of the kind of reply that would provide the boost he required. In the first part of his memoirs he goes so far as to say:

For to please women became my deepest real delight—and one or two I did please. Yet often I felt it was all acting—not real . . .

He had no time for people who were not outspoken and fearless, and he liked those who treated him as their equal, provided that they respected his only love—the theatre. So it was that he found Italy to be the land in which he was happiest.

He was a sensualist, and as he ran his sensitive fingers over a piece of Genoese damask, an African mask, or a penny wooden toy, his eyes would glow as, in his imagination, he communed with the mind of the artist or craftsman who had made the object, participating in the idea that the object celebrated.

He always enjoyed the simplest food, provided it was beautifully cooked—he could never understand why he could not get herrings and mustard sauce in Italy!

While smoking an ordinary Italian Toscana cigar, or listening to a street musician, he would follow the smoke, or the sound, and travel into realms of fancy such as others can only know when stimulated by drugs. He liked wine with his food but did not care for spirits.

In Tuscany or Liguria, as we silently walked the ancient Roman roads shaded by olive trees, he would stop and listen to the cicale, breathe deeply the olive-scented air, and say, "Ah, I can smell ancient

Rome," then, quite easily, begin to talk about one of the Caesars as though he had known him intimately. He was a voracious reader and had a wonderful memory; without hesitation he could locate a passage in a book that had once interested him, even when he had not looked at the volume for some years.

When he was working on some idea, anything irrelevant to that idea would not be tolerated: "Get rid of that chattering fool; she's getting in the way of my thoughts"; "Light some incense in the other room . . . ah, that helps"; "Read me that piece of Ariosto in Italian" . . . "that's enough—that's enough—now run away." Later, listening, one could hear the deep voice intoning the last few words of the poem over and over again, as a drawing or engraving developed at incredible speed in the green light reflected through the shutters of his workroom.

Under the self-assured façade that most people encountered was a man that few ever knew: the real, tragic, despairing, self-doubting artist, struggling with perspective and sciagraphy, trying to teach himself to write and to draw. Nor did many know the happy man, divorced from his disguises, trying to forget his work as he played bowls with Italian peasants, or rocked with laughter in a third-rate music-hall, or rowed a boat across the Gulf of Rapallo, singing Cockney and Florentine songs alternately, or the child let out from school, when we all played silly games together.

Whatever faults Gordon Craig may have had, whatever his deceptions, however thoughtless he may have been in his treatment of people, one thing will for ever redeem his character: the inspiration he gave to others. The imaginative quality of his designs will remain an almost spiritual stimulus to young artists in the theatre, and among his writings are passages that will always encourage them, for his ideas were big, he had great courage in pursuing them, and *his mind raced years ahead of his time*. That he died without demonstrating the major work of his life leaves us with an inheritance that is still a challenge to the future.

Recent Books on Gordon Craig

Mention should be made here of some of the books already published on Gordon Craig's life and work, among which the outstanding ones are:

Gordon Craig and the Theatre, by Enid Rose; Sampson Low, 1931.

Edward Gordon Craig, Designs for the Theatre, by Janet Leeper; Penguin Books, 1948.

Gordon Craig, by Ferruccio Marotti (Italian); Capelli, 1961.

Edward Gordon Craig, by Denis Bablet (French); L'Arche, 1962. English translation: Heinemann, 1966.

Of these, Marotti's book is the first to show that original sources of information have been tapped. With the others, there is evidence that Craig himself had guided the writers, and, for some unknown reasons, had often withheld documents or supplied them with incorrect information, some of which he himself incorporated in his own memoirs.

I have had to start my account long before Gordon Craig's birth because it is only when one knows something about his mother, Ellen Terry, and father, Edward William Godwin, that one can *begin* to understand him. In the light of more recent evidence I have also had to correct certain stories concerning this relationship. The two most recent books bearing on this subject are either too romantic or the authors were unaware of the wealth of material that is still waiting to be examined: Marguerite Steen's delightful story entitled *A Pride of Terrys* (Longmans, 1962) is the work of a famous novelist and not of a historian; Dudley Harbron's interesting book *The Conscious Stone— The Life of Edward William Godwin* (Latimer House, 1949) is written from an architect's point of view, and reveals a lack of biographical information.

My Sources of Reference

At the end of the text the reader will find a list of sources consulted. Among them appear the following references: E.T. Personal, E.G.C. Personal, Elena Personal, and Edy Personal; these indicate that the source is from first-hand memories passed on to me by Ellen Terry, Gordon Craig, Elena Gordon Craig, and Edith Craig.

The various groups of manuscripts and other documents in my own collection will be referred to as Author's Collection; but, together with other material such as scene designs, models, photographs, copperplates, wood-blocks, etc., it has been referred to elsewhere as the Craig Archives, Bledlow. To give a detailed list of all the documents which I have consulted would take too many pages, for they run into thousands, but I can at least give an outline of the main groups that make up this collection.

For information concerning my father's early days I have used many of his boyhood letters to his mother and his sister, Edith Craig, but I have chiefly used the hundreds of letters from mother to son which only came to light after the death of Christopher St. John, who had once had access to them when, with Edith Craig, she re-edited Ellen Terry's memoirs.

For the early days with his first wife, May, and later, with Jess, I have had to refer to the bundles of their respective letters (preserved, until her death, by my mother). Covering this same period are letters from Henry Irving, William Terriss, James Pryde, and many lesser-known companions of his youth.

In 1897 my father met Martin Shaw, who became his closest friend, collaborator, and confidant. Through the hundreds of letters that he wrote to Martin (who died in 1958) I have not only been able to follow my father's work in all its details, but even his very way of thinking. I owe an everlasting debt of gratitude to Martin's widow, Mrs Joan Shaw, for the generous way in which she has helped me by putting these letters at my disposal.

Covering one of the most exciting periods of his life, between the years 1900 and 1904, when he first made a break with the conventional form of theatrical production, I have many files of correspondence which include letters from W. B. Yeats, William Rothenstein, Haldane MacFall, P. G. Konody, etc. There are also prompt-books, note-books, sketch-books, and scrap-books, as well as his private correspondence with my mother which started in 1901 and continued whenever they were apart until her death in 1957. His manuscript "Book of Confessions 1901–2–3" is, in itself, a most fascinating study of the inner workings of an artist's mind.

Gordon Craig went to Berlin in 1904 thinking he would be back in a few months; instead, he stayed on in Europe for the rest of his life, only visiting the land of his birth occasionally. In 1905 he met Maurice Magnus, who became his assistant, and also tried to look after Isadora Duncan's business while Craig was her manager. Years after Magnus's tragic suicide in Malta in 1920, I acquired a number of his files of correspondence covering the period with my father: this material has proved of extreme importance since it includes letters to and from Dr

Otto Brahm, Max Reinhardt, Count Kessler, Eleonora Duse, and Stanislavsky, along with folders of bills, receipts and bank returns, and a tremendous amount of information about the Isadora Duncan–Craig business partnership. I also have a copy of Magnus's manuscript outline for a *Life of Gordon Craig* written in 1907, which contains a lot of interesting contemporary records of Craig's remarks on various subjects.

For the more intimate aspects of the Craig-Isadora relationship I have referred to the many little Note-books in which he recorded their times together; these he gave into my safe keeping a few years before he died.

From 1908 until his death he kept Day-books in which he recorded his thoughts about all that happened. He gave me those volumes that covered the years 1908 to 1943 when I first talked about writing an account of his life, and instructed me to edit the contents, for he realized that he had written some rather unkind remarks about a few of his friends, and many libellous ones about his enemies!

Dorothy Nevile Lees, who was associated with him during the entire period in which *The Mask* was published, wrote me many interesting letters, before she died in 1965, telling me of their early work together. I also have the files of correspondence relating to the publication of *The Mask* for 1907–08–09, and other files for 1927 when I was associated with its publication.

From my mother, I inherited all the correspondence concerning the School and the Society for the Art of the Theatre, both of which she took such a prominent part in forming, and a fascinating folder of illustrated notes by my father on all the subjects to be studied by the pupils at his school.

After I left home and married in 1928, my father and I wrote to each other regularly, and this correspondence continued until a week or so before his death, when he could no longer hold a pen and just sent me his thumb-print and a kiss. These letters, which display his beautiful calligraphy at its best, fill many boxes.

He left written instructions as to what should happen to his collection, should he die before it was properly housed, and in a special reference to the model stage on which he conducted all his experiments, he wrote:

The only man who can set this model up . . . is Edward Anthony Carrick (Craig) for he worked under me in 1919–20–21 etc. . . . He should then teach some young men and women how I worked it and why . . . if he remembers.

This experience would be very difficult to forget, in fact it stands out in my mind as one of the happiest and most inspiring periods I spent with him, when, as his assistant, I recorded each day's work with notes and plans as we went along—but this information cannot be included in a volume devoted to his life.

His notes about his great idea for *Scene* are preserved in two places, namely, the Bibliothèque de l'Arsenal in Paris, and the University of California, Los Angeles—but of course I was familiar with them before they became the property of these institutions. The working model that I made of this, his masterpiece, was, unluckily, destroyed many years ago, although fortunately I was able to preserve some of the notes about the experiments we made with it.

Lastly, I have letters to and from his publishers in regard to most of his books, starting with *The Art of the Theatre* in 1905, finished and unfinished manuscripts of plays for *The Drama for Fools*, numerous projects for unfinished books, unexpurgated typescripts of the "Shaw–Terry Correspondence," and so on. All the above material has helped me to know still better a man whom I thought I already knew . . . and loved.

Although this book has been at the back of my mind for many years, I did not make a public appeal for help until after my father's death. Quite a number of the subsequent replies were most enlightening, enabling me to fill in the missing pieces of the giant jig-saw puzzle that I was trying to put together. I would like to record my special thanks to those people whose letters were particularly helpful:

Mrs Maggie Dale, the original "Little Maggie Adamson" who danced in *Acis and Galatea* and was also in *Bethlehem* and *The Vikings*.

Miss Lilian Bishop, one of six sisters who appeared in *Acis and Galatea*.

Mrs Dorothy Rhodes, who was also with the Purcell Operatic Society, and whose husband appeared in *Bethlehem*.

Mrs Norah Paget, daughter of the late Mrs N. F. Dryhurst who, with Martin Shaw, started the Purcell Operatic Society.

Mrs Violet M. MacDonald, who was so helpful concerning the first performance of *Dido and Aeneas*, and drew me such an accurate plan of the old Hampstead Conservatoire of Music.

Mrs Maud Barfield, once Miss Maud Douie, who so kindly lent me the manuscript of her memoirs, full of the most vivid pictures of those early days in Hampstead when she was rehearsing for *Dido and Aeneas*, and later, for *Bethlehem*. She is also the only person, to my knowledge, who ever signed on to join Gordon Craig's first school in London.

Mr Stanley Watkins, who gave me such a lucid description of Rose Cottage, Hackbridge, where he also used to live.

Mr C. R. Snow, the grandson of Mrs Jane Ellis, "Teddie's" first nurse, (the much adored "Essie"), for sending me copies of family letters about "The Feather of England."

Mr Derek Hudson, who so generously lent me all the letters that my father had written to him about Jimmy Pryde.

Mr Howard C. Rice of Princeton University Library, who drew my attention to their valuable collection of papers relating to Sylvia Beach in which Gordon Craig is mentioned.

Mr Stanley Scott, who helped me with very interesting material about the production of *Bethlehem*.

Miss Nelly Pocock and Mr Paul Sheren, who were both so helpful over the George Tyler production of *Macbeth*.

I am also grateful to Monsieur André Veinstein, Curator of the Bibliothèque de l'Arsenal, Paris, and to Mr Wilbur Smith, Curator of Special Collections, University of California, Los Angeles, who now holds important documents that I have used in the past.

Very special thanks are due to:

Heinrich Heim, who not only secured my father's release from internment during the last world war, but has since been most generous in helping me with details of his experiences at the time of the German occupation of Paris.

My sister Nelly (Miss Ellen Gordon Craig), who sent me such wonderfully vivid letters about all that was happening in Vence while she did such a fine job looking after Father during the last nine years of his life.

Miss Maudie Gibson, who helped me with notes and photographs of the Gibson family.

And to Rosie, my half-sister (Mrs Unsworth), who also helped with information, family photographs, and encouragement.

Then there are two special people, Olive and Lee, to whom I owe so much:

Mrs Olive Chaplin, Ellen Terry's favourite niece, who over the years has added to my collection of family anecdotes and has so often handed on invaluable information concerning my father. In her presence one is still aware of the spirit of Florence Terry, her mother, and of Ellen.

Lee Freeson of Hollywood, a fervent admirer of my father's work, who has always found me any books I needed and to whose encouragement, generosity and friendship I owe more than I can possibly express here.

Last, but not least, come thanks to those special people without whom this book would never have been done at all:

Patrick Gregory of New York, for his encouragement and valuable advice.

Mrs Christina Towler, who copied the hundreds of my grandmother's and my father's letters so that they could be referred to more easily in typescript, and battled with bits of illegible script in abnormally quick time.

And, in true theatrical tradition, at the foot of the bill in large letters, comes my wife, MARY, who has helped me in so many, many ways while I have relived the ninety-four years of my father's extraordinary life; her encouragement and criticism and hours of work late into the night have been the most important factors of all in the realization of this work.

Gordon Craig

CHAPTER ONE

Ellen Terry and Edward Godwin
1872–1875

I⊤ WAS Tuesday, January 16, 1872. Ellen was staying at the midwife's little house on the outskirts of Stevenage. It was nearing four o'clock in the morning, but the room was golden from the light of the oil-lamps and the large coal fire that burned in the cast-iron grate. Outside, snow was falling in the silent night; inside, there was a quiet, confident bustle, for a baby was coming into the world.[1]

When Ellen was handed her baby and realized that it was a boy, she was as happy and proud as any little girl with a new doll. He was so light that she immediately christened him "The Feather of England"[2]—part of Ellen's loveliness was her whimsical streak. When she had recovered from her excitement she decided to call him Edward after his father, whom she adored, and soon he acquired the nickname Teddy; later, Teddy was to become Ted, and finally, sixteen years later, the Church was to christen him "Edward Henry Gordon Craig."

His mother, Ellen Alice Terry, was then a little-known actress of twenty-five. His father, Edward William Godwin, F.S.A., was an established architect.

In 1861, when Godwin was twenty-eight, in open competition and against great opposition, his designs had been selected for the enormous town hall at Northampton.[3] He was already well known as a theatre critic whose writings had torn many notable productions to shreds. His ideas about furniture and modern dress were discussed by all those who were interested in the new aesthetic movement which, while being ridiculed by *Punch* as "too utterly utter," finally led the way to what we now describe as Art Nouveau. Oscar Wilde referred to him as "one of the most artistic spirits in England."

Although Godwin was nicknamed "The Wicked Earl" by some of his lady friends, he was rather unapproachable and an introvert. He was essentially an Anglo-Saxon, with an aloof exterior that few could penetrate, but he was greatly admired by a close circle of friends which included William Burges, the architect; W. G. Wills, the dramatist; and later, by Oscar Wilde and Herbert Beerbohm Tree. Ellen was very much a Celt, and a complete extrovert loved by all who came in contact with her warm-hearted nature.

Godwin was pleased when he heard that they had a boy, for they already had a little girl called Edith. He would have liked to spread the news of the birth among his friends, but although he was a revolutionary concerning many things in life he was a little self-conscious about his relationship with Ellen: when they had eloped, his first wife was dead, but Ellen had only been separated, not divorced from her first husband, George Frederic Watts. He had one friend to whom he could tell the exciting news and that was Whistler—James McNeill Whistler, the delightful but irascible Bohemian—the only real man friend he ever had; so these two met at the Arts Club in Hanover Square and drank to the health and the future of little Edward.[4]

Ellen Terry is now such a well-known personality in the history of the English theatre that it would seem almost unnecessary to retrace her life again, but it is essential to this story that we know a little more about her, and her relationship with Godwin, during that period in her life which is still shrouded in mystery.

She was born in theatrical lodgings in Coventry in 1847, while her father was on tour in a small part with Miss Acosta's company. Mr and Mrs Terry liked Coventry and had often stayed at the homely lodgings in Market Street, conveniently near the Theatre Royal.[5]

Ben Terry was a carefree, imaginative Irishman from Cork, who had spent most of his life in Portsmouth. He played the fiddle, and would try his hand on almost any other musical instrument that was available. He told wonderful yarns, was very handsome, and had a twinkling eye. He was a born entertainer and as a young man would willingly perform for hours to please the customers at his father's public house, The Fortune of War, where he would place a chair on one of the large tables, and from this lofty position young Terry would play to the sailors and their girls while they danced around him. Eventually, to placate his father he took a job at the Portsmouth theatre. It was then that he persuaded Sarah Ballard to marry him, and, because he liked the carefree life of the theatre people, he was ready to throw his luck in with theirs and take to the road.[6]

No one will ever know how Sarah found the courage to marry Ben. She was a Scot, a Wesleyan, very pretty and very Victorian in her outlook. She had been taught to distrust all men, but Ben she had known since childhood. In 1838 these two spirited young people realized that they were both twenty-one and therefore officially "free," and this realization may have precipitated the wedding. Anyhow, Ben was so full of Irish humour; to him, the future rose in the east, and why should he turn to watch it set in the west? So they went off with the players and started to build one of the most celebrated families in English theatrical history. Ellen was their fourth child. Kate, who was three years older, was to be the cleverest actress in the family; Ellen was to have the most charm.

In 1862 this family of players, who had been wandering over England, got a more or less permanent job with a stock company at the Theatre Royal in Bristol. By that time they had six children. Being with a stock company meant that they could plan a year ahead, and that was very heartening. James Henry Chute, a much respected man, was lessee of the Theatre Royal Bristol and the Theatre Royal Bath; he had already engaged Kate, and now Ellen was to join her. The whole family could certainly afford to settle there for a while.[7]

Bristol was a beautiful town with stately tea–clippers sailing slowly up the Avon and anchoring very close to the theatre. The centre of the town was engulfed in a forest of masts, while the air was full of the smell of tar, spices, tobacco, and leather. On the surrounding hills, looking down upon the harbour, were the many beautiful houses, villas, squares, and churches where the wealthy merchants and their families lived.

The Theatre Royal was in King Street, only a very short walk away from Queen Square, where, at No. 51, Ben found some attractive rooms for his family.[8] Queen Square, surrounded on three sides by ships' masts, reminded him of his earlier days in Portsmouth and his parents' home in Cork.

B

The Terry girls were soon regarded with some affection, and the number of young men waiting at the stage-door to catch a glimpse of their natural beauty grew to a crowd. Sarah Terry was worried about this attention paid to her daughters, for she was ambitious about their futures and hoped that they would all marry "gentlemen" and be "looked up to" in the world. She had learned that raising children in theatrical lodgings was a hard way to live; she began to rebel against the theatre. Ben, however, was delighted by the profession; the glorious sound of words, the scenery, the costumes, the orchestra tuning up— the whole idea of make-believe pleased his romantic soul.[9]

Among those in Bristol who took an interest in the family was a well-known architect and his delicate wife, Mr and Mrs Godwin. The girls often saw him by himself at the theatre, particularly on benefit nights, and one day they were invited to a "Shakespeare Reading" at the Godwins' house in Portland Square, for Mr Godwin was Secretary of The Bristol Shakespeare Society. While Kate behaved like a well-bred young lady, Ellen, who was only fourteen, could hardly contain her excitement at seeing the many treasures that filled the place. Apart from the Oriental carpets there was an impressive collection of blue china. Ellen asked about everything, and Godwin, who most people found aloof and reserved, responded with delight to her enquiries. He told her about his friends among the skippers of sailing ships, and how they brought him, from the Far East, many of the things in his house. He showed her his drawings of the archaeological remains around Bristol. In the hall downstairs he played some Bach for her on the organ.[10] He was twenty-nine, he treated her as an equal, and she thought he was marvellous. To add to her excitement, she learned that he was the mysterious "G" who, under the heading of "Theatrical Jottings," had been writing such interesting and helpful things in *The Western Daily Press* about their performances.

Before Ellen left the Chute management to come up to London where she had an engagement, she was to go over to Bath to play Titania in *A Midsummer Night's Dream* and The Spirit of the Future in a dramatic prologue for the opening night of the *new* Theatre Royal, which had just been built to the design of Godwin's friend C. J. Phipps. The programmes were to be printed on silk!

She told Mr Godwin about this coming event and he immediately became interested, telling her all about the ancient Greeks and their clothes. He demonstrated how a Greek woman's dress was washed and then pulled lengthways and slowly screwed up until it looked like a bundle of knots—when it was dry it had the wrinkled surface of *crêpe* that made the whole garment cling to the body. Together they made her dress for Titania. She loved it, but the management wouldn't let her wear it.[11]

Shortly after that she went to London—back to disenchantment and the drudgery of a theatre with uninteresting parts, filthy backstage conditions, rat-infested scene docks, Green Room gossip and scandal. The only bright spots were Sunday visits with Kate to Tom Taylor, the theatre critic of *The Times*, at his handsome house in Wandsworth.

The house was in a crescent called Lavender Sweep. Here she met exciting and intelligent people, rather like the Godwins. Tom Taylor seemed to have all the Terrys' futures at heart, and was impressed by what his friend Charles Dickens thought of Kate, and predicted a great future for her.

Tom Taylor was a journalist. He knew the power of the press and intended to make use of it. He was also a barrister, and knew everyone —including the eminent painter Watts. George Frederic Watts, R.A., was forty-six, a pampered guest in the vast Kensington home of his friends the Thoby Prinseps, who regarded him as the reincarnation of some great Renaissance artist. They built him a studio in their house and waited on him hand and foot, as did Mrs Prinsep's sisters, Lady Somers and Mrs Margaret Cameron.

In those days artists were always looking for models who would "inspire" them. The Pre-Raphaelites, then in full cry, were searching for that "perfect face," and Tom Taylor thought he had found the perfect face for Watts, and asked Mrs Terry if he could take Kate round to meet the famous painter. Some say that he was thinking only of Kate's future . . . Mrs Terry agreed, provided that Kate was chaperoned by her sister.

Watts was enchanted, and shortly after suggested that the girls pose for a combined portrait, to be called "The Sisters." Very soon his attention was focused upon Ellen alone and the picture now remains with Kate only roughly sketched in. Ellen was always thrilled by everything at Little Holland House; like Mr Godwin's house at Bristol it was full of attractive things, but they were more ornate—most of them came from Italy, and Mr Watts was so kind and let her roam about as though she was at home.[12]

Watts was impressed by Ellen's simple, extrovert personality, her beauty, and her youthful charm. She was at the age when she bestowed on all whom she liked an unaffected love as naturally as the sun gives out its light and heat; it bathed all who were near her in its warmth. Her eyes were wide and sincere, her mouth was large and curvaceous and always ready to smile, and when she encountered anything that she thought was lovely her mouth parted slightly as she murmured a soft "oh" to herself. Her eyes danced like her father's, and her hands were always the hands of an eager, beautiful child that longs to touch the things it loves. She was also capable of great outbursts of joy, which she showed in a very un-Victorian way! She would suddenly dance in the middle of the room, or make "an appearance" dressed in someone's hat and coat, which she had found in the hall.[13]

Watts felt she ought to be taken away from the theatre and all its horrible surroundings and the doubtful characters that inhabited the shadows behind the stage. He talked about it much to Tom and to the Prinseps—that is to say, to Thoby Prinsep, his wife, and her two sisters, all of whom, like the witches in *Macbeth*, stirred the cauldron of Watts's life and decided on his future.

Shortly afterwards Mr Watts called on the Terrys and suggested marrying their daughter Ellen. This was a shock to Ben, but not to Sarah. She had been worried ever since the girls went to "pose" for this "artist," however celebrated he might be, and when Ellen had once told her mother that Mr Watts had kissed her good-bye, she became quite anxious. Now she thought that marriage was a very good idea and the sooner the better. Ellen felt it was an honour—fancy being "married"—it was like being offered a new, exciting part in a play.

This girl of sixteen was married on February 20, 1864, to a cosseted artist of forty-six, and went to live in a house that was not even her husband's, and of which she could never be the mistress. There she was to be treated like a wayward child, a young actress who must forget the stage and learn to be circumspect and a proper wife for the "Signor." She was scolded for doing the most natural things—when she appeared with her long hair flowing loose over her shoulders she was accused of being improperly dressed. Her new life had about it the worst aspects of

Victorian snobbery. But it pleased Mrs Terry to think that her daughter was now well placed.

Ellen grew ill posing incessantly for Watts, and although she admired him and loved her surroundings, she inwardly loathed her position in relation to the ladies who organized his life. It was a travesty of what marriage should be.

Then it happened—no one knows what, but suddenly Ellen was in disgrace and she was returned, bag and baggage, to her family at 32 Stanhope Street near Regent's Park, like a piece of merchandise that had proved unsatisfactory. There is only one person who can tell about this period without dramatizing it, and that is Ellen herself:

When it suddenly came to an end, I was thunderstruck and refused at first to consent to the separation, which was arranged for me in much the same way as my marriage had been. The whole thing was managed by those kind friends whose chief business in life seems to be the care of others. I don't blame them. There are things for which no one is to blame. "There do exist such things as honest misunderstandings," as Charles Reade was always impressing on me at a later time. There were no vulgar accusations on either side, and the words I read in the deed of separation, "Incompatibility of temper" —a mere legal phrase—more than covered the ground. Truer still would have been 'incompatibility of *occupation*," and the interference of well-meaning friends. We all suffer from that sort of thing. Pray God one be not a well-meaning friend one's self![14]

I think that one day she could stand the situation no longer and told the interfering ladies of Little Holland House what was on her mind, and that was the end. She was back home, a failure within a year of her marriage. The deed of separation followed in due course, dated January 26, 1865.

Back at Stanhope Street, her mother gave her a room apart. After Little Holland House she loathed the furniture and the drabness of it all. The younger members of the family wondered why she had come home.

A family of artists, known as the Casellas, took her with their daughters to Paris for a holiday. Then Tom Taylor, who perhaps felt a little responsible, tried to make amends; he found her a part at the Olympic in *The Hunchback*; Kate was there, and concentration on work helped a little.

Just after Ellen had returned to her family, Edward Godwin took offices in London at 23 Baker Street, where he established his business.[15] He was at that time designing the Town Hall at Congleton and collaborating with Burges on the designs for the new law courts in the Strand. Sometimes he stayed in rooms above his office, sometimes with Burges's father at Blackheath. He was also interested in Crisp's report about a new theatre project for Bristol. Godwin had always been interested in the theatre and it was not long before he was going to the plays. He also went to see the New Queen's in Long Acre: it was a brand-new theatre designed by his friend C. J. Phipps and he wanted to know more about it. Outside the theatre the posters told him that little Ellen of the Bristol days, now twenty, was appearing in *A Double Marriage*.[16]
After the show he went round to reintroduce himself: Ellen was overjoyed; her mother was not, particularly when she heard that Mrs Godwin had died in Bristol; she had never taken to Mr Godwin. Godwin, unaware of this, visited the theatre whenever he could.
In 1866 the outlook was gloomy. Stanhope Street seemed a sad and lonely place; the soot-covered brick houses around her depressed Ellen. She had no work, and would wander into near-by Regent's Park where she could breathe fresh air and walk among the shrubs and trees.
Sometimes her walk would take her to Clarence Gate and out of the Park and down Baker Street to number 23, where she would sit talking to Godwin while he was drawing. Godwin, who was prone to loneliness, welcomed these visits and encouraged her to come as often as possible.
Her luck changed in the following year and she got a part in *The Household Fairy* at the New Queen's Theatre again, but she was no longer happy in her work . . . and then . . .
On Saturday, October 10, after the play was over, she left through the stage-door, met Godwin on the corner of Castle Street, and the two of them disappeared into the darkness of the night. She was finished with the theatre and had left without telling a soul. On Sunday, October 11, 1868, a new life started for her in the country.[17]

Edward had found a little cottage on the edge of the Gusterd Wood

Common (known locally as Gusterwood Common). The cottage was called the "Red House," though some called it "The Firs" because of a couple of trees in the garden. It had a hall and two rooms with bay-windows downstairs, a kitchen and bake-house at the back, and two rooms and a hall upstairs; the walls were painted pale yellow and the woodwork white; the furniture, designed by Edward, was slender and black. Ellen loved it all.[18]

Over a field behind the cottage was a hamlet called Mackery End, and the village of Wheathampstead was within a mile and a half's walk. Around them were cheerful country people. On the common cows and geese grazed, tended by children in white overalls. After Stanhope Street, it was heaven.

Edward's work as an architect meant that he was only paid fees; the money therefore came in fits and starts, so "when it was nice it was very, very nice, when it was nasty it was horrid." At that time Ellen thought that £2 a week was not at all bad—her mother had kept a family on a good deal less at times. She could just afford a maid-of-all-work, an outgoing of £5 a year, but it left her free to help Edward with his work. He taught her to trace his plans and elevations, which she soon did beautifully. She had found a new life and never wanted to go back to the theatre.

She soon made friends, amongst them a Mr and Mrs Robert Gibson, who lived near by on the common, and Dr and Mrs Rumbold over by Wheathampstead. Edward brought her a bulldog to protect her when he was away, then a parrot was added to the company, then a goat and, finally, a little monkey that liked to perch upon her foot when she sat by the fire at night with one leg balanced on the other—swaying to and fro, he would doze off to sleep and her leg would go numb, but she hated to wake him![19]

Godwin sometimes spent many days with her in the country, working on one project or another, then he was quite likely to disappear for a day or two in order to survey some distant site, or stay with a client to discuss his plans. When a project for Dromore Castle took him to Ireland, Ellen went with him, thrilled to be in her father's native land. Edward took her education in hand and explained the beauties of Celtic art, making it come alive for her.

They had been together for just over a year when a daughter was born. She was called Edith after Edith (or Eadgyth), daughter of

Godwin, Earl of the West Saxons—for Edward was an archaeologist as well as an aesthete, and liked to believe that his family were descended from those Saxon kings. With her baby Ellen felt her happiness was complete.

As time went by they found that there were disadvantages in living so far from London. When Edward lectured, or attended meetings at the Architectural Association and the Royal Institute of British Architects, or stayed late with clients, or got lost in conversation with Whistler, he would miss his train to Hatfield. There was no way of letting Ellen know; there were no taxis; only the slow horse cabs called "growlers"; no telephones to say "I can't make it," no telegrams to the common, so he would have to stay in London and she would wait . . . wondering. In the summer it was fun to go across the common, down through Wheathampstead, follow the course of the river Lea and, skirting the lovely wooded park of Brocket Hall, pop over the bridge and drive into Hatfield Station; it was 6½ miles in the pony trap, and she generally had young Sam Wilmot taking the reins one way— but when Edward wasn't there it was disheartening, and a sad drive home. When the nights grew cold and dark, disappointment could turn into a night of absolute despair.

Soon after her arrival at Gusterd Wood, she had met Dr and Mrs Rumbold (who used to keep a private lunatic asylum on the other side of Wheathampstead). Dr Rumbold died, and his widow occasionally visited Ellen to keep her company. Gradually, her visits increased until she became part of the household, staying on for the next thirty years. Mrs Rumbold became known as "Boo" because that was how Edy pronounced her name.

Eighteen-seventy-one came along and Ellen was expecting another child. As Dr Rumbold was dead, arrangements were made for her to go to Stevenage where there was a good midwife, and where it would be easier for Edward to be with her when he came up from London. Orchard Road was opposite the station (some people even called it Railway Street), and here the midwife lived. Boo stayed on at Gusterwood Common looking after Edy.

On Tuesday, January 16, 1872, a little boy was born.

Edward now had a family—he would build them a home! He found a plot of ground known as Fallows Green over at Harpenden, a village they both liked, and settled down to design "the perfect house."

It could have been a reasonably priced building, for in those days a very good country house could be built for £600, and a large, double-fronted suburban villa for two families would cost only £1,000 ... but Edward's house was to be of three stories with an enormously high pitched roof; the studio was huge, and there was a lych-gate that could have housed a porter, had they been able to afford one. As things were, so much was spent on the house and its decorations and the specially designed furniture to go into it that there was not enough money left to pay the tradesmen.

"Fallows Green," the house that E. W. Godwin built for his family at Harpenden. A line drawing made from J. Forbes-Robertson's painting.

Edward was quite oblivious of the value of money; it came and it went, and he knew it would come again. He loved his new house with its floors covered in Chinese matting, which was still supplied to him by his merchant friends in Bristol; there was no other house like it in the country, and there wouldn't be until he built one for Whistler in Tite Street. He loved to play the organ, and bought one for the studio: there, he and Ellen used to play Bach's "Prelude and Fugue" late into the night.[20]

Up in London he now had offices at 29 Craven Street.

Although there was no money to spare, Edward suddenly decided on a summer holiday in France, where he wanted to study the Bayeux tapestry as part of his unending research into the origins of the Godwin family. Little Teddy was left with Boo and her niece, Miss Bocking, whom the children called "Bo," and Edward and Ellen and little Edy went over to Normandy, staying at Bayeux, then at Lisieux, Saint-Lô, Rouen, and Affray. This experience was wonderful for Ellen, who watched in admiration as Edward made the most detailed sketches of buildings and hundreds of notes about craftsmanship, all in fine silver-point. Edward loved an admiring audience. Little Edy was happy picking flowers or "listening to Angels" in the big churches they visited. It was a happy holiday for them all.[21]

They returned to find that things were not so good at home: a pile of bills and letters demanding instant payment awaited them, and a little boy aged twenty months who had nearly forgotten who his parents were.

The return was a miserable anticlimax and things grew worse as the autumn approached. Fallows Green was now mortgaged, and a helpless feeling was intensified by the falling leaves and the autumn mists.

One day Ellen decided to go over to Gusterwood Common to see the Gibsons, who had a little daughter the same age as Teddy. On the way down a narrow lane leading to Batford Mill, a wheel came off the pony trap. Young Sam, the groom, who was with her, went to get help and while she was waiting in the cold she heard hunting horns and the yelp of approaching hounds.

She loathed the hunt, and had once defied the huntsmen at her cottage on the common. It had been surrounded by baying dogs and the huntsmen asked if they could look in the bake-house at the back; she barred the way and put on an act of outraged indignation that would have gone down well at the Olympic. When they had called off the hounds, and all was quiet again, she let the fox out of the great bread oven.[22]

Thinking of this, she waited for the hunt to pass. Over the hedge they came: fox and hounds, huntsmen and followers and . . . her old family friend, Charles Reade, playwright and theatrical producer.

"My God! It's Nelly!" shouted Reade, overcome with joy. "Where have you been all this time?" She told him she was the happy mother of two children, living in the country.

Reade continued to look at her in amazement; he could recognize luck when he encountered it, even in a Hertfordshire country lane.

"Nelly, would you like to come back to the theatre?" he asked, hopefully. "No, never," she laughed. "You're a fool," said Reade, so she
thought she would say something absurd and remarked casually, "I
might think of it if someone offered me . . . forty pounds a week."
Reade was a clever man, and he now saw the solution of a problem that
had been worrying him for weeks. "Done," he said. Ellen could hardly
believe her ears.[23]

In 1852, Reade had written a most successful play, *Masks and Faces*;
nine years later he had written a magnificent historical romance,
The Cloister and the Hearth. His latest play, *The Wandering Heir*, had
been tried out in the provinces and had not been well received, but he
was determined to put it on in London, where he felt that the public
interest in the Tichborne trial (on which it was based) would turn it into
yet another success.

Reade had been persuaded to continue with Mrs John Wood as his
leading lady, but she did not think she was right for the part—neither
did he—and he was desperately anxious to find another actress for
London: leaping a Hertfordshire hedge in the wake of some hounds,
quite by chance he had found her.

The last time that Reade had seen Ellen was at the New Queen's
Theatre the year she so dramatically "disappeared"—some said she
had been drowned, others murmured "suicide," though she had been
forced to reveal her existence to her mother to save further unhappiness.

Reade now begged Ellen to discuss his offer with Godwin and let
him know, *at once*. She needed no prompting, she only wanted to get
back and tell Edward about this astounding piece of luck. As if by magic,
Reade had appeared and she had the offer of a part at £40 a week—
FORTY POUNDS A WEEK! A star's salary! They would be so rich that they
could pay off all their debts . . . in four weeks she could make enough
money to cover the housekeeping for a whole year! Edward must have
been deeply affected by the sudden joy that swept into Fallows Green;
the logic must also have appealed to him, for he agreed.

Preparations were made at once for a move to London. Edward
found a house—20 Taviton Street, just off Gordon Square, and not too
far from King's Cross Station, the terminus of the Great Northern
Railway that would take them back to Hatfield, and so to Fallows
Green when they wanted a rest.

The Wandering Heir was to open at the New Queen's Theatre in Long Acre on February 28—the very theatre she had left for Godwin, six years earlier . . .

The children were left at Fallows Green in the care of Mrs Rumbold's niece Bo, as Ellen did not want them to be brought up in the London fogs. Mrs Rumbold, from then on Ellen's faithful "companion," accompanied her to London, where she organized the household at Taviton Street and acted as her chaperone at rehearsals.

The Wandering Heir opened on February 28, the day after Ellen's twenty-sixth birthday. Ellen's charm as Phillipa Chester captivated the critics, who welcomed her return to the stage. The play ran for 130 nights, then Reade decided to take the play on a tour of the provinces, this time under his own management, and, while working out the details of the tour he made use of the intervening time by featuring the cast in *It's Never Too Late to Mend*, another play of his which was always a "go" with the public: this, he put on at Astley's, over the river.

When Godwin heard of the projected tour, with Ellen's salary reduced to £25 a week for the provinces, he was furious, for he realized that he was to be left alone, a situation he had not calculated with; an easy prey to depression unless he had people around him, he soon went to pieces; he needed youth, energy, and enthusiasm on which he could feed. Ellen, always a generous character, felt that she owed Reade some allegiance in return for what he had done for them. She also liked the company. Perhaps, too, she realized that as so little work was coming into the Craven Street office, her salary, however small, would continue to be their mainstay for quite a while. So she went.

While Ellen was away, Edward spent much of his time at the Arts Club with Whistler and other friends. He went down to advise the architects Hine and Norman on Plymouth Town Hall; he moved about restlessly, going to exhibitions and society meetings. A chance encounter with Miss Emily Faithfull, the editress of *Woman and Work*, was to make quite a difference to his future—in fact to the future of the family. She asked him if he would write on woman's place in architecture. He agreed, and wrote a long article listing all the things a young woman could do in an architect's office, such as designing private houses, wallpapers, carpets . . . in fact everything "for the creation of beauty."[24] This was at a time when the emancipation of women, whilst being ridiculed in *Punch*, was considered seriously by a lot of far-thinking people, Miss Faithfull being one of them. At the Arts Club, John Bernie Philip, the sculptor, best known for his work on the Albert Memorial, met Godwin and told him that his daughter, Beatrice, had been very interested in what he had written and asked him if he could fit her into his office as a pupil. Beatrice Philip is said to have been a lively young creature of twenty who liked the idea of an artist's "Bohemian" life, and according to the artist, Mrs Jopling, "had a dare-devil look in her eye."[25] Godwin started her at his office. He also started spending more money on entertainment away from Taviton Street, which was no longer a home for him without Ellen or the children, who were still at Fallows Green. He also moved office from Craven Street, Strand, to 6 John Street, Adelphi, nearer Charing Cross.

When Ellen returned from the provinces, she found that the situation in London was no better than it had been just before they left Fallows Green, in fact things were worse—the broker's men were in. Godwin was "ill" and in a highly nervous state. Thinking that it was better for him to get out of the way of creditors, he decided to go and stay with a friend in the Isle of Wight. Ellen stayed on at Taviton Street, with instructions from him to open all the letters and "detain" all the unpleasant ones.[26]

Once again, Chance was to play an even more important part in Ellen's life.

Mrs Squire Bancroft, *née* Marie Wilton, had recently done the im-possible: she had turned the Queen's Theatre in Tottenham Street, commonly known as the "Dust Hole", into London's most fashionable little theatre. She re-christened it Prince of Wales Theatre (now the Scala), and there, Tom Robertson's "cup and saucer" dramas had brought a new kind of realism to the London theatre. Now the Ban-crofts felt that it was time to have a change.

Irving's *Hamlet* at the Lyceum had electrified London audiences, so the change they thought of was a revival of another of Shakespeare's plays, *The Merchant of Venice*. Their first idea for the part of Portia was Mrs Kendal, but as this came to nothing, Mrs Bancroft then thought of Ellen, whom she had known in Bristol, and went in search of her.

She found her at Taviton Street, a dejected little figure in her almost empty yellow rooms. The Chinese matting was still on the floors, because no one considered such eccentric items to be of any value, and a full-size plaster cast of the Venus of Melos, which was too heavy to move, was still at the far end of the hall. Mrs Bancroft could see that things were not quite as they should be. She asked Ellen if she knew *The Merchant of Venice*, and if she was interested in the part of Portia at £20 a week.[27] Ellen forgot all her troubles and was enthusiastic—of course she knew *The Merchant*—she and her husband had been working on it only the year before: he was an archaeologist and knew all about the period, the architecture, and the costumes—he was writing about it. Mrs Bancroft was most interested to hear this—she would mention it to Mr Bancroft—and perhaps Mr Godwin could help them also. (She may even have thought that it was the same Godwin who had often advised Charles Kean on *his* memorable revivals of Shakespeare).[28]

Mrs Bancroft's visit left Ellen with a feeling that the sun was rising again. She wrote to Edward, telling him the good news, then to Bo, telling her to bring up Edy and little Teddy—she longed to see the children after the long tour. Edward came back from the Isle of Wight. All was settled: Ellen was to play Portia, Edward was to help with the production. Beds they still had, some more bits and pieces came up from Fallows Green, and nothing else was thought of but Venice in 1590.

While Ellen was studying and rehearsing, Edward was helping the scenic artist and designer, George Gordon, who he had known from the old Bristol and Bath days. Godwin was enthusiastic about this work which was so near to his heart; he even made one or two of the props with his own hands.

Then, just a month before they were due to open, something happened—no one knows what—but in a towering rage Godwin left Taviton Street, never to return. Was he piqued at playing such a secondary part in a theatre where Ellen was so obviously the professional while he was the amateur? Did he resent the attention paid to her by other male members of the company . . . or did Ellen remark upon the amount of attention he was paying to his assistant, Beatrice Philip?

In spite of this fearful domestic upheaval Ellen still carried on, and emerged after the first night acclaimed as a great and beautiful actress. Her future career was securely established and she was never to look back.

CHAPTER TWO

A Stepfather and Failure at School
1875–1888

LITTLE TEDDY was only three years old when he lost his father. Godwin wasn't dead, but it was much the same thing for he went out of their lives. The following year he married his young assistant, Beatrice Philip. Ten years later, he died, leaving behind him a "legitimate" son.

Teddy never was to know the cause of the break, and it was only when I was putting together this book that someone came forward with the following letter from Ellen to a Mr Wilson, which seems to explain so much . . . there is a pencilled note that reads "before March 6th."

221, Camden Road Villas
N.W.   Saturday night.

Dear Mr. Wilson,

In all gentleness and kindness of feeling, I must beg you not to act as mediator between Mr Godwin and myself. Our separation was a thing agreed upon by *both* of us many weeks before it actually took place. The first steps were taken by *him* and I certainly am much astonished to hear that he professes any strong feeling in the matter. Part of our compact was that we should always maintain a kindly, friendly relation to one another—He has since Tuesday last made this an IMPOSSIBILITY. He tried by unfair means to get my little girl from me (I *had offered* to let him have the boy) and I now distinctly refuse to hold any communication whatever with him.

I do feel sorry that he is ill—Glad that he has some good friends—

may he CONTINUE to appreciate them through his lifetime. I thank
you for many kindnesses you have shown me and my children but I
thank you still more for the fact that you are Mr Godwin's friend
now.

Your letter arrived AFTER your departure last evening.

If Mr Godwin's friends knew his temperament as I do and the
effects of change of scene upon him, they would advise his leaving
London and *staying with friends*, for a time at least. He should not go
alone as he is apt to brood and imagine all kinds of ills which do not
exist. You say in your letter—*"I really fear for his reason"*—When I
knew him in his home life 13 years ago I had the same idea, and at
that time he had an *utterly sorrowless life*—a devoted help-mate—
success—friends—*everything*. He never was happy—he never will be.
If you choose to show him this letter I will find no objection. At the
risk of being called utterly heartless I again say I will hold no further
communication with Mr Godwin, and I also say that this hard behaviour on my part has been brought about entirely by his own rash
conduct since the last time we were together in Taviton Street.

I apologize for taking up your time with this lengthy letter and
remain sorrowfully in spirit tho' stronger in health and purpose

Yours sincerely,

Ellen Terry

Both children have colds, but are otherwise well.[1]

When Edward walked out of Taviton Street Ellen knew that her
whole life must be replanned. She removed to 221 Camden Road, "next
to the Breknock," a famous old inn near Camden Town.[2] It was on a
hill and the air was fresher and there was a big garden for the children to
play in. That part of London was described by Frederick Pardon as
being in a neighbourhood where "lie the villas and mansions and
pretty houses in which reside the wealthy among London's middle
classes . . . and as rural and pleasant a scene as can be found in any part of
England."[3]

Godwin's attempt to take Edy away had frightened Ellen. It
frightened Edy also, and she hated her father for ever afterwards.
Teddy was at that age when food mattered a lot, and the person who
gave him the food was a very important person—Bo, not his mother.
Although Ellen adored her children and wanted them near, she thought

now that they might be better off away from all the strife, so Bo took them to Brancaster on the Norfolk coast, where she had relations and friends.

There was no permanent home for the two children until she settled in 33 Longridge Road, S.W.5, in the following year, and as the financial situation improved she also found a tiny cottage at Hampton Court where they could spend the summers running around the Park and Gardens, and this was the place where they were happiest.

Ellen's life was in the melting pot. Her return to the stage had been acclaimed by all. The audiences loved her because of her love for them —she longed to please, and was willing to spend hours of study and thought in order to succeed in doing just that. She had no ambition as an actress, unless it was to be useful in the theatre. It was her "brilliance and loveliness" which outshone all the shortcomings of the Bancroft's *Merchant of Venice*. At one performance Henry Irving was in the audience. He had just shaken the prejudiced structure of the English theatre to its foundations with the most superb and revolutionary performance of *Hamlet*. He was impressed by her personality as an actress, very impressed, but Ellen was not to know that yet.

She carried on with the Bancrofts in various other parts and then went to the Court Theatre to work for John Hare, where her first play was *Brothers* by Charles Coghlan, followed immediately by *New Men and Old Acres*. This was an important production for the Court, as it is supposed to have made Hare a rich man. For Ellen it produced a "husband" . . .

Playing the part of Mr Brown to her Lilian Vavasour was "a manly bulldog sort of a man possessed, as an actor, of great tenderness and humour"—his name was Charles Kelly (a widower thirty-six years old, whose real name was Wardell). This was not her first encounter with him; he had been a member of Reade's company at the Queen's when she returned to the stage three years earlier; they had toured together; she had tried to get him a part in *The Merchant of Venice* but failed. Now he appeared as an old and understanding friend.[4]

The playwright Tom Taylor, a man whom she loved and greatly respected, was at the Court too. Tom adored Nelly, and there was nothing that he would not do to help her. He had always felt a bit responsible for her marriage to Watts and was very worried when she eloped with Godwin. When she had been parted from Watts there were no grounds for divorce, so Watts could only ask for a separation.[5] Moreover, Ellen's family would not speak to her after she "disappeared" so disgracefully with Edward on that October night in 1868. She had been forced to keep her children in the background because it became more and more difficult for her to explain who their father was. Tom realized this was a great weight on her mind and that it could seriously jeopardize her future, about which he was now more confident than ever.

Tom Taylor, the barrister, left Tom Taylor, the playwright, at home and went to see his friend Watts. Ellen was suddenly set free by a divorce in which Godwin was cited as co-respondent. At the same time Taylor talked to Ellen seriously about marrying again—he told her that she needed a "father" for her children. Ellen had loved once and knew she would never love another man the same way again; in her pocket-book she still carried Edward's photograph under which she had written: "It is better to have loved and lost, than never to have loved at all."[6]

Kelly thought he understood her feelings . . . But, poor man, he didn't. During the run of *Olivia* (W. G. Wills's play based on *The Vicar of Wakefield*) at the Court, and following her divorce from Watts, they were married and shortly afterwards went on tour together.

At Longridge Road there was great jubilation—the children had a new "father." They were already very fond of him, because he was fond of them. Teddy, who was five and had been surrounded by women, thought he was marvellous; he practised writing his new name on everything—"Edward Wardell" (not Kelly, which was only for use on the stage).

Although Kelly was acting as a father to Ellen's children, he was only her husband in name; but he knew that would change—at least, he *thought* it would change . . .

Then came the last great move in Ellen's life—a move that was to set the whole pattern of her future, and thus establish a firm structure on which the children could grow.

In August 1878, while she and Kelly were away on tour in Liverpool, she received a letter signed "Henry Irving," asking her if she would be interested in joining him in his new venture at the Lyceum Theatre.[7] This must have been a very exciting moment.

Irving, whose real name was Brodribb, was born a simple West Country lad in 1838. Surmounting every obstacle in his path, he succeeded in becoming the most acclaimed actor of his time. His dedication to his art was almost fanatical, and his efforts to raise the status of the actor as an artist later acquired for him the first knighthood ever bestowed on one of his profession.

It was twenty-two years since Ellen's first appearance at the Princess's Theatre, and she had played over eighty parts. Through Watts and Godwin she had come to know men of taste and learning like Burne-Jones, Tennyson, William Morris, Whistler, and Oscar Wilde, all of whom had contributed to her appreciation of art and beauty. Her childhood and her tragic love affairs had taught her much about life —she had learned patience and simplicity. She was the right material from which to make the actress who was to reign supreme at the Lyceum for the next twenty years. But Ellen, totally devoid of personal ambition and quite without conceit, would never in her wildest dreams have aspired to the position of Irving's leading lady. Now it was all to happen—in double-quick time. By the end of the year she was signed up for the Lyceum at forty guineas a week and "half a clear benefit."[8] (In those days at the Lyceum that could mean a bonus of £200.)

For the first time in her life she could begin to understand the warm feeling of security. From now on the children that she adored would be properly cared for. It meant hard work—very hard work—but this she had never shirked. A new life would begin for them all.

Her first part with Irving was Ophelia in *Hamlet*. Rehearsals began in November and the first performance took place on December 30. Eighteen-eighty saw her rehearsing during the day and acting at night, with very little time for rest.

When Irving was preparing *The Cup*, Ellen suggested that he employ Edward to design the costumes and properties and advise generally; he took her advice. It was obvious that she still admired and loved Edward.

Kelly at last saw plainly that he was only playing the part of "Miss Terry's husband," and that she would never love him any more than she loved so many of her closest friends. He began to drink more and more, and, forsaking his friends in the theatre, returned to his old companions who had served with him in the 66th Regiment in the Crimea.[9] He was disgusted with the theatre; many times recently he had been offered parts that he considered unworthy of him—he had actually turned down the part of Burchell with Ellen in *Olivia* because he thought he should have been offered the part of the Vicar. He knew that, now she was with Irving, he would never have an opportunity of playing leading parts with her again. When he left the army with ambitions of becoming an actor he had great ideas about his future—now they were all smashed. He stayed away from Longridge Road more and more and finally left for good—a year later there was a judicial separation. He died in 1885, a year before Godwin.

In 1880 little Teddy was eight, his sister was eleven. He could not remember his real father—he had seen so little of him. One day his sister Edy came into the room with something held behind her back. "Would you like to see a picture of the Devil?" she asked. "Yes," said Teddy eagerly. She showed him a photograph of Godwin that she had found in her mother's bedroom. Teddy was puzzled, and never forgot the incident. He knew who it was in the photograph—his mother had often shown it to him herself, but always connected with stories of happy days gone by, when he was a "little boy," and he had looked at the picture as a child looks at a favourite illustration in a book of fairy-tales. Edy's little outburst had such malignance behind it that he was quite frightened—and he wondered—and the incident haunted him in his sleep.[10]

Edy could only remember Godwin as a man with a beard who tried to steal her away one day when her mother was out; she also remembered the rows and her mother's tears.[11]

During his first three years, little Teddy must have been subconsciously aware of his father and mother, but probably more of Effie, who looked after him and loved him.

There were happy moments on Gusterd Wood Common when he used to play with his pal, the bulldog; he even tried to cock his leg against a tree like his friend but found that he fell over and so gave it up.

When they left the cottage and went to the big house called Fallows Green, his nursery was on the first floor, where his father had also placed the kitchen so that it should be near by.[12] Sometimes his mother would sing him to sleep with Orlando Gibbons's "Silver Swan"—later, in his dreams, it used to come back to drive away a nightmare.

Then suddenly, both father and mother got very worried and then went away, and a new person was prominent in his life—this was Bo, Boo's niece. Lovely Bo gave him so much to eat that he became very fat, but he was always hungry and she could not deny him anything. Perhaps he wanted attention more than food, but the right people were not there to give it to him, so he asked for more and more food instead.

One day there was a terrific stir, everything was new and different: they were all up in London. Teddy was transported with excitement at seeing so many carriage wheels taller than himself; he pointed at them and shouted, then clasped his head with both hands—it was all too much for his small brain.[13]

In London, Bo was still his mainstay, for his mother was busy rehearsing in the day-time and acting at night. He seldom realized that it was she who was leaning over his cot when he awoke in the small hours . . . Then there was more commotion (he was three now), and his mother was sometimes in tears, which made him cry too. Then Godwin left, and the house was populated only with women. He and his sister went away with Bo to the sea, where things were calmer. The trains up and down to London were fascinating. There was lots to interest a child—but no real peace.

At last, when Teddy was four, they all went to live in a house in Longridge Road in which all the rooms seemed very high, and his room seemed the highest of all; it was up flights and flights of stairs, and there were bars at the windows. This was a new house and had no inheritance, no humanity; he didn't know this but he knew he hated the place. Going up all those stairs to a room lost at the top became a torture. When left alone he couldn't sleep; he imagined the Devil was there and he would shriek in terror, but there was seldom any answer from the great rooms far below, though sometimes Miss Harries would have to come up; she was a kind-hearted creature . . . but more often than not he would fall asleep from exhaustion—in those days there were very rigid ideas against pandering to the whims of children. Routine gradually benumbed his fears and gave him some sense of security.

But there was one new and exciting thing about the place—Charlie Kelly; he was fun, and seemed pleasantly rough after all the women. "He is your new father," he was told.

A lot of artists and writers lived near-by, among them Oswald Sickert, father of one of England's great modern painters, Walter Sickert; there was also Edwin Arnold, scholar and poet, famed for his *The Light of Asia*. Children of both these families attended a little school run by Mrs Cole in Foxton Road, where Teddy and Edy joined them. Teddy was then six and found this first school most exciting; Mrs Cole was "very advanced" and actually believed that one could safely mix boys and girls in a class together.

In the summer they went back to the seaside with Bo, and that seemed as much like home as anywhere. There was the blacksmith, Joe Powell, and his forge with the great bellows that Teddy was allowed to pull and help make the fire glow. Joe didn't make a fuss over him—just treated him like any other man.

When they came back from Joe's, there was a new place to go to—Rose Cottage, Hampton Court, which Ellen had bought as a retreat for week-ends and holidays. From this cottage he and his sister wandered in the park, played with the keepers, watched the stags fight, amused the visitors, romped and played, and for ever afterwards the thought of Rose Cottage brought him only the happiest of memories.

Although Teddy and Edy had once been allowed to mingle with the crowds on the stage in *Olivia*, Teddy had never become properly acquainted with the theatre until he was eight, when one evening his mother took him to see *The Corsican Brothers* at the Lyceum. They went behind and down under the stage and could hear the play going on above them, and there Teddy saw the men preparing the trap for the apparition; the men worked silently, with only a few whispered commands. Then his mother hurried him back to the stage level, and suddenly a long hole opened silently in the stage and the apparition of Louis dei Franchi, whom he had seen down below, rose slowly and advanced towards his brother, calling for revenge; the stage was dark except for some blue lights. Teddy could think of nothing else for days and wanted desperately to go back to the theatre.[14]

Why did she take him to the Lyceum just then? Was it, perhaps, so that Godwin, who was often there helping with the production of *The Cup*, could see their son?

At home there seemed to be lots of rows; no one seemed very happy, and one day he saw Kelly putting some bags into a cab. He never saw his friend again.

But there were occasional visits from a very quiet man called "Henry." Whenever he was about everyone seemed eager to please him, and Teddy, too, sought to win his affection. Henry didn't play games with him like Kelly had done, like Lewis Carroll and other visitors had tried to do; he was grave and self-assured, but he had a twinkling eye, and his smile was generous. He was not emotional, but he was exciting to watch. Ellen saw the change that took place in little Teddy when Irving came to see them, and she was happier than she had been for a long time.

Henry Irving was a dedicated man; he was like a priest whose temple was the theatre. He was trying to win the public's respect for what he considered to be the actor's art; he counted on using all other art forms to further his aim, and believed that he was engaged on a sacred mission. Such men are rare; they have many enemies but they are generally loved and respected by their fellow workers who discover that, by association alone, they are inspired to undertake tasks that they had previously regarded as impossible.

This "Henry" was the first man to come into Teddy's life who was stable, and on whom he could focus, and whose bearing he might wish to emulate.

Those preceding years of pampered insecurity surrounded by adoring females and a continually changing background had effected him profoundly, and it would be many years before his subconscious reactions could be readjusted—and some of them never were. Like so many children, he was a neglected seedling that circumstances had forced the gardener to overlook, and a bit late he had been "potted out" and was expected to make good growth. Henry Irving was the firm stick up which he would now try to climb.

Another feature in his new life was the sudden acquisition of a family background. Ellen had been ostracized by her entire family since 1868; in running off with Godwin she had offended respectable society. Since she had been respectably, if only superficially, married to poor Charles Kelly, they could all accept her again without seeming to condone her "terrible behaviour." They were happy, too, because they could now talk openly about the children. Their happiness could be felt by the children. Grandma and Grandpa came round to Longridge Road with tears of joy, and Edy and Teddy learned all about Uncle Ben, Uncle George, Uncle Charlie, Auntie Kate, Auntie Polly, and darling

Auntie Flossie. And there were many more relatives, all exciting, all part of their new and very own family.

In acquiring a background, Teddy discovered that he had also acquired a future, and it now remained to be seen if he could eventually overcome the many doubts and fears that had troubled his growing mind over the last nine years. He was very short-sighted and wearing eye-glasses had added to his sense of insecurity (later he fancied himself in pince-nez that were the same pattern as Irving's and which he wore until the 1930's).

Now a big problem faced Ellen—how to establish a desire "to do" in a boy who had no father figure on which to model himself, how to keep him free from all those dangers which a woman fears in a growing boy's nature—cowardice, cruelty, selfishness, and laziness.

Laziness was going to be the most difficult "vice" to overcome, for 33 Longridge Road contained his mother; his sister Edy; Boo, his mother's companion; Bo, his and Edy's special guardian; Miss Bindloss, for a time his governess; Miss Harries, the housekeeper—and his own special admirer; the cook, and the housemaid. Passing to and fro like the weaver's shuttle in this wonderful web of women were more women—his mother's understudy, Audrey Campbell; his mother's self-appointed helpers; his sister's girl friends—and . . . all "The Admirers." Why should he work? What at? What for? How? Sometimes his sister would try to encourage him to do something with "Come on Teddy, be a woman!"

The hours and rules were so strange, too—one had to keep quiet in the morning because mother was asleep after the late night's work at the theatre; then there was a late-morning rehearsal, sometimes lasting through lunch-time, which meant you could not see mother; then there was mother's rest in the afternoon in order that she would be able to cope with the evening's performance—so there was only a short talk and a kiss before she went. Sunday could be great fun with visits from Grandma and any other members of the family, or from admirers like young Stephen Coleridge, Johnston Forbes Robertson, or Graham Robertson. Best of all were the days spent with her alone at Rose Cottage, Hampton Court.

School was decided upon, to keep him occupied—school, which so often provides parents with an escape from responsibility, but would only provide Teddy with stock answers in preparation for a professional career . . . "how to play cricket with words and football with lives," as W. R. Lethaby so aptly put it.[15]

It was young Stephen Coleridge, who had been in the navy and was then in the Diplomatic Service, that Ellen picked on for advice in this matter. She went a step further and made him Teddy's "guardian," a responsibility that Coleridge took very seriously, poor young man; he was not blessed with humour, only with sarcasm, a characteristic he may have inherited from his father, a Lord Chief Justice.

Life was passing, and Teddy was being fêted on his visits to the Lyceum, where he was treated as a V.I.P., and was able to watch plays with Bo and Edy from the Royal Box. He would write to his mother from the seaside, addressing her as "dear old Mother." He was then ten years old.

Just after Teddy's eleventh birthday, Coleridge thought that he had found the "right school." It was near Tunbridge Wells: Southfield Park, Southborough, and was kept by the Reverend Ernest Wilkinson and his wife. Teddy wrote home in despair about the other boys: "only two out of the twelve are gentlemen, that's the boy that came down with me and myself." Later came a letter saying, "I feel so unhappy, Mother"; three weeks later he wrote, "we have fine larks now"; a month later, "I like this school very much." Mr Wilkinson was fond of marmalade, and was always very pleased when parents sent it to their boys—at breakfast he would sit at a top table, and looking down at the little ruffians below would say, as though it was another Grace: "Any boy want marmalade—no?—*good!*"[16]

That year there was to be no Christmas holiday with his mother; she was going away on a tour of America with Irving's Lyceum Company.

Before her departure Teddy and Edy joined her for a long week-end in Glasgow. As a treat they all went for a cruise on the *Lady Torfridra*. It was a misty morning and the captain pointed out a mysterious little island to starboard—"Watch the island," he said, and gave an order for firing a small signal cannon. Thousands and thousands of gulls swept off it and into the sky, swarming and circling above it like smoke, their shrieks mingling with the wind that whistled through the rigging. "That's Ailsa Craig," said the captain—"and that's what I shall call myself when I go on the stage," said Edy. Edy was very forthright, very practical and, unlike her brother, could make up her mind at once. She was fifteen and was just beginning to think of becoming an actress.[17]

Teddy felt that he was already an actor when he performed in *Bluebeard* at school. He had sent lordly instructions to his mother to get Arnott the property master to:

> make me a wooden sword nicely finished and curved a good shape and give him something—a present for making it.[18]

This was the first of many letters that he was to write, asking people to get things done for him and telling them to remunerate a third party—always ignoring two important things: Where was the remuneration coming from? Had the first person time to spare to get the second person to do the job? Simply because time never meant anything to him until his last few years, and money . . . that was just a useful commodity that most other people had in quantities but of which he had none . . . and which could always be counted on to turn up when things got too difficult. He was also finding that "Ellen Terry" was a magic word that could always help him: late, as usual, he had once run on to the station platform at Tunbridge Wells crying, "Stop the train—stop the train—this is Miss Terry's son"—and the train had stopped.[19]

When the following Christmas was approaching Ellen felt so lonely in far-away America that she wired Coleridge to bring Teddy; he had the thrill of crossing the Atlantic in *The City of Chicago*, and in New York he was "pursued by all the little girls in the hotel." In Chicago, Irving, to please Ellen, gave him a small part as a gardener's boy in the first act of *Eugene Arram*—this was just two days before his thirteenth birthday; later he was allowed to mingle with the crowds in some of the other plays.

For his birthday Irving gave him a copy of *Robin Hood*, illustrated by Howard Pyle; Teddy feasted on these illustrations day after day and never forgot their first impact, for their influence can be seen in the stance of so many figures in his costume designs in later years; Howard Pyle was an important man to him for ever afterwards, and he always cut reproductions of his drawings out of magazines to preserve in his scrap-books.

Back in England, Ellen was called on one day by a rather beautiful but untidy young woman—"Miss Terry, would you come quickly," she said, "Mr Wardell is very ill and wants to see you." The young woman was the new "Mrs Wardell." They went at once by cab to some very poor lodgings; there lay poor Charles, dying. He had asked to see her again and died just after her arrival. Ellen left in tears, and for days suffered "a fit of melancholy which I cannot conquer."[20]

Irving was now preparing *Faust*, and part of his routine was to take the designers, the scene-painters, the costumiers, property-master, stage-manager, and so on to Nuremberg to make drawings and collect materials and inspiration. He made the party a happy one by taking Ellen and her children.

It was here that young Teddy one night witnessed something which greatly impressed him.

Together with Irving and Joe Carr, they had penetrated deeply into the slums and a party of roughs hung threateningly about the prosperous-looking sightseers. Joe Carr, foreseeing an ugly situation, began a strategic withdrawal. Irving stood his ground for a moment and then, assuming the most fearsome posture from his catalogue of grotesque attitudes, advanced on the hooligans who, in terror, took to their heels.[21]

Forty years later Teddy remembered this and scattered a crowd in Italy by advancing on them in the same way, but with his stick held high and shouting, "I am the demon dwarf of blood"—a line he had once heard in a pantomime—and the crowd rapidly dispersed.

When Teddy was fourteen, Stephen Coleridge thought it was time he went to a public school. Bradfield College was chosen.

Ellen and Irving were now off on yet another tour of America. "Do give my love to it," wrote Teddy. He thought it was a happy land and would have dearly liked to have gone again.

At Bradfield he gained nothing in the way of knowledge, but he made a chum of Paul Cooper, who remained afterwards one of his closest friends. For a short time he became sports-conscious, so as to please Robert Temperly, his master. He picked up all the rude jokes he heard—on returning home for a holiday he was disappointed to find that they amused no one. On entering the sitting-room one day, old Boo asked him where he had been. "Ask me-arse," he replied. This was thought to be a good reply at Bradfield, but, together with some other stories that he wrote out for Edy, only got him a caning from his guardian while his mother cried in another room.

Eventually they thought it expedient to send him abroad, this time to an English school run by a mixture of English and German mast rs in Heidelberg, which went by the pompous name of Heidelberg College.

Meanwhile, unknown to Teddy, his father, who had been spending all his money and energy on various theatrical ventures in which he was helped by his admiring lady friends, suddenly became ill. On the morning of October 6, 1886, Whistler, who had been with Godwin to the end, asked Mrs Jopling, the artist, to go and tell Ellen the news of his death to spare her the shock of seeing it announced in the newspapers. "When I told her," she wrote, "I shall never forget her cry: 'There was no one like him.' "[23] He was only fifty-three.

Now that both Godwin and Wardell were dead, Irving no longer tried to hide from Ellen that he was deeply in love with her, but Ellen still knew that Godwin was to remain her only real love, and the tragedy of Wardell's death, which she must have realized was partly caused by her trying to believe in an impossible marital situation, was still fresh in her mind. She loved Irving, and admired him above all men, but she knew that their love could only prosper in the theatre, for it was only there that they had an interest in common—an overpowering interest which amounted at times to complete self-abnegation. They knew that they would be together in their work and that was all that mattered.

A month after his last term at Bradfield, Teddy left London for Heidelberg. On September 18, 1887, he wrote, "I'm here at last and it's a very jolly place."[24] He liked Dr Holtzberg, the head. He loved Heidelberg; the romance of the surroundings, the town, Krall's little café in the old town where the boys used to gather on their days off and gamble like real Heidelberg students—this was all grand. But in the school it was Bradfield all over again. Mr Laurence, one of the English masters, an unpopular man, soon showed his resentment to young Teddy, who, he considered, was an over-privileged pupil because of his mother's celebrity. (She had asked that he be allowed to go to the theatre whenever there were any good plays to be seen.)

Away from the atmosphere of the theatre, he yearned to go on the stage. He wrote to his mother, pleading for the "boy's part" in *The Dead Heart*, which he had heard they might do at the Lyceum: "Do, oh do, send me a copy of it—I will promise to study it."[25]

From far away in Boston, Ellen now started to write long letters to her growing boy. She tried to be mother, father, companion, guide, everything. One sees from her letters around this period that she is becoming more and more aware of a parent's great responsibility for a child's future. She includes little stories about Irving and his dedication to work, hoping that Teddy will "get the message" and be fired with a desire to emulate him. January 26, 1888, she writes from Boston:

> Knowing this was a terrific big theatre I begged and prayed that I might be "let off" the first night in Boston because of my voice and that Miss Emery might play Margaret—No—he was like iron—like a rock about it, and I got mad and said, "I do think that if your son, or your mother, your wife, the idol of your heart were to die on the stage through making the effort to do the work you w^d let it happen"! "Certainly I would," said he to my amazement: I expected he would say, "Oh, come now, you exaggerate"—So now I know what to expect. He certainly w^d *drop himself,* before he'd give in, and there my Ted is the simple secret of his great success in everything he undertakes. *He* is most extraordinary."[26]

He got this letter during a period of "confinement to school." After this he was "kept in" by Mr Laurence for another four weeks. This was more than he could stand and with two other boys who suffered under the same master he escaped one night from the "college". Using his Gordon plaid as a rope down which to slide, and taking to their bicycles they rode off into the glorious, free night, all along the banks of the Necker, up to the Schwarzer Adler at Zieglehausen . . . lovely, lovely freedom at last . . . !

When she returned from America, Ellen went to rest at Margate. There on October 23 she found a letter from Heidelberg College:

Dear Mrs. Wardell,

I regret very much that the school career of Edward Wardell should be terminated this morning by summary expulsion from

Heidelberg College. You are aware that your son has tried our for-
bearance over and over again. . . . Yesterday evening he broke out of
the house with two others and absented himself until 3.30 a.m. . . . He
has a very ill-disciplined nature with an impulsive temper. His actions
are marked with utter disregard for consequences.[27]

This was signed by Laurence.

Coleridge had a letter too, and wrote off to Ellen, almost in a panic.

Meanwhile, poor Teddy arrived in London, sad and ashamed, and
went straight to his grandfather's house. Ben, with the vestige of a
twinkle in his old eye, wired Ellen in Margate: "Ted with me will be
well looked after nothing serious but most idiotic write tonight."[28]

Stephen was worried about what had happened while these wicked
boys were out on the rampage—was there . . . perhaps . . . something
immoral? Ellen wrote to him, "Sometimes I think you are the silliest
gentleman I ever met with."[29] Coleridge's wife wrote emotionally: "I
implore you to stop and consider how you are bringing them up. . . .
Oh, Nellie, do forget yourself and think what you owe to them. . . .
You used to let me say things to you sometimes, till Henry came and
took your love away from me."[30] There were eight pages of it and
many more from Stephen.

Then, slowly, all became normal again. The monster, after all,
looked like any lad of sixteen.

Ellen wrote to the Reverend Wilkinson and asked him if he would
take young Edward back as a private pupil and coach him for a while.
Old Wilkinson, who admitted having "much affection for him,"
welcomed him to Southfield, and at the end of October reported:
"I believe him to be a good boy—Flighty, but good. . . . Guided right
I have every confidence in him."[31] His advice was not to try to find
another school but a tutor with one or two other pupils; best of all, he
thought, would be a tutor who could travel with him "showing him
other places and peoples." They read *Macbeth* together, an experience
which was to make a life-long impression on his pupil. Rather sadly
they parted on December 21.

While all this was going on Irving could see that Ellen was being
upset and that it was reacting on her work. He made the only sensible
suggestion . . . "perhaps . . . eh . . . Teddy could be made useful at . . .
The Lyceum."

CHAPTER THREE

The Lyceum · the Provinces · Herkomer

1889–1892

In 1889 Teddy was seventeen years old. At last his mother was beginning to call him Ted, and gradually everyone else did so too.

To keep him from becoming idle and despondent at home, Ellen decided to take old Wilkinson's kindly advice and find him a temporary tutor elsewhere: this turned out to be a rather pompous fellow, the Reverend Gorton, of Denchworth Vicarage, near Wantage.

The Vicar patronized "Readings" at the local Shakespeare Society; there, Ted rather fancied himself as a professional amongst a lot of amateurs, and he wrote to his mother giving very amusing, though rather unkind reports on how the plays were read . . . by the others.

He gained nothing from his stay at the rectory, except that once or twice a week he would walk a mile or two and visit a Mrs Cook, who was the daughter of Theodore Cook, the writer, and editor of *The Field*. Mrs Cook was the only person from whom he ever had "drawing lessons"; she was an amateur and taught him, as best she could, the genteel art of "copying." This was one of the pastimes of Victorian young ladies; they copied drawings or water-colours for each other's scrap-books. Ted just copied Gordon Brown's illustrations to *The Henry Irving Shakespeare*. He had inherited an eye for proportion and found it child's play. Drawing helped to pass the few months at Denchworth.

Meanwhile, Ellen was tense with excitement now that Irving had shown some interest in her boy's future. She bombarded Ted with letters full of news, love, and advice; she so wanted him to "succeed" that she almost overdid it. Above all, he must please Irving by his conduct and his attitude to work; in one letter she writes:

> . . . Yes, your writing was *much* better my dear Ted—bolder—clearer—and not so affected as it has been of late.
>
> . . . Henry is well, but looks sadly tired—he works so *very* hard, and *has* worked all his life—that's the meaning of such a brilliant record of successes. Nothing great is done without it, Ted, and oh, believe me, if you were not blind and foolish, you'd understand and *will*

One of the many copies of Gordon Brown's illustrations to *The Henry Irving Shakespeare* made by young Teddy in 1888. He signed them all "E.W."

some day, and regret, how wicked it is of you not to take the golden opportunities you have and profit by them. *Work* is a blessed Saviour —If *now* you had improved your time and had got something into your big head you might have been with us playing Malcolm—it's a small, but *very* important, *very difficult* part—anyhow you'll have to play Malcolm before Macbeth—or Macduff. I'm off to rehearsal.

Edy was *singing in a chorus* at a concert given in Berlin on Monday. *Singing*!!! think of it!—God bless you— . . .

Your loving Mother.[1]

In another letter, apart from news about Sargent's portrait of her as

Lady Macbeth, there is a suggestion that he might copy some better drawings than those made by Gordon Brown:

Dearest boy—

. . . Last night Sargent's picture of me was hung up in the Beefsteak room to show to a few friends—30—! The whole thing was a great success. The picture—the supper—the whole party—*all*. I sat between John Sargent and little Mr Edwin Abbey and had a very good time—by the way I wish you w^d study and copy *his* drawings— they are so beautiful I feel, and he scorns *trick* so entirely—Mr Parsons too, his flowers are just perfect, and as (when you come home you will most likely see a good deal of both of these artists) it w^d be a very good plan to try and find out about their work *first*![2]

Then, on May 27 (1889), she had some real news. At last it looked as though the day was near when he would be allowed to act at the Lyceum.

My dearest boy, I hope you are enjoying this splendid hot weather— it is a little *too* hot for town and Lady Macbeth with her heavy dresses—nevertheless it is lovely. . . . Now work away *well now*, *every minute*, and who knows but I may induce Henry after all to let you play that part—but, *Hush—Hush—Hush*!!! But much depends on this quarter's record of your conduct—Get mastery over your own little *self*. Compel *yourself* to learn this or that, and you'll learn a great deal at school, and get happiness out of life which can't be had in any other way. . . . If you read and study Dickens *Tale of Two Cities* just at present it will be very profitable, for the story of Sydney Carton in that book is the story of *The Dead Heart*, and is of the same period. . . . I conclude with a blessing upon your fair tho' fat-ish "chops," and a suggestion that you have y^r head shaved—I mean cut off—I mean your *hair cropped quickly*, so you can train it again—the heavenly hour when we twain shall happily meet—it will cool your BRAINS (?) also—

Your loving old
Mother[3]

Realizing that before he could be of much use at the Lyceum he'd

c

have to have some lessons in elocution she sent him another letter
three days later:

> . . . Now a bit of business—Get to work *at once and study* (first the
> words, and afterwards the whole meaning of the character and play),
> *Falconbridge* in King John—You're *not* going to *play it:* but I mean you
> to have a dozen lessons, for a dozen guineas, from Mr Walter Lacy,
> in Elocution the very first opportunity which occurs—and you must
> be prepared beforehand for the lessons—*Falconbridge* was one of his
> best parts—(Falconbridge the bastard of course I mean).
> "And hang a Calfskin on those recreant limbs"—
> Now set to work at once—*don't ask people about the part* at all, do it
> yourself *and then*—Mr Lacy—4

At last he was going to be spared any more schooling and the chance of
proving himself as an actor was near at hand.

Ted spent the first part of that summer with Boo and Joe Powell at
Brancaster, reading *King John* and *The Tale of Two Cities*; then Irving
invited him to Ramsgate; he was to go on his own and spend the rest of
his holiday there. This was a delightful gesture on Irving's part, making
it possible for them to get to know each other better, and he also foresaw
a good opportunity for them to go through Ted's forthcoming part in
The Dead Heart, thus saving time with him at rehearsals later.

At Ramsgate they stayed at the luxurious Granville Hotel, Irving's
dresser, Walter Collinson, being the only other member of the party,
and apart from occasional visitors they had the time to themselves. They
explored the neighbourhood and visited Canterbury. Ted began to
feel quite a man!

Life really was beginning for him in earnest. He had failed miserably
at all his schools, but now, as by magic, he had suddenly won a "scholar-
ship" to the Lyceum Theatre!

After his happy stay with Irving he returned to the Powells at Brancaster for his final visit before his first real job. Here, on August 27, he
got his last briefing from his mother:

> *Now remember*, I have the *highest hopes* for you, and the *fullest trust* in
> you, that you will now aim high, and always endeavour to do your
> best in your new calling—You'll find many temptations, but *with
> help* and determination to go right instead of *wrong*, you *will* go right,

will succeed—*will remain a gentleman*—and your Mammy's own lad—
with the respect of everybody in the theatre—and the affection too,
I'll be bound.

Be simple—truthful—and industrious and as *straight as a die and
you'll never get into trouble*, but if you go *ever so little out* of the straight,
you will get into trouble—One thing, too, remember—it's very
difficult to go *quite* straight always, but directly it *begins* to go wrong
go back and set it right—To have a friend is a good thing in need—
but *friends* to stick by one, and "hide the fault they see", are not
common as blackberries—they must be tried for years before one can
be *sure* of them—Such a friend *I* will be, if you want one in any difficulty—a cleverer friend than *younger* ones could be, if they wanted to,
ever so much, for I have *great experience in suffering* and great belief in
endeavour to be straight, and no belief whatever in fundamental
evil—evil right away down deep—It's our strength, or weakness—
I fear you have not shown much strength hitherto—when I was
young I was weaker than I am now—and suffering had made me
stronger, but I've always found a helping hand, the best thing in the
World in a difficulty—Now here's mine ready for you and *don't
forget* it—If I'm cross that's *nothing*—(the mere weakness of body)—
and never fear me, I love you and that means everything as you'll find
—Remember by the way to always say "Mr Irving" *in the theatre*—
not "Henry"—

I'm *so* glad when I think of your coming back—Give my love to
your friends—God bless you my dear dear Ted—You know who this
is from—

Mum

Rehearsals started; from now on, mother and son would see each
other daily. *The Dead Heart* was to open the season on September 28,
coinciding with the centenary celebrations of the capture of the Bastille
—a scene that would thrill the audience when they saw it on the stage.
This play, set against the background of the French Revolution, had
originally been written by Watts Phillips and was one of the successful
melodramas played at the Adelphi Theatre in 1859; but Irving engaged
Walter Pollock to rewrite the whole thing, after which he cut it and
rewrote many parts, as he did with most plays.

For weeks Irving had immersed himself in the French Revolution.

He spent large sums of money on prints, books, manuscripts, contemporary documents, swords, and so on. He wrote to Ellen, "I am full of the French Revolution, and could pass an examination." Ted observed all this, and bought a few books himself—after all, Irving was going to pay him £5 a week, which was really too much for a young man living at home.

He had never seen any reason for buying books before, except for casual reading. Now he discovered that books could help him to relive the life of past ages, and this knowledge would give him a special bearing in historical plays. He bought and read other plays and, in imitation of his master, cut and rewrote whole sections in order to "improve" them, make them more dramatic, but generally more melodramatic.

In August 1889 Ellen moved yet again—this time to a happier house that would always be associated with her great days at the Lyceum; this was 22 Barkston Gardens, only a few streets away from Longridge Road, but very, very different, chiefly because it overlooked beautifully kept trees and lawns. The house stood out from the others in the square because of the window-boxes at every window, so that the front of the house was literally draped in flowers. Here Ted and Edy had their own work-rooms. Some of Godwin's furniture still had pride of place in the dining-room and sitting-room; there was a piano, a settee, two arm-chairs, and a lovely sideboard with panels painted by Burne-Jones . . . all of which he had designed . . . all that was left of days gone by.

The elocution lessons started with Walter Lacy, a most handsome old actor who had been the dashing hero in many plays at the Princess's when Ellen first appeared there as a girl. Walter Lacy also knew a great deal about Charles Kean's methods, so Irving had engaged him as an "adviser" on his early Shakespearean productions. He was gratified to find that his young pupil actually knew the part of Falconbridge in King John—that reminded him . . . and a delightful afternoon was spent talking about the beauties of past productions.

Another tutor was Leon Espinosa, who also worked for Irving and was responsible for the dances in his productions. He had been a ballet master and a great name in his time, and still had the bearing of one who had inherited the traditions of the eighteenth century. He showed Ted how a young gentleman of 1798 should carry himself.

The "great" Jem Mace, who had retired from boxing, now taught fencing; from him Ted learned to be light on his feet and never to take his eyes off the eyes of his opponent.

At home his mother had arranged for him to have French lessons. His teacher was a young man named John Sankey, who later became Lord Chancellor, but at that time found it difficult to teach his pupil anything—Ted just could not cope with book learning.

Most mornings, Ted and his mother would go to the Lyceum in a one-horse landau, passing broughams, cabs, victorias and horse-drawn buses on the way. The streets smelt of sweating horses and the stable, for, as yet, there were no motor cars. As they returned at night, the lamplighters would be seen going their rounds lighting one gas-lamp after another, aided by a long pole with its protected flame at the tip.

A new quiet excitement and a sense of purpose was building up within. Ted found that the regular "good evening" and "good morning" to Barry, the stage-door keeper made him feel established. Arnott, the property-master used to tell him little stories about great transformation scenes in days gone by and, when no one was around, he would get the men to show him how the traps worked.

Among the actors whom he met, there were two that stood out, and whose characters he admired. They were both a lot older than himself. One of them was Mr Toole, the other was William Terriss.

Toole, with his twinkling eyes, was a much-loved man—"The Prince of Comedians." Whenever he visited the Lyceum everyone was delighted and wanted to have a word with him; many of the older men liked to reminisce with him about the good old days at the Adelphi Theatre down the Strand. Irving was always happy when his old friend called, and so the chain reaction reached young Teddy. Once, when he and his mother had gone to Brighton for the week-end, Toole called upon her at her hotel, but as she was still in bed, he took young Teddy for a walk and talked to him about life as though he was his equal. The subject drifted to "charity" and, coming to one of the many Regency crescents that are dotted about the town, Toole said, "Observe this group of identical houses—in each dwell individuals, let us see how *they* feel about charity." Then, mounting the steps of the first house, he knocked. A maid answered; "Good morning," said Toole seriously, as he raised his top hat, "would you, by any chance, have a little groundsel for a sick bird?" The girl looked sympathetic and asked him to wait; she returned with some crumbs in a little paper cone, saying that she was sorry they had no groundsel, would the crumbs do? He thanked her and left. As he knocked or pulled the jangling bell at different houses round the crescent, he either had the door slammed in his face, or he was laughed at, or some, like the first girl, went in search of a substitute; "which only goes to prove that we are all different," said Toole as they returned to the hotel, distributing little packets of crumbs and bird-seed to the delighted sparrows as they went along.⁵ Toole made Ted feel that older people were not only approachable but, in a way, heroic—fancy being able to go up to an important house, knock, and ask such a question in all seriousness! Toole was four years older than Irving and nearing sixty; Ted was seventeen.

William Terriss, his other hero, was very handsome, and the darling of the gallery girls. He had served in the navy, had tried tea-planting, had been shipwrecked, then had a go at sheep farming in South America where he had been embroiled in a local revolutionary upheaval. After two unsuccessful attempts he finally became an actor and a popular idol.

Ted first met him in the company of some other young actors at Rules in Maiden Lane, a favourite London eating-house for the profession; there he was amazed to see Terriss consume a whole duck and most of a bottle of port for his lunch!⁶

After *The Dead Heart* Irving put on *Ravenswood*, and Terriss was with the company. He and young Ted then became inseparable companions. Terriss used to tell him, "Watch the Governor and you'll learn everything, and remember—time flies."

If Ted was to remember anything it had to appeal to him through his emotions. History meant nothing to him unless presented in the form of pictures or personal memoirs of some person in whom he could take an interest. Pictures made the biggest impact. Books on the arts and crafts taught him nothing, but he could watch a scene painter like Hawes Craven and take in the whole technique in a flash; and, what is more important, his fertile imagination would run ahead adapting and developing the possibilities of what was to him a newly discovered medium of expression.

So Ted devoured rehearsals and watched Irving and everything he did—his craftsmanship, his bearing, his mannerisms—he was to use them all later.

The Dead Heart was another of Irving's successes, and although

Ellen's part gave her very little opportunity to sparkle she was happy to see her son received so well, and, of course, the audience seeing them together playing mother and son were delighted and allowed their emotions to run away with them. There were 183 performances during the season, the last performance taking place on May 9, 1890.

During the week-end before his eighteenth birthday, Ellen took Ted out to Harpenden to look at Fallows Green, then over to Gusterwood Common and all the old familiar places. She was to do this often during the remaining years of her life, and when I was a boy of thirteen I too was taken on the same pilgrimage, and at every shrine in her memory she would stop and would tell vividly and beautifully the story that was associated with the place. Old people would come from their cottages and say, "Hello, Nellie, how you doin'," and her mind would fly back to 1872.

Ellen often spent her week-ends with her other old friends from Gusterwood Common days, the Gibsons. They had lovely Ashwell House in the quieter part of St. Albans. Ted, and sometimes Edy, would go too. The Gibsons' daughter, May, was a handsome girl the same age as Ted, and they enjoyed each other's company. May was quite a competent though unimaginative little artist herself. She had considerably more strength of mind than he had and this he rather liked, as she could always be counted on to suggest a pleasant pastime. Sometimes they were allowed to go to the theatre together—provided little Maudie, May's niece, went with them.[7]

Soon after the last performance of The Dead Heart Ted joined the Haviland and Harvey Company and went on tour until September 4. Irving had encouraged him to do this because he thought it would give him an opportunity to gain experience in a number of parts with a good repertory company, a very different thing from the luxury of a run at the Lyceum, but in return for allowing them to bill him as "Mr Gordon Craig (of the Lyceum Theatre)," Irving insisted on selecting the parts that young Ted should play.

Throughout the tour his mother wrote him letters of advice, and was obviously still worried when he was out of her sight. She and Irving were filling in time with readings from Shakespeare which were very profitable in the provinces in those days. Ted wrote to her in Manchester telling of a cut that he had received during a stage duel. She replied at once.

Very glad to get your letter—oh, the poor hand! Keep the wound *clean*, and keep it *from the air*—if you neglect a cut like that, it may give you a good deal of trouble—You will get on quite well during this tour, and be quite happy if only you *keep your head*, on *all* occasions—I suppose you were very nervous on the Caleb night— *I hope so* or I'd not give 2d for your chances as an Actor— . . . think all the while, all you can of your work—I fear *Henry* doesn't believe *you think of it at all*!!

He says you have "natural ability" but have no *idea* of what "*work*" *even means*, so far—and he says if there's not the *necessity*, as in old times, that young actors should *make* it—that they should *Imagine* performances and make ready for that.[8]

Ten days later when she was back in London she wrote to advise him on his part of Gaspard in *The Lady of Lyons*.

Glad you are going to do "Gaspard"—you sh^d try to be in *deadly earnest* and the earnestness of a moody discontented reserved nature and the make-up might be either *very* short (almost shaved hair— brown & *dead pale face or*—the same hair black and a face as brown as a berry—*straight brows*, anyway, and a hard jaw)—I think perhaps it sh^d be quiet with the fires underneath breaking out through the eyes, and fists, and quivering lip—it's a wonderful little part—*very* difficult (to play *properly*) and you sh^d *get into the mood*, before you go on the stage—Remember—[9]

Ted did his best to keep her informed of the company's progress and to send her all the notices and tried to take in all her good advice.

Ellen kept his bank-book for him and insisted that while he was on tour he sent her £2 a week to put away as savings. That left him with only £2 a week but it still gave him no idea as to the real value of money. In London, book-shops, tailors, tradesmen of all kinds were only too delighted to give "Miss Terry's son" credit, and at Barkston Gardens he did not contribute towards his food and lodgings; there, he had two most beautiful rooms overlooking the Gardens, with Miss Harries, and Boo, plus two servants always in attendance. He was "treated" everywhere, and if his mother thought he needed anything she would make him a present of it. The £2 a week must have seemed like a whim on his mother's part, not a necessity for his survival in the future.

On August 25, the company was booked to perform at Northampton. This town had nostalgic memories for Ellen and for a moment she allowed herself to dwell upon them:

. . . You'll like *Northampton*—You must *notice well the Town Hall* there—and go over it—I will tell *why* some day—*I want you to make some* sketches of it for me 3 or 4 careful ones—
The tower, and three quarter face, &c, &c.—It is a beautiful design—and was chosen from dozens of others in a *competition* amongst architects a good number of years now ago—when there were not nearly so many beautiful buildings, and when all Art was in a dull almost hopeless condition—A young fellow of 21 or 22 won the competition, and amongst the competitors I think *Street & Scott* were included—but the design chosen was this young fellow's—and your Father was the young fellow—It, and heaps of other work he did afterwards, shᵈ have made his fortune, but he was very careless of money and wasted it and died very poor—But there was no one like him, none—A man born long before his time—Of extraordinary gifts, and of comprehensive genius—Until lately you have had so little understanding of the world, I have not been able to speak with you of many things but when you come back we must have some nice long *quiet* talks—and you will *understand*, and *feel*, I am sure.[10]

The tour ended on September 4, and on the whole his notices had been very good; so much so that he was able to reprint some in a little folder as a handout to other interested managements in the hope that, following the next "Lyceum season," he would be able to tour the provinces once more. Some of the notices are interesting, for they give an idea of the estimation of his acting ability at the time; here is a selection from four different newspapers:

. . . He has much of his distinguished mother's talent, and he loves the profession he has chosen with the love of an enthusiast. . . . Mr. Gordon Craig is tall, has a fine voice and good presence, and there is a world of progress before him.

as Alexander Oldworthy in *Nance Oldfield:*

> . . . He has mannerisms, but he has the true GIFT. He acts from within . . .

as Mercutio:

> . . . His rendering of the character of Mercutio was instinct with life and spirit. His laugh was natural and catching, and he fairly revelled in the wit and fancy that the master mind of Shakespeare has put in the mouth of the gay gallant . . .

as Caleb Deecie:

> Mr Gordon Craig's impersonation of the blind man Caleb Deecie, was touching, true to nature, and Mr Craig is certainly a finished actor in every respect.[12]

On September 20, the curtain went up on *Ravenswood*, in which Ted had the part of young Henry Ashton and the pleasure of being with his hero, Terriss, who played Hayston of Bucklaw.

In Act IV, Scene 4, called The Sea Coast, Hawes Craven had designed and painted such a simple yet impressive scene—showing a cove with some cliffs rising from the sands on one side—that the memory of it remained with Ted for the rest of his life and kept on re-emerging in many of his own early designs. In 1908 it was reflected for the last time as a superb wood engraving showing two Greek warriors fighting at the foot of a cliff—called, simply, "Design for a Stage Scene."[13]

Ted's mind worked very much like a musician's, who, travelling here and there and hearing a song sung by a peasant, or the tune of a passing band, would later adapt the air as a basic theme and develop it into a symphony. Isadora Duncan used to think it was shortsightedness that made him stop before some ghastly piece of architecture and draw it as a beautiful composition; he was, in fact, only using it as a theme. It is interesting however that Hawes Craven's scene was the first piece of theatrical scenery to affect him so strongly.

Towards the end of the run of *Ravenswood*, young Ted became ill with jaundice. Martin Harvey, his understudy, took over, and Ted went to recuperate at Hastings. Returning to Barkston Gardens for Christmas, he found himself sharing an old-fashioned railway carriage with a couple of navvies. The day before, Ted had read the ghastly details of the hanging of Mrs Pearcey for murder. As the train proceeded one of the navvies produced an enormous sandwich, bit into it, and as he pulled the sandwich away from his mouth, it took with it a long piece of gristle which suddenly snapped back into his face. Through a mouthful of meat and crumbs he remarked, with simple British humour, "Ello, ello, 'ere's a bit o' Mrs Pearcey!" This had such a profound effect on Ted that he was never able to eat a sandwich again, but the navvy's remark became part of his repertoire, and out it would come whenever he found something doubtful in his food.[14]

While he was ill, Terriss had written him a letter that is worth quoting because it is so typical of Terriss's manner:

Lyceum Theatre,
December 4, 90.

Dear friend and companion,

May these few lines when they meet your eyes—find you in a cheerful mood and spirit. Remember life at best is but a day and altho' now you are passing thru a misty atmosphere yet the bright sun will burst forth again and your bright smile and cheery laughter make the welkin ring.

We have many acquaintances but few friends—class me with the latter contingent and when called on shall not be found wanting—A cheery word makes the heart pulsate—Nothing is as bad but it might be worse—Thank the stars that if you hadn't been laid up as you are, you might have been run over and killed in the Strand instead of a comfy bed and home surrounded by all that's nice a good mother and plenty to eat.

God bless you—
William[15]

Soon after this, during a luncheon at Rules, Terriss was holding forth to Ted and some other young actors. He proclaimed that one could never play a part unless one believed in it; if one believed in it intensely, only then could one make the audience believe in it, too. The argument went on and he took a wager that by his acting he would stop the traffic on Waterloo Bridge by gathering a crowd to see something that wasn't there. The party started across the bridge, wondering what Terriss would do. Suddenly he stopped and looked across the river gasping, "My God!" The others stopped; what had he seen? He grasped the parapet and peered still further—"My God, it moves," he murmured, as in a trance. More and more people gathered to see. Then, pointing slowly and dramatically towards the enormous lion on the brewery across the water, he gasped, "The tail... *the tail* ... it MOVES!!" His arm was rigid, his eyes starting out of his head; all were straining their eyes and murmuring. The police came along—"Now then Mr. Terriss, what are you up to?" Terriss smiled and turned back to Rules, pocketing a £5 note which he gave to the waiters.[16] A man who could do a thing like that fascinated young Ted. It was not as subtle as Toole and "the groundsel for a sick bird," but it was marvellously spectacular!

The 1891 season saw Ted in many small parts with Irving and his mother. The plays: *Much Ado about Nothing, Charles I, Olivia, The Corsican Brothers, Nance Oldfield*, and *A Regular Fix*.

When the season was over he joined a travelling company again; this time it was with the famous Sarah Thorne. Sarah, who was then fifty-four, was quite a personality. She ran a stock company at the Theatre Royal, Margate, where she also trained young actors. The tour took him to Canterbury, Tunbridge Wells and Deal, and as far away as Edinburgh. When it was over he returned to the Lyceum to rehearse the part of Cromwell in Irving's version of *Henry VIII*. Irving, by way of encouragement, raised his salary to £7 a week.

The last two years had been exciting, and every moment that he was with Irving he found intensely interesting and exhilarating, but when he was away from his master's magic, life became drab.

The first night of *Henry VIII* was on January 5, 1892. On the sixteenth he was twenty years of age. He sent his photograph to his old nurse, dear Essie of Gusterwood Common days; with it he sent a letter in which he said:

> You remember Mrs Gibson don't you—Mother's great friend: well, her daughter and I hope some day to be married. . . . I thought you would care to hear this and perhaps from me . . .

This was his first mention of marriage; it was followed by a P.S.

My stage name and the name I shall always use will be Gordon
Craig.[17]

Although he had followed Edy's lead in adopting Craig as a stage
name, Henry, Edward, and Gordon had been added when he was christened at the age of sixteen—Edward after his father, Henry after his
godfather, Irving, and Gordon after his godmother, Lady Gordon.

He had found the christening service very impressive—a bit too
emotional, though. He always found church services rather overpowering, and later in life when he was in Florence, he would go into a
church to look at a painting and become spellbound by the ritual, the
lighting, the singing, the slow movements of the priests, and the
obvious inspiration of the congregation. Suddenly, he would wrench
himself away from the spectacle and sit a long while, silently thinking.

It was not until after his twenty-first birthday that his stage name
became official when it was registered by Deed Poll on February 24,
1893.

After Irving's generosity in paying him £7 a week, he was very
discontented when Sarah Thorne would not offer him more than £5 a
week for the 1892 summer tour, but it was, after all, the top salary in
the provinces. However, the company stayed most of the time in
Margate, which made things easier as he grew to know and like the
place. Mrs Thorne was also generous enough to let him have a benefit
performance at which he cleared £20 and that made him feel enormously rich!

That year he also made some extra money, and gained extra experience by doing recitals with Violet Vanbrugh at "At Homes."

Fashionable hostesses were "At Home" on fixed days every month
during the season and musicians, actors, actresses, even young poets
were paid to give recitals. You arrived in a cab or carriage and were
relieved of your outer garments by footmen, or maidservants in white-
lace pinafores, then ushered into a lower room where you feasted upon
piles of sandwiches and tiny cakes, all marked with little flags describing
them, or tasted little custards and ices handed round by other footmen.
Behind this mountain of food and epergnes of sweet peas and asparagus
fern officiated the parlour-maids, who fluttered excitedly if you were
well known. From the rooms above could be heard the distant applause
rewarding some favourite who had just entertained the gathering. Up

the stairs you went, to be announced by some enormous voice at the door; the hostess, never far away, swooped upon you, and repeating your name aloud, said how delighted she was to see you. All round the front drawing-room and spilling over into the inner drawing-room sat the senior guests resplendent in their afternoon attire, and behind them stood the younger people, murmuring to one another—there was very little floor space left. You were introduced to some special guests, then, as though the idea had just occurred to her the hostess would say: "Mr Craig, I wonder if you would care to recite something for us? We did so enjoy seeing you in *Ravenswood* last week." You said yes, you did have something that you hoped would amuse, and all were silent as you went through the ordeal. Then came the patter of applause again. Later, when you were leaving, you were handed a little envelope like a spy being handed some secret papers—in it you found a cheque for the sum agreed by you or your agent. All *so* polite and—terrifying.

Recitals were, nevertheless, very well paid; one performance could bring in the equivalent to a week's tour, or more. Ted, though slightly feminine in appearance, was much talked about because he was "such a beautiful boy"—Oscar Wilde once wrote and told him so, but Ellen commandeered the letter.

None of this, however, was helping him much with his future. Only one thing impressed him deeply that year. He went to listen to the Bavarian artist Hubert von Herkomer, who had settled in England at Bushey in Hertfordshire, when he gave a lecture on "Scenic Art" at the Avenue Theatre. Herkomer emphasized certain defects in modern theatrical productions. He pointed out that theatres were built so absurdly that figures on the stage looked like deformed dwarfs from any view-point in the gallery, and that footlights—a convention inherited from the past—cast unwanted shadows over the actors' features, so that the eyes of a person with prominent cheek-bones were completely blacked out if he or she stood near the front of the stage; that the raising of a curtain disclosed the actor's feet first, and revealed the scene from bottom to top. He also attacked the absence of movement or atmospheric effects in the skies, conventional scenery, and so on. All this was demonstrated with real lights, scenery, and lantern slides.

Herkomer had his own little theatre in his Art School at Bushey and there he amazed his audience with his impressions of moonlight, misty glens, sunrises, etc., all done by the most careful use of *electric* lights and painted gauzes. His curtain did not go up but parted slowly from the centre outwards. There were no footlights—only side-lights . . . at a proper distance. A lot of the scenery was in relief. The orchestra was hidden.

Most important of all, Herkomer had written his own plays and composed his own music "reminding the audience of Purcell and Arne in the songs, and Wagner in the orchestration." He acted, danced and sung in the chief roles, and designed his own scenery; his pupils helped him to build it, and acted in the remaining parts. They printed their own programmes, and their most magnificent invitation cards. His shows were in no way amateurish and many theatre people went to see them in order to pick up ideas.[18]

Ted had been to Herkomer's theatre before, with his mother, and was much impressed by all he had seen and heard there. When Herkomer's talks appeared later as articles in the *Magazine of Art*, Ted bought them and, together with one or two other articles on Miracle plays and costume, started another scrap-book. He was convinced about one thing—should he ever be an actor-manager he would do away with footlights and open his curtains sideways . . . and use electric light. Why didn't Henry Irving use electric light? He often wondered, but evidently never asked.

The end of the year saw him back at the Lyceum rehearsing the part of Oswald in *King Lear*. The show opened on November 10. Then came Christmas. The next year was to see a major change in his life.

CHAPTER FOUR

May Gibson · Jimmy Pryde · Despair
1893–1896

IRVING WAS planning the 1893 American tour, his company's fourth, to begin in March, when Ellen came to him full of anxiety—her boy was talking vaguely of marriage. He would be twenty-one in January, free to do as he liked, and she feared he might be foolish and tie himself to the wrong girl.

Ted's name was already down for the tour, and just after his birthday he received a letter from Irving apologizing for missing the date by two days. The letter went on:

> I have heard with regret that you do not think of going with us to America—Is not this a pity? You have a prospect of playing some splendid parts, which would certainly give you a great experience.
>
> Should you take another engagement in London, you will be tied down, as now, to one part and could not possibly get the practice which you would have with us—for you would have understudies besides your own repertoire.
>
> I hope you will think better of it and come with us—but if you should be married (as this is not impossible) there would be nothing but to leave your wife behind in England.
>
> The hard work and anxieties of such a tour as ours could be very great and to drag about a young wife on such an expedition would be positively dangerous—a responsibility *which I* would not undertake with anyone in whom I was interested. Say you had to leave your

wife behind, in a town, there would be great risk in that—and if *you* stayed behind it would cause the greatest inconvenience to us.

Of the anxiety to (your) Mother I say nothing. Such a mother as yours has no peace when you are disturbed—or your interests are at stake.

This tour will be a very hard one for her, and her work, as much as she can possibly bear, and your presence would be a comfort to her I know.

Now I would advise you to leave your wife behind or wait for your marriage until you return—when you would have less work, less anxiety and less discomfort.

I would very much like you to come with us as you told me you would—And I should not only like you to be with us for my sake but more for your mother's and your own—for I know it would be for your good. God Bless you old fellow—I am glad to hear you are feeling all right again—H. I.

18th Jan. 1893.[1]

Irving's reference to it being "positively dangerous" to drag a young woman about on such a tour was echoed by Ellen a few months later, when she wrote: "This rushing, tearing America, so full of hope! but oh, so rough—so rough"; in Boston there was "no decent bread, and the water was filthy"; later, she writes of the Southern states, "Poor places! Defeated." . . . "In New Orleans they say water is found (at) three feet . . . they can't bury their dead here but have to take them away to the hills."

Pinkerton's Detective Agency was busy offering rewards for the capture of such men as Bill Doolin and his gang, Butch Cassidy, and the Wild Bunch: there might be surprises for anyone who thought High Street, Dallas, and High Street, Uxbridge, were in any way similar.

Irving followed up his letter to Ted with a present of a superb gold watch with an inscription. Ellen gave him some original manuscript poems by Walt Whitman and a first edition of *Leaves of Grass*; these she had bought in America during the last tour, knowing he loved Whitman, although she herself did not like his work.

The watch may have reminded him of Terriss's warning that "time flies" . . . But after reading Whitman, he would hardly feel more amenable to discipline—

> Walt Whitman am I, a Kosmos,
> of mighty Manhatten the son,
> Turbulent, fleshy and sensual,
> eating, drinking and breeding.

This was stronger stuff than Rossetti's translation of Dante's *La Vita Nuova* which he had just been reading. He had given May Gibson a copy of this, marking such lines as:

> With sighs my bosom always laboureth
> In thinking, as I do continually,
> Of her for whom my heart now breaks apace.

He was already aware of a feeling of revolt in the arts. Apart from Whitman, he had read Victor Hugo and seen his exciting drawings; Whistler's paintings fascinated him; Monet's pulsating colours and suggestion of form without any rigid outline excited him too— especially the pictures of Rouen Cathedral of which he had seen reproductions. All the Impressionists were exciting, but in his circle of friends there was no one to whom he could talk about such men and their work. There were also Ibsen and Strindberg, whose plays he had found and read, but their names were not mentioned at the Lyceum. There were Wagner and Sibelius, and so many others whose works he had glimpsed or heard about. Under the stage at the Lyceum, in the fluttering gas-light, members of the orchestra sometimes spoke about "the rebels," and played a bar or two to prove a point. Mr Fillery, the machinist, told how they actually used electric lights *on the stage* at the Savoy. He knew that outside this magnificent temple of tradition there were other joys and he yearned to know more about them.[2]

May reminded him that he had talked to her about marriage once or twice; now that he was of age he no longer had to ask his mother's permission. He had some money, why not? It would be a step in the direction of self-assertion.

While Ellen was enjoying the spring weather at her Winchelsea Cottage, she received a telegram, dated March 27, to say that Ted and May had been married at a Registry Office. She made the entry in one of her note-books and added, "This is the 19th Century!"

May, being a practical girl, had probably thought it wise to get Ted to make up his mind, for at that time there were two other girls who also thought him a desirable partner; one of them was pretty Lucy Wilson, about whom he was always talking, the other was Jess Dorynne, a beautiful young actress with a far-away look in her eyes, who Ellen very much liked.

Ted thought of marriage as a poetic state of being—it would be *romantic;* one would have a house of one's own . . . and he thought no further. Money? Oh, he had that, and more would turn up—in respect to money and beautiful women he thought along rather the same lines as his father.

Through his mother's efforts as his banker, he had in the last five years amassed a sum of about £700. This was a good capital on which to start married life: in those days £260 a year was a reasonable budget for a young couple.

Ellen had written to remind him that the American tour would see him richer by about £300, and surely May could, and should, wait that little bit longer? She ended by reminding him:

> You are of age now—a man—and must look the matter in the face— not excitedly like a hysterical girl, but calmly, and dispassionately.[3]

But spring was in the air. Marriage to May seemed much more tempting than the hard slogging of a tour in America.

For some time Ellen had noticed that he took his work at the Lyceum far too lightly, and when Irving had more or less pushed him out on tour Ted was resentful and went grudgingly, just to show his master that he could do it.

He was spending a great deal on books, pictures, stationery, and clothes, and could always be persuaded to buy a new hat—he loved hats. He never bothered to pay bills until they arrived with an accompanying letter requesting, "Immediate payment—or else."

Ellen had a little cottage at Uxbridge, as well as those at Winchelsea and Hampton Court. The cottage, once known as the Audrey Arms, was a delightful seventeenth-century building in half timber and brick; it was at the bottom of the hill near the Treaty House and Flour Mills, and beside it was a bridge over the river Coln, where ducks quacked merrily, waiting for bits to be thrown. She used this cottage, like the others that she collected, for odd week-ends when trying to forget the theatre; now she told Ted that he and May could have it as their first home for five shillings a week. She would have liked to have made him a present of it, but did not think it would be good for him to get it for nothing; he needed to be reminded of his responsibility.

Uxbridge was on the St. Albans line of the Great Western Railway. It was a prosperous little town and beyond it was the densely wooded Buckinghamshire countryside—a painter's paradise. The near-by villages of Chalfont St. Giles, Fulmer, and Ickenham were places Ellen loved to drive to for peace and quiet.

It was when Ted was returning to Uxbridge one summer evening that he got to know the painter James Pryde, whom he had once met briefly at the Lyceum, where Jimmy's parents were always welcome guests. On the train, their conversation ranged over many subjects. They spoke of Herkomer, Irving, the theatre, and finally of Alexandre Dumas; this man, they agreed, was the greatest writer of historical novels; each could quote incidents to the other's delight—what Gorenflot had said, what Chicot had done, and d'Artagnan, and Porthos—what superb characters! By the time they arrived at Uxbridge they were old friends. Together they walked up from the station to the High Street, turned left and down to the Audrey Arms; they agreed they would all meet the following day. Then Jimmy walked on to Denham where he was going to stay with his sister who had just married the painter William Nicholson.

Thus began a friendship that was to take Ted's attention away from acting and centre it for the next few years on the graphic arts.

William Nicholson was from Newark. James Pryde came from Edinburgh. Nicholson was the same age as Ted; Jimmy Pryde was six years older.

Pryde and Nicholson were gay Bohemians who were about to achieve universal fame as the most outstanding English poster designers, comparable only with Toulouse-Lautrec and Alphonse Mucha, the great French artists. Pryde had remarkable inventiveness and saw the world as a vast stage full of forms and shadows, enlivened by little figures here and there, suggesting that something dramatic was just about to happen. Nicholson went in closer; he loved characters, expressions, shapes. He was a great master of technique, and whether engaged on oil painting or wood engraving, always found a way of expressing what he wanted with bold shadows and highlights, and a few exquisitely simplified details. Together they made poster designs which they signed "Beggarstaff" or "W. J. Beggarstaff," but were often referred to as "the Beggarstaff Brothers."

These two artists came together through James Pryde's sister Mabel, who had fallen in love with Nicholson at Herkomer's art school where she was also a student.

When Ted and May descended on them at their cosy cottage, The Six Bells (another one-time public house), they felt very welcome. The atmosphere was homely; the walls and floors were covered with bits of drawings and cut-outs, samples of lettering, pots of paste, pots of colour. Nicholson was doing most of the work, Jimmy having bright ideas, Ted being enlightened. He was also enchanted by Mabel, who was thrilled to have Ellen Terry's son as a guest.

Ted knew nothing about drawing beyond what he had gleaned from his "copying" lessons with Mrs Cook. Now, watching Nicholson the whole conception of making pictures appeared to him in a new light; the magic of it caught him.

Nicholson had a trick that fascinated him: you scribbled and scribbled away at an idea, then put a piece of black (not blue) transfer paper under the scribble, and, selecting certain lines from amongst the scribbles, transferred them on to a piece of sugar paper; then, with a paint brush dipped in water, you went over these few lines and gave them a soft edge; the result was delightful, and so simple. He also had a way of pencilling in a design very lightly and, with waterproof Indian ink, filling in all the shadows very boldly. When it was dry, he touched up all the highlights and put in the details with Chinese white; the result looked liked a woodcut. In fact some of his so-called woodcuts were made that way.

When Nicholson actually engraved on wood, Ted watched, spell-bound, as the design slowly developed: the wood was cut away and a light pattern emerged on a dark ground, first in bold splashes by using a large tool, after which the minutest details were added with a small tool; one could then print a copy and go on altering the block until one achieved the desired result; then one could print, or have printed, hundreds of copies . . . thousands . . . The idea of starting with a black background and slowly introducing light was what captured Ted's imagination.[4]

At this time simplification in design was beginning to appeal to public taste; Victorian over-elaboration had reached such proportions in the hands of tradesmen with no artistic appreciation that it was becoming monstrous. The desire for the simple approach led many artists and their friends to collect the work of country craftsmen: horse brasses, country pottery, shepherds' smocks, wooden toys, and so on.

In 1883, Joseph Crawhall, a little-known pen-and-ink artist from Newcastle, produced for Field and Tuer at "The Leadenhall Press" a quite remarkable book of ballads and short stories, *Olde Tayles Newlye Related, enryched with all ye Ancyente Embellyshmentes*. It was printed in quarto on a coarse buff paper, using very fat and well-inked types, and

Craig's wood engraving of Walt Whitman, made from a photograph.

the "Ancyente" engravings were in fact, bold, humorous designs by Crawhall himself, all engraved on wood. The whole approach was joyful and robust, and appealed instantly to Nicholson, Pryde, and Craig, as well as to many other artists in England and America. The idea of the bold woodcut caught on. They were such a delightful change from the prosaic wood engravings made by men like Swain, whose work featured among so many contemporary book illustrations.

Ted went up to London and in Red Lion Court, off Fleet Street, discovered old Lacy Evans, a strange character who resurfaced old woodblocks. From him he bought some tools and a few small squares of boxwood. He struggled to make one or two woodcuts, but had little success until one day Nicholson suggested that he take a photograph in which the highlights were in great contrast to the shadows, trace it, transfer it to a wood-block and just cut out the highlights. Ted tried this with a photograph of his beloved poet, Walt Whitman, and the result looked so professional that he was encouraged to go on.

This sudden contact with the graphic arts must have awoken some dormant artistic sense inherited from his father, for he seemed to assimilate all that he now saw happening around him with astonishing rapidity and with apparent ease.

On September 4, 1893, Ellen and Henry Irving set off on their tour, which was to last until March 17 of the following year. Ted and May were alone at last, except for visits to and from their new friends at Denham and to May's parents at St. Albans.

Time passed carelessly. Ted occasionally tried his hand at sketching, but was not happy with the results now that he had seen Nicholson and Pryde at work, so he returned once more to an art in which he considered himself to be something of a master: the preparation of plays for acting. This was something he had seen Irving do so brilliantly—you took a play with a good plot and cut it, then rewrote whole passages, transposing lines, and finally produced what you considered to be a good play from the *actor's* point of view. After all, you argued, it was meant to be performed, not read in a corner. Garrick had set an example some time before by slashing Shakespeare's *Macbeth* and *The Taming of the Shrew* to ribbons, and then, by introducing music and ballets here and there, had actually made the great bard popular in the eighteenth century. Ted started on *Henry IV*, which he hoped to adapt in such a way as to make it possible for one actor (himself!) to play Hotspur as well as Prince Hal. Then he tackled Robert Browning's *A Blot in the 'Scutcheon*; *Peer Gynt*, he thought, had great possibilities.

Then one day there was a knock on the door; the Reverend T. W. James was calling. Ted, who was probably expecting a little homily on "Married Life," was agreeably surprised by what his visitor had to say. The Reverend James was trying to raise funds for the National Schools in Uxbridge, and wondered if Mr Craig—connected as he was with the Lyceum Theatre—would care to help by giving a recitation or acting some little scene in a performance they were hoping to put on at the

Town Hall in November. Ted said he would be delighted and told the
Reverend James that he would most definitely help. Then he sat down
to think of all the recitals he had done with Violet Vanbrugh. As one
idea gave way to another, it suddenly occurred to him that instead of a
recitation or a duologue he might produce a whole play! And with the
help of the remaining Lyceum staff there was no limit . . .

The following day he was up in London talking it over with Violet
Vanbrugh. Then he lunched at Rules and met the actor Tom Heslewood. Tom, who loved anything with a mediaeval background, said
why not put on Alfred de Musset's *On ne badine pas avec l'Amour*, known
under the English title of *No Trifling with Love*. They read it through
together and Ted thought it a magnificent idea. He would be Perdican,
Vi would be Camille. While Ted set to work, cutting the play into
shape, Tom sounded various friends about playing other parts.[5]

Since the action of the play was supposed to take place in France in
the Middle Ages, Ted studied his father's copy of Viollet le Duc, and
then wandered round the National Gallery looking at the early masters
and making notes.

Then there was the incidental music—that must be correct too, so
Jo, a girl friend of Edy's, was called in to help. Jo, who looked more
like a pretty boy, was also known as "Jimmy" Overbeck; she was also a
baroness.

The announcements, which looked rather like invitations to a wedding, were printed and sent out—proclaiming:

> We intend to give as *thorough* a performance as possible, and to that
> end all the costumes are being specially made, the music specially
> written, and the scenery specially painted.[6]

Although Ted did not actually design the costumes, he took little
sketches along to the Lyceum wardrobe, giving details of all that he
hoped to get so that the right things should be put together—the
trimmings to the dresses, the pearl on the cuff. The few people left in
the department did their best.

The scenery was mostly damask hangings; the furniture was from a
collection of old props left over from *Louis XI*.

All this cost money, of course, but Ted wanted everything perfect—
accurate in every detail.

The cast was advertised on November 2, 1893 as:

Mrs. Gordon Craig,   Mrs. J. Fountain,
    Miss Miller,   Miss Wortham,
and
Miss Violet Vanbrugh
(of Lyceum & Daly's Theatres, London)

Mr. Heslewood,   Mr. Fountain,
Mr. Barnett,
Mr. E. Woodbridge,   Mr. A. Bird,
and
Mr. Gordon Craig
(of Lyceum & Daly's Theatres, London)

The programme also included a comedy by Benjamin Buckstone called *A Rough Diamond*, and two duologues, one of these being *Au Revoir* by the poet Austin Dobson.

Unluckily, when the time came, Vi could not play the part of Camille, and it was eventually taken by Miss Italia Conti.

Full of enthusiasm, Ted wrote to his mother telling her that he was "in control" of the entire production. Unimpressed, she replied:

I hope the Uxbridge performance is progressing—I fear those sort of affairs tho' "*for charity*," turn out to be full of trouble and with *no* result or benefit to "The Charity" or anyone else—and generally it is thus—like—

Expenses............... £13 11 9
Returns £12   0 0
Profit ....Ah   !   !
Loss.................Oh!

If you'll tell me the result exactly I will—Well—tell me the result —I don't think it's the best practise for you either my Ted—for it is the best practise to be under control in one's work—until one is mature at least—and often *then*.[7]

Ellen was right: when it was all over there was nothing to show. He wished he had been able to print a proper programme; he knew he'd made many mistakes, but he'd enjoyed himself; it had been his first production; he had done it alone.

By Christmas it was only too obvious that May was pregnant, and they wrote to tell Ellen. After this, her letters seemed to be devoted to May's well-being and the coming baby, except for continual reminders to Ted that he must get a job and earn some money—and spend less on luxuries like hand-made writing paper.

It appears that, in less than a year, they had almost run through their £700—a lot of it, of course, had gone on the production. Ellen, far away in America, was very concerned about their lack of money and began to send £3 a week to help them—

> I could let you have £5 as easily as £3—but my dearest darling you had better try the £3. . . . Remember that at the Red House on Gusterd Wood Common your father and I lived on £2.[8]

On April 8 a little daughter was born; they called her Rosemary. As soon as the baby could be taken out they went up to Window & Grove to be photographed.

Window & Grove, in fashionable Westbourne Grove—"Photographers to the Royal Family"—had photographed Ellen Terry and Henry Irving in nearly every part in which they had appeared; later they included young Gordon Craig and his sister, Ailsa Craig; now, here was the third generation: they considered it an honour. It was also good business, for the demand for mounted photographs of theatrical celebrities was prodigious. Families had vast albums full of half-plate or *carte-de-visite* photographs of their favourite stars, and compared them like stamp-collectors; as soon as a new one was out, a copy had to be obtained.

Ted was very proud of his little daughter and sent copies of the photographs to all his friends and relations.

By July, Ted, who had done nothing in the way of acting for over a year, suddenly realized that he had no more money. He was stung into action by his mother and the pleadings of his wife . . . he must do something to keep the home together and help pay their way. He started scanning *The Stage* and *The Era* and at last came across an advertisement that interested him:

THE W. S. HARDY SHAKESPEARE COMPANY

were looking for experienced members of the profession to make up their touring company. Ted applied and found, to his joy, that they had not decided upon their young lead. They were as happy as he was: in the provinces, "Gordon Craig of *The Lyceum Theatre*" would look good on the play-bills, especially when associated with plays like *Hamlet*, *Othello*, and *Richard III*, which were part of their repertoire. They intended starting with *Hamlet*, and this was the main attraction for Ted.

Ever since Irving's famous revival in 1874, the part of Hamlet was every actor's ambition. Ted, when in a melancholy mood, saw himself as a young Hamlet: his father was dead, his mother had been married to another—sometimes he even wondered if his father had been poisoned, Hamlet's father had been . . . Yes, *Hamlet* just suited his mood.

He rushed back to tell Pryde and Nicholson, and they set to work designing him a magnificent poster, which they were to deliver to Hereford in time to advertise the first performance. When the parcel arrived and was unrolled, Ted was overjoyed; the design was bold and impressive. On turning to look at Mr and Mrs Hardy, he could see that they were . . . well . . . really rather horrified—it was so very *modern*. A six-foot length of brown packing paper on which was stencilled in black the side view of a young Hamlet looking at a skull, his face and hands in a light ochre colour; underneath, in capital letters was written "Hamlet," and the famous signature, "Beggarstaff"—nothing more, no time or place or date! Ted arranged, at his own expense, to have the posters stuck up all over Hereford, and two outside the theatre. It was, after all, the very first Beggarstaff poster to be used in public—some had been seen at a great exhibition of posters and others would soon be acclaimed where ever they were shown—but in distant Hereford, and for Mr Hardy's company, it was a bit of a shock.[9]

The company played at Ludlow, Rhyl, Wolverhampton, Wellingborough, Rugby, Salford, and ended up at Uxbridge. It had been an exciting trip full of experiences typical of the old travelling companies, such as playing to a theatre in Wellingborough with "only eighteen shillings in the audience."

Ted was very disgruntled when, after playing the lead in *Hamlet*, he was only given the smaller parts of Cassio in *Othello* and Gratiano in *The Merchant of Venice*. He mentioned this in a letter to his mother, who replied:

Oh, Ted, you're quite wrong in thinking that either Henry or I ever went touring and playing big parts before we played little ones, and we *never* either of us went touring on *our own account* until about 15 or 16 years ago—We played in provincial *engagements* parts like Hero & Claudio— Nerissa & Lorenzo—(or Gratiano) and then minor parts in all the melodramas such as "The Mutiny at the Nore" "The Angel of Midnight"—"Giselle" and all the *bigger* parts in *Farce*, but go on tour with the responsibility of our own company we never did. You say "the art has not changed, tho' the times have"—Henry says the man who sets himself *against* the times in an Art as old as the dramatic art wᵈ be a fool, and get left"![10]

When he returned home he found Rosie grown and his wife rather melancholy—she had found life lonely except when she had been visited by the Nicholsons or when she had stayed with her mother at St. Albans.

The next four months at home were very difficult and he could not settle down to the domestic distractions of family life. He was constantly being asked to help with the baby, and at night she cried. There was no running water; it had to be fetched from a pump. He tried to engrave and managed to make some of his first book-plates. But the cottage seemed far too small for the three of them.

Then he found that May was expecting another child. This perplexed him: why had she decided to have another child just when she knew they were so short of money? He thought it was just a little inconsiderate! Although he was not such a fool that he did not know how babies came into the world, he was always firmly convinced that women could, somehow, decide at what time they would allow themselves to become pregnant. In later years, he would say: "Women know how to look after themselves if they want to," and he actually believed that they all possessed some jealously guarded secret.

In the following year, 1895, some newcomers to the theatre world, Hubert Evelyn and his pretty wife, Mina Leigh, were looking for a young actor to play Cavaradossi opposite her Tosca in the play of that name. Gordon Craig's name was suggested to them. They read his "notices" and saw photographs of him in *The Dead Heart*, which was set around the same period as *Tosca*, and that decided them. Evelyn was having special scenery designed, and new costumes—everything was to be perfect for his young wife. As expense did not seem to matter, Ted asked for £10 a week and, to his delight, got it. The tour was to last from March till June. At first Evelyn, who took the part of Scarpia, felt pangs of jealousy watching Ted play opposite his wife, but when he saw that Ted had found an old girl friend in the company he felt more at ease. The friend was pretty Lucy Wilson, and Ted found her even more attractive than he had when they were last together just before his marriage; he now accompanied her everywhere. There was a month's rehearsals at the Victoria Theatre in Waterloo Road, and then they took to the road: Eastbourne, Bath, Coventry, Stratford, Yarmouth, Norwich, Ryde, Southampton.

While they were at Coventry, Irving sent him an invitation to attend the first night of *A Story of Waterloo* and *Don Quixote*. He dashed down to London and sat in the stalls, feeling "no great sadness" at not being with the company on the stage.

The next day, while he was visiting May, she gave birth to a son. He stayed another day, then, leaving May with her mother, rejoined the Evelyns at Coventry, the very proud father of Robin.

The tour ended on June 18, but he did not go home, for he had discovered that Lucy was joining another company in Paisley. Instead, he arranged for his agent, Mr Tate, to get him a job with the same company, although this entailed a fifty per cent reduction in his salary. To his mother he wrote:

> . . . I'm afraid I must come down to £5. That blessed £5 which I began with as a sort of earnest of what was to come. It is better to earn (that) than have an earnest of what you're not going to get . . .[11]

They started with *The New Magdalen* by Wilkie Collins, Lucy playing Mary, and Ted, the Reverend Grey. By this time he was becoming positively ill with longing for Lucy, who had always had a soft spot for him, but now that he was "happily married," did nothing to encourage his amorous inclinations. He put poems by Heine to music for her; he had flowers sent to her at the theatre: she remained as sweet and immovable as ever.

In July, while they were in Edinburgh, Jimmy Pryde decided to visit his native city. He joined Ted, who got him one or two small walking-on parts with the company; Jimmy was as excited about acting as Ted was about drawing; he was in heaven!

Jimmy, seeing how his young friend was suffering, did what he could to help. He showed him round Edinburgh and Glasgow, Aberdeen and Dundee, and stayed with him until they reached Newcastle in September. When they were not discussing Lucy, or Irving's knighthood, they talked again and again of Alexandre Dumas, and one day Pryde suggested that Ted might try to illustrate some of Dumas's novels starting with *The Vicomte de Bragelonne*. He advised Ted to copy some figures from Jacques Callot's seventeenth-century plates, of which he had a small collection, and to make up the backgrounds by tracing bits from other sources; that way, he would gain confidence. Ted was soon absorbed in this new interest, and Lucy became merely his "inspiration."

When he returned home, May's attitude toward him had changed; she seemed hurt and aloof. In theatrical circles scandal spreads fast—she had heard stories about his attention to Lucy, and the fact that he had taken such a cut in salary just to follow her around infuriated her. They were both miserable.

They decided that they needed a change and moved to London to be nearer things. They found a place at 20 Addison Road, and were soon followed by their friends the Nicholsons. Other neighbours were C. B. Cochran, and a character called Ranger Gull, a journalist whom Ted liked at once; he made him a book-plate, then went off him just as quickly because he resented his familiar manner with Mabel Nicholson.

Ted had only one desire now, to have more time and space in which to draw and practise engraving. This had become the only occupation that brought him real satisfaction; in taking his mind off his many worries, it admitted him to a world of his own that was full of romance. But the babies took up all the room, and May was resentful if he spent a lot of time with the Nicholsons up the road.

He began to feel that he could please no one. From his mother came letters of advice, always advice—with just a bit of love tacked on to the end. He could not see that all this advice was meant to steer him away from trouble and future suffering, and that it was prompted by deep affection. He could not understand why his mother, who, after all, made so much money, should worry about the small sums he kept asking for—like a child asks for a penny to go and buy sweets. Another letter arrived in which she pointed out:

At my time of life with my regular work to do I *must* expect *help* from you, rather than all these added little worries and added responsibilities. . . . I look upon this £3 per week as helping May and your babies, and *you must not put it to any other use*—and for yourself you must make your own living. . . . *Do you see the doubled responsibilities which await you in the near future?* Give up dreaming of the future, and make your *bread and butter for today.* The rest will follow *if you do this now—not else*! . . . You will have your wife— you *will* have your children—Well, they are joys—then work for them, deny yourself other joys—*books*, and *pictures*, and feed and wash them—yourself—*I* did—and it did me more good than any other thing. They are helpless—when *you* were helpless I was your servant—I had no servants for you—and I cooked and baked, and washed and sewed for you—and scrubbed for you, and *fainted* for you, and *got well again for you*, as my mother did for me—You talk and talk, and don't *do*—"*He who would rule the day, must greet the morn—There is no hour to lose.*"[12]

This letter saddened him—especially the picture of his little mother cooking, baking, washing, scrubbing . . . and fainting *just for him.* He went the rounds again but it was too late in the year—managements were only thinking of pantomime.

The year 1896 came along and suddenly there was new hope: his old friend Sarah Thorne offered him the leading parts in *Hamlet* and *Romeo and Juliet*, with star billing on all the posters—but the best she could do in the way of salary was £2 a week; this was a terrible comedown, but together with his mother's £3 a week, life would be a lot easier—at least, he thought it would, for he did not know what "chance" had in store.

CHAPTER FIVE

Jess · the Dawning of Ideas
1896–1899

SARAH THORNE'S offer of £2 a week was very small, but the engagement was with her stock company so there would be no travelling from place to place and no looking for doubtful lodgings. During the two months at Chatham he would also share in a benefit performance with two other actors, and that alone could be worth another £10 to £15.

The parts offered were the great attraction: Petruchio in *The Taming of the Shrew*, Fabien and Louis in *The Corsican Brothers*, and the title roles in *Hamlet* and *Macbeth*—this was an opportunity not to be missed when one was only twenty-four.

May, who had a flair for designing costumes, made or remade all that he required for the parts he was to play. This occupation brought her into the picture and she felt happier—she needed cheering up with a third baby on the way. Also, she was aware that Ted had a lot on his mind—he found all sorts of reasons for staying away from his home and family; yet he obviously loved his children, particularly his little daughter Rosie, of whom he was always making drawings.

When he left for Chatham he did not tell May that among the members of the stock company he had again found an old friend; this time, it was Jess Dorynne, whom he had not seen for six years. Jess had always hoped that Ted would see that she loved him; now, when he was yearning for personal attention, chance had thrown them together in dreary Chatham lodgings where she was "playing sentimental music on a poor piano," and it dawned on him at last that she was very fond of him. At the end of two months they were talking of love, and of how they could correspond with each other in the future. Another young actress was there as well—Gertrude Norman, known by all as "Tommy"; she felt lonely too, and sought Ted's companionship.

At this time, Ted was in a state of confusion regarding himself and his future; he had not yet discovered what he really wanted to do; he had great ambitions but no money and no staying power. Compared to his new artist friends, actors began to appear pompous and artificial. He found the actor's life extremely arduous, and hankered after the Bohemian life of a painter. He thought Jimmy Pryde was the most wonderful character he had ever met, in many ways a bit like his friend Terriss, only Jimmy was always having magnificent and imaginative ideas, always enjoying himself—in fact, he seemed to be at home in the world.

It never occurred to Ted that if it had not been for Nicholson and one or two other friends Jimmy would have starved. Nicholson generally shared his fees with Jimmy, even when he had only contributed to an idea verbally, Nicholson having done the actual job. Friends at pubs or clubs would sometimes buy a sketch or two for a couple of guineas to help tide him over a bad patch.

Dear Jimmy, with his long coat and yellow gloves *looked* so splendid and treated life as though it owed him a debt that would be paid in full . . . tomorrow or the next day.

Ted had already noticed that Irving seemed to be losing interest in him and his future, and he could not understand why. When Ellen had tried to get him a part in *Faust*, Irving had said, "No, it is better for him not to come back to the Lyceum, at least for a while."[1] She wrote and told Ted this, and it hurt him to read it.

To him, May seemed a changed person. They had more and more rows—generally over clothes; he never bought her any, but was always buying himself new hats. One row ended in a struggle in which the porcelain door handle broke in his hand, cutting it deeply, and he had to go about for a couple of weeks with it bandaged and was unable to draw. May could not see why he wasted his time drawing anyway—why didn't he take a part with a London management, however small the salary?

It seemed to him that the children took up most of May's time and energy, and life at home was no longer fun. His mother, whom he

loved more than any other woman in the world, seemed to be continually criticizing him. He had once written:

> I wish to live until the evening of my mother's death, when I should
> wish nothing more enjoyable than to die out before the next day
> waked.[2]

But although he knew she loved him too, he found her very difficult
to talk to because she generally had such strong ideas about men, whom
she thought should do a lot more for women.

From Chatham he had hinted to her that all was not well at home,
and she had replied:

> I can gather simply *nothing* from this letter written half to Edy and
> then to me from Chatham—I can only read *between the lines* of
> several of your later letters, and I feel myself very helpless for I may
> *chance* to read wrongly—*I hope so*—But anyway, were I in England
> even, what c^d I do? *Forseeing the probability of all this*, I tried my
> hardest, my softest, my most threatening, and my most appealing
> prayers to you a few years since—a prayer to you to be *unselfish*, to
> heed my words, to listen to my advice, for the sake *not* of myself, nor
> of May, nor of you, but for the *general right*, for the *principle* which is
> always in the end the best—You would not heed me—when I loved
> you so you sh^d have listened—and it is of no use to speak now.[3]

All this he found to be very cold comfort.

During the return journey from their American tour Ellen did her
best to persuade Irving to think again about Ted and perhaps fit him in
to their provincial tour, which was planned to start as soon as they
arrived in England. Irving agreed, and Ted joined the company, taking
small parts at £8 per week. He travelled with them till the end of
May, stopping at Liverpool, Manchester, Glasgow, Edinburgh, and
Newcastle. The regular salary and the deference paid to Miss Terry's
son was soothing, even if galling at times.

When he was in Newcastle, he was lucky enough to meet Gilbert
Tate, and jumped at the offer to play Hamlet and Romeo for him at
the Parkhurst Theatre in July. Ted was now having ideas about producing, and was so insistent on how this and that should be done that
Tate suggested he rehearse the whole company himself, which he was

only too glad to do: he could now refer to them as "my company" . . .

In August, Irving had a nice surprise for him—the parts of Arviragus in *Cymbeline*, and Edward IV in *Richard III*. *Cymbeline* had to be ready by September 22, *Richard III* was to follow on December 19.

During the run of *Cymbeline*, Ted stayed with his mother at 22 Barkston Gardens. It was more convenient for getting to and from the theatre. May was still at St Albans and was there when her third child, Philip, was born on November 22. It was a Sunday and Ted was able to go over, but his presence could not have been much help to May, for his mind was elsewhere.

One night, when Jimmy Pryde was visiting Ted at the Lyceum, he pointed out Max Beerbohm and William Rothenstein, who were seated in the stalls. Max, later to become dramatic critic for *The Saturday Review*, was immaculately dressed, gazing ahead with a far-away look in his big round eyes, whereas Will Rothenstein, with his beetling brows and broad grin, seemed to be holding court with everyone around him. He met both of them later at the Café Royal.

Max was already established as a brilliant caricaturist and his slow, dry humour was the envy of many of his friends. Completely unpractical, he was incapable of anything apart from his genius for writing and drawing, and looked on Ted as a bit of a magician who could engrave, act, and play the piano. In one of his earliest jottings he summarizes Ted's character as follows:

Playing piano—leaping up—throwing back hair—flowing cloak. German student—Heidelberg—one expected sabre cuts—Unearthly —The Young Bacchus—His amours, almost mythological . . . pure type of artist—*Genius*.[4]

Ted admired Rothenstein, not only because of his precocious talents as a painter, but also because he seemed to know everyone of potential importance among his contemporaries in the sophisticated world of art and letters, and like a "superbly intelligent bee, he always knew where to find the finest nectar."[5] Shortly after they met, Rothenstein started an interesting portrait of Ted as young Hamlet, but he never finished it for Ted was a bad sitter—always "leaping up," as Max had noticed.

In December, when Irving produced *Richard III*, Ted put his heart and soul into the part of Edward IV. He wanted to prove to Irving that he could do a good job and act the part of a much older man. His mother said later that it was a fine performance—but after the first night, Irving had an accident and hurt his knee so badly that he was out of the play, which subsequently came off, and Ted, bitterly disappointed, was once more at a loose end.

During the Chatham engagement with Sarah Thorne's company, he had met a "couple of chaps who had a bit of money and were willing to put £100 apiece into a production," and another "who wanted to put a good deal of money into a tour for me": this he confided in a letter to Edy, suggesting that she might come in on the scheme, as costumier. However, there was an important proviso—this "good deal of money" would not be available until 1897 when "the chap" became twenty-one. This wasn't long to wait, and soon Ted was able to enter in his diary, "January 18 to 23, Croydon Theatre Royal—under my own management: *François Villon* and *The New Magdalen*." He produced the plays and shared the leading parts with Lucy Wilson. For a week he felt grand as an actor-manager, and invited Max Beerbohm, Jimmy Pryde, and other friends to come and see the show. But when it was all over he found once again that most of the money had gone on the hire of scenery and costumes, and the printing of special posters that he had designed.

Again despondency set in and he tried to forget himself by sketching and engraving. Jimmy encouraged him, and he managed to sell one or two book-plates at £3 a time.

He had reached a point when mere acting had no further attraction for him; it seemed a dead end and he felt he could never even hope to be the supreme technician that his master was. He had also learned more about art in general and had begun to feel that there was more to the Theatre than just the art of acting. The other actors at the Theatre Royal, Croydon seemed a useless, conceited crowd after the well-drilled members of the Lyceum Company. To his sister:

I wish I were dead at the present moment. All seems agoing wrong— work—affection—position—can't write a note of music—can do nothing . . . [6]

An old copy of the *Era Almanac* shows that at this time he had been reading Charles Mathews's article on "Actors of the Past"; he had marked the passage:

> . . . of all earthly things the actor's triumphs are the most fleeting, the least demonstrable. There is nothing positive that can be established respecting his talent, no point of excellence that can be proved, beyond the questionable opinion of contemporaries; . . . Authors, painters, sculptors, leave behind them positive evidence of the genius which obtained for them the admiration of the public of their day . . .[7]

Three or four years back he would have tossed Mathews's article aside, but since meeting Nicholson and Pryde his whole approach to art had changed. He had noticed, too, that these artists and their friends were so different from young actors and actresses. They didn't lie about waiting—they invented; they were continually inventing and they had some beautiful results to show for their efforts; they were their own masters. He started to think of freedom for himself—and of creating beautiful things that would leave behind "positive evidence."

He decided that he would go away into the country; Jess would come with him and they would live on "practically nothing" while he worked away designing posters and book-plates. After all, he had already sold four or five book-plates at three guineas a time . . . and had made one or two posters, even if these hadn't been paid for; he felt sure he could get plenty to do and Jess had a small allowance that she was ready to share. She also had the spirit of adventure, which helped a lot.

At this moment he received a telegram from Ben Greet. He went over to the Olympic Theatre and Greet told him that Nutcombe Gould had been taken ill; would he play the part of Hamlet that night? Irene Rooke was Ophelia . . . This was a wonderful opportunity—a chance of playing Hamlet in a famous London theatre. There was no time to think; he said "Yes." So his plan for escape was shelved.

Irving lent him one of his old costumes and a dagger. When he put them on he thought he felt the magic working. He gave a magnificent performance and carried on for seven more. His mother and Irving actually came to see him; she was very proud, writing in her memoirs later: "unconsciously he did everything right—I mean all the technical things, over which some of us have to labour for years."[8] The Hon. Gilbert Coleridge also recorded later that it was, in his memory, the finest of many great performances of the part.[9] Irving smiled and joined in the applause—he was pleased . . . for Ted's sake.

But it was soon over, and old Charles Mathews's words haunted him once more. He found a small cottage in Summers Road, Thames Ditton, and named it Rose Cottage—for luck. It was near enough to Hampton Court where his mother had once had a Rose Cottage, the only place that brought back memories of a happy childhood.

Sometimes he wandered around the Palace with Jimmy Pryde, who often stayed with him—for May and the children seldom came now. Jimmy was continually changing, or being asked to change his residence and he liked nothing better than to spend whole weeks with Ted, who was such an obvious admirer. Ted never failed to welcome "beloved Jimmy" with open arms, for his buoyant nature drove out all depression. Better still Jimmy always *seemed* to encourage him, instead of seeing the pitfalls in advance and dashing his hopes of success. When Jimmy wasn't there, Jess was, and the presence of another woman had been noticed by May.

Ted talked to Jimmy about starting a magazine, illustrated with woodcuts and containing amusing extracts from his favourite books; there would also be contributions by Jimmy and all their friends— Nicholson, Max Beerbohm, Rothenstein. Jimmy suggested he could sign some of his work by other names and so invent new "blokes" like the Beggarstaffs. They tried to think of other names: Ted's favourite "Bath Oliver" biscuits were lying on the table—"There you are," said Jimmy, "Oliver Bath," and this became the first of the many pseudonyms that were to follow.[10]

Money was terribly short. His mother, on whom he had always looked as someone with "lots and lots of money," wrote and told him that she was "overdrawn by £7. 0. 0." for the first time in her life. She was already sending £3 a week to May, and had been for some time, because he couldn't.[11]

The situation between May and Ted was tragic; they had grown too far apart ever to be happily reconciled. And something more: certain letters sent to Ted c/o Pryde—which Pryde in his haphazard way had redirected to various provincial theatres—had found their way to Ashwell House, where May had opened them only to find her suspicions confirmed. There *was* someone else, and now she knew her name was Jess.

In July, there was an offer of a week's engagement at near-by Kingston-on-Thames, and he took it because the money would pay for a holiday which he felt he needed. He played young Marlow in *She Stoops to Conquer*, and then he and Jimmy went to the east coast. They chose Southwold in far-away Suffolk, and in doing so, Ted took one more important step in his life, for at Southwold he was to meet Martin Shaw, the musician.

While Nicholson and Pryde had opened one door and introduced Ted to the beauty of form and colour, Martin Shaw was to open another and introduce him to the magic and power of great music, and to an unswerving and life-long friendship based on a mutual appreciation of each others' qualities as artists in two different mediums.

But to start with Shaw was only going to play the piano, delightfully, at the local pub as an introduction to a scene from *François Villon, Poet and Cut-throat* by S. X. Courte, in which Ted and Jimmy were going to perform for the villagers in the hope of raising funds for some stranded players. Ted, as Villon, was to be turned from evil ways by Jimmy who had the part of a priest! Jimmy took his part very seriously, and spent as much time on his make-up as he would have given to painting a portrait.

The whole episode at Southwold was full of fun and gaiety, something they would talk about for years afterwards. The entertainment over, Jimmy sketched and made eyes at the postman's daughter, while Ted went for walks or bicycle rides with Martin Shaw, who lived near-by with his family. Martin opened his eyes to some of the homely things around him: the pierrots who entertained on the sands, children playing, old bathing huts on wheels and so on; Martin was very English and, like a poet, saw beauty in these everyday things which Ted would never have noticed because his training at the Lyceum had always taken his interest in the direction of the melodramatic.

Martin was a great lover of English music and the English rural scene. He considered himself a cockney. His parents were both musicians. His father, a Yorkshireman, was "a simple soul, generous, quixotic, impulsive . . ." They had come to Southwold in 1877. Martin had studied at the Royal College of Music under Professor Villiers Stanford, Walford Davies, and Charles Wood. With him at the College were

Coleridge Taylor, Vaughan Williams, Gustav Holst, John Ireland, and Rutland Boughton—all to be renowned in the history of English music.[12] One side of Martin's face was disfigured by a birthmark, and this may have accounted for his lack of drive; otherwise, he was a most cheerful and rather handsome young man. Ted was able to encourage him. Martin explained the secrets of the musician's art to Ted, and also taught him that "if you get the simple beauty and naught else, you get about the best thing God invents."

Back at the inn where they had rooms, Ted began to make plans for his magazine; he had nothing to say yet, but plenty to show. He had by now engraved about ten designs on to wood-blocks, and he had also engraved about ten book-plates. He had the actual blocks so they could be printed from direct—that would save making reproductions. He'd write something about . . . Hamlet—and could fill in with a few quotations from Walt Whitman or Dumas or one of his other favourites. As soon as he got home he'd ask Phillipson's, the printers in Kingston-on-Thames, how much they would charge to do it monthly. Jimmy told him that if he hand-coloured prints from some of the blocks in an edition of, say, ten or twenty, he could call it an "Edition de Luxe" and charge a lot extra, as well as selling hand-coloured woodcuts separately. It all sounded very hopeful.

But after the holiday came a return to realities.

The pierrots that Martin had pointed out to him at Southwold still haunted him—he didn't see them as they were, but as strange beings in his own dream-world. He made many sketches of them in their black skull-caps, black gloves, voluminous white trousers, and smocks with two enormous black woollen balls for buttons, and they were to figure prominently in many of his designs for quite a while afterwards. He now devised an entertainment based on a Hans Andersen story, and called it What the Moon Saw; this he planned to recite, dressed in white as a pierrot, against a night sky with a moon. His new friend, Martin Shaw, composed some appropriate music to go with it. They got an audition at the Palace Theatre in London, and when it was over Ted asked Charles Morton, the veteran music-hall manager, what he thought of it, and he replied: "It's all right for what it is . . . but what is it?" This was to become a family saying, but it wasn't very encouraging at the time.[13]

All these experiences were helping to toughen him. Although

disappointed, he thought he could see a gleam of hope; even if his ideas for simple black-and-white settings were turned down by theatre manágements, he could at least capture some of them as drawings or engravings, and, above all, he was finding his way as a graphic artist— so he felt freer, and therefore happier than he had been for a long time. He just wanted peace and quiet in which to sort out these ideas, then he thought he might be able to get something done—the art of wood-engraving was teaching him to simplify and in that direction he wanted to know more. There was to be no peace, however.

May wrote to Ellen to complain about Ted, Ellen wrote to Ted to remind him of his responsibilities, and Ted wrote back saying that he had no work and therefore no money.

Then, as if to lend emphasis to the heart-breaking state of affairs, another little boy was born; he was called Peter. Poor child; what a sad world to come into—his father wasn't there to greet him, and his mother can hardly have felt that a fourth child would be a welcome addition to the family.

At the beginning of December Irving told Ted that there were to be big changes at the Lyceum: he added that he would not be able to afford him any more, and he should no longer count on the Lyceum as a possible source of income. Ted didn't want to go back to the Lyceum but the news was still rather a shock to him because of its finality.

A few days later in the gas-lit streets, he heard the paper-boys shouting "Six-'irty Evenin' Noos—pypur—Terriss stabbed to death— read all abart it" . . . Poor Terriss, who never wished anybody any harm! It had happened at the hands of a maniac as he entered the stage-door of the Adelphi Theatre.[14] The date was December 17, 1897. For Ted this was a tragic end to a very unhappy year. It also marked the end of Ted's life as an actor. The mooring ropes had been cast off; with no charts, but with much hope, his barque was slowly drifting away from the home shores that he knew, and out into the open seas.

Early in the new year, Mr Holme, the editor of *The Studio*, found amongst his mail a "review copy" of a strange new magazine in a cover made of coarse brown wrapping paper—it was called *The Page*. It contained a fable by Tolstoi on one page and a quotation from Marcus Aurelius on another; then a woodcut by an unnamed artist, followed by two pages about *Hamlet*, unsigned; another woodcut showing the back view of the sub-editor in his top-hat, and a woodcut illustration to a Dumas novel; two book-plates, one of which was "the property of Gordon Craig"; there was a loose hand-coloured plate of a Falconer, and a portrait of "The Editor," who seemed to be a woman. It ended with this announcement: "The illustrations are original and are designed and cut in our offices. . . . Each month we shall publish two book-plates, one already in use, one looking for a master."

This was Ted's new magazine. Mr Phillipson, the printer, had given him credit, and allowed his address to be used for "all communications." The colophon stated that there were "only 140 copies printed." The price was 1s. 2d.

Only one side of the paper was printed on, so the bulk was a little deceptive; but it was fresh and imaginative. One hundred and forty copies didn't suggest competition . . . the editor liked it and wrote to say so. So did Mr Konody, the editor of *The Artist*, and Mr J. M. Bulloch, of *The Sphere*.

Of course Ellen thought it was beautiful, but was immediately worried about the cost, and the debts it might incur. Even May was pleased with it: she saw *The Page* as an occupation that might keep Ted out of trouble, possibly bring in some regular money and thus bring the family together again . . . The next number was issued from Ashwell House. Then it went back to Phillipson's, and so on until finally, in August, Ted found a new cottage. This became his headquarters for the next two years, and with a newly designed cover, the magazine's new address was announced:

"At the Sign of the Rose—Hackbridge—Surrey"

The property belonged to a Miss Sheppy, who lived next door. The rent was £30 a year. "The cottage was smothered in ivy and birds' nests, and the roof was the meeting place each autumn of the house-martins who gathered there for their autumn departure. There were thousands of them and you couldn't see the roof or hear yourself talk, until they took their way off."[15] Inside, Ted redecorated it with brown packing paper up to the wainscoting and cream manilla paper above; the woodwork was a rich laurel green, the floors black and shiny.

He designed Miss Sheppy a book-plate and presented it to her. From now on this was to be a special honour which he bestowed on people he liked, loved, or wanted to impress. Although he had presented his mother with most of the book-plates that he had designed for her, she generally insisted on paying generously; she also commissioned them as Christmas gifts for relatives, and friends in America. He had already made presents of book-plates to Lucy Wilson, "Toto" Norman, Jimmy Pryde, and Martin Shaw, and had recently bestowed one on Phillipson, the printer.

Ted had so enjoyed his holiday at Southwold the year before that he had gone there again in June, and from there had meandered through other Suffolk villages, sketching as he went; then he found a little place on the coast called Dunwich. Not having Jimmy with him, he was desperately lonely. He suddenly thought of Jess and wrote to ask if she would like to come down for a holiday; she answered by appearing the next day: this was an unexpected joy. He was staying at the Barne Arms, but soon found a kind woman at Ivy Cottage who let them have two bedrooms and a sitting room for 7s. 6d. a week.

At last he felt the New Life was starting.

Jess had no job and was happy to be away in the bracing air of an east coast village. Everything around them seemed beautiful and homely, and they lay in the shade of the trees taking turns in reading aloud from Rossetti's translations of the Italian Renaissance poets.

> This fairest one of all the stars, whose flame forever
> lit, my inner spirit fills,
> came to me first one day between the hills.

Ted was sketching quite freely, quite differently; he wasn't trying to be like anyone else, he was just enjoying the shapes he saw, and the act of translating them to paper gave him a sense of achievement—*and* he had something to show for his efforts.

One happy day followed another; then one morning on the breakfast table he found an envelope marked "Private." The handwriting was in the expressionless copper-plate style used by clerks. The writer was staying at the Barne Arms. He wrote: "I am staying at the above address in order to make some enquiries personal to yourself . . ."

There was also a note from May at the same address, giving Ted "five minutes" in which to decide whether he wanted to speak to her or not. She had come to see if "it was true" . . . someone had spread the news. The pastoral scene was suddenly shattered; now, all was misery, and the presence of an enquiry agent, a disinterested third party paid to be a sneak, made the whole situation nauseating. It was the end.[16]

After they had gone, Jess said she was ready to stand by him—help him—anything. This roused him from his depression and he was soon bursting with a feeling for adventure.

They returned to look for a cottage near London in which to celebrate a new life—Miss Sheppy's cottage was just the thing . . .

In the October issue of *The Page* was an announcement that the edition would be increased to 400 copies. Also included was a reproduction of the book-plate he had just engraved for Jess Dorynne—a little plan for a theatre of the future.

The following year, the last one of the century, was a year full of happenings. Ted was now making bold drawings, good ones. That year he engraved over eighty boxwood blocks and about twenty-six book-plates. By the end of the previous year he had made seventy-two blocks and about twenty book-plates. A lot of the blocks were done, at Jimmy's suggestion, with the idea of illustrating Dumas's novels. With this stock of blocks *The Page* didn't worry him.

He had also wandered around the theatres making sketches of various friends in the parts in which they were appearing, or in which they were about to appear. He found these simple line drawings appealed to the editors of illustrated papers like *The Sphere*, *The Tatler* and *The Lady's Pictorial*, from whom he got ready cash: not much, but often equal to a week's slogging on the stage. It was easy for him to gain admittance to dress rehearsals and sit in the stalls watching the actors. He felt rather grand on the other side of the footlights, and appreciated the actors' eagerness to see what he had made of them—and their admiration at his ability to draw.

He also made a poster advertising *The Dome* for the Unicorn Press. *The Dome* was a magazine rather like *The Page* but published on more commercial lines. Full of interesting reading matter and good plates reproduced from old, as well as contemporary work, it had given *The Page* a fine "write-up," and that was encouraging: so were the "write-ups" from Italy, France, and Germany: they all seemed to appreciate the vigorous effort behind this youthful work . . . it was something new.

William Nicholson's success with his *Almanac of Twelve Sports*, published by Heinemann in 1897, was followed by his *London Types*, and in this year by an even more successful *Alphabet*. They were full of lovely, bold designs, some cut on wood and others made to look like it: they looked. as though they had been hand-coloured but the books were reproduced lithographically. Jimmy, of course, had helped with "ideas" and scribbles.

One of the most popular designs from *Gordon Craig's Book of Penny Toys.*

Ted, who had watched these books being prepared, decided to make a book for children in roughly the same format. This would be for *his* children—for now that he was further from them, he found that he missed them, and often went to see them on neutral territory at 22 Barkston Gardens or at Winchelsea when they stayed with his mother, who adored having them. May would not allow them to stay with him while Jess was there: this he could not understand and thought it cruel—forgetting the nightmares and unhappy bewilderment that he had suffered as a child under similar circumstances.

For quite a while he had been collecting the wooden toys sold at a penny each by passing gypsies, which he added to a few that a friend had brought him from Holland; most of them were beautiful in their simplicity of design. Edy had also collected some which she had brought back from Germany, and together, they thought out *The Book of Penny Toys*. There were twenty bold designs, each design preceded by some verse describing the toy, and an amusing little wood-cut of yet another toy as an endpiece. The cover was a beauty, but at the last moment the title had to be changed to *Gordon Craig's Book of Penny Toys*, because someone else, who had seen the announcement, had pinched the title and used it.

The printed matter was all in a very bold type which the printer, Mr Farncombe of Croydon, called "Elephant type." It was the same type that had featured in all the old play-bills some twenty years before. In the Foreword one reads that "the verses are by E. C., S. D., J. D., E. A., G. C., and O. B.": these initials covered the identity of Edy Craig, S. Downing, Jess Dorynne, Edward Arden, Gordon Craig, and Oliver Bath—the last three, of course, being all the same person!

The whole book was printed on what was known as sugar paper, a thick, buff-coloured paper that was generally sold for the manufacture of sugar bags, or for wrapping purposes in grocers' shops. All the illustrations were to be coloured by hand—and forty, in each copy, would take a long time: Jess undertook to do the majority of them, though they asked friends to help if they thought them capable. They had to get at least fifty sets done before the binder would handle them, so they could not publish the book until the end of the year.[17]

Meantime, for a summer holiday that year, Ted and Jess turned their backs on Suffolk with its unpleasant memories and went as far west as possible, finally reaching Bristol. From there, they found the small village of Cleeve, near Yatton in Somerset: here, they stayed at a cottage in Plunderers Street, because the name fascinated them. Every day they were out and about, and drawings came easily. Better still, Ted started to read lots of new books; among them the works of Blake, Nietzsche, Wagner, Goethe, and Ibsen. *Peer Gynt* he read aloud, shouting it into the wind as they sat on the hill-tops and looked down into the valleys. He had always seen himself as young Hamlet, but now he saw himself as Peer Gynt. When he had read this play years before he had thought it needed rewriting, but now he became so engrossed in it that he began to make sketches for a future production. These designs were entirely unrealistic, quite free of any tradition or influence, strong imaginative work—most of it done on Broadfield Downs looking towards the distant sea, as turbulent skyscapes built up in the evenings, with purple clouds touched with pink and yellow.[18]

The Cleeve holiday brought him in contact with the hospitable west for the first time; it was warmer too, and the people were kind. Jess had done everything she could to make him feel happy and free. He had left the theatre into which he had been born, had severed all connections with the stage as a place in which actors ruled supreme, and was beginning to see on a distant horizon a new conception of the theatre. Nothing to do with archaeology—no realism—but something nearer to poetry. Ideas made manifest by suggestions. He suddenly realized that he was quite ignorant of all that he wanted to know about the arts—he must learn quickly. Spurred to action, they packed up and returned to Hackbridge. He was going to WORK and LEARN, so that he could capture some of the new ideas which had begun to flow through his brain.

CHAPTER SIX

Martin Shaw—Music and "Dido"
1899–1900

BACK AT "the Sign of the Rose" he tried to plan his future.

He went to the printers and got them to make up some copy-books measuring ten and a half by seven and a half inches: each contained a hundred sheets of a cheap straw-coloured paper, glazed on one surface and rough on the other; either side could be used, but it was nicer to write on the glazed surface and draw on the rough. These were to be his new school-books, his copy-books, his sketch-books, scrap-books, and note-books.

In one book he listed some of the things he intended to study:

This list is to stand as a well from which I may choose some work to do which suits the mood I may be in.

Then comes another note:

Read Plato. Horace—Cato 1 & 2. St. Augustine, drink these in at all opportunities.

Then:

Work out *Perspective* with the help of books, but most from old Italian perspective drawings—see Leonardo da Vinci page 25.

Then realizing how little he really knew about the actual working of a theatre, he put down:

Work a lime for a month, super for a fortnight—scene-shifting for a month when preparing a play—fortnight in flies—fortnight on stage.

("Lime" was short for lime-lights, somewhat like our arc-lights; "super" was short for supernumeraries—what we call "extras.") Then came:

Practice to draw with all kinds of materials . . . keep drawing whatever flies quickly to the imagination—practice and *keep attempting to record what you see in the mind's eye.*[1]

He was now twenty-seven, the beginning of one of the most fecund periods in any man's life, a time when the untamed imagination of a young artist sees no barrier to achievement—except his own inability.

In his mind's eye he saw so much that he wanted to record: it was like a never-ending fountain of ideas. Some of these he had already captured, and they come to us in his woodcuts; others became notes and sketches for masques, plays, and ballets; yet others became unfinished drawings of passing events, views, or fantasies—all material to be used in later years. He became involved in an ecstasy of work.

He also realized that he was committed to *The Page*, and would have to shut his "mind's eye" and get on with the job of editing—but this was helpful to him in a way, as it kept him in contact with realities. He felt he must keep *The Page* going at all costs, since it was his only contact with the public, however small: he knew that if he did not keep before the public, he would perish—this much he had learned from Irving and from Irving's manager Bram Stoker. He sought to enlarge the scope of *The Page*, also to get it published by someone who could take on all the responsibilities, but the various publishers or printers that he approached realized that his personal touch was the quality which was making it a success, and further, that there was no big market for such a magazine if it was produced commercially. So, hoping to make his own work easier, he wrote to all his friends inviting contributions.

Amongst others, he wrote to Martin Shaw and asked him if he could let him have a piece of music to reproduce in a forthcoming number. He ended his letter:

I heard from Pryde some days ago for the first time since I saw you last—He is at Bexhill on Sea, *Painting*!

(He had no notion that he was soon going to lose the "beloved Jimmy" as a companion, for Jimmy was just thinking of getting married . . .) The letter goes on:

> Shaw—Shaw—Shaw—how I yearn for the stage again. . . . All the duffers I meet think I have left the stage—Because one leaves the the woman one loves too well, it does not mean one loves any less— It means *more*.[2]

Shaw let him have a piece of music for *The Page*, and at the same time wrote and asked if he would ever have time for a cup of tea over at his place in Hampstead. Ted replied:

> Let me know what day—then a theatre after, if possible, or a walk, talking about the German Emotionalists.

That was in May 1899—from then on they were to see each other more and more often, Ted generally making his way to Hampstead, where together, they roamed the Heath talking about music, the theatre, Nietzsche and Heine, Shakespeare and Purcell.

Shaw was living a bachelor's life at Fortune Green. Like Ted, he was, in his own words, "undisciplined by nature." But the art of making music was in itself, one of the severest disciplines that any artist could submit to. The art of acting had no such disciplines; the casual passing on of traditions had been a very haphazard way of developing an "Art," which in any case, had no established rules, and Ted had realized this.

Slowly a bond of friendship grew between these two, and Martin became the man to whom Ted could unburden his soul, the man to whom he could confess his shortcomings and to whom he could impart his wildest dreams, a man from whom he could learn, for he was a musician, and was not music the Mother of the Arts? Martin was fired by Ted's sparkling imagination and, together, they felt they could achieve great things.

Up to now Ted had enjoyed music only in a casual way and he had even written a few tunes; but his attitude towards it had been much the same as Irving's . . . how useful would such and such a tune be to the play? As a boy he was bored by it, even when his mother had taken him to hear a Handel concert at the Crystal Palace—the reason being that he was *expected* to enjoy it. Shakespeare, he had begun to understand because his works and words were discussed daily at home, and he had watched scenes rehearsed ten and sometimes twenty times in order to put over the full beauty of every line. Now Martin was to talk about music in much the same way as Irving and his mother discussed the dramatic qualities of a play.

Martin was a keen walker, and it was during one of their many jaunts across Hampstead Heath that he told Ted of the genius of Bach. He was describing the *Matthew Passion*—the story as developed by the different voices and the dramatic underlining of certain phases by the great choir—when they reached an old inn called Jack Straw's Castle; asking if there was a piano available, they were shown into a back room. Martin, without any music, went through whole passages of the *Matthew Passion* banging away at broken keys and giving impressions of the choir by shouting la-la-la's, all the while delivering an inspired commentary on the development of the story as expressed by the moods of the music. He did all this in a standing position, while Ted, almost in a trance, lay on a moth-eaten old chair, discovering for the first time that music, by its combination of sounds and form, could express emotion.

He was intoxicated by it—and from that day, he was haunted by a desire to produce the *Matthew Passion* with visual accompaniment, for in his mind's eye, as Martin played, he had seen visions: great flights of steps, crowds of moving figures, crowds that opened up as a single figure ascended to His destruction, figures wandering in darkness, shafts of light appearing as great chords brought them forth, pink skies turning to blue, then to purple and indigo, against which a solitary figure stood out in gold.[3]

With the help of a few pen sketches he described these ideas to Martin, and he too began to see with *his* mind's eye.

Shortly after this, Martin, encouraged by a Mrs Norah Dryhurst, started the Purcell Operatic Society. Its initial aim was "the revival of the works of Purcell, Arne, Handel, Gluck, etc.," and "the chief object of the Society would be to select for stage representation their best works."[4] Mrs Dryhurst was to be the secretary. She was a most energetic woman, whose house was the centre of the large circle of artists and writers who had taken refuge in Hampstead—in those days still a village on the outskirts of London where one could buy a small house for £80 and a cottage for £50.

The Society's first presentation was to be *Dido and Aeneas*. Martin, recalling Ted's inspired talk of coloured lighting for Bach's *Passion*, approached him about devising a new way of putting over Purcell's short opera.

Because Martin was engaged with his music, and Ted with *The Page* and his *Book of Penny Toys*, they couldn't meet as often as they wanted to. Ted in Hackbridge near Kingston-on-Thames was miles away from Shaw in Fortune Green, Hampstead. Telephones were still strange new machines, so they had to be content with writing to each other. The correspondence started in October.

Ted, because of his past experience of the theatre, immediately took control of the Society's future! The membership was limited to 250, whose annual subscriptions of a guinea each formed the Society's only resources. That wouldn't go very far, so the first thing he did was to design a prospectus for general distribution. They then decided to elect honorary members in "the expectation of plenty," and Martin asked Ted if he could get his mother and Irving interested "as we want some good names to send out with the letter, to catch subscribers." Ted's reply is interesting:

> I will ask Mother for her name—Irving we can do without; he has little sympathy with anything of this sort, and *none* with younger artists.[5]

This was on October 14, 1899. Two days later Ted writes that he is "dreaming of Dido nightly."[6]

But trouble was brewing at Hackbridge: May wanted to go and stay there while she sorted out furniture and books that she claimed were hers, so Ted decided to move, with Jess, up to London, where in any case he would be nearer to Martin and the new work. To do this, he had to clear out his belongings and let the cottage. The interruption put him into a fury, and he burnt a whole lot of the uncoloured sheets for *The Book of Penny Toys* and many of his wood-blocks, drawing-books, and manuscripts. Jess snatched some of the drawing-books from the flames, thus preserving the *Peer Gynt* designs for posterity.

They found a flat "over the river" at Battersea, 25 Norfolk Mansions.

From this new address, with Jess's help, he continued to edit *The Page* as a quarterly. She also filled in every moment colouring the remaining *Penny Toys* sheets for the binders.[7]

Ted, thinking only of *Dido*, used to walk down the road to Battersea Bridge and watch Whistler's "Nocturnes" come to life on the sleeping Thames as the barges and tugs with their twinkling lights went up or down on the evening tides. At one time he even wondered if they could use the river as a background to the opera, with a moored barge for a stage and the indigo sky and distant lights as his backcloth.

Except for the two leading performers, who were professionals, all the chorus and assistants were amateurs recruited from amongst Martin Shaw's and Mrs Dryhurst's friends in and around Hampstead: they eventually managed to muster about seventy-five. These amateurs were enthusiastic singers, but few had any training and none had trained as dancers.

Ted had visualized no particular setting as a background to the opera; what he saw was a pattern of colours and movements, groups of figures emphasizing the mood of the music.

The early rehearsals were taken only by Martin; his job then was to teach and encourage his chorus. They rehearsed wherever they could find premises in Hampstead: to begin with Dr Boulting let them use the big room at Guyon House in Heath Street; they moved later to Lested Lodge, a wonderful old house in Well Walk. Then Ted joined them, for the "movements" were becoming clearer in his mind as he became more familiar with the music, and he wanted to study these amateurs to see if they were capable of carrying out the kind of movement he had in mind. The group soon required larger premises, and these they found at the Drill Hall at the top of Heath Street (now the Everyman Theatre).

Of course Robert Maitland and Grace Wike, the two professionals, found the amateurs slow to learn, so did Ted, but as a result of some of their shortcomings he was forced to develop certain new ideas that helped make the last scene memorable. He writes to Martin:

I see Dido (is) in the dumps and chorus pretending to be sorry,—I'm trying to turn dancers out while making my book. Dances are devil- ish fishy things for any but professionals to attempt. One dance I'll make a dance of arms—white *white* arms—The rest of the scene

dark—and out of it, the voices—with arm accompaniment—exciting
if done well.[8]

This dance of arms was to come in the last scene at Dido's death.

By December, Ted was pleading again for an assistant. When he
started he had asked for two: "an under stagemanager and another as I
shan't always be able to put aside my work."[9] Although they were five
months away from the actual performance, there was a lot to do and
none of them were being paid . . . Little Maggie Adamson (now
Maggie Dale) was his most spirited dancer, Mrs Oswald Cox was
organizing the making of the costumes, but materials had to be selected
and purchased, and armed with tracings of Ted's sketches, the performers, or their parents, had to make them up.

Christmas came and Martin still hadn't found the hall that would
suit them, and Ted was worried because he must know into what area
he was to fit his movements and backgrounds. He asks Martin to "try
and accustom the singers, chiefly the chorus, to walk as they sing, so
that it doesn't become a difficulty later."

While waiting for news of the hall, Ted lay in bed at night and,
"watching the shadows on the walls and ceiling," worked out new
patterns for his chorus—"but I want to hear the music more before
fixing anything."

Early in the new year, Craig and Shaw visited the Hampstead
Conservatoire of Music (known later as the Embassy Theatre) and
spoke to the director, Cecil Sharp, who lived on the premises. Sharp, an
enthusiastic admirer of Purcell's music, agreed to let the hall to them at
the inclusive fee of £29. 3s. 6d. for three performances and preparation
time.

On February 21, 1900, there was a committee meeting, and Martin
had to inform Ted:

At present we have £60, of which £16 or so have to be paid away
—therefore the scenery (independent of costumes) must be cut down
to £60 unless we get in much more money.[10]

But this did not worry Ted any more than it would have worried his
father—they had started . . . they would finish, money be damned!

Martin now moved to a flat over a shoe shop opposite the North London Station in Finchley Road. Ted joined him there in March; time was getting short and they needed to be together as much as possible so as to share ideas. As a relief they would sometimes spend the evening at the Café de l'Europe in Leicester Square, where Ted would make sketches of all the pretty girls, and in these noisy surroundings he could also work on the opera.

He based most of his ideas for the costumes on the traditional conception of Greek warriors and Greek maidens, but greatly simplified the design. Aeneas was to wear a gilt helmet, a garment that looked like a short toga, and garlands of flowers for his departure; his followers were also to wear simple helmets and were to carry circular shields and long spears painted a light tone of Venetian red. The sailors wore Phrygian caps and short tunics. Dido's attendants were to be in garments made of cheap materials like mutton cloth and gauze, cross-laced at breast and hips, and in the first scene they too were to wear garlands of flowers. The witches were to be swathed in strips of grey gauze. Most of them wore slippers or sandals. Dido's beautiful hair was dressed to look like one of the Grecian heads in the British Museum.

After his first visit to the Conservatoire, Ted realized many of its defects. Although it covered the same areas as the present Embassy Theatre, it had originally been built as a concert hall and there was no proscenium, so there was nowhere to conceal the lighting. It had the most up-to-date concert platform, over forty feet wide, which would take two grand pianos, and behind them, on other raised platforms, a complete orchestra of strings, woodwind, brass, and percussion. The job had been done properly and the platforms were part of the structure —immovable! So they would have to be worked into his scheme. But he had to have a proscenium, and the proscenium would have to be low enough and deep enough to hide the top of the backcloths which were to be an essential part of his design.

He now recalled some interesting points about Herkomer's performances at Bushey. Because of the absence of footlights the actors had looked less artificial. Herkomer's side-lit gauzes, placed six feet or more in front of his backcloths, had achieved a depth of colour such as he had never seen before—he only knew of the painted gauzes used in pantomime transformation scenes. He decided that whatever happened he would have gauzes too, and side-light them with different colours, the rest of his light coming from *above* the proscenium.

He consulted Mr Judson, a local builder, who knew nothing about the theatre, but after visiting the hall said he could easily build a proscenium-cum-spotting rail in one; this he proposed to do by erecting two six-foot-square towers of sturdy scaffold poles on either side of the platform, and from them, cantilevering longer scaffold poles until they met in the centre—this would form the framework of the oblong opening that Ted required; it would measure about thirty by fifteen feet. Those at the back of the hall would get a remarkably oblong picture, whilst those in the front would get an almost square picture because they would see a greater proportion of the sky. Slender poles were lashed across the joints in the centre, and any slackness that might arise from the weight of men and lamps was taken up in the middle of the proscenium by wire ropes which went up through the ceiling and were secured to the main timbers of the roof. The whole structure was cross-braced with light timbers and was then covered with painted scenic canvas.

Immediately above the soffit of the proscenium the scaffold poles were slatted over to form a platform for six lime-lights equipped to take coloured gelatines—blue, amber, and green. On either side of the stage were less powerful electric lights, with changeable gelatines; at the back of the auditorium were two small spotlights.

A frame was erected at the back of the "stage" behind the orchestra platforms from which could be suspended two backcloths, one painted bright ultramarine blue, the other a medium grey; there was also a small cut cloth to be suspended close to the proscenium: these were all taken up or lowered like the sails of a ship, with the aid of block and tackle. Another frame was erected just in front of the backcloths on which was stretched a grey gauze.

The only portable structures, or scenery proper, used upon the stage were a charming little throne for Dido—which resembled one of the tall four-posted beds at Hampton Court, but with a domed top on its four slender pillars—and four walls of trellis work, six feet high and about ten feet long. This trellis, formed of twelve-inch squares, was covered with a mass of imitation deep green vine leaves and great bunches of imitation purple grapes. With these few elements, some sacks of paper rose petals and the simplest of costumes, plus his chorus,

Craig was going to attempt to give a visual background, or accompaniment, to one of Purcell's operas.[11]

There are fewer records of the stage movements devised by Craig for this first performance at Hampstead than there are for some of his later shows, but it is obvious from notes made at the time that these movements were more like those of a Greek chorus than those for a ballet.[12] Haldane MacFall and a few others have left us some idea of what took place. The music we know from Purcell's score.

Today, a dancer and a musician, provided they were limited in a similar way, might be able to recreate what Craig and Shaw achieved then, but the danger would lie in the professionalism of the chorus. It is obvious from all written and verbal records of what happened that the beauty of this production depended to a large extent on the great simplicity of all that was done, coupled with the suggestion of infinity in the background.

The curtains parted to disclose Dido seated on a pile of red cushions under the domed canopy of her throne, tended by her hand-maidens, flanked on either side by the trellis of vines laden with purple grapes, which hid the chorus. Above her rose a sky of pure ultramarine; six feet in front of this was stretched the gauze, lit by a pink light—from some angles in the hall the effect would be lilac, from others sky blue, plus depth. This scene, described as "Dido's Palace—the Arbour," opens with the beautiful song "Shake the Cloud from Off Your Brow," and ends with the chorus singing "To the Hills and the Vales," accompanied by a delightful floral dance.

In the following scene, where the Sorceress plots the destruction of Aeneas at sea, Ted imagined that this deity inhabited "some long, low waste of dunes to which had drifted all the wreckage of the world," and there she plotted among the skeletons of ships. For this scene, which was described as "The Witches—Wreckage," the orchestra platforms were lost under an old grey stage-cloth. Now he used the grey backcloth and had green and blue lights playing on the gauze, in front and behind which were grouped the Sorceress, and the chorus, who, "like sea devils, crawled about her feet, and rose and fell like clouts of raggy seaweed." Close to the proscenium was a "cut cloth" that gave the impression of some wreckage. The whole effect was a dull black and white, with a touch of green and blue coming from above. In this setting the chorus sang: "Harm's Our Delight and Mischief All Our

Skill" . . . ending with a "dance of furies"—some of whom wore masks made of *papier mâché*. (This was a scene they all loved doing!)

Act II, which was supposed to take place in a "moonlit grove," was played at Hampstead on the bare stage with green lights on the gauze against the grey cloth. (A special backing was painted for this scene in the following year when it was performed in a proper theatre.)

Aeneas' departure and the joyous chorus of "Come Away Fellow Sailors" was played against the simple blue backcloth, but with yellow light upon the gauze. Aeneas, decked in garlands and accompanied by his followers holding circular shields and tall red spears, ascended the orchestral platforms towards the background where three or four masts and a few ropes suggested his waiting ships.

The last scene, "The Palace—Death," was again in Dido's palace, but not in the throne-room; dressed in black, she reclined on a pile of black cushions, surrounded by her hand-maidens. The scene started in green light, which gave way to the blue backing, which in turn grew darker as the light was taken off the gauze, and against this ever-darkening ultramarine sky, she sang her death song, "When I Am Laid in Earth"; then, as the chorus got to the line "Scatter roses on her tomb," there descended from the heavens an ever-increasing rain of pink rose petals —they did not come down all over the set, but in a vertical shaft of light upon Dido alone, until they blotted her out; finally, in the deep indigo night, all that could be seen were the arms of the chorus seeming to wave her a sad farewell . . .

This performance was given three times only, on May 17, 18, and 19.

At that time, the government in power was waging war with the Boers in South Africa, and the whole country was waiting to hear the fate of the garrison of Mafeking, where, under Baden-Powell, the British were gallantly trying to hold out. During the latter part of the last performance, shouts and screams could be heard in the streets outside the hall. Someone slipped out to see what was happening. The news-boys were rushing about madly, with piles of paper slung over their shoulders, shouting, "Relief of Mafeking . . . Mahon breaks through!" The news filtered back into the hall and half the audience rushed out to buy papers and join in the mass hysteria, afterwards known as Mafeking Night.[13]

But even with popular interest focused on this war, the press still found time to praise, even to acclaim the work done by Shaw and Craig and the chorus at a little Hampstead theatre on that memorable occasion: *The Sporting & Dramatic News* wrote of "one of the most original presentations of opera ever witnessed." *The Lady* reported: "The scenery of *Dido & Aeneas* at Hampstead was, in one word, mythical.... I have never seen amateurs move about the stage with so much skill as the chorus in *Dido & Aeneas*." *The Musical Courier* referred to "the bold pioneers of a distinctly new movement in stage productions." *The Review of the Week* gave considerable space to its account of the performance, its writer having stopped to consider what Craig and Shaw had done at Hampstead, and how it could affect theatre production generally; his comments, published on August 11, 1900, were very far-sighted:

For a long time the question of the representation of Shakespeare on the stage has been a burning one, solved in one way by the Elizabethan Stage Society, and in another by Sir Henry Irving; but a performance of Purcell's *Dido and Aeneas* gave hopes of a third and better solution, which, as the opera is, I believe, shortly to be repeated may be worth a little consideration. This opera was staged by Mr Gordon Craig, and by its simplicity, breadth of effect, and delicate strength of colour, was the work of one who added to the imagination of an artist the skill to make it visible to others. The main idea was never lost sight of, no detail was allowed to detach itself from the picture, and every touch was of importance in the gradual development of the tragedy. This was achieved by a broad simplicity of treatment applied to scenery, dresses, lighting, and grouping, and was given full value by being set in a frame of like simplicity.... The real triumph of the setting was, however, in the use of light and shade; it was as carefully considered as in a wood engraving, and added immeasurably to the tragic simplicity of the whole performance.... If this was possible on a small stage, with little help from the art of the stage machinist, does it not point out the way for which we have looked so long—the way in which we may see Shakespeare and Maeterlinck in all their poetry? No lavish expenditure could have added to the restfulness of such a spectacle, and the complaint of want of funds may now be put aside, while we take the middle path between ugly pedantry on the one hand, and superfluous detail on the other. The main principles acted on by Mr Craig can be applied to work on a scale as big as that of Covent Garden, or as small as that of the amateur stage; but it does demand one thing—it demands a director such as this performance had, a man who is at once an artist and a stage manager. And since such a man has been found, why should we not see more of his work, and have other memories of harmony of colour and form—in other words of a perfection of beauty?

Both Craig and Shaw were unanimous in their praise of the chorus, those enthusiastic amateurs, who, over seven months, persevered at rehearsals and tried, with their voices and *movements*, to put over ideas quite new to them.

These two young men had given London a performance which, although on a very small scale, was proof of the existence of a new approach to the conception of theatrical presentation. It was a break with the established order, with the Irving tradition of a romanticized pictorial background still lit by gas-light. It was a break with the Gilbert and Sullivan approach to opera and its vulgar use of the new electric light. It was a break, above all, with sham realism. It liberated the imagination of the audience but was powerful enough to guide them in the direction conceived by the designer, not only of the setting but of the whole mood of the production.

One more standard would now be seen flying in the wake of the big new movement that was erupting throughout Europe among the younger creative artists. Where were they going? Many didn't know—but together they knew that they were leaving the decadence of uninspired realism, which, thanks to new researches in photography, phonography, and all other forms of mechanical reproduction, could soon be supplied by skilled mechanics. Like all young artists with new ideas they had to find a way, make new rules, and, in the process, be misinterpreted and maligned, copied without credit, laughed at whenever they failed, and if they succeeded have their successes ascribed to the influence of some remote predecessor; but they were going somewhere—they were no longer content to do as was done before.

One thing must be remembered, an important factor that favoured this particular breakaway movement: most people knew that Edward Gordon Craig was Ellen Terry's son, so the press, at least, would regard this rebel with a certain respect due to one descended from a family of such renown in the theatre—the son of the most loved actress of those times.

At the Lyceum, Irving had fought for the re-establishment of the actor and his "art." He had been the first actor to be knighted. Ellen had made Irving's task easier by helping to bring in the vast audiences, many of whom came out of sheer love of her personality. Now her son was going to prove that the actor was not a creative artist, and that the theatre as an art had still to be born; to some, this seemed like sacrilege; to others, like the poet W. B. Yeats who witnessed the performance with awe and admiration, it seemed like the dawn of something great.

The last performance of *Dido and Aeneas* was on Saturday, May 19. On Sunday, they rested and celebrated. On Monday they all foregathered at the ivy-clad Georgian house belonging to Charles Woodward's father, No. 10 in Church Row, one of the most beautiful streets in old Hampstead. Charles Woodward, always cheerful, was their honorary treasurer, but what he had to tell them was not very cheerful. The production had cost £373. 10s. 6d. "By the sale of tickets and subscriptions" they had taken £192. 15s. 6d. The deficit was £180. 15s. The comparatively large sum of £28. 15s. for printing was an extravagance that Ted had felt to be essential: it was spent on the Souvenir Programme, illustrated with his woodcuts and containing the names of all concerned in the production, which would be the only record left when all else was forgotten.

Various members and honorary members gallantly advanced money to help pay their creditors; Woodward himself advanced £50, Martin £20, Dr Danford Thomas £20, and Mrs Dryhurst did her best with £5; Ted had nothing, but wrote for help to his mother and sister; altogether they collected £153. 2s.

As such ventures will continue to be embarked upon while there are still young men and young women with courage but little hard experience, it is interesting to see where the money went. Here is a copy of Mr Woodward's accounts on the "expenditure" side:

	£.	s.	d.
Scenery: Mr Hemsley	80	10	0
Costumes & Properties: Elkam B.	44	1	0
Erection of stage: canvas; men's time and materials:			
Mr Judson	63	19	0
Hire of Conservatoire	29	3	6
Lime light: Messrs. Maskelyne & Cook	12	0	0
Hire of stage carpenters: C. Tanant	8	10	6
Printing: Farncombe & Baines & Scarsbrook	28	15	0
Artists & Orchestra	31	9	0
Hire of Score & Parts		13	6
Advertisements, papers	8	0	0
Bill-Posting	4	7	6
Paper leaves: Mr Haviland	4	0	6
Hair Dressing: Mr Plenty	2	4	6
Blocks for Programme		15	1
Hire of Piano		10	6
Hire of Rooms for rehearsing	2	0	0
Dress Material, time etc.	10	11	8
Stamps	11	4	10
Salary to Business Manager	7	0	0
Return of Subscriptions	1	11	6
Petty Expenses, Telegrams, Stationery, Travelling etc.	12	19	10
Hire of man to make up	5	0	0
Printing: Messrs. Goldridge	2	7	0
Commission to ticket agents		17	1
Lamps for stands in orchestra	1	0	0
	£373	10	6[14]

Ted and Martin had received nothing, not even their expenses for their work over the last seven months, while they had designed the production and trained the chorus.

Ted was convinced that with the press notices they had received they could now go on to greater successes; they had acquired a fine chorus, and they themselves had gained a lot of experience; they only needed to find a management.

He had learned from Terriss that "when you are down, then is the time to ride in a hansom cab—it makes you feel better" . . . So while Martin paid off his old lodgings by selling many of his books, Ted pawned the gold watch that Irving had given him and set out in search of a *house* in Hampstead. He found one: No. 8 Downshire Hill—near Mrs Dryhurst, who lived at No. 11. These premises were to be their offices, studio, and living quarters.

New letter headings were printed, one announcing the Purcell Operatic Society's new address, together with quotes from the press about their recent production: it read well. This method of attack, using past press notices as a boost for future productions, he had learned from Irving's manager, Bram Stoker, that burly Irishman who, with his gift of the blarney and a shrewd sense for business, had steered the "governor's" ship through many a rough sea. Now, at Downshire Hill, Ted tried to recollect all that Bram had taught him. He remembered: "you must always seem to be dressed well"; "you must only be seen in good restaurants"; "you must always be talking about the production after the next"; "you must preserve everything that the press writes about you, for we live in a world governed by journalism."[15] So, at the bottom of the new letter heading there was a panel that read as follows:

Dido and Aeneas, produced in May 1900. Some Press Opinions: Quite admirably done . . . worthy of all praise—*The Times*. Very commendably rendered; wonders in pictorial detail—*The Chronicle*. Of the costumes, masks, scenery, and general mounting there can be nothing but praise—*The Standard*. The whole work was carried through with a sincerity and conscientiousness deserving cordial recognition—*The Musical Times*. Bold pioneers of a distinctly new movement in stage production—*The Musical Courier*. It was certainly a great undertaking—*The Artist*. This really striking performance of a beautiful work—*The Lady*. The whole performance was impressive and beautiful—*The Gentlewoman*. A fantastic and highly artistic representation of the whole work—*Lady's Pictorial*. Does it not point out the way for which we have looked so long?—*Review of the Week*.[16]

Ellen had received her son's plea for help while she was on another tour in America, but, in the light of previous experience, decided against sending him a lump sum of money. At this time she was only interested in his personal health and well-being, so she sent him £2, and a promise of £2 weekly to follow. There was also a little note:

> I enclose the first £2, *not* for trying to pay off any futile debt, but for *necessaries*. A chop—A toothbrush—A Boot—A Bed.[17]

With signs of summer showing all around him and a couple of pounds in his pocket, Ted, forgetting any other responsibilities, thought his most immediate need was a rest, so he and Jess went west again.

He hoped that once he was back on the Broadfield Downs, he'd be able to develop many of the new projects that he and Martin had discussed as the right follow-up to *Dido and Aeneas*. There was *Acis and Galatea*, a new play by Ford Madox Hueffer, Dryden's *King Arthur*, with Purcell's music . . . *Hamlet*, which he now imagined with a lot of music and a masque called "Hunger" which he was writing himself.

Away in Cleeve, far from all worries and cares about past debts or future projects, he wrote to Martin in Southwold, where he too had gone for a rest.

> It's night—11 o'clock. Silence on all sides. A high-up rustle of trees in the wind—and the door being open; and my room being a few feet square, the scents from the stocks, flox, geraniums and roses drift into the place and on to my table—The pen dips into stock scented ink and the paper has a covering of scent from the roses. It's all most perfect. It makes up for all—You must get another £5 a year cottage here—or somewhere. It is cheap, and the way to live. I hope you will enjoy Southwold. . . . Let them all know that you and I are waking up creation.
> Think up a Hamlet motif for me and command me to some action when ever and what ever.[18]

Back in these pastoral surroundings they both loved so much and where they had found happiness and inspiration a year earlier, Jess thought she would tell Ted the marvellous news—she was, at last, expecting a baby. But, although he tried, for her sake, to seem pleased, this news was for him a spectre from the past. The last thing he wanted at that moment was any feeling of responsibility. He supposed that Jess had wanted a baby very badly, otherwise why had she decided to have one just now? Why at this time?

They left the little cottage in Plunderers Street, and found another still further out of the village. This was Hill Cottage, which Ted tried to

The cottage at Cleeve where Craig lived with Jess.

visualize as the little country retreat with Jess and a baby to which he would be continually returning for relaxation after producing plays in London. He designed some new letter headings incorporating a pretty view of the place, which he engraved there and then. But all the time he was haunted by the new responsibility that would soon be thrust upon him . . . He tried to console himself with the knowledge that the allowance of £100 a year which Jess got from her family would be enough for all her wants at Cleeve. Then, turning his back on the west, he dashed back to London—where he suddenly felt he must be, if he was to profit from the success of *Dido*.

He wasn't really in the mood for work, but he wanted to occupy his mind to free it of other problems . . . He must not let anything come between him and his work . . . Why did women always want to have babies? He supposed that they decided to have them, thinking they would thereby have a hold on their men . . . No one was going to get a hold on him . . .

CHAPTER SEVEN

Birth of Ideas · A "Masque" · A Dream
1900–1901

He had run away. At a moment in his life when he needed the tangible love of a woman to bolster his ego and lend him confidence to take the next step, he felt that Jess had let him down.

He was twenty-eight, with a superbly flowering imagination, but with a very immature approach to life and, therefore, little self-assurance.

When he should have been roughing it with youngsters of his own age he had preferred to saunter down the Strand, wearing a fashionable topper, in the company of men like Terriss, who liked him as a companion but had neither the time nor the inclination to start teaching him about life.

When he became "of age," this handsome, even beautiful boy had found himself looking longingly at all the pretty girls in his mother's circle, like a penniless child looking at the cakes in a shop window. He imagined himself as a "Romeo," and talked of love and read poetry to them. He liked their company and relished their admiration, but found them difficult to approach and would always wait for them to break the ice.

On discovering that there was a physical as well as a romantic or mental approach to love he was carried away, but while this new discovery stimulated him and intensified his vision, he was surprised and rather hurt when he was subsequently reprimanded for his "animal passions."

Through Jimmy Pryde's companionship he had developed as an

artist and become more worldly, and in the company of this gay Bohemian he had gradually been able to get love and sex into perspective. But he soon discovered that while he preferred the intellectual company of men, the mental exhilaration derived from physical contact with women was essential to the development of his imagination.

He had to have an eager and admiring audience with whom he could communicate his thoughts, plot the overthrow of his enemies, and celebrate every little victory.

Jess, whom he had known before he was married to May, had come to him later at a period when he was in despair, and a new life had started for him. In her company he had discovered himself as a graphic artist, free from outside influence; he had let his imagination run wild and she had encouraged him. She had given him the helping hand he needed, relieving him of much of the editorial and administrative drudgery on *The Page*, and taking over most of the hand-colouring of *The Book of Penny Toys*. She really loved him—very much.

Then, when Pryde had married and had almost gone out of his life, Martin Shaw had come into it, bringing with him the discovery of music—a new, almost overpowering stimulant to his imagination. Martin had also taught him to enjoy all kinds of simple things that he had not noticed before; from him, he had learned to smoke a pipe; in his company he felt on top of the world. Martin, who was three years younger, was in need of just such a friendship too; he possessed great artistic perception but was inclined to be overcautious; Ted, whose brain was overflowing with ideas, was always encouraging Martin to follow—deriving courage for himself in so doing: they were ideal companions.

Ted had loved Jess—as much as he had loved any woman—ever since they had started living together in 1898. She fitted into his romantic scheme of things; she read poetry to him while he worked, or obliterated herself when she was not required; she was beautiful, and the French blood that flowed in her veins made her seem more vivacious than most other women that he knew.

Jess, however, had not noticed that in the intervening years he had discovered a new LOVE—this love was the theatre; not the traditional theatre in which he had been brought up, but an exciting, new kind of theatre which was beginning to make itself visible in his mind's eye;

as yet, it was like a faint light seen in the distance, but he was determined to reach it. This love was to grow stronger and stronger as the years passed, becoming the all-consuming passion of his life; any obstacle in his way would be surmounted or destroyed.

He began to think that Jess was trying to obstruct his progress by keeping him to herself in a country cottage, and the first signs of a neurosis began to show itself: this was suspicion—and it haunted him for the rest of his life. The more he thought about his present predicament, the more he believed that he was the victim of some deeply laid plot to divert him from the new path that he was treading and which he felt sure would lead him to great enlightenment. He dared not think who the plotters were; when he did, he was horrified . . . Perhaps his mother was involved; she loved Jess and wanted Ted to be happy with her; she also wanted him to return to the stage as an actor—Jess had once suggested that they might get small parts in a play together! He imagined he saw Jess posting secret letters . . . thought he saw sinister figures in the village . . . it *was* a plot . . . they were trying to trap him. So he fled.

The journey to London cooled his brain, and he found No. 8 Downshire Hill quite exciting to return to. When he took this house it was in a miserable condition, but he had given instructions to the builders . . . and now he thought it looked fine—they thought it looked terrible! The front room downstairs had been painted black all over, then varnished. All the other rooms had black floors, skirtings, and doors, and the Morris wall-papers had been replaced with white lining-paper.

But Martin was missing, so he had no one in whom he could confide, no one to whom he could talk about his immediate projects and his ideas for the future—he wrote to him at once:

This dear old place looks lovely—smells much better—and is really most nice altogether.[1]

Then he hired a piano, and waited.

While he waited he went back to his school-books and continued to fill them with notes:

When drawing remember not to Reason,
That only comes during the preparation,
not when doing the thing.
Design: Scenes, Costumes, Props, Movements
and the rest for: Hamlet—Lear—Macbeth—
Othello—Romeo & Juliet—Merchant of Venice—
Tempest.
Bach's "Passion" (Matthew & John)
Peer Gynt, Faustus.
Tannhauser, Lohengrin, Tristan & Iseult.
The Fairy Queen (Purcell)
Pantomimes and Masques.
Symphonies by Mozart and Beethoven
The Serenade for wind instruments
Rewrite "Hunger" for speaking and dumb show.[2]

August in London was very lonely; he found that most of his friends
were away at the seaside, or on provincial tours. However, he wasn't
lonely for long, for in response to the new prospectus for the Purcell
Operatic Society, people were continually calling to see if they could
get parts. Most of them were the usual young women who thought
that their beauty alone had cut them out for the stage. They amused
him for a time, then he grew sick of them. They generally talked so
much about themselves that he wrote in large letters on the wall of his
studio: "Stand Still . . . and listen."

But Hampstead was a happy place, and Downshire Hill, with its
houses nestling amongst the trees, its little church, and the skittle
alley at the bottom of the road made it seem like a small village on its
own; and the great stretch of heath, with its old trees, ponds and pretty
walks brought the countryside closer.

Down the road lived the writer and critic D. H. Nevinson, the
artist Carline; Mr and Mrs Dryhurst lived at No. 11, and at No. 39,
Signor Gaetano Meo, another artist, who had three handsome sons and
three beautiful daughters. One of the daughters had the loveliest eyes
that Ted had ever seen, and each time he passed the house he looked to
see if she was there.[3]

Suddenly he remembered that Volume III of *The Page* had to be
prepared for the printers. This was another hindrance, in fact *The Page*

was becoming a burden. However, he realized that it could still be useful, so he approached his friend Paul Hildersheim, a solicitor, to see if he could get some people interested in forming a syndicate to run the magazine. No sooner had he broached the question than he was writing to Martin:

> Did I tell you that a syndicate is being formed to run "The Page" for several years. . . . I shall only remain Art Editor with a good slice of power at the wheel. . . . It will be a capital place to insert articles about the plays and operas. If (as I suggest) it's made a popular and good magazine it should become a power for us.
> The wheels begin to turn for us, Mon Ami.[4]

Martin returned from Southwold and they began once more to plan the future of the Purcell Operatic Society. Martin had once suggested that Purcell's incidental music for Fletcher's *Prophetess, or, The History of Dioclesian* would make a beautiful masque, and Ted had been working on this subject, devising ideas for the chorus. He thought they could call it *The Masque of Love*, and, together with *Dido and Aeneas*, it would make a splendid show for a West End theatre. To make the whole programme even more acceptable, he said he would try to get his mother, if she was free, to put on *Nance Oldfield* as a curtain raiser. They wanted to do it as quickly as possible while they could still gather the chorus together.

Ted wrote to his mother, telling her that they needed £300, and explaining that it would help *him* if she could help the P.O.S. She received his letter in France, where she had gone to the Haute Savoie to try to cure her rheumatism. She replied:

> I hope to Goodness my dearest Ted that all the work you are doing will bring you some profit commercially—for what enthusiasm I have left in me I invest in *you* and not in the Opera Co—I know many pleasanter investments than *that*. It is entirely with a view to benefiting *you* that I part with £300 of my very hardly-gotten gains, and if you don't personally benefit by it I shall feel savage.[5]

This seemed wonderful news, and they went ahead with rehearsals of *The Masque of Love* so that they could show her what they were doing before asking her for help with *Nance Oldfield*.

Nearly every day Ted received a letter from Jess, chiding him, professing her love and asking him to come back to Cleeve. The letters grew sadder and crosser, and his replies became more and more irritable, for she was upsetting his work; she was convinced that another woman, and not work, had taken him back to London. The pathetic situation was punctuated by the arrival in November of a beautiful little girl, who was to be called Kitty. Soon afterwards, Jess returned to London and took rooms in Camberwell. They met occasionally, but generally resorted to correspondence, where they vied with each other in recriminations coated with occasional endearments.

The Gordon Craig Book of Penny Toys was in the book-shops in time for Christmas, but the praise of the critics hardly compensated Jess for the hours of work she had put into colouring them. For Ted, the book held no further interest.

In January of the new year (1901), Ellen came to see one of the rehearsals of *The Masque of Love*, and was delighted; what pleased her most was seeing her son putting the chorus through its paces. Ted now asked her about *Nance Oldfield* and she said she would love to do it, provided that it did not clash with Irving's programme. At her suggestion, he approached Mr Saunders of the Coronet Theatre, Notting Hill Gate. Mr Saunders liked the idea, and agreed to fit them in the week beginning March 25; Irving agreed to let Ellen go—everything seemed to be in their favour.

The new presentation of *Dido and Aeneas* and *The Masque of Love* was a great success. There is no doubt that the majority of the audience had come to see their beloved Ellen in *Nance Oldfield*, but some of the critics saw that the work of the two young men, Craig and Shaw, was important. The suggestion, at a later date, that the work went un-recognized is nonsense; they could not have hoped for better notices.

W. B. Yeats sent Ted a warmly appreciative letter on the production. Not knowing Ted's address, he addressed it care of Mrs Dryhurst, and in his accompanying letter to her he said: "I think you know Gordon Craig, and I want you to send him the enclosed. It is about his wonder-ful scenery at the Purcell Society, the only good scenery I ever saw ..."[6]

The stage at the Coronet was larger, enabling Ted to get even more depth into his blue sky, because there was a greater distance between the backcloth and the gauze in front of it. Many of the critics differed in describing the colour of the background, some calling it lilac, others purple or blue—in fact, this variation in shade was achieved by changing the colour of the lights directed on to the gauze in front of the same ultramarine cloth.

It is interesting to note that a number of the critics realized that one of Craig's biggest contributions lay not so much in the scenic effect as in his composition of beautifully thought out *movements* and colour effects.

For *The Masque of Love*, which formed part of the entertainment, he devised an entirely new form of presentation. There was no painted scenery, just three walls of light grey canvas and a grey stage-cloth. In this box, what might today be described as a modern ballet took place. The plot was outlined as follows:

The Scene is a hall in a mansion. Cupid sends forth children to fetch masks, by which we understand that they are playing at being Gods and Goddesses—Flora, Comus, and the rest. Three groups, representing Blood, Riches, and Poverty, enter at different points; their wrists bound, and they are dragged in, in a typification of the stern mastery of Love. Their fetters are loosened. The rod of captivity becomes a maypole of merriment, whereon a solemn movement follows—"Hear mighty Lord!" At the conclusion of this chorus, we hear outside a rustling and the sound of feet, which create mingled fear and expectation. Bacchanals enter, and the maskers flee like startled fawns. A hymn to Bacchus follows, with lively movement of hands and bodies, and an interweaving dance. While the eyes are fed, the measure of a bright country dance enchants the ear, the masque closing with the usual procession.[7]

The main colours were black and white, with little touches of colour here and there. The grey box set was filled with pools of coloured light, and the figures moved in and out of different fields of colour as they went through the beautiful movements that Craig had devised for them.

Martin Shaw remembered the first night with his usual dry humour:

In the Masque, the children upset the infant Bacchus in his car and while the unlucky babe (where was the L.C.C.?) hung perilously downward, howling, his attendants shrilly disputed the question who was to blame for his ungodlike position.[8]

Max Beerbohm remembered:

Whitefrocked children dancing beneath a flight of pink and white air balls, and those slow-moving harlequins with surcoats of dark gauze over their lozenges, setting the huge candles in the candelabra of the Prison of Love—they and the rest are ineffaceable pictures in my memory.[9]

Ellen wrote:

Nothing can take it away that spite of all obstructions and small anxieties we had a lovely week with Dido and The Masque at the Coronet. I enjoy thinking of it *now*—altho' at the time I was very ill —The Music of Dido's death haunts my memory . . .[10]

Once more they all met at Mr Woodward's home, and this time the news was better: the expenses had been £534. 6s. 8d., including Ted's and Martin's "fee" of £10 each, and the receipts £938. 17s. The takings had been as follows:

	£	s.	d.
1901. March 25	105	18	0
26	138	11	9
27	134	0	9
28	138	6	3
29	133	12	6
30	164	18	0
30 (Matinee)	123	9	9
	£938	17	0 [11]

There was good cause for celebration, and it was decided to go right ahead with plans for *Acis and Galatea*.

With thoughts about *Acis and Galatea* pushing into every moment of his time, he now realized that it would be impossible to carry on with *The Page*. The syndicate had not materialized. Also, he must get rid of Hackbridge, which had become only an address of convenience. He therefore prepared the last number for the press. He filled it with contributions from Joseph Crawhall, Pamela Coleman Smith, Haldane MacFall, J. W. Simpson, Mrs. Barbauld, Fritz Endel, C. V. de Rozsnyay and . . . Alexandre Dumas, and some thirteen of his own wood engravings, as well as some half-tone reproductions. One of the engravings was a scene for the future production of *Acis and Galatea*, and there was also a portrait of Jess Dorynne—as it were, in memoriam.

He found then that he still needed some more blocks for this volume and since he had a few unfinished ones that he had discarded, he used them all, describing them as the work of Oliver Bath.

As he could not see any future use for poor Oliver, he decided to get rid of him too, so, under the pseudonym of Samuel Drayton, he wrote his obituary notice! He even announced that there would be a posthumous exhibition of his work in "the charming watercolour galleries at the Sign of the Rose." Of course, no such galleries existed, but he knew no one would go, and this "make-believe" was all part of the fun he so delighted in.

August came and, as usual, everyone was leaving London for their summer holidays. Martin also left, joining his parents in Margate. His mother had extended an invitation to Ted as well, but he was in one of his mad moods and wanted something to stimulate his imagination.

Hearing that the Dryhursts were going to Brittany he conceived the idea of going there himself, but in disguise. Whom should he take with him? He wondered if he could persuade Jimmy Overbeck, the beautiful girl who had helped him with the music at Uxbridge, to come, disguised too—as a boy. Just "adventure—no lovemaking—sheer fun."[12] The sheer fun appealing to her, she agreed, and the play-acting went on . . .

Being in France was intensely exciting. Enraptured, he wrote to Martin from the tiny village of Samer, near Boulogne:

Aug 22 1901

Mon cher Martin—I write in or rather outside a café. . . . Fine place France—Fine people the French—can't speak a word of English. . . . It's the nearest approach to an Arabian night . . . no single sound resembles any I have heard before—nothing that I can see can I recognise . . . and here at my side—well, I'm not quite sure what sex sits there. It's extraordinary and I would give a deal to express it.

Here's a dog at last. He understands me. I pat him—a square lump of sugar . . . it is extraordinary. You and I must come here to France— I am as a virgin in the land and the land as a vestal to me, and it would be the same to you . . . we should have a splendid time and add a cubit to our artistic stature.

I'm *bursting* to put down what I see and feel—and can't. . . . Tom Browne could though—

Carts here have two wheels—That in itself sends me crazy—I see one across the road. It's been there 10 minutes—am still wondering at it —all this difference . . . wonderful . . . Beautiful . . .[13]

Craig's sketch of the young Baroness Overbeck disguised as a boy, 1901.

This holiday was a complete success. "Jimmy" O. kept up her disguise until her return, even in the face of being flirted with by another girl! To pay for it all, Ted wrote and illustrated an article which he sent to *The Artist*, and for which he received four guineas.

The article, which was entitled "Samer," and signed by one James Bath, related a local legend connected with the ancient abbey and church. It ended with some bars of music, which the writer described as all that remained of a traditional folk-song telling of the monks who had once inhabited the priory. The two illustrations were coloured views of the village, one by James's late brother, Oliver, and one by Gordon Craig. Needless to say, the drawings, the article, and the music were all imagined by Ted, and dashed off one afternoon when the rain kept them indoors.[14]

Back in London, and the glorious bout of make-believe over, a reaction set in. He became morose and introspective, and started filling one of his new note-books with "confessions." These were to be the records of his troubled mind.[15]

In his first notes, he is merely preoccupied with the various girls that call in the hope of getting jobs with the operatic society. Who are they? What do they really want? What are their real intentions? He is sure that beneath their beautiful exteriors lies something sinister: "I know not if she be a girl or a harpy . . ." Then, of another: "She reminds me of J.D., without that girl's brains or character—Her eyebrows are much the same—her eyes too and seem to suggest—But wild mules shall not drag from me what they suggest . . ." Then again: "It appears she is a humbug—a woman. I can almost guess her to mean the very opposite of what she says." Then: "Bach's Passion—that is wonderful and gives one all one longs for . . ." and "Samer!—There *was* a town—there I spent a few splendid days." Then, suddenly, the entry: "Never mind, I shall be dead if I do not discover myself in the next three or four years"; then: "I do not believe I shall ever be in love with any woman."

After this comes a note complaining that the art critic MacFall "only writes in *The Studio* about my twopenny-h'penny drawings," followed by another note in bold pen strokes:

> I am wrong—I find he writes about
> The Theatre—Good
> The Theatre, C'est Moi!

He gives pages to recording his impressions of Irving's performance in *The Bells*; he begins with: "Irving in The Bells. . . . "*Christian*" the cry of a trapped animal . . ."

He develops this later:

At the end of the play what is it that rings in my ears—not The Bells —not the final words of the death agony—not the "howl" of the dogs at Daniel's farm, though they sound faintly in the night at the heels of the haunted soul, but it is the cry *"Christian"* that pierces me to the very heart—a life long hope dying at each utterance . . .

These notes were later to be the basis for his book on his master, but at the time he had to record them because the memory of the performance obsessed him so.

He seems to reach a climax at a point where he records a fantastic dream about his father. It is of particular interest because it gives an indication of the turbulent state of his subconscious mind:

One night I thought that I saw and spoke with my father. Although I had never seen him whilst he lived I fancied in my dream that his face was as familiar to me as Mother's—But it was terribly sad. We sat on boxes that floated on a calm sea. At times he would rise from a sitting position and standing on his floating box would pour out a torrent of praise and love addressed to his lost lady, my mother. . . . All the time his eyes would rain tears which ran down into the salt water and spread round him in rings of crimson, purple and black which with the green of the sea combined to make a most pleasing effect that delighted us (my father and myself) exceedingly. We were both astonished at the colours for after all said he "they cannot be tears of blood"—and laughed—And I replied "nor coloured tears, father." And he said—"I think not."
And by and by as we sat without speaking, the sky grew darker and darker—and from the three circles of colour came thousands of voices all like drowned voices—a mixture of sobbing and laughter flung up from the deep.
All the while I remained wonderstruck and a feeling of deep sorrow took hold of me.
My father remained seated, his head leaning on the palms of his hands, and the curve of his back seemed in some way to be the side of a hill. I cannot tell how long it really was that this singing lasted—it seemed like an age, and all the while I sat and looked and looked, first at the circles of moving colour and then at my father. He did nothing, but it seemed as though he wanted something to take place and I could feel the appeal of his averted eyes. And I rose to my feet and took in one long breath, then I stepped into the first circle of black drops—and grew deathly cold, for they clustered round my feet like mussels that cling to a rock and seemed to suck the life from my limbs—they stung me like a nation of bees. Then I moved forward to the second ring, which rose like a fiend and bound itself on to my hips and breast and grew ever tighter and tighter till I though my head would burst. I saw there remained but one ring—that of crimson tears—and my heart seemed to extricate itself without a struggle from my breast, and I moved forward till I reached the last circle.

As I came near to this I heard strange old fashioned tunes around me. Old English airs, madrigals and glees—all of which sounded familiar to me—then I heard the prattling of babies, and last of all, four childrens' voices rose and fell singing "The Silver Swan." And on the last note I stepped on to the rim of the crimson circle—and it rose and smote me in the face and twined itself round and round my throat till only my eyes remained uncovered.

I looked around me.

The sea, the boxes, my father—all had disappeared— and there in front of me sat thousands and thousands of gods and goddesses as in a huge theatre. . . . All the walls were made of white wood and everyone was dressed in white, and a white crystal bunch hung from the centre of the place and contained a thousand lamps which gave a soft light to the whole scene. From the centre of this bunch of light floated the sound of instruments—flutes and harps and violins—and again the song was "The Silver Swan."

And I looked into the great audience once more in search of something . . . and there I found a smile for which I had waited, it seemed ten thousand years—Into it I fell and knew nothing more but heard two voices whisper "My Son—and felt four arms laid over my shoulders——"

Shortly after this he was laid low with a fever, and his kind neighbour, Sylvia Dryhurst, came up to see him: he was in a state bordering on delirium. He told Sylvia that he thought some enemy of his was sticking poisoned needles into a wax image of him (he had read about this in one of Dumas's novels). Sylvia, being a clever woman, returned the next day with a box, saying: "This contains a well pricked image of your bad enemy"—immediately he felt better.

But he was still worried about Jess, and money, and the future . . . and still haunted by thoughts of his father: "he who failed so much when he had the gifts to succeed—he is remembered as a failure—and they say 'see his son—another failure—like father like son, . . .' This won't do."

CHAPTER EIGHT

Elena and Peace · "Acis"

1901–1902

HIS SANITY was saved by Martin's return. He at once took Ted to a promenade concert at the Queen's Hall, where Mr Henry J. Wood was conducting Mozart's *Symphony in C Major*: this was balm to his troubled mind, and he wrote in his book that it was "one of the most beautiful and faultless blessings I have heard—quite wonderful."[1] With Martin back there seemed to be some reason for work, and once more he tackled *Acis and Galatea*. At nights they sat late, talking about the theatre of the future: a theatre which, like music, would be an art on its own—not just a hotch-potch of the other arts exhibited by a theatrical producer "like a monster at a fair." As a special treat Martin would sometimes play him whole passages of the *Matthew Passion* while he worked out ideas on the white walls of Martin's room.

They were both desperately short of money, so Ted devised a scheme for presenting a version of *The Masque of Love* at the Alhambra. The management said they would "consider it"; Ted's hopes were raised beyond reason, only to crash a few days later when they turned it down.

He wrote to his mother—who was again on tour in America—explaining that he was only appealing for help, this time, because he wanted to get on with his next production, and he sent her some of his designs to show her what he was doing. She was enchanted, and promised to stand guarantor for a loan of £200, at the same time telling him that he was crazy to think his productions were cheap: if the composer-arranger-conductor received no salary, and the producer-designer and a chorus of sixty or seventy were unpaid too, it might *appear* cheap, but it would be very different in the account-book of a professional theatre. She also pointed out that expensive productions were only paid for by a long run, not by "a one week stand."[2]

Among Martin's friends in Hampstead were the Meos, who lived down the road at No. 39. Gaetano Meo, friend of Rossetti, Burne-Jones, and Samuel Butler, was a painter. All his children had been trained as musicians. His twenty-two-year-old daughter, Elena, was one of those virtuoso violinists who, in two days, could learn by heart Paganini's *Moto Perpetuo*, then play it without music at a concert. She had played in public since she was nine years old. Her sister Margherita or her Uncle Antonio usually accompanied her, but at times she had asked "kind Mr Shaw," and he had come along: now, the occasion had arisen again, and she ran up the hill and knocked on the door of No. 8. The door was opened by Ted, who at once recognized the beautiful eyes.

They looked at each other for what she later described as "a very long while, neither saying a word." Then Elena asked for Martin. He was out for a moment; would she come in? Ted showed her round the studio, an environment in which she felt quite at home.

She knew that artists did not like people to enthuse over their work, so she looked quietly at Ted's pictures, one after another, allowing herself to take each one in, then said which one she liked best. It was an enormous white cloud, with a minute line of landscape at the bottom and a hint of blue sky round the edge—it was, in fact, the backcloth for *Acis and Galatea*.[3]

They talked about Handel—she loved Handel, except when Mr Thingumy asked them to play the same piece every time he called . . . Who was Mr Thingumy? Oh dear, she could never remember names . . . yes she could, it was Mr Butler, Samuel Butler . . . no, she had never heard of Ellen Terry. That was his mother. Had he ever heard of Gaetano Giuseppe Alfonso Faustino Meo? No. Well, that was her father—and they laughed like children.[4]

Martin did not turn up, so she said she must run home, or "Pupsie" would be cross, and she disappeared.

Ted sat for a long while, then made this entry in his book of confessions:

December 1, 1901

I ring down the curtain on the play. It was a failure. Act I passable. Act 2 better. Act 3 abused. Act 4 foolish. Act 5 idiotic. The Theatre is now about to be razed to the ground. When this is done, and all fresh and clean again, and when all trace of the old place is destroyed and the foundations of the new place laid, a new Theatre shall be built and then a new play enacted—I will take the one part and she will take the other.

The next day she called again and saw Martin, who agreed to play for her.

As she passed No. 8 two or three days later, she saw, stuck up in the ground-floor window, a picture of an enormous teapot and a question mark. She called in and asked, "Did you put that there for me?" "Yes." By the time she left they knew they were in love. She explained that her father would be most suspicious if Ted was to call, and she found it very difficult to get away from home unless she was going out to give violin lessons; they agreed to write to each other.

One day she learned from Martin that Ted was married. She was in despair; she already loved him so much. Ted then told her he was expecting a divorce, but as she was a Roman Catholic she did not see this as a solution. Before they had met she was already discouraged by the world that she had encountered since leaving her convent school and had seriously thought of becoming a nun, but Cardinal Vaughan had advised her to postpone such an idea for another two years. Now, as spontaneously as she did everything in her life, she came to a decision —quite simply, that only Ted mattered; she would love him for the rest of her life . . . and she did.

Seventeen days after their first meeting Ted wrote:

It is the privilege of one man in ten millions to work for such a being. . . . She has black hair—magnificent black eyes—a deep voice —noble brow and clear cut nose—firm and good lips—strong and kind chin—clear white skin—and the manner of her ancestors— —the grand and simple manner of the dead times—nobility and courage in every gesture—and generosity spread *over all*.

It is such a woman *that demands as much as she gives* and *no more*, and who receives more than she demands and from whom *no return is asked.*

This is a woman for whom kings might die, and to whom gods shall bow—I would *live* for her.[6]

Then he adds:

The proper definition of the verb "to live" is not to be found in any of the present dictionaries.

After another meeting he wrote:

I am the last person to deserve what meeting her means—but by all that I love and honour I will raise myself up to her whatever it may cost—*cost, cost,* why what is there I cannot pay for, I who am now the richest man alive!!! She has brought me new life new love new trust, and *a belief.* And I *trust, love, live,* and *believe* HER.[7]

At last he had found a woman whom he really loved and, at the same time, with whom he could find peace—and that inherent understanding that has nothing to do with knowledge, but is possessed only by people whose forbears have inherited it from some ancient culture.

They corresponded every day, sometimes two or three times, and, like conspirators, found all sorts of amusing ways of concealing letters, to be picked up. Whenever she passed No. 8 there was a picture message in the window which only she would understand.

The rehearsals for *Acis* were now under way, and Ted found that his work was easier—ideas were flowing again. He worked right through Christmas, sometimes making designs for Bach's *Passion* as well; at other times he went on trying to capture what he saw in his mind's eye, giving the resulting designs such arbitrary titles as "The Tents," "The Cloud," "Enter the Army," "The Arrival."

At the beginning of 1902, Martin went to see W. S. Penley, whom he had known as a singer rather than as an actor. Penley was a charming man who was chiefly remembered for his creation of the leading role in *Charley's Aunt.* He had made quite a lot of money and had invested much of it in a theatre in Great Queen Street—known as Penley's, or the Novelty (its old name), or the Great Queen Street Theatre. He agreed to let it to Martin for the ridiculous sum of £40 a week.

When Ted wrote and told his mother about this marvellous offer, she replied, "Penley's Theatre, my dear, is of no use to anybody I fear, including himself"[8]—but they thought it was too good a bargain to miss, and closed the deal.

In the meantime, Mrs Dryhurst, Martin, and Ted were trying to interest everyone they knew in supporting their next effort. The P.O.S. had a sum in the neighbourhood of £300 left over from their successful run at the Coronet Theatre. They all realized that it was greatly due to Ellen Terry's generosity in putting on *Nance Oldfield* at her own expense as an added attraction, which had brought them their very good audiences, so Ted approached Mrs Langtry and asked her if she would help with their next production: at first she seemed interested, then said she could not manage it. Walter Crane, the artist and illustrator of childrens' books, gave them £10, and with one or two other donations this completed their meagre working capital.

Ted was all for a great burst of advertising: "How say you to huge posters all over the shop, instead of, or as well as circulars?"

Great Queen Street
Theatre
ACIS & GALATEA
&
The Masque of Love
will be performed at the above
Theatre in May 1902
IF THE ENGLISH PUBLIC
will instantly signify their
intention of supporting their
Greatest Musician
HENRY PURCELL
Etc. Etc. Etc.[9]

He had another idea for raising money, which was to transport the chorus to the various universities on Saturdays and give performances of *The Masque of Love* on the railway-station platforms "using a plain cloth background and the platform made to look *mysterious* some way or other."[10]

Who was to arrange it all and pay for the transport of fifty or sixty people, he had not thought about. However, the idea could have been developed; the colleges *might* have provided space in a great hall, and Tillings *might* have done the transport for the advertisement value. But the P.O.S. had no organizer with drive; only Ted had the drive.

All the time he encouraged the P.O.S. to have more rehearsals, racking his brain for ideas for the background; as he listened to the chorus practising, the ideas slowly materialized.

At this point he decided on a trip to Curtain Road in the city, and spent hours rummaging through wholesale houses to see what he could find in the way of cheap materials. It was when he discovered a big supplier to the upholstery trade that the basic idea for all his scenes and costumes came to him. He would use *webbing*—upholsterers' webbing —and tape; he could buy it wholesale in all colours and all sizes. He would fashion transparent tents out of the two-and-a-half-inch-wide webbing (in those days generally used for supporting sofa springs), and he would make dresses out of the inch-wide tapes. The tents would seem transparent because he would leave gaps between each length of webbing. The costumes would look like drapery one moment, and then would break into hundreds of flying ribands the next.[11]

The costumes for *The Masque of Love* were already in store. He had based a number of them on the pierrot costumes that had so enchanted him at Southwold in 1897, and they had been very cheap; he had made a lot of the masks himself.

Ted was apprehensive lest Martin's natural caution would cause him to lose enthusiasm. He wrote to him in the new year:

> Move we must my dear fellow—They won't help us if we stand still, dignified though it may appear. . . . And remember two of 'em got the Duc de Beaufort out of prison—two of 'em put Charles on his throne again—and two of 'em produced Dido and the Masque. En Avant ☞ if that means forward.[12]

The "two" who helped the Duke and Charles were, of course, two of the three fabulous musketeers from Dumas's novel!

By February, bills were beginning to come in for props that were being made, and the printers were asking for payment for the prospectuses and announcements, and the wig-makers wanted payment for work they had done for *Dido* the year before. Ted wrote to his mother, telling her of these continual "pin pricks" that worried him and prevented him working. This time he got a stinging reply:

I send cheques to pay *half* the amount of five *pressing* bills you tell me about—"*Old* Bills" you say!! Why, I have been paying your "old bills" these ten years!—I sh^d not send this but that I fear *just as you* want to make a public appearance with the "*Acis*" at the Coronet you will be disgraced publicly by having the whole thing stopped by your creditors—meanwhile you are running up bills every day by speculating in a theatrical enterprise with *no means*—Do you call this anything but dishonest? You have strength and talents and opportunities, and you must *finish* this *bill paying* by yourself. Sixty Pounds just before I came away—Thirty afterwards—Two hundred I stand for, in honour to Saunders for you, & now Sixty-three Pounds—it is in all about upon £400— & you say in your letter "these pin pricks worry me"—Good Lord!.. *Pin Pricks*!! my patience is fast going—[13]

She had taken it for granted that they were returning to the Coronet, and could not imagine that after her warning they would be so foolhardy as to try and use Penley's "unlucky" theatre.

On March 7, thirty-six sandwich men (a familiar sight in London in those days) were walking up and down the main thoroughfares displaying the posters announcing the new production at the Great Queen Street Theatre—but the "English public" did not know the whereabouts of the theatre nor had they heard of this composer, Mr Purcell.

When the curtain went up on March 10, the effort had not been wholly wasted, for a few critics managed to find the place. What they saw proved that yet another milestone had been passed in the direction of a new kind of theatrical representation, and again they heralded the advance. Graham Robertson, the artist and writer, gives the most vivid impression on record of what the performance was like:

Many who went to hear the familiar and ever welcome pastoral came away uncertain as to whether they had heard or seen *Acis and Galatea*.
The music was given delightfully, but was only one delight

among many—a part of a curiously complete, strangely harmonious whole.

Round it and out of it was woven an ever-shifting maze of colour, form, and motion, through which the music tripped daintily, more lovely than of old, and happy in its native land of Faerie.

"O the Pleasure of the Plains!" sang the chorus, and the fierce mid-day light beat down, tempered softly by the draperies of the white tent under which they lay. Of scenery, in the ordinary sense, there was none; all was suggestion, but such skilful suggestion that into the cool, white shadow came the very heat and glare of mid-summer's meadows under a burning sun.

And among the drowsy nymphs and shepherds wandered a fantastic, childish figure, bearing many-coloured balls which hung suspended from a hoop, held high above her head. And to each dreamer she gave of her wares, purple and green and red and blue— little bright dreams to be had for the asking—and she seemed to whisper to each, "What would you?" and one seemed to answer, "Mine shall be blue, full of blue night and the deep sea"; and another, "Green for me, a dream of green pastures and running streams"; and a third, "Mine to be the red, a world of roses and of fire." And to each she seemed to smile and say, "Here—catch!" and she snipped the thread and flicked the painted ball through the air to the dreamers, till the whole scene grew gay with colour and magical with the floating and tossing and whirling of the many-hued balls.

And here people said, "How silly. For these are air-balls, and children buy them for a penny at the gates of Kensington Gardens."

And truly it was very silly indeed, and, for that very reason, it was exactly right; for what can be sillier—or more charming—than the opening chorus of *Acis and Galatea* with its silly tinkle of sheep bells, its silly words and its wonderful picture of the silly Arcadians "sporting the hours away." It was silly. It was also curiously beautiful and imaginative.

The vision of the dream-seller may or may not have been thus named by its designer, but that is of little matter; for it is the particular property of true vision (which is the highest imagination) that to all it means something and to no two people the same thing.

And so, through the setting forth of the story, song, action, and dance went hand in hand, none claiming the mastery, among a setting ever appropriate and suggestive; whether in the first great hint of Polyphemus when, in a dim wood of dark overhanging shade, one single fold of a vast purple mantle, sweeping down from the darkness, trailed heavily upon the ground; or when the monster himself became visible, a huge, brooding form upon a throne of heaped shadows, a haunting shape, never clearly seen, yet difficult to forget; or in the beautiful moment towards the close when, at the transformation of Acis into a fountain, the flow of a running stream was so quaintly echoed in the bending, swaying forms, floating scarves, and waving arms of the chorus, that music and singers alike seemed to melt together and ripple in a silver flood round the feet of the new-born Water God.

Nor was the *Masque of Love* with its clear harmonies of white and ivory and faint yellow—so at one and of a part with the music—less striking in its completeness, its dainty directness of statement.

As in the Handel Cantata, neither the music, the dancing, nor the setting were first or last; each was for all; and for the actors it is the highest compliment to say that they were forgotten. Acis and Galatea loved and sported in the plains of Arcady, the Lover and the Beloved met and parted in the Great White Chamber of Dreams, but names and personalities of today were lost.

And here Mr Gordon Craig, the Deviser and Executor of these fair imaginings, had achieved his great object—that the Sister Arts of Music, Painting, and Pantomime should make up their little differences and cast away their jealousies, and, by a united effort, should create anew a Forgotten Art—the Art of the Theatre.[14]

They had divided the opera into four scenes, which they described in the programme as:

The White Tent—The Shadow—The Giant—The Grey Tent.

In the sketch-book that Ted carried around at rehearsals he had noted down for Act I:

White—Pink—Grey and one touch of blue.
Costumes white, pink and silver?
Haze of white over all.[15]

The effect of a transparent tent was achieved by hanging hundreds of lengths of the two-and-a-half-inch-wide webbing from just behind the proscenium and draping it back over a bar: the webbing was not close together and through this curtain of strips, which opened and closed as figures came and went, could be seen a simple backcloth with tones that graduated from "white at the bottom and went through pink and blue and finally ended in Indigo at the top." A note beside the diagram reads "Japanese."

For the scene called "The Shadow," in which the wretched lovers are warned, "Behold the Monster Polyphemus, see what strides he makes," he placed his lovers on a formal mound in the centre of the stage. Years before, he had pasted into his scrap-book a photograph of just such a "lovers' mound": it was a fountain at Versailles; there reclined Ceres, carved in stone, surrounded by little cupids on a little island rising from the waters.

The idea for the grand *shadow* of Polyphemus came from the Lyceum, where, tired out one night after rehearsal, he had sat in the stalls, still covered in their dust-sheets. There, he had watched the scene shifters preparing the stage for the following day, and as the figures moved forwards and backwards, the "working light" cast their enormous shadows all over the back wall of the empty stage.[16] Max Beerbohm, in his criticism, referred to: "the cunning adjustment of shadows over light, making Polyphemus in *Acis and Galatea* a real Giant—the only real and impressive giant ever seen on any stage."[17]

When Acis was transformed into a fountain in the last scene, the tent of grey streamers slowly disappeared, and in the vast expanse of blue sky, a "Water God" gradually materialized in the form of a great fountain where the sparkling beads of water rose and fell. This beautiful effect—erroneously reported recently as having been "projected"—was, in fact, achieved by piercing holes in the backcloth and back-lighting them; then, by revolving large perforated discs in front of the lamps, the spots of light came and went, producing the cascade effect—a trick used in pantomimes at the Princess's Theatre from the time of Charles Kean.[18]

The old traditions of the Lyceum and the Princess's were coming to the aid of their young offspring, whose exciting vision was charting a route to a "new world" of the theatre.

While men like Max Beerbohm, W. B. Yeats, Arthur Symons, and

Graham Robertson were carried away by the beauty and the "suggestion that strikes straight to the nerves of delight," Haldane MacFall, the writer and critic, was writing Ted a letter full of admiration and frank advice:

March 13, 1902

Dear Craig,

Splendid!

Will write when I can squeeze the windbag of Time.

Meanwhile—Terrific.

The Polly Phaymous was simply godly; and the colours in the first act were good enough to eat.

What cow dung the criticis are! Think I saw Symons wildly applauding.

Kidlings! Wonderful—wonderful!!

Why did Penley build his theatre *there?*

... God, to think you have to gather in the deadheads, (and things like *me*), to fill a house for such glorious achievement!

Again, the critics are but vain cow dung. What a blithering world is this beneath our feet!

I am going to make one or two suggestions—

1. Put some brass bracelets on the man Acis. The hands look raw and unwieldy in gesture when the arm is naked as all women know. What a superb piece of colour, his robes!

2. Don't drop the string of balls in the love scene—it doesn't mean anything; and what it *does* mean is indelicate. Otherwise all the balls were very nice. If you *must* leave the balls in the love song, for God's sake not so many. Damn it all Acis wasn't a pawnbroker!

The tapes were terrific.

3. There is a difficulty you must take in hand at once in these operas. Between the acts, you lose your public, whom you have captured, three times by having no music. Anything is better than that. Shaw giving an emotional fantasia on the Jews' harp, or showing the tragic potentialities of a toothbrush upon the harmless but necessary slopcan. Anything. Is there no bridging over this gap? Anything to prevent the audience lapsing into what it is pleased to call thinking—the critical attitude. Of course, I quite allow that your bawling behind the curtain was wholly delightful, but whilst vibrant with

suppressed emotional intensity it was not in the picture. You very
nearly got an encore once, all the same. It was when you told the
carpenter he was ruddier than the cherry and a vegetarian and his
feet smelt—or words to that effect.

4. You must make Acis and Galatea do their love-making *standing*.
A love affair, sitting on the floor is pobbly on the stage—however
nice in reality. With amateurs particularly, love is very dangerous.
They can always do a passable cuddle standing—vide *Masque of Love*
and *Acis and Galatea* first love scenes.

. . . I liked Acis's dress in that first act, it was fine colour, as was every
touch of colour in it, to that glorious white watch-tower affair. And
that splendid yellow background!

It's glorious, my son, glorious, glorious!!![19]

MacFall was a good friend, and although Ted was often furious with
him, he always had to admit that he found this blunt Scot's criticism
very useful.

There are no records of what Mr Woodward's "Treasurer's Report"
showed at the end of the week. We do know that the broker's men were
in the theatre on the last night, and to make sure that nothing of value
was taken away they even searched the bags of the chorus as they left.
Martin Shaw remembered later that

The Purcell Operatic Society expired in a blaze of glory. The bills
had to be paid and Ellen Terry came to the rescue—though why she
should have done so, seeing that it was more my affair than Craig's,
I being the founder and prime instigator, her own kind heart only
knew. The creditors were all most kind, and even the electric light
company read the meter *ritenuto e diminuendo* for the first time
in history.[20]

The wonderful chorus now had no future to look forward to. For
three years they had slaved for Shaw and Craig, endeavouring to reproduce the beauties of Purcell's and Handel's music accompanied by
Craig's "movements" and dances—all this they had done for love.
They were now "amateurs" only in the literal sense of the word. It
had not been a sacrifice, for they lived in a period when people made
their own fun and became more familiar with the arts in the process. At

that time there was no magic box to hold them by the eyes and ears until their senses were dulled by a surfeit of pre-selected entertainment. This work had been an exciting part of their lives, and, as the years passed, they must have felt proud of their efforts which had helped so much to bring a new kind of Impressionism into the theatre.

CHAPTER NINE

"Bethlehem"·"The Vikings"·Frustration

1902–1903

W HILE PREPARING *Acis and Galatea*, Ted had ignored all envelopes that looked like bills and only opened those in Elena's hand.

Elena wrote daily from her old convent school in Sussex, where she had gone to stay for a couple of months, hoping to find the peace of mind that was so necessary before she decided on her next move, which could play such a big part in Ted's life as well as her own. She knew she loved him with all her being, and she sensed the power of his love for her. They had talked of eloping, and the idea appealed to her adventurous spirit, but she had been brought up to fear the wrath of God if she ignored the rules laid down by her Church.

Ted was risking nothing, for he believed in nothing. The mystery of the Church intrigued him, but it also overpowered him and so frightened him away.

Elena believed in her Church like an Italian peasant. She knew it would be sinful to run away with Ted, even if he married her later, and she would suffer terrible punishment in her after-life: she believed this so sincerely that she needed enormous courage to take such a step, and once she had made her choice there would be no turning back, for it was in her nature to see anything she started through to its conclusion . . . Convinced that Ted was worth any sacrifice, she prayed hard for forgiveness, and on March 13, holding tightly to her violin, and a crucifix given to her by one of the old nuns, she returned to London.

Half-way through the run of *Acis and Galatea*, they met early in the morning at the bottom of John Street (now Keats' Grove), and disappeared in much the same way as Ellen and Edward had done thirty-four years earlier.[1]

Elena, like Ellen, was rejected by her family as she embarked on her new life which was to be filled with happiness and despair, all of which she would accept because of her undying love. She was twenty-three.

Martin found a note from Ted, telling him what they had done; then, nearly every day for the next two or three weeks, a postcard would arrive with such messages as:

> We are at Chorley Wood. What ho—at No. 1 something or other. I write this at Rickmansworth and have forgotten the name of the street. Organ striking up so please excuse—Send a thousand pounds to me at Post Office, Chorley Wood if you *can*.[2]

One day Martin got a registered letter enclosing the inscribed gold ring that Ted's mother had given him on his "first appearance." He asked Martin to pawn it and send him the cash!

The lovers then hired a pony and trap so that they could drive through the countryside and over the border into Buckinghamshire. They were enjoying a new sense of freedom and the first signs of spring. At Chorley Wood, when it rained, they delighted in watching the trains from the cottage window, imagining silly stories about the people they saw in the carriages.

Ted introduced Elena to all his favourite characters in Dumas's novels, reading them aloud to her, and impersonating the characters as though he was acting in live melodrama—she listened wide-eyed, a magnificent audience, gradually getting to know the characters as well as he did.

With Elena he could be quite at ease, he could be a child again. There was no need for pretence. He left behind his Romantic and his Artistic make-up, knowing that whatever he did, however he appeared outwardly, she had a link with his real self, the self beneath all his disguises —the man struggling to find his way in life, and impelled by some strange magnetic force towards an ideal that was developing in his mind day by day.

She realized that his theatre was *his* religion, and that she would have to embrace it too, and learn to love it, for inevitably she would have to share his love with his ideal.

He began to turn to her for advice instead of to his mother. Her simple intuition was to be his future mainstay in judging character, and whenever he disregarded it he always had reason for regret.

Now that Ted had a woman beside him with whom he could share his secret fears as well as his childish joys, and hopes, he found life easier. He knew that *whatever happened* she would stand by him, and he felt he could tackle anything the future had in store. Martin would always co-operate with him in his work, but Elena was his secret talisman—and her second name was Fortuna. He called her Nell, but in hundreds of notes about her she appears generally as N., sometimes as Nellie.

On returning to London they took rooms in Kensington. Ted went over to Hampstead to see if Martin had returned from a much needed rest at his parents' place in Margate.

He found No. 8 Downshire Hill in a state of siege—and recognized his old enemies, the bailiffs; they had been prowling about for some some time, waiting to effect a "lawful entry." Ted, who was an expert bailiff-baiter, succeeded in entering unnoticed and found more trouble: a vast pile of bills, including one for £28. 7s. from the London & Suburban Advertising Company for the services of the "36 Boardmen in Uniform" who had paraded the London streets for nine days. It was they who had called in the bailiffs.

Down the road, he heard from Mrs Dryhurst that Signor Meo had at last put two and two together and discovered that it was Ted who had "stolen his favourite daughter." Meo was in a terrible rage and had only one desire, to kill Ted. Mrs Dryhurst had to remind the frantic father that he was now a naturalized British subject, and would have to forget his Calabrian code of honour.

Martin and his brother, Jules, soon joined Ted, and they tried to think out how they could carry on, and get in and out of the house without letting the bailiff in too. While they were devising a compli-cated system of keys and passwords, young Jules, who was often absent-minded, heard a knock at the kitchen door and asked who it was: an old woman's voice replied, she had come to clean up; Jules opened the door and in walked the bailiff!

They discovered that they would have to feed him while he was there, and also supply him with a light and a bed at night. They decided to make life so unbearable that he would leave, so they told him he could sleep on the couch in the otherwise empty studio downstairs—the black room with varnished walls.

Here, at night, by the light of one candle stuck on an old saucer, Ted walked up and down, telling Martin of his ideas for *The Masque of Hunger*. As he paced the uncarpeted floor in the eerie light, describing the "procession of beggars, holding aloft their dead and starving children, while voices chanted 'Pain . . . pain . . . pain and sorrow,' " he added, "reduced to this misery by men such as these." The bailiff huddled on the couch showed visible signs of unrest, but stuck to his post.

They eventually raised some money to clear up the debt that got rid of him, and later, felt that they had scored some kind of victory when they heard that he had given up the job as bailiff and had become a caretaker.[3]

Ellen was experiencing a certain urgency that comes after middle life. She wanted her children, Edward's children, to be safe.

Irving was now sixty-four, and was finding it increasingly difficult to get plays that would suit him, let alone a part in which she too could shine—after all, she was fifty-five.

She had slaved all her life and needed a little rest, apart from which she was frightened about her eyes. Unknown to her, a cataract had been developing for some time; she was becoming partially blind, and suffered from frightful headaches, which the gas footlights at the Lyceum made even worse.

For some time she had discussed the possibility of Ted undertaking a production for her. She had taken a delight in everything that he had done in *Acis and Galatea*, and particularly in *The Masque of Love;* she felt sure of his artistic ability—after all, he was Edward's son—but she also knew that he shared his father's disregard for anything to do with money. Ellen felt sure that if she could give him a free hand with the production while being there herself to guide and advise him over the practical and financial side, she could launch him successfully as the brilliant designer-producer she thought him to be.

At the same time, it would give her an opportunity to put Edy's costume business on the map: she had financed this business for some

years, as well as giving her a good allowance, and she felt it was time
that the business supported Edy.

In fact, she longed to see her children making headway independently.

Ellen invited Martin and Ted to Winchelsea and talked things over
with them. She liked Martin, whom she felt might have a restraining
influence on her son.

They spoke of different plays that she might put on, such as *Peer
Gynt*, or *Griselda*, which Laurence Irving was translating from the
French, but she longed for a good part in a "powerful play," and
thought often of Ibsen's work—Ted suggested *The Vikings*, and she
started to read it.[4]

Meantime, Laurence Housman, who had seen *Acis and Galatea* and
admired the simplicity of the production, got in touch with Ted to see
if he would design and produce a Nativity play that he had just written,
called *Bethlehem*. His friend Joseph Moorat had written music for it,
and he had the necessary finances—the proceeds from his very successful
book, *The Love Letters of an Englishwoman*.

He was quite ready for Martin Shaw to train the singers and conduct
the orchestra. They would each receive a fee of £50, part of it on
account and the rest at the end of the production, which Housman only
visualized as a short run at Christmas.[5]

The idea appealed to both Ted and Martin as something they could
get on with while waiting for Ellen, who in turn was faithfully waiting
for Irving.

Fred Terry was embarking on a production of R. G. Legge's *For
Sword or Song*. Ellen thought there might be some work here for Ted,
so she wrote to her brother:

> I must tell you that *Ted* is a most wonderful hand at *Fairy Scenes*—
> arranging—lighting and clothing them, and being very full of
> original ideas might be of use to you.[6]

Fred asked Ted to go and see him, and it was agreed that he should
design some of the costumes and two of the scenes, the first and the
last, because Fred wanted them to make a particular impact on the
audience. The idea of merely designing a couple of scenes for a production did not appeal to Ted, but the £20 did. He wrote to his mother:

—it's very amusing and not a bit interesting because the play demands nothing but the usual treatment.

I am finding out through this what Harker, Telbin and Craven do their scenes for . . . For instance, I have designed Act III "Sword and Song", Harker's men paint it, and I get £10, Harker £50.[7]

Ted was also putting together an exhibition for John Baillie, a friend of MacFall, who had a pleasant little picture gallery at No. 1 Princes Terrace, in fashionable Bayswater. It was to open in October. He had about fifty original drawings and a similar number of woodcuts, and it was just a question of getting them mounted, designing the invitation card, and printing the catalogue. Edy had agreed to decorate the gallery with sprays of lavender and dried leaves.

In fact, there was plenty to do. *Bethlehem* appealed to him, *For Sword or Song* did not interest him at all, the exhibition would be fun but he was already thinking far ahead, and talking to Martin about incidental music for *The Vikings*.

While waiting to hear which theatre or hall Housman was using for *Bethlehem*, Ted drew scenes for his theatre of the future. They were not exactly scenes—he called them movements, for that was how he imagined them. He found that places under different lights and conditions evoked different moods: these moods when coupled together became movements, and acted as a kind of "figured bass" or basso continuo through which other forms could wander in a given pattern—and the beauty lay in contemplating this visual counterpoint in the same way that one would enjoy a piece of music.

In the very early morning, or late at night, Ted and Elena would walk across Hyde Park, then up the Mall to the Duke of York's steps which they would stand and watch in the changing light, while Ted would make notes. Elena would be the figure that moved up and down or across the steps—sometimes quickly, other times majestically. Occasionally a group of children would accidentally give the necessary pattern he sought, and one night, when the road-cleaners were using hoses and the jets of water were back-lit by the street-lamps, Ted was overcome with joy.[8] In his note-book he made the entry:

F

THE STEPS.   Up and Down
                      1st Movement—2 Children
                      2nd   —20 Children
                      3rd   —Man & Woman
                      etc. ad infinitum.
         The Scene (The Steps) The form—The Movements
                      The colour and rhythm.[9]

These were short-hand notes, to serve him at a future date. Kinetics now became his chief interest.

When he and Elena went to Dunmow in Essex for a summer holiday they would watch the standing corn being blown by the wind, and as the rhythmic waves swept across the field Ted would see in it the marching of great armies. The sight of children playing traditional ring games and skipping games, and the local Morris dancers held him enthralled.

At the same time he started to notice the beauty of the surroundings in which they were living. They hired a "governess cart" and drove around the Essex lanes stopping here and there while he made the most joyous pictures of the English countryside. Then, in order that no one should know where they had been, he would write imaginary names on his sketches; Billericay became Hayworth, Danbury became Mortimer Wood, and Stansted Heckfield.[10]

From Essex he wrote to Martin:

I am full of a lot of feelings that I cannot express—Doesn't one ache to achieve a tremendous something or other and then at the end it looks like so much rubbish. One *is* so much more than one can do— and so much less than one can dream. I sometimes see that one can arrive as far as one can dream in a flash—in some sudden way— chance.[11]

They had found a studio at No. 15 Pembroke Walk, Kensington, but before leaving Downshire Hill, Ted had traced his best Bach *Passion* design from Martin's wall and then painted over the original with whitewash.[12]

Gradually, as Laurence Housman and a newly formed London drama league got organized, Ted became absorbed by *Bethlehem*: he had to prepare designs for sixty or more costumes which his sister was making in her workrooms, as well as work out the four simple scenes.

Following the search for a large enough hall, Housman had settled on the Great Hall at the Imperial Institute, but, like the Hampstead Conservatoire, it had no proscenium. As the one for *Dido* had been such a success, Ted repeated it again here.

Meanwhile, Joseph Moorat, who had never worked on such a performance, began to take offence when Ted suggested cutting out certain pieces of his music and inserting pieces by Palestrina, and traditional airs, one of which, "God Rest You Merry, Gentlemen," he had never heard! This happened quite often, until only two or three pieces of his music were left.

After the proscenium was built they held a rehearsal on the stage and discovered that the acoustics were terrible. Ted asked the advice of Paul Cooper, his boyhood friend from Bradfield days. Paul was an architect, and he suggested hanging the hall with some cheap material; through Edy Craig they found a quantity of blue cloth that did the trick, and the auditorium now resembled a great tent.[13]

Bethlehem had been refused a licence by the Lord Chamberlain because it showed the Holy Family; therefore it could only be produced "privately."

The cast was anonymous, and the programme, which was a single sheet of paper, simply credited Housman, Craig, and Shaw, then listed the cast of seventy-five without saying what parts they played; many of them had been recruited from the ranks of the faithful P.O.S. chorus.

There were four scenes:

The Shepherds in the Fields—The Coming of the Kings—
Outside Bethlehem—The Cradle of Bethlehem.

There was another little scene, "Outside Bethlehem," which Ted thought necessary as an introduction to "The Cradle of Bethlehem." It was acted in front of the curtain, which was drawn apart, only a few feet, to show a view of the town, painted to look like an early woodcut. The chorus sang: "Come little town, your narrow doors undo ..." This scene is not included in the published version of *Bethlehem* that appeared at the same time as the production.[14]

This production was a very new experience for Ted. With all his previous work he had music to inspire him, and music to control every movement. This time it was poetry, the music was only incidental; nor did he have Martin working with him months before.

Instead of the sunlight and shepherds of Arcady he had starlight and the shepherds of Bethlehem. In place of the gay dances of the nymphs and shepherds there was the solemn procession of the Magi and their retainers—and in their wake Ted added a great throng of followers, such as he had seen in so many of the paintings by the great masters at the National Gallery: there were beggars, musicians, a murderer, weird cripples, and so on. In dressing this motley array, his sister had proved to be wonderfully inventive.

In the first and last scenes he made a radical break-away from the traditional representation of the Nativity, and this must have been quite startling to the audience who would have gone to the performance expecting to see the images that had long been impressed upon their minds by hundreds of Victorian Christmas pictures. But the curtains parted to reveal something entirely new.

In the indigo night there were stars, actually twinkling; beneath them, in a pool of light, the shepherds sat in a sheep fold with what seemed to be their flock. A young shepherd was singing one of Moorat's beautiful songs, "The World Is Still Tonight," punctuated by a watcher's voice singing out, "Ay oh, Ay oh, Ay oh." There was a blind shepherd called Abel, who has some fine lines to speak, and for this part Ted got his friend from the Margate Theatre Royal, Percy Rhodes, who delivered them superbly.

The scene was made from a few sheep-hurdles, some sacks, and a boxful of old crystals. There was an indigo backcloth; the stars were the crystals taken from an old chandelier, and suspended at different heights on black cobbler's thread, they sparkled every now and then as they caught the lights. A number of Essex sheep-hurdles, placed so as to form an irregular rectangle, represented a sheep-pen. The sheep, indistinct in the darkness, were represented by many sacks filled with wood-wool, the suggestion of sheeps' ears made by tying off two small sections near the point of each sack. The shepherds lay about waiting in the soft light, dressed in ageless garments—cloaks and slouch hats made from shaggy sheepskins and sacking, each carrying a long pole or shepherd's crook.

In the last scene, Ted made use of the existing formation of platforms at the back of the hall, and on these he arranged Joseph, the shepherds, angels, and worshippers so that they built up a large group of figures and faces that looked down on Mary and the Holy Child, who was not visible'but whose Presence was recognized by a light that came from the crib at Mary's feet, illuminating them all. The Magi and their retinue, some of whom played old musical instruments, entered from the back of the hall, forming a great slow-moving procession down an aisle on the left side of the audience. They came in a blaze of rich purples, greens, and gold, but because of this very richness of colour, when they mounted the stage they were kept in the shadow, forming a fine silhouette in the foreground.[15]

The whole ensemble and lighting had been influenced by Rembrandt; Ted had just bought a book of reproductions of his etchings, and in his excitement had scribbled across the wrapper, "Rembrandt is the born dramatist, though he writes no words."[16]

On the last night Martin and Ted received their cheques, and letters of thanks from the author. Ted, forgetting the pile of bills at home, changed his into golden half-sovereigns, and gave them away to the chorus as tokens of his affection and gratitude—they called them their "medals," and Maude Douie kept hers as a memento for years afterwards.[17]

Christopher St. John (which hid the identity of Christabel Marshall, who was Edy's lifelong companion), gave a fine review of the performance in *The Critic*, otherwise it went almost unnoticed compared with the wonderful press for the previous operas and the masque; this was probably because it had to be produced as a "private performance," or because it came at the beginning of the pantomime season.

Ted hoped that at least some of the more enterprising theatre managements might have seen their work or read their notices, and would invite them to produce something similar for the big London theatres.

But the theatre managers of 1902 did not want to speculate on new ideas; they were just businessmen who wanted to invest money in something safe, and since they had no imagination they could only go by what had succeeded before—one week at the Coronet Theatre was not sufficient recommendation. Unluckily, Ted looked on this attitude as a concerted plot to bar his way in the theatre and he started writing to the papers about "The English Theatre" as though it were a united body opposed not only to him, but to the development of the theatre as an art.

While preparing *Bethlehem*, he had bought a copy of Horn's *Ancient Mysteries* (1823), and in it was delighted to read about the old English "Harvest Festivals." The idea appealed to him—he immediately published a delightful prospectus called *The Harvest Home,* telling of the old

✲ A MASQUE ✲
THE HARVEST HOME
DESIGNED AND ARRANGED BY MARTIN SHAW AND EDWARD GORDON CRAIG.

The prospectus for *The Harvest Home*, 1903.

custom of accompanying the last load of corn to the barn with singers of harvest songs, Morris dancers, hobby-horses, and musicians. The last line in the prospectus read, *"the performers number 30 to 40 and the time taken is $\frac{3}{4}$ of an hour, or longer if required."* He had visions of spending the following summer in the English countryside accompanied by a group of singers and dancers from the P.O.S, the costumes being those used in previous productions . . . they would go from one great house to another . . .

He started sending the prospectuses to anyone he thought would pass them on to friends amongst the landed gentry. He was full of enthusiasm—until his practical sister Edy remarked, "the harvest doesn't go on all through the summer you know, and you'd never be able to afford the transport for thirty or forty people all over the country for three quarters of an hour's work!" He consoled himself by thinking how nice it would be to do a Harvest Home one summer at Smallhythe, his mother's farm in Kent.

Ted and Elena spent Christmas together in Essex. And on January 16, 1903, for his birthday, his mother sent him *Roget's Thesaurus of English Words and Phrases*, a book that was to herald a new phase in his life.

In March of the previous year he had written his first article for the press—"The Production of Ulysses." Before that, he had only written odd bits and pieces for *The Page* and *The Artist*, either anonymously or under various pseudonyms. Recently he had developed a profound desire to write seriously about the theatre; for during the last three years, while he and Martin had been working together, he thought that he had discovered why the contemporary theatre was so behind all the other arts. He agreed with Leopold Eidlitz, who had written in his *Nature and Function of Art*:

> To produce a work of art the artist must have a clear and definite understanding of the idea which is to be celebrated and a thorough knowledge of the methods required to represent it in matter. The artist must, from the beginning of the work and throughout every stage of it, be the master of the means and methods of accomplishing this object.

He therefore concluded that the artist in the theatre should be the director and the producer as well as the designer of the backgrounds and of every movement on the stage, and he should light the stage and the actors in a way that would develop a mood—convey an emotion. Above all, this should be done impressionistically and not realistically. In fact, there was no need for dialogue or even for a play. This would be nearer to his conception of the "art of the theatre"—all this he wanted to write about in order to find out more.

He had asked his mother how to set about putting down these ideas: she had replied, "sit down and write." Now she had given him Roget's magic book. It was soon to rank among the most important books in his library; he revelled in it, and even intoned it aloud to Elena:

> oaf, lout, loon, lown;
> dullard, doodle, calf, colt;
> buzzard, block, put, stick;
> witling, dizzard, donkey, ass!

He wrote a note on the fly-leaf: "To teach oneself to write—to draw, so as to be able to *express*, if not to *do*, for expression is the Deed of the Artist."[18]

By the end of the year he had written five letters to the press, and six articles for which he had been paid. These articles had such titles as "Stage Management," "Theatres and Actors," "Stage Scenery," "Theatrical Art," "Theatre, Trade or Art." Most of them came out in the *Morning Post*.

The arrival of *Roget's Thesaurus* introduced him to the meaning and power of words—this was to be a new medium for him to experiment with, and he hoped that with its aid he would get his ideas recognized all the quicker.

He had to leave Pembroke Walk and had found a splendid studio in Chelsea—No. 13 and 14 Trafalgar Studios, Manresa Road, which was down the road opposite 215 King's Road, where his mother had gone to live. He had also found a big cottage for Elena and their first baby at Maldon in Essex.

The baby, a girl, was only a few weeks old, and it pleased Ted that she looked like her mother. They had hoped for a boy, but perhaps they would be luckier next time.

Ted now turned his attention to *The Vikings*—his first treatment of a play in prose, and by one of his favourite modern playwrights, his only regret being that the translation was by William Archer, whom he did not like.

His immediate job was to design all the costumes so that Edy could go ahead and set her women to work making them. There was a cast of fifty-six, including fourteen principals, so a large number of drawings would be necessary. There were also the properties to be designed for Louis Labhart to make: shields, spears, helmets, caskets, musical instruments, and an enormous candelabra some fifteen feet in diameter for the banquet scene, great eating vessels, and so on. All these were being made in wood and metal by a fine craftsman, and not of the usual *papier mâché*. He had always believed that properties, especially those handled by the actors should be made as beautifully and with as much detail lavished on them as the actor lavished on his own make-up.

Then there was what Ellen referred to as the "gutting of the Stage," which had to be put in hand and supervised: this consisted of taking up all the lines and battens so that nothing would be visible between the stage and the grid. Then, just over the proscenium arch he erected a bridge to take the lamps for his main source of lighting, as he had done at Hampstead. Here, however, there was a difference that he had not calculated on; the proscenium was three times as high and the lights lost a lot of their intensity before they reached the stage.[19]

He found the atmosphere of Trafalgar Studios very helpful. He didn't feel so pent up and there were other painters, sculptors, and musicians all around—struggling, like himself, to capture their ideas.

Chelsea in those days was, like Hampstead, a community on its own. Interesting river-craft were moored to jetties all along the mud banks, trees lined the waterfront. An artists' colony had long been established, and there were pubs and inns on the embankment, like The Black Swan, where the evenings could be passed in the jovial company of Vaughan Williams, the composer, or painters like Augustus John and William Orpen, their models, and the occasional bargee or ostler. In the King's Road there was the comparatively modern Eight Bells, where Pryde and Nicholson could be found—Nicholson always on the look-out for "blokes" that he could draw. Across the road was the Chelsea Palace of Varieties, where, for a shilling, one could enjoy the performances of "naughty" Marie Lloyd and Chevalier's superb cockney songs, mixed with juggling, *tableaux vivants*, Chinese acrobats, and all that made the old time Music Hall such wonderful entertainment.

The inhabitants of this new world wore slightly different clothing to that which he had got used to in Kensington. This was a very hat-conscious period and most actors wore "toppers," which they seldom

removed, even for lunch in a restaurant; but in Chelsea many of the
artists sported bowlers or soft felt hats or large French berets. Hats
were distinguished by special names, such as "The Argyle" for the
West End topper; "The Brighton," a bowler chosen by the young
sparks; and "The Woolwich," which was neither a top-hat nor a
bowler and was worn by those who were undecided as to which group
they belonged. Ted decided to join those few artists who favoured a
broad-brimmed felt hat; he also started wearing a cloak.

But trouble was in store for Ted at the Imperial Theatre in Tothill
Street; there were all sorts of obstacles that he had not anticipated. To
begin with, his mother was the most loved and the most experienced
actress of her time, but she was a traditionalist; most of the actors—
particularly Oscar Asche and Holman Clark—were established members of "The Profession" and felt they owed their allegiance to her, and
not to Edward the rebel. Then there was Edy the feminist, who was not
particularly imaginative, and knew it, but was very practical, very
stubborn, and generally got what she wanted by appealing to her
mother when they were alone. There was also Alfred Courtenay, a
rather punctilious man; he was "Miss Ellen Terry's Business Manager."

When Ted wanted a piece of action performed in a different way to
that suggested by the author, whose stage directions he had completely
disregarded, the profession at once appealed to Ellen.

If Edy felt that anything in the play should be changed, or if she
wished to simplify a costume, she would mention it to her mother on
the way to rehearsal, and the suggestions would then seem to be Ellen's.

Alfred Courtenay, ignoring family ties, set about his job as though
this was a routine production: he wanted estimates in advance and
receipts for petty cash, and even asked "Mr Craig" to sign a contract
with "Miss Ellen Terry." Ted was outraged.

All this produced an undercurrent of intrigue and subversion, and the
atmosphere in the theatre was electric with tension. Ted, sensing the
opposition, became increasingly resistant to criticism. His only trusted
collaborator was Martin, who had written some magnificent incidental
music for the play; among the actors only Hubert Carter seemed eager
to interpret his ideas.

The correspondence between mother and son over the cast shows
considerable disagreement. There were continual reminders in every
letter from Ellen: "It strikes me that the interlaced pattern on the

curtains may look far too civilized and grand." (This was obviously Edy.) "Remember to get Estimates"; "Remember it will have to travel"; "I cut the third act tremendously"; "Don't call any Principal until I am there too," and so on.[20]

Ted was now thirty-one, and had the experience of three productions behind him. Financially they had been failures, but artistically they were way ahead of everything in the contemporary English theatre— even in the European theatre. Mr Courtenay was there to see to the finance, and Ted should have been given a free hand with the rest, but he was still Ellen's boy, and that was a tremendous handicap. She was still treating him as her pupil.

In the first act there was an exciting rock structure that had to be rolled on to the stage; it looked like a great landslide, at an angle between thirty and forty degrees. On this, Ted wanted Oscar Asche and Holman Clark to fight with swords, but these traditionalists, thinking of the usual broadsword technique used in *Macbeth*, where they delighted in prancing about the stage, said it was impossible. Ted explained that it should look more like the ancient Samurai fighting with their enormous swords; great slow movements, with sudden flashes. That, they thought, would make them look absurd—Ted, using Carter to help him, showed them how, and they were furious that it could be done so effectively.

Someone told Asche that, in his costume, he looked marvellous. "It's not the ruddy costume, it's me damn fine figure," he remarked, and stalked away.[21]

Looking back on the production at a later date, Ted wrote to Martin:

My feelings about the Vikings are just yours. But I feel convinced that no *Vikings* can be done unless each character will listen to the stage manager and hear what character he is to play. What the hell is the use of Act I—what's all the bother about on the rocks, the ROCK and the Giants, the swords ten inches thick and blood flowing, wrestling of limb and brain, if Hjordis is not the exact opposite of all this exterior might.

What is the *storm* of the play but the counterpart of the storm inside her heart, and what has exterior storminess to do with her—absolutely NOTHING. "to side with the wild sisters" and all that is the cry of her soul not the instinct of her physique. Soul is to her what physique is to every other one in the play. Sigurd is little short of God, Gunnar absolute man.

But I may be getting mixed. I've been fiddling with a scene for the last 6 hours and it goes wrong and I'm losing the ounce of touch I had.

You did the *Vikings*—and I did the *Vikings*—and the rest were doing jokes—and never got rid of their skins, much less into any others. And only because, as it goes today, that is an impossibility—

The stage is uʍop ǝpᴉsdn.[22]

The press attended the first night on April 15 in great numbers. The attraction was, of course, to see Ellen Terry in her first big part by a modern author of repute. But it was not a success. There were too many conflicting interests—"beautiful Ellen Terry"; "controversial Ibsen"; "revolutionary Gordon Craig"; and so on.

The Imperial Theatre was in Tothill Street (behind what is now the County Hall, Westminster), miles away from the Strand, which was then the centre of "Theatreland and High Life." It was pretty, but had no reputation, and again, few people knew where Tothill Street was.

Ted's life-long friend, William Rothenstein, wrote to the *Saturday Review*, using phrases like "perfect marriage of dramatic suggestion," "perfectly noble expression of the tragedy of men's and women's lives," "everything seemed terribly but simply inevitable," and ended by saying he felt sure that in a very short time Craig "will have won the foremost place in the modern Theatre he has already shown his right to."

James Huneker, the American dramatic critic, was there, and was probably the only person to leave a fairly accurate account of the production; it is therefore well worth while quoting two of his seven pages on the play in order to give his impression of Ted's contribution:

. . . I went to the most beautiful theatre in London, the Imperial, to hear, to see, above all to see, the Norwegian dramatist's *Vikings*, a few days before it was withdrawn, in May, 1903. For one thing the production was doomed at the start: it was woefully miscast. The most daring imagination cannot picture Ellen Terry as the fierce warrior wife of Gunnar Headman. Once a creature capriciously sweet, tender, arch, and delightfully arrogant, Miss Terry is now long past her prime. To play Hjordis was murdering Ibsen outright.

But the play had its compensations, Miss Terry's son, Edward Gordon Craig, exercised full sway on the stage, lighting, costumes. He is a young man with considerable imagination and a taste for the poetic picturesque. He has endeavoured to escape the deadly monotony of London stage problems. Abolishing foot and border lights, sending shafts of luminosity from above, Mr Craig secures unexpected and bizarre effects. It need be hardly added that these same effects are suitable only for plays into which the element of romance and of the fantastic largely enter. We see no "flies", no shaky unconvincing side scenes, no foolish flocculent borders, no staring back-cloths. The impression created is one of real unreality. For example, when the curtains are parted, a rocky slope, Nordish, rugged, forbidding, is viewed, the sea, an inky pool, mist-hemmed, washing at its base. From above falls a curious, sinister light which gives purplish tones to the stony surfaces and masks the faces of the players with mysterious shadows. The entire atmosphere is one of awe, of dread.

With his second tableau Mr Craig is even more successful. It is the feast room in Gunnar's house. It is a boxed-in set, though it gives one the feeling of a spaciousness that on the very limited stage of the Imperial is surprising. A circular platform with a high seat at the back, and a long table with rough benches, railed in, make up an interior far from promising. A fire burns in a peculiar hearth in the centre, and there are raised places for the women. Outside it is dark. The stage manager contrived to get an extraordinary atmosphere of gloomy radiance in this barbaric apartment. He sent his light shivering from on high, and Miss Terry's Valkyr dress was a gorgeous blue when she stood in the hub of the room. All the light was tempered by a painter's perception of lovely hues. This scene has been admired very much. For many, however, the third act bore off the victory. A simple space of hall, a large casement, a dais, the whole flooded by daylight. Here the quality of light was of the purest, withal hard, as befitted a northern latitude.[23]

When Ellen had read the play the year before, she had written to her son:

. . . As to the Vikings—the scene between the two women where they discourse of their lovers—!! *how how* cᵈ that be managed— Except at the Stage Society subscription performances it would not be allowed! Then a part like that for me would be like *3* Lady Macbeths—It's superb and I'd like to—but I'm afraid I could not get at it—could not do it—but it's wonderful—and as *I think of it* I feel like getting up and *trying*—but nobody would believe in me in such a part and I'm too old now to experiment *handicapped*. Of course I might say I wanted to *have the thing done so much*, and could not think of anyone who could do *the part* better.²⁴

She braved it, and had to suffer the consequences. Three weeks before they "rang up" on *The Vikings* her professional self warned her again, and she wrote to Ted:

"*Red are the rocks, white is the sand. Blue are the waters of Helgeland*"— —but what about Much Ado? I've only £500 to spend on it—and if I had 5000 it would be impossible to *scene & dress* the Play in three weeks in your way, let alone drill supers and rehearse everybody. Then again, I believe in the *old* play, and the *old me* in it, would not be acceptable to the Public in a *different style* to the one they know— Lose no time dear, please, in telling me if you see yʳ way to stage managing the thing with *existing scenery & dresses* (wherever we may be able to pick them up)—as slight as possible and with nice lighting —to make it all look as beautiful as may be—A *dance*, in which I dance too, during the scene with Benedick, and all going very merrily—and then if 'The Vikings' *doesn't* go, *pop* it on, as if we meant to, all the while, and there are *2* plays at least for America. This is the only way in which I can do it.²⁵

Three weeks after the opening night she realized they were no longer covering expenses and alerted Ted to go ahead with *Much Ado About Nothing*:

Thursday morning—Private
Now whilst there is time to simplify the scenery and lighting for Much Ado, I want to impress upon you that *everything* depends upon

the *quick changing of the scenes on the first night*—it's no use afterwards, for the newspapers speak of the *first night*. It will mean *ruin* to me if this play don't succeed and I shall close the theatre and finish up on the following Saturday if things don't go smoothly on the Tuesday— It w^d mean ruin to me if this Play don't succeed, for I should with *that* play be losing about £150 or £200 a week—& for *you* it would be ruin, as making *"impossible" from an all round point of view to do Craig's beautiful work*. . . .

To get through this season quietly without *obvious* disaster must be our united aim.[26]

There was a two-week break in order to allow time for rehearsals and mounting the show. On May 23 they opened again, with *Much Ado*. The costumes were by "Gordon Craig and M. Racinet"—they were all traditional.

In despair over the failure of *The Vikings* but spurred on by the urgency of the situation, Ted dashed out to look for reference books which might help him with the Italian Renaissance and came back with a copy of Serlio's *Five Books of Architecture*. This beautiful work, with its simple woodcuts showing the orders of architecture, streets in perspective, and ornaments, not only gave him the answer to his present problem, but became another of his main sources of inspiration in later years. In 1545 architecture was treated reverently, simply, and with great affection, and Ted, who had never thought about it before, felt that in Sebastiano Serlio he had found a friend.

In this volume was a simple design giving the true proportions of a Tuscan pilaster, and he had five of them made, each eighteen feet high. By altering their positions and filling the spaces between them with curtains, balustrading, or formal garden backcloths, he had an adaptable scene and with these few elements was able to produce "Leonato's house" and also his "Garden" in Acts I and II, and the "Monument of Leonato" in Act IV. "A Street" in Act II was just a simple front-cloth —also inspired by Serlio.

But it was the church scene in Act III that created the most lasting impression. For this his main source of inspiration had come from the paintings of Taddeo Gaddi. Against a backing of grey curtains decorated with a *varnished* pattern that sparkled in the dim light, he built a long platform, reached by four wide steps. On the platform was a great altar, crowded with enormous candlesticks. High over the altar hung a giant crucifix, part of it disappearing into the shadows above (this was like the Cimabue crucifix in Florence). In the foreground he suggested two great columns by gathering together two clusters of enormous grey curtains. The only illumination in this dimly lit "church" came from an imaginary stained-glass window above the proscenium arch that cast a great pool of light upon the floor below, while the distant candles twinkled mysteriously on the altar in the background. The characters were only lit when they entered the acting area which was the pool of coloured light; outside it, they too became silhouettes like the columns.[27]

The description of the scene in *Modern Society* is most interesting, because it shows that the critic really *believed* that he had seen "arched mosaic columns," and refers to the "Byzantine splendour."

Even Bernard Shaw, writing to Ellen on June 3, had to admit that ". . . as usual, Ted has the best of it. I have never seen the Church scene go before—didn't think it *could* go, in fact."[28]

According to some of the papers, even Sir Henry Irving "was impressed by Mr Gordon Craig's lighting effects."

Ted was saddened by the whole affair: the idea of working with his mother at the Imperial Theatre on a production of his own had been so exhilarating, but as time went by, the intrigue, the resistance to all that he was trying to do had sickened him. When his mother left the Imperial and took *Much Ado* on tour in an effort to regain some of her lost investment, he went once or twice to see the show, and from a letter to Martin one can see exactly how the feeling of discord grew between him and the actors of the future:

When I want a sound bracing now, I visit a suburban theatre and witness "Much Ado"—I cannot tell you how painful the operation is, or how much good it does me.

Each time I see it a viler gaiety is added—speech is noisier & action floppier—thought infrequent, and taste unknown.

One part of course flashes brilliantly, the rest is dull heartrending vulgarity—unrest everywhere. You could get the full fervour of my feeling if you could hear Bach's Passion interpreted by the Gaiety Chorus under Raymondiana—And add to this "contentment" on all the faces—contentment shrieking in their purses—

E. W. Godwin.

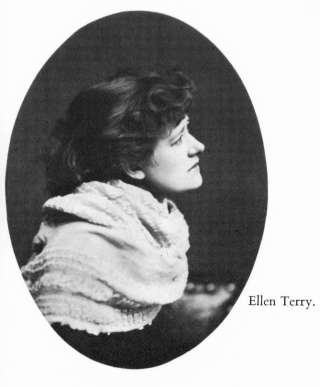

Ellen Terry.

Teddy, aged three.

Opposite page: Top,
Teddy in Chicago in 1885.
Bottom, Teddy with Henry Irvi
returning from America in 1885

A page from Ellen Terry's notebook.

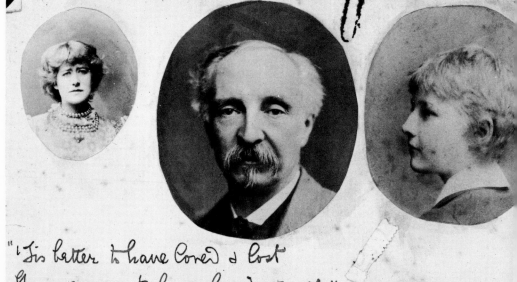

" 'Tis better to have loved & lost
than never to have loved at all " =

Henry Irving in 1878.

May Craig with Rosie in 1898.

Edy Craig.

Martin Shaw.

The house in Hampstead
where Craig and Shaw lived and worked.

Gordon Craig with his mother, Ellen Terry, in *The Dead Heart*.

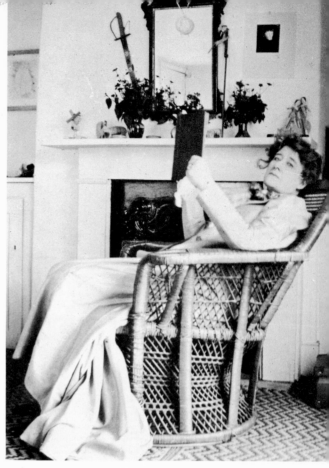

Ellen Terry at her cottage
in Kingstone Vale in 1899.

Opposite page:
Top, The chorus in
Acis and Galatea, 1902.
Bottom, The opening scene
in *Bethlehem,* 1903.

Elena Meo in 1888.

Isadora Duncan and Gordon Craig, photographed by Elise de Brouckère
three days after they met in 1904.

Gordon Craig wood-engraving in
his hotel bedroom in Holland, 1906.
From a photograph by
Isadora Duncan.

Gordon Craig in Berlin in 1905,
from a photograph
by Isadora Duncan.

A moment of arrested motion in Craig's conception of *Scene*.

Gordon Craig in Florence, 1907.

Maurice Magnus.

Constantin Stanislavsky
and his wife, Maria Lilina.

Craig with his assistant
Sam Hume in 1908.

The Arena Goldoni, Florence.

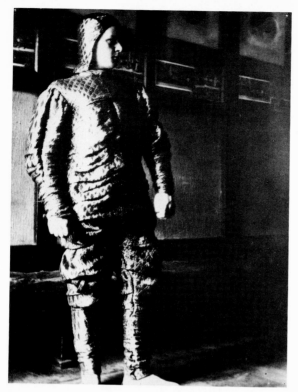

One of the costumes for *Hamlet*, made from Stanislavsky's famous gold fabric, 1910.

One of Craig's models showing an arrangement of screens for *Hamlet*, 1909.

Gordon Craig wood-engraving in 1910.

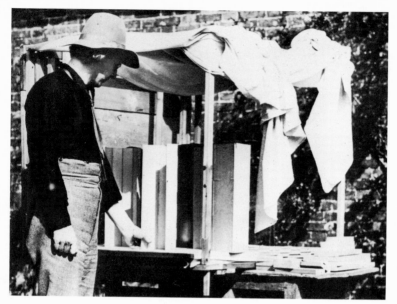

Gordon Craig work[...]
with his model stage[...]
in 1910.

The model for Bach'[...]
St. Matthew Passion.

Gordon Craig with Elena and their
two children, at Smallhythe, 1910.

Edy Craig with her niece, Nelly,
at Smallhythe, 1910.

Opposite page:
Gordon Craig in 1925.

Lord Howard de Walden,
the man who financed Gordon
Craig's school in Florence.

Craig, Max Beerbohm, Elena, Edward, Florence Beerbohm, and
Nelly at the Villa Raggio, near Rapallo, 1925.

Gordon Craig, Douglas Ross, and Ian Leffcott working on the Tyler production
of *Macbeth* at Craig's villa near Genoa, 1929.

Opposite page:
Top, Gordon Craig in Russia in 1935.
With him are Mr. Arosev, President of the Society
for Cultural Relations, and Vsevolod Meyerhold,
the famous producer.
Bottom, Gordon Craig in 1935.

Gordon Craig, aged seventy-nine, at Tourette sur Loup.
Photographed by his son, David Lees.

They come off the stage and seriously take as the final verdict, the applause of a kind audience.

This is Hell—I know of nothing more tormenting.[29]

Financially, he gained very little from the whole enterprise, for in the previous year he had agreed to his mother's proposal that she would settle his debts on *Acis and Galatea*, which amounted to over £200, then deduct this sum from the salary he would eventually receive for his work on their forthcoming venture. However, he was better off by about £200, plus a few more pounds which were the proceeds of his exhibition of pictures in the Imperial foyer and another at Baillie's Gallery.

In May he was elected a member of the Society of Twelve. This he considered a great honour, since among the other eleven members were no lesser artists than Augustus John, Charles Ricketts, and Charles Shannon, William Nicholson, Lucien Pissaro, and, of course, Will Rothenstein, who had proposed him. He exhibited with them at the Obach Galleries in the following year. This gesture from a group of notable artists pleased him, but at the same time made him feel bitterly aware of the comparative indifference of his fellow workers in the theatre. Then he remembered that at least Hubert Carter had shown signs of friendship at the end of *The Vikings* run—he had presented him with two York hams. One of them hung in Trafalgar Studios, the other in the kitchen at Maldon; Elena and Ted were to live on ham for weeks!

Towards the end of 1903 his thoughts turned to the formation of a school. There he would train young enthusiasts, such as he had found amongst the P.O.S., to become a new generation of actors. He started working out a course of study . . . when suddenly a note arrived from Will Rothenstein, suggesting a meeting at the Café Royal—it was important. Ted went along and Will introduced him to Count Harry Kessler.

Kessler, four years his senior, was an aristocrat in the old sense of the word, a diplomat, and an eminent person in the Court at Weimar in Germany. But above all, he was a patron of the arts whose taste was way ahead of his time, and he was already collecting the work of the Impressionist school, and had some fine pictures by Cézanne, Gauguin, and Seurat. There was a beautiful theatre at Weimar that was financed by the Court, and Kessler's interest extended to this too. His mother was Irish, he loved England, and often found reasons for coming to London, where he kept in touch with the world of art. This, of course, made him interesting to Rothenstein, and it was from Will that he had originally heard about Craig.

Kessler had seen *Acis and Galatea* and *The Masque of Love*, and he had appreciated the beauty and simplicity of Craig's work, as well as its particularly English quality. But when he saw *The Vikings* he was even more enthusiastic, for this time there seemed to be Wagnerian tone in the whole conception of the production which he knew would appeal to German audiences. He wanted to meet Craig in order to tell him how much he admired his work and to see if he would contemplate visiting Weimar and producing something in the theatre there.[30]

Ted, who had long admired Goethe, immediately thought of the time when he had walked out of the Weimar theatre because they had insisted on having a live poodle on the stage! All the same, a possible escape from all that was sickening him in the English theatre intrigued him. He could remember a little German from his Heidelberg days, so he would not feel lost . . . But he told Kessler that he would certainly not accept the invitation unless he was given full power to carry out his ideas: when he had been in control, *Dido* and *Acis* and *The Masque of Love* had been good—only the lack of finance had hampered them— but *The Vikings* had been a battle for artistic control all the time and the results had suffered. He had learned a lesson that he would not forget.

Kessler returned to Germany and Ted returned to the "school" idea, wishing that Martin was with him so that he could discuss the part he would play on the "staff."

Ellen talked to Ted of the possibility of his producing *The Merchant of Venice* for her in America. Also, a suggestion came through Kessler that he might do something for Duse. "I go to see Duse in Milan in six weeks—I am to do something for her—an act or a scene or a stage-cloth or a play—something . . ." was how he put it in a letter to Martin![31]

Autumn in Chelsea was very depressing, and the river mists made him brood. The only work that seemed to fit his mood was *The Masque of Hunger*, and another called *The Masque of Lunatics*, both of his own invention. More bills arrived and the weather turned colder. Nothing was to be gained by hanging about in London, so he joined Elena in Maldon and tried to forget the theatre for a while. They sat by the fire, read Dumas and played with the baby.

CHAPTER TEN

A Letter from Berlin · New Life · Isadora

1904–1905

THE YEAR 1904 came along, and, with many misgivings, Elena left their little daughter in Maldon in the care of an old nurse, while she returned to London with Ted: their second child was due at any moment and she was going into a nursing home for its birth.

Ted tried to concentrate his attention on drawing up the prospectus for his proposed school. Not knowing what fees to charge, he consulted prospectuses from the Royal School of Music, the Slade School, and one or two others, eventually deciding that "twenty-five guineas a year" *looked* good. He sent some to the press, and to those among the P.O.S. whom he thought might be interested. His mother received one, and wrote to him saying that she thought the fees were much too high.[1]

At that moment a notice arrived from the gas company informing him that the gas would be cut off if the bill was not paid immediately, and, simultaneously, the landlord's solicitor sent a letter demanding nine months arrears of rent.

Ted was furious at the landlord's failure to appreciate his difficulties, then began to view his demands as a plot to wreck his school. He immediately ordered some more prospectuses, this time giving the address of 167 King's Road, Chelsea, which was Paul Hildersheim's office, down the road.

Paul and his sister, Gertrude, were old friends from the Hampstead days; he was a solicitor, she an artist and enameller; they had both worked enthusiastically with the P.O.S., and Gertrude had made most of the beautiful props for *Bethlehem*. They had great affection for Ted, and although they could see his shortcomings as a businessman, they admired his flashes of genius, and did their best to help him.

On January 11, another little daughter was born, and Ted gave Elena a most beautiful green and blue enamel crucifix which he had designed specially for her, and which Gertrude Hildersheim had made. At the same time, they heard from the nurse at Maldon that little Nellie, their first child, was not well. As soon as she could get about, Elena rushed back with the new baby.

No work was forthcoming. The only sign of interest came from Kessler: still keen that Ted should go to Germany, he suggested that he send over some of his "delightful drawings" for an exhibition in his private gallery in Weimar; he was convinced that if he could show some of Craig's work to Dr Otto Brahm, the new director of the Lessing Theater in Berlin, he could persuade him to give Craig a contract, especially as Brahm had a production of Thomas Otway's *Venice Preserved* in mind, obviously a play for an Englishman to design. (The play had been translated into German by the poet Hugo von Hofmannsthal, whom Kessler had also introduced to Brahm.) He felt sure his diplomacy would work.

Although Ted had liked Kessler when they met at the Café Royal, he was not particularly enthusiastic about leaving England to work in Weimar under what he imagined would be the control of some archduke, and he did not expect to hear any more about a Weimar production. But Kessler was one of the most persevering of men, and he intended to get Craig to Germany somehow.

While Ted prepared a selection of stage scenes and costumes for the packers to send to Kessler, he also collected together all the drawings he had made of the Essex countryside, having decided to exhibit them in his studio to help pay the rent.

He wrote to Martin:

All sorts of things are on the boil and I don't think the fire looks like going out. . . . I have just lost the engagement of my life (Weimar) and am just about to found a school—a school of my *belief*.[2]

But while he was regaining his courage he received distressing letters from Elena—little Nellie was getting weaker and going off her food; then a telegram arrived: "COME AT ONCE NELLIE I THINK GONE." He was with her in a few hours, only to find it was true. They were both heart-broken.

They looked for another cottage, and further along the coast at Southminster, they saw an attractive little house in the centre of the village, but it was still occupied. There was a coach-house attached that could be converted into a studio; a village pump was near by. They met the local doctor and his wife, Dr and Mrs Light, whom they both liked at once. They agreed to take the place as soon as it was free. They also decided to call their new little daughter Nelly.

Back in London, on top of his other troubles, Ted heard that May was at last filing her petition for divorce. Poor Jess was desperately unhappy—she had not even won Ted, and now she knew that he intended to marry someone else as soon as he could. Her only consolation was her little daughter, Kitty.

Once again Ted sank into a state of depression, and spent days wandering round Hampton Court, trying to recapture the few happy memories of his childhood. He always shirked emotional upheavals and rushed, for relief, to a change of scene where he could forget, as he chased new sights that would engage his mind in new fancies. He longed for Martin's company, but he was busy teaching music at a school in the country in order to make a living. Jimmy Pryde was married and no longer such a carefree Bohemian.

On June 13 a letter arrived from the Lessing Theater in Berlin; it was signed by Dr Otto Brahm. He dashed round to Paul Hildersheim, who translated it for him, roughly—very roughly! It began as follows:

> I have heard your artistic capabilities very well spoken of which you have put to use on the London stage so that you may now lend us artistic support . . .[3]

Brahm went on to suggest that Ted should go to Berlin for a "*trial period*" from September to October, and after that make a contract for a yearly salary, to be paid monthly. The reference to a "trial period" infuriated Ted: "It suggests doubt in your mind as to my work," he wrote. After much further correspondence, Paul Hildersheim succeeded in getting things straightened out, and it was agreed that Ted should go to Berlin for a period of four months, during which time they could discuss the production of *Venice Preserved* and he could prepare the designs for the scenes and costumes. For this he would receive £200, some of which would be paid in advance. If they found they worked well together a contract would be prepared, with a starting fee of £500 a year.

His exhibition at the Trafalgar Studios between June 27 and July 2 had produced only a few sales. There was no sign of work in England so, paying up a few immediate bills and leaving money with Elena, he bequeathed his studio to Martin and left for Berlin on August 23. In his last letter to Dr Brahm he said, "I cannot fix exactly on what day I shall arrive but I dare say it will be on August 27th at the latest, when I shall call upon you and settle everything." Here, he thought, was an unexpected deliverance from all the worries that were haunting him.[4]

Except for a few short visits, he was never again to live in his native land. He did not want to leave England, for although he inherited his imagination and temperament from his Celtic mother, he was essentially an Englishman like his father; he loved England: its history, its countryside, its traditions, above all the monarchy. He knew nothing about Europe apart from what he had learnt of Italy from Rossetti's translations of the Italian Renaissance poets and the pictures in the National Gallery; all he knew about France came from Alexandre Dumas' romances, and a trip to Boulogne; he had distant recollections of Germany from Heidelberg days, and that was all.

It is ridiculous to suggest that he chose voluntary exile in Europe. He went there because the idea of designing *Venice Preserved* appealed to him; it meant some ready cash and the solution of his immediate problems; he also hoped to see Weimar where his beloved Goethe had lived and worked. In the interim, he hoped his divorce would be finalized, and that he could return to Elena and his idea for a school; without an opportunity to experiment he knew that his ideas would never materialize, and he felt that a school would make this possible.

In Berlin, he found to his delight that artists and intellectuals were treated with esteem. Artists were not frowned upon as a group of useless Bohemians, but regarded as people with something to contribute to contemporary society. Because officialdom sometimes regarded them as *dangerous* intellectuals, even revolutionary, it added an air of audacity and importance to their discussions on Impressionism, Art Nouveau, and other movements.

Ted also rather liked being called Craig by everyone; it was a pleasant change from "Ted" and "Teddy."

But think who chooses clever names - this & this

Still even then it's curious that it hasn't been altered by a King or by the public.

"But think who chooses these names . . ." From Craig's letter to Martin Shaw in 1904.

He wrote excited letters to Martin telling him that:

. . . here beauty is not held to be above the heads of their audiences . . .
Popular music is played on Sundays !!! without anyone being shocked . . .
Oscar Wilde is thought of very highly . . .
Beardsley considered one of our best artists . . .
One thing illuminating too—streets are called this way: Bach Strasse, Goethe Platz, Schiller Strasse, Kant Strasse, Beethoven Platz and so on —In Germany the creative artists are honoured—in England, Generals and public men. . . . Suppose they missed you and me and even Hildersheim—one could understand it, but one would think that

Shakespeare would be jumped at for Streets and Squares. . . . But think who chooses these names—⁵

All the same, his letter ends with: "Dying to get back to the English lanes."

He soon discovered that many of the critics considered they were entitled to a special reverence, since they were the mentors of this highly developed public taste. One of them was the director of the Lessing Theater.

Otto Abrahamson, who found it more profitable to be known as Otto Brahm, was sixteen years older than Craig, and had approached the theatre as a dramatic critic. He had started a journal called *Die Freie Bühne*, and had written: "I am a fighter by nature, and I am working wholeheartedly to put over new forms of Dramatic Art and to regain for the Theatre the fullest significance in our intellectual life." He was against traditionalism, and in favour of a *natural approach to acting*—"to show the picture of a complete human being to the audience." His method was to plan nothing and let the actors develop their parts within themselves while he, with his fine perception and highly developed critical faculty helped the play to take shape "as a rational whole."⁶

Looking back, it is only too obvious that Craig and Brahm could never see eye to eye on anything.

When Craig first called at Brahm's office, he found that Brahm was away at a rehearsal and did not wish to be disturbed. He met instead Emil Heilbut, a most friendly man who was editor of *Kunst und Künstler*, the German equivalent of *The Studio*; because he could speak English, Dr Brahm had asked him to be his intermediary. He asked for the designs to show to Dr Brahm. Craig, taken aback, said he did not make designs off the cuff—he wanted to meet Brahm and to know how the play was to be produced, and he also wanted to meet the actors. Heilbut said he would speak to the Doctor . . .

Meanwhile, Craig looked round Berlin and found a bookshop run by a Mr Meyer. It was the most wonderful bookshop he had ever seen; on the shelves there were literally hundreds of books on the theatre and art, including *The Page* and his *Book of Penny Toys*. Mr Meyer was very friendly, and told him how to find a studio. Over by the Tiergarten, in the north-west district, Craig found an enormous block, No. 11,

Siegmundshoff. He took Studio No. 33, which was high up on the third floor and had a fine view of Berlin. It was twice the size of Trafalgar Studios, and the rent was only £25 per annum, compared to the £75 per annum he had been charged in London. He immediately left his hotel and made himself at home in his new surroundings.

From Meyer he bought a book by Manfred Semper, the fourth volume of the vast *Handbuch der Architectur*, devoted entirely to theatre construction. It was the first book on the subject that he had ever seen, and it played a very important part in the development of his future ideas. In this book he found reference to the Asphaleia System of hydraulic lifts as used in the theatres at Halle, Prague, Budapest, and Vienna. According to some of the plans and sections, this system made it possible to raise or lower platforms in almost any section of the stage; the sections could also be tilted to any angle. There were also diagrams of a Cyclorama that could be run round the whole stage at a moment's notice. He became enthusiastic about the idea—he could see more in it than just mechanized rostrums, and he longed to work in a theatre where he could play with such a system.[7] He called to see Heilbut and asked if they used the Asphaleia System; when he heard that they did not he said that he felt it should be installed, as it would help him with his ideas for *Venice Preserved*! This message was passed on to Dr Brahm, who was furious and wrote to Craig, saying that it was impossible and would he kindly get on with the designs which must be made to suit the theatre *as it was*. It was obvious that he regarded Craig merely as a designer of scenery.

Away from the theatre, Craig was becoming a figure of interest among a large group of artists and intellectuals. He had been asked to give an exhibition of drawings, and was interviewed by art critics who had not only heard about his work, but some of whom had actually bought copies of *The Page* and his *Souvenir* programmes. Dr Bredt was writing a long and profusely illustrated article about him in the July number of *Deutsche Kunst und Dekoration*. In fact he was feeling rather elated and less and less dependent on Brahm's patronage.

Brahm then sent him a message asking him to get in touch with the stage-manager, the scene-painters and mechanics, and to discuss all technical points with them regarding his settings for the forthcoming production in order to make sure that he understood the workings of their theatre.

From his new studio Craig wrote to Heilbut:

"Nothing can come of nothing" says King Lear—And as Dr Brahm has nothing of mine either scene or costume how is it possible to discuss how it shall be carried out—

I am doing the scenes, costumes, properties, and lighting scheme for "Venice Preserved". I hope to deliver them soon—Then Dr Brahm's mechanics can tell him how they propose to manipulate the production—

If they then find it an impossible riddle I shall have much pleasure in showing Dr Brahm how it is to be done.[8]

Brahm tried new tactics. He said Von Hofmannsthal wanted to see the designs. Craig said he would take them to him. Brahm said they must be sent through his office. They were getting nowhere.

Meanwhile, Craig was being very pleasant to Heilbut, and made him a gift of some sketches. Heilbut, when writing to thank him, pleaded ". . . I beg you only to send the drawings for *Venice Preserved* to Dr Brahm," then, hopefully he added, "perhaps you *did* already send them."[9]

It was then October 13, and only two designs were finished. He left these for Brahm to see, but said he would prefer to send all the designs together. He also pointed out that he had only received the play eight or ten days before (this, of course, did not matter because he was using Otway's version, not Von Hofmannsthal's), and that he had not met the cast, so how could he design the costumes? He ended his letter with: "It will be a very easy play to manipulate. I have the idea for an invention which will simplify the SKY. But it will need to be made."

Then, thinking of the plotters and schemers who might be shadowing him, he added: "I must secure the patent, as it will mean a fortune —every theatre will adopt it once it is seen."[10]

He had already told Heilbut about the "endless sky" effect obtained in *The Vikings* by "gutting the stage." This new idea was not quite so drastic, but Brahm refused to consider it.

Realizing that they were getting nowhere, and with little time left to get the production under way, Brahm ordered his resident scene-painter, Herr Impekoven to go ahead with designs of his own, trying to incorporate the only two scenes for which Craig had produced drawings, Act II, Scene 1, and Act III. At the same time he wrote to Craig terminating their agreement.

More letters of recrimination followed, each proving that the other had caused the delay. Finally, Craig wrote to Brahm insisting that his name should only be associated with the two settings he had designed and asking for printer's proofs of the programme in order to make sure that his request was carried out.[11] The first night of *Venice Preserved*, or *Das Gerette Venidig*, was announced as January 27.

On January 10, Craig wrote to the *Berliner Tageblatte* giving his account of what had happened in order to vindicate his position as a designer-producer; the letter was very long and not particularly accurate.[12] Brahm was interviewed by the press and gradually the argument was lost in the winter snows.

Craig had been in Berlin for five months and had seen Brahm only briefly two or three times, all communications having been second hand. Brahm was a critic, *interested* in the theatre as a cultural force. Craig was *in love* with the theatre as an art; he had no time for critics and did not try to hide his feelings. It seemed a pity that Kessler had ever brought them together.

During this very involved period in Berlin, Kessler invited Craig to Weimar. The princely splendour of Kessler's beautiful house put him at ease. Here he met the Belgian architect Henry van de Velde, one of the most prominent men in the Art Nouveau movement in Europe; with him was the Austrian architect Joseph Hoffman, whose beautiful designs for a modern theatre fascinated him. Together they discussed the shape of the theatre of the future, and both of them encouraged Craig to make a model of what he wanted. In this atmosphere ideas came fast and a model was soon made.

Kessler's plan was, in fact, succeeding: he had got Craig to Germany, he believed in him and his ideas and recognized him as a man of vision who could revitalize the theatre of Europe, and he hoped that Germany would be the first to benefit.

In Weimar, Craig was happy. He wrote to Elena, telling her of the town's beauties, and of his excitement about future prospects. To Martin he spoke of Goethe's house, and walks in the park at night where he tried to capture the spirit of the past.

In Berlin a long article about him appeared in Heilbut's magazine,

Kunst und Künstler, and preparations were going ahead for an exhibition of his stage designs and wood engravings at Friedmann and Weber's new gallery. Kessler was writing the introduction to the catalogue: it was a fine essay on Craig's ideals for a theatre of the future, an essay which did much to establish him as a man of genius in the minds of the art critics and the more advanced members of the theatrical profession in Europe.

At that moment a new personality entered Craig's life: this was Isadora Duncan, and through her art he was to discover the final ingredient necessary to the formula that was to be the basis of all his future ideas for the theatre.

Isadora Duncan's approach to life was much the same as Craig's. They shared the same insensibility to other people's feelings, the same vague attitude towards money matters, the same disregard of man-made morals, the same reverence for beauty, the same love and dedication each to their own art, and the same desire to make known to the world the magic that they had discovered.

They found it easy enough to "fall in love"—both regarding sensual gratification as a necessary spur to artistic inspiration, and over the next two years they were bound together in a fitful dream of adventure, love, art, and disillusionment, from which only one of them would escape unscarred.

The names of Isadora Duncan and Gordon Craig have been coupled as "lovers" for so long that their real significance to each other has been lost under the fast growing weeds of sentimentality and sensationalism.

It was not Isadora's physical appearance that particularly attracted Craig (Martin Shaw even said that she was lacking in sex-appeal).[13] But she had the plump prettiness of a Colleen, "the tip-tilted nose and the little firm chin, and the dream in her heart of the Irish, who are so sweet to know"; most important of all, she was "full of natural genius which defies description."

The year before they met she, too, had encountered true, passionate love for the first time. A young Hungarian actor, "of Godlike features and stature," had transformed her from a "chastened nymph into a wild and careless Bacchante"—she, too, had sworn "fidelity until death."[14]

To her, Craig's outstanding feature seemed to be an electrifying personality that made her "psychically aware of its presence," and, she remembered, "there was something feminine about him, especially about the mouth, which was sensitive and thin-lipped—he gave the impression of delicacy . . . only his hands, with their broad-tipped fingers and simian square thumbs, bespoke strength."[15]

The December snows were falling when Craig accidentally met Elise de Brouckère, whose sister, Jeanne, he had known in London during the production of *The Masque of Love*. He lunched with her at her flat in the Spichernstrasse, and talked much about his forth-coming exhibition, and his school where "Movement" would be one of the main courses of study. Elise asked if he had seen Miss Duncan dance at the Kroll Opera house. No? Hadn't he seen the hundreds of posters that smothered the hoardings, advertising her performance? He hadn't even noticed them! The idea of sitting through an entire evening watching an American woman dancing in some scanty raiment did not appeal to him.[16]

Elise said the Duncans were a charming family, all working together. They lived at 11 Hardenburg Strasse, quite near. The family consisted of Mrs Duncan, Isadora, her brother Augustin and his wife and their daughter, and a rather severe sister, Elizabeth; they were *Irish-*Americans. She was sure Craig would be interested in Isadora because her kind of dancing was more like movement to music than dancing . . . in fact, just what he had been talking about. They went round to see them—it was December 14.

When they arrived at the Duncan's place, a Mrs Maddison had just sat down at the piano to play a piece by Gabriel Fauré. Craig and Isadora stood behind her, listening. Isadora's face reminded him of some of his previous loves; "at one time it seemed to be Jess, at another time exactly like Lucy Wilson." "We became friends and lovers from the moment we stood there at the piano," he wrote in his note-book.

Isadora was most impressed to learn that Craig was the son of her "most perfect ideal of woman,"[17] the great Ellen Terry. She wanted to see some of his work, and the next day she turned up, dressed entirely in white, with a white fur-coat, at his exhibition in Friedmann and Weber's Gallery. Craig was delighted with her enthusiasm, and almost overpowered her with his commentary on the various designs: he pointed out their significance, explaining that they were static pictures of something conceived in motion—the movement of light—colour—form. Isadora seemed to understand.

She invited him to come and see her dance. He described the performance later in these words:

She came through some small curtains which were not much taller than herself; she came through them and walked down to where a musician, his back turned to us, was seated at a grand piano; he had just finished playing a prelude by Chopin when in she came, and in some five or six steps was standing by the piano, quite still and, as it were, listening to the hum of the last notes. . . . You might have counted five, or even eight, and then there sounded the voice of Chopin again, in a second prelude or etude; it was played through gently and came to an end and she had not moved at all. Then one step back or sideways, and the music began again as she went moving on before or after it. Only just moving. . . . She was speaking in her own language, not echoing any ballet master, and so she came to move as no one had ever seen anyone move before. The dance ended, and again she stood quite still. No bowing, no smiling—nothing at all. Then again the music is off, and she runs from it—it runs after her then, for she has gone ahead of it.

How is it that we know she is speaking her own language? We know it, for we see her head, her hands, gently active, as are her feet, her whole person. And if she is speaking, what is it she is saying? No one would ever be able to report truly, yet no one present had a moment's doubt. Only this can we say—that she was telling to the air the very things we longed to hear and until she came we had never dreamed we should hear; and now we heard them, and this sent us all into an unusual state of joy, and I sat still and speechless.

I remember that when it was over I went rapidly round to her dressing-room to see her, and there too I sat still and speechless in front of her for a while. She understood my silence very well; all talk being unnecessary.[18]

His silence was induced by a mixture of overwhelming admiration and furious resentment—admiration for what had been to him the greatest artistic experience in his life, resentment that this revelation should come from a woman. Unknown to him, she had been travelling the same path as himself, and it was her unique genius that made it possible for her to show him something about abstract movement which he was still struggling to understand.

Stanislavsky, who was also spellbound by her, wrote later:

When I became acquainted with her methods as well as with the ideas of her great friend, Craig, I came to know that in different corners of the World, due to conditions unknown to us, various people in various spheres sought in art for the same naturally born creative principles. Upon meeting, they were amazed at the common character of their ideas.[19]

Isadora had discovered someone who could say all that she thought, and Craig, someone who held part of the secret for which he was searching.

When Martin helped him to understand the secrets of music, a life-long friendship resulted from their association. Isadora helped him to understand the secrets of "Movement," and because she was a woman and he a man, a love affair resulted which momentarily swept them off their feet in a whirlwind of mutual enlightenment and admiration.

He was thirty-two, she was twenty-six.[20] Chance had brought these twin spirits together in a foreign land at a moment of susceptibility when both were intoxicated by public acclamation. The glowing embers of their previous loves were suddenly blown into a mighty flame again and it *seemed* to consume them.

To him this "flaming love" was exhilarating, and the naturally polygamous male found it easy to succumb to Isadora.

He could not get Isadora from his mind and, after seeing her dance again, he went round to the Duncans' flat, where Mrs Maddison again played Fauré. When she left, he and Isadora ran downstairs to see her off. Then, thinking that it would be fun to go somewhere away from the family, they were about to enter the cab with Mrs Maddison, when Augustin, who knew his sister's ways, "descended like a thunderbolt" and begged them "to desist"; but they managed to slip away later, when Dr Federn and his sister left in a vast motor-car that could seat four in the back. They all decided to drive towards Potsdam, and had to stop for coffee once or twice when the car broke down. The two lovers, sitting in the back, did not care—for them it was a fairy-tale adventure in which the car seemed to be a carriage and four.[21]

They got back to Berlin at eight o'clock the following morning and breakfasted with Elise de Brouckère, who afterwards went to see how the land lay at the Duncan home. She reported that the atmosphere was frigid, so Isadora decided to stay the night with her, promising to go to Craig's studio the following day, December 17, "for tea."

When she arrived it was as though two long-lost lovers had been reunited.

The studio, on the third floor, was an immense place with the traditional skylight on one side, and on the other, a kind of mezzanine-gallery, or balcony, reached by a flight of stairs; artists usually slept and cooked up there because it was generally warm. But Craig had neither couch nor stove, for he slept in a rather drab room down the road at No. 6 Siegmundshoff—and the gas in the studio had been cut off!

While there was still light they went for a drive in Isadora's carriage. When the early darkness of winter fell, they went up to the gallery, and there made themselves a bed from two old carpets covered with Isadora's fur-coat, while his coat was rolled up to serve as a pillow; an old sheet and a couple of rugs provided their only covering.

"She kissed as much with her eyes as with her lips," he wrote.[22]

The next day Isadora had to attend a small reception at her own place, so she waited until she knew it had started before leaving for home, hoping, in that way, to avoid a scolding. They walked across the park, she "dressed in their bed," he "wearing their pillow"; on the way, she laughed and said, "It's remarkable how independent and free virtue can be and feel."

At the reception she behaved like a queen, but afterwards, feeling the chilliness of her family towards her, she disappeared again and returned to the studio and stayed there, hidden, for some days. The Duncans sent notices to the press saying that Isadora could not appear as she was ill.

The good-natured porter at Siegmundshoff 11 was kind enough to bring Herr Craig his food from the near-by delicatessen, paying for it himself as he knew that Craig was temporarily out of cash. But gradually the food must have palled and the cold must have been unbearable, even for two lovers; also, Isadora was due to leave for St. Petersburg, where she had an engagement—so they descended from their paradise to the snow-clad world below.

From their first moment of meeting Craig has recorded all that they said and did in one of his secret little books of confessions. He even remembered telling her that he was expecting to marry in a few months time—she said she did not believe in marriage:

> She tells me about her life and whom she has loved before—then laughs, and laughs, and laughs . . .
>
> Do I love her?
>
> Does she love me?
>
> I do not know or want to know.[23]

CHAPTER ELEVEN

Eleonora Duse, Italy and Freedom
1905–1906

Two months later, when the heat of passion had cooled a bit, his conscience prompted him to reason with himself about the relative places which Isadora and Elena occupied in his heart and mind. He generally found that writing about such problems in his private notebooks helped him to understand them better. How could he love Elena as he did and yet find room for Isadora?

> . . . I am in love with one woman only, and though others attract me how could it ever obliterate what exists of her in my heart and soul, or how could it alter my heart and love towards her—But I am keenly attracted to another woman, who may be a witch or a pretty child (and it really doesn't matter which) and I find it hard to be away from her. She not only attracts me, she revolts me also. One moment I instinctively smile with her and love to be with her, and the next I want to be away from her and I shrink from her. It is not that she is at all ugly or repulsive—but merely that I am delighted with her or bored.
>
> When she talks about herself incessantly for a quarter of an hour—when she drinks more wine than she needs or wants—when she cuddles up to other people, men or women, relations or not relations—it is not that she does so repulsively but I see they are equally attracted as myself—and I object to be equally anything in such matters.
>
> And my confession is that I have a contempt for her and do not

like to feel I have a contempt—because I find her so dear and delightful.

Still I cannot trust her, and even friendship, much more love demands absolute trust.

Not that I love her—it is not possible to "Love" twice.

And that is where perhaps a clever idiot would get mixed, for though I do not love her, I tell myself and her that I do—Still I also tell her that I am unable to tell what love is—

So I am—Love is something a bit less restless and wayward than this. Love regards no other thing or person except through the eyes of the loved one . . .

Love which torments is not love. Love is all which is dear and beautiful, without fluster or excitement, without excess of laughter or tears, something at ease and gravely sweet—And where love is there is no room for any other thing."[1]

But what about Isadora—how did *she* feel? She danced nearly every day, and at each performance she expended a tremendous amount of physical energy, as well as the continual mental exercise that is required by improvisation. She found that she was slowly being consumed. Her only stimulus was the exhilaration she derived from her wild and ecstatic audiences and, in between, she counted on the company of admiring friends and a liberal flow of champagne to recharge her exhausted spirits in readiness for her next public appearance. Her thoughts about Craig ran parallel to his, resulting in similar conclusions; she wrote later in her memoirs:

His love was young—fresh and strong—he had neither the nerves nor nature of a voluptuary, but preferred to turn from lovemaking before satiety set in and to translate the fiery energy of his youth to the magic of his Art.

. . . he was in a state of exhilaration from morning to night.

. . . he was always in the throes of highest delight or the other extreme, when the whole sky seemed to turn black and a sudden apprehension filled the air. One's breath was slowly pumped from the body, and nothing was left anywhere but the blackest of anguish . . . as time progressed these dark moods became more and more frequent.[2]

Furious discussion about the relative qualities of their work "resulted in thunderous and gloomy silences" . . . ."all women are a damned nuisance," he said, but she adds:

And yet Gordon Craig appreciates my Art as no one else has ever appreciated it. But his *amour propre*, his jealousy as an artist, would not allow him to admit that any woman could really be an artist.

A point was reached when she admitted that she "adored Craig"—

I loved him with all the ardour of my artistic soul . . . yet I had arrived at that frenzied state when I could no longer live with him or without him. . . . I realized this state of things must cease; either Craig's Art or mine—and to give up mine I knew to be impossible. [3]

Meanwhile, what was Ted telling Martin—his best friend—about her:

Artist or not—this is a marvellous being—beauty—nature & *brain*.
I don't like brainy women but brains and intelligence is a rare & lovely thing.
If you could see *one* dance you would understand how wonderful it is. Beauty & Poetry is art when it is created, no matter how, by a living being—
I have seldom been so moved by anything—It is a great, a rare rare gift, brought to perfection by 18 years of persistent labour—& we may all agree to worship such things.
. . . Inspiration is given out by the thousand volt per second from Miss D. And I am alive again (as artist) through her—You know how life giving or taking one artist can be to another.—We gave each other some darned stunning inspiration once—. [4]

A new feeling of adventure took hold of Craig and whirled him off into a mad dance. Ideas came and went. Books were planned, even started, then shelved; productions were discussed and the discussions broken into so that he could dash across Germany to help Isadora with a dance recital; projects for schools and theatres loomed large and faded—it was a period of a hundred schemes.

I wonder would you know me if you met me now? [he writes
to Martin].

I am no jot altered—but am more myself than when I left
England.

They've watered me well here & I grow—Expect to receive
wonderful news within 3 months. I may then have my own theatre
& my own company. NOT ACTORS but a CREATURE of my own
invention—a blessed marvel my BOY!

I have rec^d wonderful encouragement in letters from Hauptmann &
Sudermann. . . . They & 6 or 7 other head artists & poets are joining
together to make a *call* for me to be given a theatre, and a committee of business men have already approached me about said
theatre—

It will mean a tour through Germany starting at Dresden (6
months there) in my own (new built) wooden theatre.

Pray to old Jupiter for the idea—sacrifice a pipe of shag to it—!

Kessler has proved a brick—Gerhardt Hauptmann's son has
already asked to be in my company.

No women in it boy. Only comrades! whish! but we're getting
at it. I almost think I'll insist on your coming over when I start—
if only to see you—& help me with your company for a fortnight—
at my blooming expense.[5]

While he was still spellbound by Isadora, ideas filtered through his
mind, some of them remaining to become the embryos of other ideas
that were to play a big part in his main theory later on.

One was this conception of a supremely beautiful creature—something like a Greek statue—which could be made to move, and could
be controlled like a marionette, but would not suffer from, or be
affected by emotions—like Isadora. At first he referred to this figure
as "a being," then he used a word compounded from German and
French and called it the Über-marionette.

Such ideas were coming so fast that he decided to record some of
them for a future book. He wrote to Martin about an idea for "three
to six puppet shows which I intended to produce, . . . an immense
affair warranted to stir all Berlin—first play is by Maeterlinck."[6]
Later in a letter he again remarks: "*These puppet shows engross my
attention.*" To his mother he wrote of a new project for three

productions: "If it succeeds, as I trust it will, I shall this time have final success as I have arranged to dispense with actors—and am *not* using marionettes. The marionette is only a doll—the actor (for me) only an unsuperable difficulty and an expense." Then, again to Martin: "The actors must cease to *speak* and must *move* only, if they want to restore the art to its old place. Acting is Action—Dance the poetry of Action."[7]

Slowly, he was evolving his great idea for a new kind of kinetic theatre—a synthesis of form, light, scene, figures and sound . . . movement. Two years later the idea became fully developed and his experiments started, but in 1905 he had too much to think about to give all his time to any one project.

He met Max Reinhardt, who was then just thirty-two. He was Brahm's rival in Berlin. Like Craig, he had trained as an actor; and he was intrigued by all he had read about Craig. He found the exhibition at Friedmann and Weber's most inspiring, and they talked of working together. Reinhardt suggested that he should design *The Tempest* and Bernard Shaw's *Caesar and Cleopatra*—Craig thought *Macbeth* would be better. But they got on very well, and Craig was sufficiently enthusiastic to start making drawings for all these plays—it was a period of prodigious output.[8]

Then it became apparent that they were talking at cross-purposes—Reinhardt's idea was to produce the plays, using Craig's designs for scenery and costumes; to Craig, designing a production meant everything from scenery, costumes and props to lighting and movement.

Reinhardt was still willing to compromise within the existing set-up at the Deutches Theater. He suggested paying four thousand marks per production. Craig would design everything down to the last movement, but the final instructions to the actors and technicians must still come through him.

Craig, thinking of all that he had suffered on *The Vikings*, insisted that he must "be master of the stage, and that beyond me there should be no appeal. . . . Then success will follow."[9] Kessler was brought in to help negotiations but they were doomed to failure. Craig failed to see that the actors and technicians would naturally owe allegiance to Reinhardt, and in any case, with his inadequate knowledge of German he would have been forced to use an intermediary.

Reinhardt, convinced that Craig's designs were ideal for the kind

of productions he had in mind, told his young assistants to go to
Craig's exhibition and drink them in because that was the type of
work he wanted in the future. Craig, hearing of this, did not see it
as admiration, but as downright robbery.[10]

He now felt the immediate need to publish his ideas about the func-
tions of what he chose to call the "Stage-Director," in order to avoid
any future misunderstandings.

Except for Elena, Martin was the only person in England who knew
what he was doing. To Elena, he communicated all the complicated
inner workings of his mind, mixed with the wildest speculations on
the future. He did not write about Isadora; and in these early days, he
did not admit even to himself that he was in love with anyone beside
Elena. To Martin, he gave clearer details of his work. He continually
asked Martin to join him; now more than ever, he needed a real
friend with whom he could discuss life, as well as art—someone who
could help him solve his problems which had become as complicated
as the Gordian Knot.

Sometimes, when he got the English papers, he would read of what
was happening in the London theatres, and would write indignantly
to the editor, under some assumed name, or ask Martin to write for
him. He became aware of the extremely insular attitude towards art in
the English press. They never seemed to be aware of the serious work
that was going on in Europe.

He thought of starting a magazine again, but no longer as a shop-
window for his wood engravings: this time it would be his mouth-
piece, and would also represent all those who were tired of a decadent
theatre and who were striving, like him, for something new. He
already had a big following, and could expect contributions from
van de Velde, Von Hofmannsthal, Max Reinhardt, Count Kessler,
Isadora Duncan, Gerhardt Hauptmann, and even Herbert Beerbohm
Tree. He thought of calling the magazine *The Theatre*, then decided
on *The Mask* (the idea of hiding his identity as a writer appealed to
him more and more); he would appear on the announcements merely
as its artistic adviser! He approached publishers, trying to interest
them in the project. He wanted the magazine printed in English,
French, and German.[11]

Kessler, who was doing all he could to keep Craig busy and in
funds, asked him if he would like to illustrate a special edition of Von

Hofmannsthal's *Weissen Fächer* (or *The White Fan*); he would receive £150 for a set of four wood engravings. Craig was very interested because he liked the poet, and started on the designs for five of the largest blocks he had ever made.[12]

Once again he thought about trying to find an "agent," or "manager," who could advance all his projects for him, enabling him to concentrate entirely on the creative work. He envied Max Reinhardt, whose brother, Edmund, looked after the business side of the Deutsches Theater, leaving him free to think only of the artistic output.

In March, Kessler came to him with another proposition: he could put the wood engravings aside for a while, and instead, design the scenes and costumes for Von Hofmannsthal's poetic version of the *Elektra* of Sophocles—he was to have carte blanche, and a fee of £300. The production was to star Eleonora Duse.[13]

Kessler, who was not only Craig's patron, but also Von Hofmannsthal's, had told Duse, whom he greatly admired, that he was ready to back the author and the designer if she would present the play. He had persuaded her that the leading part was made for her and she had agreed; she hoped to be in Berlin the following month and, if all was ready, she would seriously consider the proposition.

Kessler knew Duse's strange enigmatic nature. This beautifully sad woman seemed to live part of her time far away in some dream, from which every now and then she would awaken and, coming back to earth, for a brief period would be as practical as any astute business-man; having accomplished this unpleasant task, she would return to her dream-world. Hence his desire to present her with a *fait accompli*.

She had once said:

I gave my love to "Camille" when I was young—*now* it is a past love—It is the same with plays and people—one does not love the same person and one cannot love the same play *always*, but to *renew* love—that is the secret.[14]

Craig got on very well with Von Hofmannsthal, for although their attempt at co-operation with Brahm on *Venice Preserved* had failed, they had discovered that they had a great deal in common; both were opposed to Brahm's naturalism in the theatre, both favoured the poetic drama, both were artists. Von Hofmannsthal, like Duse, lived

in a land of dreams, and his craving for beauty showed itself in his
poetry.

Isadora went off on a tour, taking in Hanover and Magdeburg, and
Craig, left on his own, designed the whole production of *Elektra*, sets
and costumes, in the space of four weeks. The fact that Kessler had
given him carte blanche put him at ease. Selma Rook started making
all the costumes, which were to be fitted in Craig's studio, using male
and female models based on measurements sent by Alfredo Geri,
Duse's agent. The scenery was being painted by Mauritz Wimmer.
The whole episode was most exhilarating and, having completed his
part of the work, Craig joined Isadora in Brussels and Amsterdam;
he was to return to Berlin in April for the fittings.

When he did return, he found that Duse would not be coming and
had asked for everything to be sent to Florence. Later came news that
the production had been postponed indefinitely. During one of her
practical moments, Duse had concluded that the play would be too
elaborate to become part of her repertoire, for which she must have
standard-type settings that were easy to pack, and as easy to light in
Buenos Aires as in Florence or Berlin.[15]

Once again, the effort had been in vain. One or two of the scene
designs still exist; all the costume designs have vanished, but may yet
reappear in Berlin, where they remained for a long time as surety for
the bill owed by Craig to Selma Rook. Craig liked one of the designs
for Clytemnestra's dresses so much that he kept it and it was used as
Plate I in *The Isadora Mappe*, published by the Insel Verlag the following
year. (It is obvious that this first plate and the other five are not
related—the figure is not even dancing, the colour scheme is different
and there is no hint of Isadora in the face.) Selma Rook's itemized bill,
describing each of the costumes, is the nearest I have come to discovering what Craig had in mind for the other costumes. The often-
reproduced *Elektra* stage-setting, with the foreground figure in black
and an enormous doorway behind, was not made for the Duse production; it was an idea Craig developed for himself—a note for the
future.[16]

Soon after the opening of his exhibition at Friedmann and Weber's,
a small, dapper man turned up, and gave Craig considerable pleasure
by actually studying every picture in detail with what seemed to be

the interest of a connoisseur—now and then closing his eyes to dwell with the picture for a moment, in the same way that some people listen to music. His name was Magnus—Maurice Magnus.

Magnus was charming, dignified, and intelligent. He said he would write to various papers in America about the exhibition. He took Craig to have a martini at a nearby café, and there they talked for hours.

Although he was an American, he spoke English without a trace of an accent. He seemed to know everyone in Berlin. Craig was fascinated by his manner, for he appeared to regard all things as possible—"one only has to know the right people." Craig asked him if he could suggest someone to manage his business for him, and he outlined his various projects: there was his Experimental School, there was a new portable theatre which he had outlined, but it needed completing—van de Velde had admired his plans; there was his magazine, called *The Mask*; a book, to be translated into every language, telling of his new theories on the art of the theatre; there were various other books—one on Miss Duncan's dancing; exhibitions of his drawings had to be arranged; then there were productions—first on his list were *Hamlet* and *Macbeth*. Martin Shaw was to be the musical adviser, and he felt sure he would have an enthusiastic assistant in Gerhardt Hauptmann's son, Ivo, who was studying at Weimar and had already shown keenness to join him. All this was like music to the ears of Maurice Magnus—he said he would think about it.

The next day he announced that the work outlined by Craig was so interesting that he was prepared to throw up his present contract (he did not even have a job) and to put his experience at Craig's disposal.

This was the beginning of an association that could have led to great achievements had not the two partners been fascinated by each other for all the wrong reasons![17]

There is a certain cunning which nature seems to bestow on those of her creatures who survive by means other than hard work: unluckily, this cunning—which can become artifice and finally art—can also become too artful and finally descend to mere trickery. Magnus was not really a trickster, but in business he considered all tactics, all weapons fair, and Craig, who had no time for businessmen, was delighted to have someone on his side who knew about "all their tricks." He felt that, with Magnus on his side, he was equipped to make a fortune—then he would return to Elena and the beautiful country lanes of England.

In the first week of the new year he had received a letter from Elena telling him that they had a little son. This gave him a great sense of completion—something that he had inherited from his Victorian background—and, like Godwin, he wanted to do something, like building a house, to celebrate the occasion. Four years earlier, when he first met Elena, he had written in his note-book: "The son of such a woman might be the greatest man on earth—physically—morally— mentally. I am the last person on earth to deserve what meeting her means."[18]

From now on he was going to watch the growth of this poor child, expecting to see signs of genius almost from babyhood!

To Martin, he wrote:

> I will win this time, absolutely must, and then I'll return with the spoils of war and lay them at the feet of my son and his mama. I was never so alive—never so fit—ready to go through hellfire . . .[19]

Five days later it was: "I see Spring is coming. Oh for a fortnight of the English hedgerows."[20]

The green lanes of England were not for him—his restless nature required exhilarating surroundings, conflict, plot, and counterplot.

He agreed to give Magnus £3 a week and, as business improved, to raise it to £5. Three pounds was equivalent to about 60 marks, and in those days you could live superbly at any good hotel for 50 or 60 marks a week. At the Hotel de Russe, the finest hotel in Berlin, the weekly bill, inclusive of three magnificent meals a day, service—every-thing—was only 80 marks.

Magnus was just twenty-nine.[21] He was born in New York; his mother was separated by only one generation from the royal blood of the Hohenzollerns. In his youth he had been friendly with the American poet Hilton Turvey. He had an insatiable desire to collect celebrities, the more illustrious, the better, so he had left New York and come to his motherland, where, although he could not boast openly of his connection with the Kaiser, he could at least feel that he was *near* the Court. He knew how to conjure with great names, for he actually believed in their power and the spells they cast. He now felt that he was wasting his time acting as a correspondent to various American newspapers and teaching at the Berlitz school. Craig was ideal material for him to work on—son of the great Ellen Terry, patronized by Count Kessler, and a friend of Isadora Duncan, the dancer who was captivating Berlin with the magic of her art— *these were names.*

He started organizing at once. First, they must have an office, separate from the studio; they took No. 42 in the same block as the studio. Then they must establish a business name that would cover all their activities; he suggested "United Arts", which, in German, became "Direktion Vereinigter Kunst"—yes, that sounded good. Their telegraphic address was "Footlights." They must hire a typewriter and get a secretary. They found Fräulein Hänsler, who understood English. Everything was done on credit, Magnus making all concerned feel honoured that he had remembered them.

Next, he suggested that they might conduct all Miss Duncan's business from their office as well; they would probably make better bookings for her, and could look after her publicity properly. At the time her bookings were being handled by her brother, Augustin, who was a lovable person but hardly a businessman.

Isadora liked Magnus, and his idea. She also felt that Craig's experience of productions could be used to her advantage. It was agreed that "Vereinigter Kunst" would take ten per cent from her receipts. Gordon Craig and Isadora Duncan then opened a joint account at the National Bank für Deutschland.

Isadora's family was dependent on her. Her brother acted as her personal manager, Elizabeth as her assistant and eventually as the manager of her school, and her mother went with them everywhere.

The existing files of correspondence show that Magnus really did his best to promote the business, but it was almost impossible to help two such temperamental people. Isadora drank champagne like water and tipped on a grandiose scale. Craig continually borrowed from the business account and then there would not be enough to pay the secretary or Magnus. The following week money would come in from a tour, and Magnus would pay the secretary and take his own salary. A few days later there would be a row—where was all the money that came in last week? Magnus would explain, but Craig could never understand; instead, he sometimes thought that Magnus was being a bit too clever. Suspicion bred suspicion, and periodically the association would come to an end, only to be resumed when Craig realized that business *was* better with Magnus in control. Maurice was too soft-hearted with the great ones that he had collected and the trouble would only start again.

There were times, however, when Craig was astonished at Magnus's ability to achieve the impossible; it was on these occasions that he was convinced of his brilliance and indispensability.

Once, Craig, accompanied by Magnus, was taking a model to show to Reinhardt at the Deutches Theater; reaching the Unter den Linden, they discovered that the road was blocked by two lines of Prussian guards in full-dress uniform—the Kaiser was expected at any moment. Craig was late for his appointment. "My dear Craig, just leave it to me," said Magnus, in his rather staccato way. He took a card from his pocket-book and looked for the most important mounted officer, to whom he presented it, at the same time indicating that they wished to pass to the other side. The officer inspected the card and gave a command—the ranks opened, Magnus bowed slightly, and they crossed the road, with Craig following. "One has to know the right people," said Magnus.

A few days later, when they were meeting Kessler at the house of Mendelssohn, the banker and music lover, they paused for a moment in the hall; in a flash, Magnus looked over the visiting cards that were lying on a magnificent silver salver on the hall table, and selecting a couple, pocketed them. Craig looked on, amazed. Said Magnus: "You never can tell—might be useful one day—names mean such a lot, you know." Those were the days when most visitors left cards, and this gave Magnus plenty of opportunity to stock his pocket-book against all difficult occasions.[22]

As Magnus was there to cope with the business side of his affairs, Craig thought that all his fondest schemes would be settled within a few weeks. He was blind to the fact that no business could be conducted at that speed and, anyhow, without trained assistants he would be incapable of carrying out so much work. Where would he even find an assistant that his suspicious nature would permit him to reveal his ideas to? This was, of course, his reason for starting a school, a place in which to find and train some faithful assistants.

Since Isadora's affairs were being run in a very casual way, and since she was the only money maker, it was obviously necessary to get her business settled first.

Craig immediately set to work redesigning her programmes, her advertising matter, her posters, even her forms of contract; at the same time they started driving harder bargains with those managements who were interested in her performances. Her great success in Berlin and the publicity given to her school of dancing there soon made her a sought-after personality. Everywhere she went her dancing was a revelation of controlled artistic abandon which had a liberating effect on the minds of the audience.

In March, Craig made a series of six designs showing Isadora in "movements" from six of her dances and these were exhibited in Düsseldorf. The idea was that these drawings should be framed and taken round with the Duncan outfit and exhibited in the foyers of the various theatres where she performed. They were also to appear as part of an advertising scheme, printed on a band of paper that would encircle those cast-iron display kiosks that were dotted about the squares in all the big towns of Europe. This last scheme did not succeed, because the printing was too expensive, so Craig thought of appealing to a higher-class audience by getting the Insel Verlag to publish a portfolio containing his designs reproduced in colour and set in grey mounts. He wrote a piece of blank verse to accompany the designs in which he tried to express his feelings about Isadora's dancing. This was printed in German and also in English to allow for copies to be sold in England and the U.S.A. When finished, it all seemed very divorced from any of his other work, and showed how totally under Isadora's spell he was at the time.[23]

He had never made any figure studies before, and although many of his designs had included figures, they had always been in costume, many of their postures being influenced by the designs of Howard Pyle, the American pen-and-ink artist, or by Jacques Callot, the seventeenth-century engraver. He had never studied anatomy or even thought about drawing in a life class. Now he was confronted with designs that showed a very lightly draped female figure in arrested motion. He got the model, Lissle Breitenpoller, to pose for him, but he found the whole process dreary and uninspiring; eventually by scribbling away, he devised some very idealized visions of Isadora gliding through the clouds, prancing in pools of light, and bouncing in the wings of an old-time theatre. The first design in the series, however, shows a stationary figure; this was the design for Eleonora Duse's costume as Clytemnestra. Isadora so loved it that it became the format on which the other five designs were based. The Insel Verlag were not at all keen about the publication, but pressure was brought to bear by Kessler, who had interests in the firm.

Meanwhile, his own projects became notes on paper, which he sent to Magnus with instructions to advance them in all directions, while he was travelling with Isadora and her family all over northern Europe, staying at the grandest hotels and eating at the most fashionable restaurants. Everywhere he went he met people who were inspired by his work and his unending enthusiasm. He, in turn, was fascinated by the various cities that they visited, with their famous art collections, their theatres, their architecture; they were all food for his imagination. He wrote, "I haven't a penny in my pocket, but I'm living like a duke."[24] He was intoxicated by this way of life and the ideas that were generating in his mind. He began bombarding Magnus with letters and telegrams telling him to do this and that, insisting on more grandiose conditions in contracts that inevitably came to nothing— blaming Magnus for the failure of his own impossible demands. Meanwhile he was having a grand spree.

Following their meeting in Berlin, Craig and Isadora travelled together to Dresden, Hamburg, St. Petersburg, Moscow, Frankfurt, Breslau, Brussels, Amsterdam, Cologne, Bonn, Freiburg, Tutzing, Zürich, Utrecht, Leyden, and The Hague. There were many return visits to these towns, and to Berlin, which still remained their head-quarters. During this time, Craig's designs for stage scenes and his wood engravings were being exhibited in Düsseldorf (March), Cologne (April), Dresden and Weimar (May), Munich and London (June), Vienna (October).[25]

Apart from the tremendous output in the way of drawings and sketches the only important work that he did in 1905 was to write his little book, *The Art of the Theatre*.

Although he had planned this booklet in 1904, it was not until after his misunderstanding with Brahm and then with Reinhardt that he realized how important it was for him to make it quite clear to all that when he spoke of "designing a production" he meant designing *everything* that was seen upon the stage, from the simplest property sword to the last detail in every actor's movements. He also had to establish in his own mind, as well as in everyone else's, what he meant by the title Stage Director. Magnus was also most insistent that he should get this book published, for he knew that the printed word meant much more to businessmen than any amount of inspired talk: they might not understand it all, but it had been *printed*.

Craig started dictating the book on April 22, and it was finished by May 4. It was written in the form of a duologue between a stage director and a playgoer, in much the same way which Leoni di Sommi had written his book on stage presentation in the 1560's when he was trying to explain his role as a stage director to the Court of Mantua.

Craig would not rest until he found a way of making his finished product in the theatre a work of art. It was obvious to him that it must be conceived by one person, and even if it was dependent, like music, on others for its execution, those others must be controlled by one artist throughout the whole performance. In 1904, he had written a preface to the book, which ran as follows:

The Art of the Theatre is the same in one respect as any other art.
ιt is the work of one man—
Unlike most other arts it can only be seen and heard during the life of the man who creates it—It cannot be copied for future generations by future Theatrical artists—
It ιs necessary, then, that it must be accepted whilst the artist is still living.[26]

In his new book he tried to make this clearer; he makes the playgoer ask:

Action, words, line, colour, rhythm! And which of these is all-important to the art?
THE STAGE DIRECTOR: One is no more important than the other, no more than one colour is more important to a painter than

another, or one note more important than another to a musician. In one respect, perhaps, action is the most valuable part. Action bears the same relation to the Art of the Theatre as drawing does to painting, and melody does to music. The Art of the Theatre has sprung from action—movement—dance.

THE PLAYGOER: I always was led to suppose that it had sprung from speech, and that the poet was the father of the theatre.

THE STAGE DIRECTOR: This is the common belief, but consider it for a moment. The poet's imagination finds voice in words, beautifully chosen; he then either recites or sings these words to us, and all is done. That poetry, sung or recited, is for our ears, and, through them, for our imagination. It will not help the matter if the poet shall add gestures to his recitation or to his song; in fact it will spoil all.[27]

Even as he was writing this he was becoming increasingly aware of certain disadvantages with which the stage director was confronted compared with the composer of music: the composer's music could always be played by instrumentalists who, provided they played competently, would produce the same combination of sounds at exactly the same instant at each performance, even years after the composer's death, whereas the stage director had to depend on the play actor who was continually subject to his own emotions which too often revealed a rather mediocre personality.

It was while he was pondering this point that he saw some of Jessner's puppets, and a new idea had began to germinate in his mind: puppets—marionettes—an *über-marionette*—a "creature" that could be controlled by an artist.

What should this creature be made to do? Since acting was action, why had there got to be a play at all? A play was perfect in itself when it was read—acting a play did not improve it, but acting must be seen to be enjoyed. Did not movement have a complete emotional appeal? The movement of light and the movement of figures, accompanied by the movement of sound? As the frontispiece of his new book he showed a design that was not for any known stage play, it was just: "*A Study for a Stage Movement.*"[28]

Again he tackled his sketches and notes made years before, when he and Elena spent hours watching the Duke of York's steps—watching the changes of mood and light, and the coming and going of people upon them. He finished four of his most exciting designs in one week; he called them *The Steps*, first, second, third, and fourth "mood."[29]

His little book was translated into German by Magnus, with a foreword by Kessler, and was published by Hermann Seeman—its German title *Die Kunst des Theaters*. He was very happy, and wrote to Martin in May, telling him it was being printed and sending him a typescript copy so that he could read it in English and share his excitement. It ran into three editions, and was followed by an English edition published by T. N. Foulis, with an introduction by Graham Robertson; later, an edition was published in Holland by S. L. Van Looy, with introductions by the actor J. C. de Vos and Marius Bauer, the artist.[30]

This little book did more to establish him as a reformer than anything else that he had attempted in the way of designs or productions, and it was soon being read all over Europe by those who wanted to see a more inspired approach to theatrical presentation. The artist's approach to painting had already changed, music was following, and Isadora was revealing that dance could be a creative force rather than a tired traditional routine; Craig was pointing the way to those in the theatre. He realized that if there was to be any rallying point he must continue writing, and to this end Magnus contacted several publishers in England and Germany with a view to launching *The Mask*, but like the rest of the commercial world they could see no great sale for the revolutionary magazine that Craig had in mind.

He hardly ever wrote to his mother now that he had Elena and Martin to whom he could unburden his soul. Elena always encouraged him in her simple, loving way, which contained no shadow of doubt as to his future. To Martin went a continual flow of letters—he was the only creative artist to whom he felt he could reveal his troubled mind. Together, they had known the excitement of producing something that was a landmark in the history of the theatre. To his other friends, like Max Beerbohm, William Rothenstein, even to Paul Cooper, he assumed the character of a fellow artist carrying on mysterious experiments abroad.

Putting together lines from various letters written at this period we can glean an impression of how his mind was working:

haven't heard from mama for 8 weeks now—not even for my
birthday.

These darned Americans make their attempts succeed.

I send everyone different reports of the people I'm supposed to be
staying with.

Reinhardt, who promised me Hamlet, is a first class man whether
he lets me do it or not.

Something may grow from all of this. I want my instrument—and
go on gathering all I feel and see and hear.

All work seems to hang fire at present . . . until I learn to make
something which lives without my actual presence.

If *I* were a musician or a poet or a painter do you think I would
bother 2 straws about advance—rather would I *retire*—live alone—
search out some *new* fountain where melody, colour or song springs,
and bathe in that fountain day and night—but success I would leave
to others.
The nearer I come to success, the more form and beauty I see in
what is called *failure*—
All this talk of ours about Art is it but the shouting out of "who'll
buy" in the market place.[31]

In October 1905 the news reached him in Amsterdam that Henry
Irving, the only man who had ever tried to help him to understand
and love the theatre, had died. He felt this loss tremendously. He
wrote to Martin: "The old Angel dead—and howling forbidden to
us of the masculine gender—and I cannot tell you the state I am in,
unrelieved—may my immortal Henry float away and away where ever
fancy allows."[32]
While he was in this broken-hearted state, Isadora suddenly became
panic-stricken for she believed that she was pregnant, and once again
he felt lost. Whenever he felt like this he would enter into one of his

day-books, diaries, or note-books, the one word "searching" and the date. Now, with the end of a gloriously hectic year, he was once more writing "searching" in his note-book, and the date, December 1905.

In the new year Craig became more and more restless. The various projects over which Magnus had been trying to help him had come to nothing, chiefly because he tried to conduct all his business with letters and telegrams while trailing about with Isadora. In Stockholm he managed to meet Strindberg and fancied that the great dramatist favoured his ideas.

The portfolio of six designs of Isadora dancing came out at last, following a tremendous amount of correspondence about the colour of mounts, the method of reproduction, and so on. Although they made a handsome show when displayed in the foyers of theatres, they were too expensive to sell well; it was also obvious that Craig was no figure artist and that the designs were conceived in far too romantic a vein—in fact, they seemed almost old-fashioned. But Isadora loved them.

She now began to reveal her very complex nature; she was either exhilarated and inspired, or so depressed that she contemplated suicide. She would sink into despair because some man had not fallen for her when she was doing all she knew to fascinate him, then would suddenly preach a sermon about respectability to her lover.[33] Her moods were always extreme, and with the realization that she was pregnant, her fits of joy and despondency alternated with greater frequency. At one moment "the divine message sang" in her "entire being," at other times she "felt like some poor animal in a mighty trap."[34]

Craig felt lost, and yearned for Martin's company. He had tried to persuade him to come to Germany since the beginning of the previous year. At last he persuaded Isadora that the only way she could maintain any continuity in the performance of the musical background to her dancing, which at that time varied with every orchestra she encountered on tour, was to have her own conductor, and that Martin was the ideal man. She had heard so much about this "Martin" that she at last agreed. She probably thought that this would help to cheer Craig who had become "strangely remote." Martin had never considered himself to be a good conductor, but work was not going well for him in England and the thought of a trip to Europe and of seeing his old friend spurred him on to accept.

They all met in Berlin, and Isadora was delighted with Martin's unassuming, joyous approach to the work. Craig was happy again; he had someone with whom he could discuss his ideas, someone who understood what he was talking about. He had never been able to do this with Isadora because on the subject of art they seemed to speak in different languages.

Together, they started on another tour, taking in Munich, Augsburg, Amsterdam, Copenhagen, Stockholm, and Göteborg.[35] Then they returned to Amsterdam where, in June, Isadora found a little place near Leyden called Villa Maria at Nordwijk op Zee. The sea was only a few yards away and this seemed to please her. She now felt too ill to dance any more.

Craig also loved the sea, but he could not stand inactivity for long; again the feeling that he was being trapped came over him and he bolted—this time back to England and to Elena.

Although he had supplied her with money and had written to her continuously while he had been in Europe, he had only paid her one brief visit after the birth of their son, Teddy, and over nine months had passed since he had seen her. In the terribly worried state in which he found himself, he knew that she was the only person who could set his mind at rest. He felt that he had let her down: he had promised to marry her as soon as his Decree Absolute came through, but when he had received the papers from the lawyers in May of 1905, he had made the excuse that he could not leave his work. Now he wanted her advice and encouragement.

He was in England between July 18 and 21, and found Elena unchanged in her devotion. He had not the courage to tell her everything about his affair with Isadora, but merely said that some woman who was infatuated with him was giving him trouble—the breach between him and Isadora was gradually widening, and he probably made himself believe, at the time, that it was a one-sided affair. Elena's simple love for him, and her tears when he left after so brief a visit made him decide, within himself, to do whatever job came next in order to make it possible for him to have her and their "little family" with him. He had brought over material for dresses and various trinkets, all of which she cherished after he had gone. He thought she looked paler than she used to, so, just before leaving, he ordered the local brewery to send a firkin of oatmeal stout to the cottage, and he told her to drink a glass every day! He promised that they would be together soon.

Back in Holland, he flitted between Rotterdam, where he was organizing an exhibition, and Amsterdam, where he was trying to get the State Theatre interested in his work through Jan C. de Vos.

He thought it would comfort Isadora to know that he was near, but he did not want to get involved, as he was terrified by emotional displays. Marie Klist, later to become one of her dearest friends, joined her, and another friend, Kathleen Bruce (later Lady Scott), came along to see if she too could help. Once, while Craig was there, she made a delightful little statuette of him in a reclining position, contemplating a little figure—his über-marionette. The cottage got overcrowded and too hot, so Craig decided to sleep on the beach. Kathleen thought it a good idea and did the same, leaving Isadora to suffer unnecessary pangs of jealousy. Marie Klist helped to fan the flames since she and Craig shared a mutual dislike, each for the other.

In September, while he was in Rotterdam, he got a message saying that Isadora had given birth to a little girl. The tension over, Craig dashed back to be with her. She was radiant with happiness and wrote, "now I know this tremendous love surpassing the love of man . . . what words could describe this joy."[36] Because it was the "Irishness" in Isadora that so appealed to Craig, he sought an Irish name for her child; they chose Deirdre—"beloved of Ireland." But neither of them could have realized that the name was associated in Irish legend with tragedy.

As soon as Isadora could get about they returned to Berlin and her School of Dance, which Elizabeth had been running in her absence. There, with her loving little pupils around her and her little baby, she felt more at ease. Her mother had already shown her disapproval of the entire affair and had left.

Shortly after this, Eleonora Duse came to Berlin, staying with her friends Mr and Mrs Mendelssohn. Kessler asked the Mendelssohns if they would invite Isadora and Craig so that Duse could meet the young artist who had impressed her with his designs for *Elektra*; she already knew and admired Isadora.

Duse was delighted with Craig's enthusiasm, and asked him if he would like to do something else for her—something beautiful for *Rosmersholm*, which she intended to present later in the year. Craig found it very difficult to converse with Duse because he could speak neither French nor Italian, so Isadora acted as interpreter. He wanted to explain that he would design the whole production, or nothing, but Isadora was translating this as "he would be very interested indeed."

By this time Isadora must have realized that unless Craig got involved in some work soon he would go mad, and it may also have occurred to her that she could not nurse him *and* her baby. Kessler was very keen that Craig should back his theories up with something tangible. Craig thought that if he designed only the scenery for a production he would be going against all his strongest convictions. Gradually he saw that Isadora had set her heart on him doing something with Duse, whom she greatly admired, and that if he did not agree she might suffer a severe setback in her health. He probably thought, too, of Elena and the children, so he agreed—and thus began a whole new chapter in his life.

They stayed on in Berlin until November, Isadora making arrangements for the future of her school, Craig working on the scene for *Rosmersholm*. He was using a new rough-textured board and a wonderful range of pastels in dark blues and greens, and as he worked he got that mysterious feeling—or what James Huneker described as that "Spiritual Territory"—into his design. Duse was obviously caught by its spell, but when she asked about entrances, and queried the size of the window in the background, it was all Isadora could do to persuade Craig to finish the work; why wasn't he given carte blanche, he asked, as he had been given before on *Elektra*?

In November, Duse let him know that the play was to be produced in Florence, and on the seventeenth he wrote from Berlin to his friends in Holland, the Van Looys, telling them that he was just leaving "to produce a beautiful play for Madame Eleonora Duse . . . it is Ibsen's *Rosmersholm*, and it shall be made into a dream—a dream—DREAM."[37]

They all left for Italy on the Nord-Sud Express—Craig, Isadora, Marie Klist, and the baby.

After going through the Brenner Pass, Craig became restless: he was

about to enter Italy. He imagined Goethe travelling the same route by
coach in years gone by, and remembered: "Kennst du das Land wo
die Citronen blühen."

He stood in the corridor of the train, peering at the grandeur of the
mountains, the ravines, and the torrents. They crossed into Italy at
Belluno, and as they descended into the plain of Lombardy the rising
sun cast great shadows across the landscape, and he felt that at last he
had come home. "Peri, Dolce . . . Domegliara; a perfect place": he
wrote their names in his address-book as they passed. During the day,
as they crossed Lombardy, he became more and more exhilarated by
the beauty of the architecture, the poplars, and the effects of light and
shade—the pictures that he had loved at the National Gallery were
coming to life! This was the ancient civilization from whence Elena's
forebears had come . . . As he progressed farther and farther into Italy,
his past life receding from his memory, he was like some insect emerging from its chrysalis; the torpid stage was over—he wanted to fly.
He felt that he could.[38]

In Florence they stayed at the Washington Hotel. There was no time
to waste; he dare not look at the city but instead went immediately to
see Signor Landi, the scenic artist, who lived in the Via Ghibellini.

Landi looked at his design: all he could see was a dark greeny-blue
interior with an opening at the back looking out on to a misty
"beyond"; the mistiness even pervaded the interior and the walls,
which seemed more like great curtains merged into the floor like the
roots of huge trees. He admired it, but said there was nothing in it for
him to do; all those graduated streaks of colour, indigo merging into
ultramarine, into Russian green, with here and there lighter tones of
the same colours. This was . . . impressionism! There was no architecture, no columns, no cornices and architraves—what was there for
him to paint? He was most courteous but implied that it would do
him no good to be associated with such work.[39]

Craig sat in a café called the Giubbe Rosse, furious and disillusioned.
He had believed that the Italians would possess the artistic perception
lacking in other countries; now he felt that tradition was even more
deeply rooted in their theatre than in Germany or in England.

On the way back to the hotel, he noticed two youths painting the
side of a house with some beautiful blue distemper. They were perched

on the most flimsy scaffold, but seemed unaware of any danger as they sang gaily and handled their brushes in time with their tune; they were not slopping on the colour anyhow, but stroking it on like artists. Here were his scene-painters at last. The following day, he got someone to talk to them: Would they like to help this celebrated foreign artist to paint scenery? They would be delighted! They were engaged.

Next, he discovered that what he knew as "scenic canvas" could not be found in Florence; paper, backed with net, was generally used by repertory companies, so ordinary sacking had to be purchased and great lengths sewn together by hand.

Craig set to work on the stage of the Pergola Theatre and, working day and night with his two lads, produced what he wanted within a week—an astounding feat since neither he nor his two helpers had ever painted scenery before. Remembering that, in England, Hawes Craven always mixed his colours with size, he had asked Signor Landi what it was called in Italian: "Colla," he said; and what proportions did they use? "Half a cup to a big pot of hot water." He entered this note in his address-book, and that was all the data that he had to work from. Powdered colours were easy to find.

Eventually the moment arrived when the lengths of painted cloth could be tacked to battens, and the whole assembled as a scene in which the only dressings were a great carpet, a circular table surrounded by chairs, and a divan lit by a strange lamp under which much of the action was to take place. With the help of some very imaginative electricians, the scene was lit in an abnormally short space of time. Finally all was ready and Duse, seated with Isadora in one of the boxes of the empty theatre, saw, at last, what Craig had given her. For a moment she seemed lost; then, true artist that she was, she found her way into her fellow artist's imagination, and the beauty it had produced. The scene was a revelation—an extension of Ibsen's imagination: it was not a drawing-room, but "a place" as unreal as the play.

At the dress rehearsal the next day Duse embraced Craig before the whole cast and told them that only through his genius would actors ever find release from "this monstrosity . . . which is the Theatre of today." The younger ones tried to feel with her, but the traditionalists felt as "out of place" in these mystic surroundings as Oscar Asche had felt with his "damned fine body" in *The Vikings*.

On Wednesday, December 5, the ornate curtain of the ancient

Teatro della Pergola went up to reveal Craig's scene to a rather bewildered audience, who were expecting a realistic setting showing the interior of a Swedish gentleman's house. In the brief silence that followed, a voice was heard to murmur, "Bella, bella," in real admiration. It was the great Tommaso Salvini, Italy's Henry Irving, who was to become one of Craig's most cherished friends. Duse, persuaded by Craig, had dressed in a long off-white sheath in which she moved like a spirit. To the Tuscan audience Ibsen's words must have seemed as strange as Craig's scene, especially when spoken by a Rosmer who probably felt, looked, and sounded completely out of place against this background which he could not understand.

Enrico Corradini, the designer, who was there and saw it all through the eyes of an artist, wrote:

> The stage seemed completely transformed. The usual wings were gone. Here was a new architecture of great height, ranging in colour from green to blue. It was simple, mysterious, fascinating, and a fitting background to the complicated lives of Rosmer and Rebecca West; it portrayed a *state of mind.*[40]

During the interval, the audience was like a disturbed beehive; although men like Salvini and Corradini were enthralled by Duse and the atmosphere created by Craig's scene, most of them were puzzled. Inserted in all the programmes was a leaflet in which Craig had endeavoured to explain the idea behind his design, but it was a bit ahead of the times and cannot have been much help to the few who bothered to read it. This leaflet, now very rare, contained the following interesting passages:

> Ibsen's marked detestation for Realism is nowhere more apparent than in the two plays *Rosmersholm* and *Ghosts.*
>
> The words are the words of actuality, but the drift of the words, something beyond this. There is the powerful impression of unseen forces closing in upon the place: we hear continually the long drawn out note of the horn of death. . . .
>
> . . . Therefore those who prepare to serve Ibsen, to help in the setting forth of his play, must come to the work in no photographic mood, all must approach as artists. . . . Realism is only Exposure,

whereas Art is Revelation; and therefore in the mounting of this play I have tried to avoid all Realism. . . .

Let our common sense be left in the cloakroom with our umbrellas and hats. We need here our finer senses only, the living part of us. We are in Rosmersholm, a house of shadows. . . .

. . . throw away all concern, enter into the observance of this as though you were at some ancient religious ceremony, and then perhaps you will be aware of the value of the spirit which moves before you as Rebecca West . . .

It ended with the prophetic line: "the birth of the new Theatre, and its new Art, has begun." It was signed, "Gordon Craig."[41]

The following day he wrote to Martin, the only person who had sent him a telegram for the opening night:

. . . It was a success, and is. Duse was magnificent—threw her details to the winds and went in—She has the courage of 25! She, Ibsen and I played our little trio out, and came home happy—

I have this morning received a lovely long letter from her. She asks me to work with her in joy and freedom to do three more Ibsen plays at once—She says "I will *never* have any other scenes— any more of that other *horrid family*"—

Is it not happiness to find this still alive in the Theatre—What I talk—and think is *necessary* to talk—is not always what I do.[42]

Duse's actual letter, which was written in French ran as follows:

Thank you—I acted last night as in a dream—far away. You did your work under terrible difficulties—so thank you. Last night I understood the strength of your help—so again, thank you.

Let us hope that we shall work together again joyfully and un-hampered. E.[43]

She had already mentioned *The Lady from the Sea* as one of the plays on which they might work, and full of enthusiasm Craig immediately started to read it, scribbling his notes in the margins as he went.

As their financial situation was critical, they all returned to Berlin a few days later. From there, Isadora went on to Holland, where she still had an engagement to fulfil. Craig remained in Berlin. Still thinking of *Rosmersholm*, he wrote to Martin, who was in Rotterdam awaiting Isadora's arrivel.

> . . .' The pleasure I got from seeing Miss Duncan watching my work with Duse was *infinite*.
>
> I care not now whether anyone approves or disapproves of one point in my plan or a hundred—because I have that which *glows* to *accept* it without approval or disapproval.
>
> I am free—
> > Nothing can affect me any more.
> > > I want nothing—
> > > > For I've found everything . . .[44]

He tried taking lessons in French so as to be able to talk to Duse, but finding it "a most queer sensation learning by rule," he gave it up.[45]

Although some outsiders may have been under the impression that this first period of collaboration with Duse was unhappy, it was not so. It had been a fight in which he had tried to achieve something worthwhile, and he believed he had won Duse over to understanding his kind of scenery.

His brief glimpse of Florence had so inspired him that he longed to go back. Since his arrival in Germany two years earlier, certain ideas had been developing in his mind, and all sorts of new experiences had helped to crystallize these ideas; now all he wanted was peace and quiet and the right surroundings in which to work, in order to make these theories visible to all. He felt sure that he would find this in Florence. He also believed that he now had one of the greatest personalities in the European theatre behind him, and consequently, the realization of his ideas would be easier. To another friend in Holland, Fritz Labidoth, he sent an enthusiastic letter from Berlin on December 17:

> It will interest you to know that Madame Duse has associated her name with mine, and will serve with all her heart the idea which my School intends to develop—That is to say, I have the spirit of the greatest actress living for the most advanced idea of the Theatre, even to the extent of getting rid of the actors themselves, which as you know, by no means implies getting rid of the great personalities . . .[46]

Suddenly, he received a telegram saying that Isadora was too ill to perform. He rushed to Holland and did his best to comfort her—she was suffering from prostration, the result of her nerve-racking experience as Craig's "go between" with Duse while she was also having trouble feeding her baby.

When Craig returned to Berlin a few weeks later he found telegrams waiting for him from Duse, who was staying at Cap Martin, in the south of France. She had been trying to contact him for some days. One of the telegrams mentioned a new production, *Tintagile*; then, on January 23, came yet another telegram:

I have a new play that is very beautiful but I must discuss it with you. Can you come to Nice? I shall be putting on Rosmer February ninth. Duse.[47]

Craig was getting tired of these continual changes in Duse's plans. Isadora who was very keen on the Duse-Craig association which she felt might lead to greater things, wrote to him from Holland, pleading with him to go.

. . . Look toward your star and be your own sweet joyous self. Don't be impatient with D, but *go* to *Nice* and you will see all will turn out as you wish. Not allowed to write any more than this . . . be wise and take the hint of your most loving Topsy.[48]

He left for Nice on February 7 and on the following day went round to the old Casino Theatre to see if all was going well. To his horror, he discovered that the stage-manager, on finding the proscenium opening at Nice so much lower than the one at Florence, had calmly cut two or three feet off the bottom of the whole set, thus altering all the proportions and bringing the window at the back so low that it almost reached the ground. His fury knew no bounds, and after telling everyone in the theatre what he thought of them in English, with the introduction of various French and German words such as "cretins," "imbeciles," and "dummkopf," he rushed off to find Duse. She could not understand any of his words, but she disliked his outburst and lack of self-control. All was over between them—they would never work together again.

Isadora, although ill, came down alone to try to heal the wounds.

Duse, who had learnt the hard way, is supposed to have written to Craig philosophically, saying: "What they have done to your scene, they have been doing for years to my Art."[49]

From his letters to Martin, it is obvious that Craig's life with Isadora was no longer running smoothly:

> . . . You write you hope Miss D. and I are good humoured—I am fighting to be so . . .
>
> I am having hell with Duse—but hush, not a word to a soul—and besides, I shall win. The Rosmer scene was CUT down—pity me a little, yet I care so little, for I want to fly far beyond that haphazard work . . .
>
> My whole being is sick by the delay of the birth of that which is burning me . . .[50]

Isadora was now joined again by her mother, Marie Klist, and the baby, and they all moved out to Mount Baron. There she relapsed into her exhausted state.

Recalling this period she wrote, "although I loved Craig with all the ardour of my artist soul. . . . I realized that our separation was inevitable." She also began to suspect that she had cause for jealousy, and continued: "I realized that this state of things must cease. Either Craig's Art or mine . . . and to give up mine I knew to be impossible; I should pine away—I should die from chagrin. I must find a remedy, and I thought of the wisdom of the homeopaths." And as everything that we wish for very much comes, the remedy came. He entered one afternoon: fair, debonair, young, blond, perfectly dressed. He said: "My friends call me Pim . . ."[51] and so her next sad adventure began.

Looking at this episode in retrospect, Craig wrote later:

> . . . all's past . . . all's said . . . all's done . . . What now? It seems that all has not been said. I loved her—I do so still—but she, the complex she, might have wrecked me, as she wrecked many—and finally herself. And did she not wreck me? No, she did not. She was a strange, lovely, strong creature, but it seems that I was the stronger.[52]

They had enjoyed life together for nearly two years. Before her still lay many triumphs and very many tragedies; before him lay the chance to fulfil his ideals. She would always go on working on his behalf; he would always worship her as a goddess who had appeared to him once, as in a dream. Through her, he had been able to see Europe, meet people, live a life of luxury. Through her art, he had come closer to understanding what he himself was trying to achieve in the Theatre. He would always have reason to be grateful to her. Even then, away in Russia with "Pim," she was already talking about him to Stanislavsky, and in so doing, was helping to write the next chapter in his life.

CHAPTER TWELVE

"The Masterpiece" · Moscow · "Hamlet"

1906–1912

ALTHOUGH THEY did not say "good-bye" to each other in Nice, Craig and Isadora parted, never again to meet as lovers. Isadora tried twice to rekindle the flames, but it was too late, because the Craig that she had left in Nice was a different man by the time he reached Florence a few weeks later; by then he had decided never again to let any person come between him and his work.[1]

His education was over. He had learned all that he wanted to know for his immediate plans, and all he needed now was time for experiment.

He had started life with the theatre already in his blood; from Irving he had learned to respect it; finally, he dedicated his life to it. From his father he had inherited a natural love and understanding of architecture—the art by which "ideas are expressed in Structure." From Pryde and Nicholson, he had learned to convey ideas through the medium of the graphic arts; from them, he had also learned about form and the dramatic powers of light and shade; from Martin Shaw, he had learned about music, and, above all—through music—about movement. Movement then became his main preoccupation. Then he had met Isadora the dancer—but she did not dance dances, she danced ideas;[2] she *moved* in sympathy with emotions called forth by the music of Peri, Glück, and Beethoven, and the audience responded to the ideas she generated; she was mistress of her own technique and controlled an art that was all her own.

Isadora had told Craig that she had based her theories on ideas that originated in ancient Greece, so he began to think back on the origins of the theatre and acting, and again came to the conclusion that in the beginning, acting was action—movement. He now concentrated upon an idea that had been flitting before his mind's eye for the last seven years; a theatre in which he would appeal to the emotions of the audience through movement alone. There would be no play or plot, but simply the correlated movement of sound, light, and moving masses. Should he want to use a figure or figures, for scale or emphasis, they were to be figures as superb as the gods in the temples of ancient Egypt, and their movements would have to be as much under his direct control as the rest of the stage. The audience would, as it were, see a symphony; it would be a kinetic experience—although he never used that word to describe it.

This idea was not, as so many thought, to exclude any other form of theatre, for he loved the theatre in all its forms, from music-hall acts, through circuses, puppet shows, melodrama, operas, to poetic dramas and even church ceremonials, but he wanted to create a new kind of theatre that was an art and on its own. He would not accept a hotch-potch of the other arts as the art of the theatre.

The climax of events in Nice left him in an aftermath of calm; a new sensation of freedom came over him, and he started to explore the neighbourhood.

He travelled on a little narrow-gauge railway through tunnels and over viaducts up to the small mountain town of Vence. This place, with its strange architecture resembling a natural outcrop of stone on the summit of a hill of olives, rekindled in him the desire to draw.[3]

Earlier in the year, when he was in Holland, Marius Bauer had shown him some of his lovely etchings in which tiny figures moved about in imaginary Eastern backgrounds and great walls were broken by a single arch that cupped some mighty shadow: Craig had admired them greatly. Bauer had given him two or three little copper plates and a dry-point stilus to experiment with, and now he found them at the bottom of his travelling bag. Suddenly, this new medium appealed to him, and his very first attempt to use it was inspired by one of the ancient gates of Vence.[4]

He still kept in contact with Martin, who was then in Florence, where Isadora had asked him to look for original fifteenth-century

Italian music to inspire some new dances. On February 15, Craig wrote a letter to him, in which we begin to see his new state of mind developing:

> Dear and lovely old friend—I'm in bed—have flung myself into it in the middle of the day—as the day was proving evil enough for the year- –I slept and am a bit better—but you know what it is and how the only relief lies in the birth of that which is tormenting me- – –Slowly but surely, just as that star outside, which is passing across the panes of my window (some 400,000,000 miles in actuality), I shall pass out of the Theatre to the new Land of Beauty. A place of my own creating. How slowly I have let hold of each rope—and now having a rope flung from the new I can draw myself slowly up.
>
> The people thought I was reckless—see how cautious my recklessness was. I threw overboard their old machine first—then their scenes—then their methods of moving the figures—then the playright—then speech—now, last of all, the figures themselves—real or pasteboard—over they go, trumpery and unworthy—until a breed can be grown which are like the rest of the thought, *hard, clearcut, passionless*—[5]

Another letter contains the lines:

> My whole being is sick by the delay of the birth of that which is burning in me—You know we talked of it, and you understood. I know that your heart and being is on fire at the delay of your own births. . . . Dear boy—I send you my love—I will assist you—assist me.[6]

The picture of the indolent artist sitting with pen or pencil poised waiting for divine inspiration has, over the years, been more or less taken for granted, but his real agony is seldom revealed as here . . .

By the end of the month he had made up his mind to return to Florence. He had left it the year before, accompanied by Isadora. "When next I came there it was without her—It was then that my hour struck." He wrote these lines many years later; something powerful about the place *had* called him back. He found the inhabitants "serious—much at ease, they seemed, not *earnest*, not enthusiastic—just serious, quietly learning each his craft or art and talking very little about it."[7]

He got himself a temporary room on the top floor of the old Palazzo Sassetti, which was just behind the Piazza Vittorio Emmanuele. In the Piazza itself was the famous old café called the Giubbe Rosse, with its *fin de siècle* decorations of mirrors and gilt, its tables spilling out on to the square. This place he remembered, with love, from his last visit; its attraction was magnetic. Here, to his great joy, he found Martin again. Here, too, were painters, sculptors, musicians, of all nationalities. Old waiters served quietly and efficiently; passing musicians stopped to play haunting old Tuscan airs; a little hump-backed man paid a visit every night, calling out "Piccolo Gobbino," and selling tiny images of himself carved in mother of pearl—he said they would bring luck.

In this café he felt at home: the waiters remembered him; here he saw Corradini, Carlo Placci, and the sculptor Maraini, and many other artists of note. Here, also, were James Gibbon, Edward Hutton, Stephen Haweis with his beautiful wife, Mina Loy, and the Tesleffs—a lovely family from Finland. Later, the rich American collector Charles Loeser arrived. He looked forward to this meeting, for Loeser had once told him that if he ever wanted it, he could always let him have an old villa to live in on the hill across the Arno, with the most beautiful panoramic view of the city. Loeser welcomed him warmly, and they agreed to meet the following day.

He saw Martin back to the Hotel de Rhin, and then spent the night wandering alone through the piazzas and back streets of the city. In many places the street-lights were suspended in great lanterns from wires strung high above, and as they swayed in the night breeze they cast enormous moving shadows of any object in the path of the light. Approaching the Ponte Vecchio from the south bank of the river along the Via Gucciardini, he met a party of twenty men all dressed in white, their heads completely covered in cowls pierced with holes for their eyes; they came down the winding road rapidly and silently, each man carrying a flaming torch, the four men in the middle of the party carrying a rough coffin on a bier. These were the Miseracordia, a group of charitable men who hid their identity, and who could be called on at any hour to bury the unclaimed dead. He was awed by these faceless silent figures: "What wonderful material for the Grave scene in *Hamlet*."[8]

This time he had leisure in which to look, and see, and he found the city almost too marvellous to be true:

> . . . towards night time all became much more grave, and really the great dead seemed to me to come to life—passing as shadows: Yes, I could swear I felt them passing. So I was filled with a courage which up north had begun to desert me. I felt that these ghostly shadows were very friendly, and when day came I went eagerly to see the works they had left behind them. To reach a palace or a picture I would have to pass through whole streets of houses, each one built by those men whose shadows swept round me towards evening. Each house was a piece of perfect building; adorned or unadorned, the building was perfect. Seeing them, I was made well aware that their makers were without the personal ambition to get on—were solely purposed to do well. Here, Florence gave me daily proof, as I walked silently and saw the evidence of the true spirit of men and artists.
>
> That was all I needed. I too would do well in my work and not care whether or no I "got on."[9]

Loeser and Craig met the following day and, passing over the Ponte alle Grazie and out through the old city gates of San Miniato, ascended the steep slope by threading through walled lanes overhung with gnarled olive trees, still green in February. At last they came to a twisting lane called the Viuzza della Gattaia, and an old, square cream-painted villa with faded green shutters and a roof that seemed to project halfway across the lane. The villa contained many rooms with tiled floors and just a few pieces of simple furniture. There was also a long terrace covered with vines and dotted everywhere with great earthenware jars in which were planted oranges, lemons, and camellias. Craig was enchanted by the place, and the generous Loeser told him he could have it for as long as he liked; an old peasant woman would come in and clean, and make coffee in the morning, and he could find excellent food in the many *osterias* in the city below. No. 4 Viuzzo della Gattaia became Craig's first home in Florence—and Florence was to remain his home for the next seven years.

His black felt hat was now battered and limp; he wore sandals which he bought from an old monk at Fiesole, and went about in open-necked shirts—happy and carefree.

Martin was still there, but could only stay for a couple of months, so he joined his old friend before returning to England.[10]

With a place in which to work, peace of mind, spring in the air, and a feeling of friendship all around him, he embarked upon the biggest programme that he had ever attempted. It was as though the floodgates of his creative power had suddenly been opened, and an unending torrent of ideas poured from his pen and pencil.[11]

He started work on his magazine, The Mask, which he was to keep filled with his writings, many of which were to be the basis for his next book, On the Art of the Theatre. He built a vast model stage in order to experiment with his moving scene. He made twenty to thirty etchings, which he first described as "Motions" and later as "Scene." He carved thirty to forty figures with which to people his models, and later developed them as prints which he called "Black Figures." He couldn't afford to have blocks made to illustrate The Mask, so he also began engraving again. Finally, realizing that he could no longer carry on alone, he once more made plans for the school where he would train future assistants and develop his theories until they became practicable. He was now thirty-five.

It seemed to him that The Mask was the most urgent part of his programme to develop first; it would take the most time and depended a lot on other craftsmen. With his own magazine, he wouldn't be lost in Italy—he could keep in contact with his friends throughout the world; and by means of it, he would establish a rallying point for all those setting out in the same direction . . . away from a derelict art, towards a new form of expression.

He needed a secretary who could speak English and Italian, who could handle proof-correcting, who was practical enough to run around and get estimates, samples of paper, and do all the necessary registration, and so on.

Through a friend of Loeser's he had met a young Englishwoman who spoke Italian perfectly, and who was living with friends in

Florence, where she was preparing her third book for publication; her first two, on the manners and customs of Tuscany, had been published by Chatto & Windus and J. M. Dent, and had been very successful—she had been asked to do more. At first, Craig thought that he would be expecting too much if he was to suggest that she give up a literary career in order to combine the work of a secretary, printer's-devil, and general factotum, but this young woman, Dorothy Nevile Lees, was fascinated by his personality and persuaded him that she *was* the right person, and thus begun a partnership which resulted in her becoming the mainstay of this remarkable magazine during the next twenty years.

Dorothy, who soon became "D. N. L.," lived in the Via Santo Spirito, and she used to climb the hill to the villa every day and try to cope with Craig's strange way of working. He lay in bed late, thinking out subjects for articles and then, suddenly inspired, he would rise, slip on one of the white linen tropical suits that he had bought in Holland, and would pace up and down the enormous terrace, dictating excitedly, pacing ever more rapidly as the ideas developed, his words sometimes being lost at the far end of the terrace where he had gone to seek inspiration from the view. This could continue for hours, then the great cannon in the ancient fortress on a nearby hill would boom out its midday signal, everyone in Florence would down tools for a couple of hours, and Craig, Martin, and D. N. L. would generally do the same, descending into the town to eat at one of many picturesque little restaurants tucked away in the side streets; Lapi's, in the cellars of the Palazzo Antinori, was a favourite. Food was cheap, and a shilling or one-and-sixpence bought a grand meal with a small bottle of wine. During lunch Craig would often be wildly elated about his morning's work, but in the afternoon when he saw it typed out on the page he would sink into the depths of despair, and would alter and deface the article until it was almost illegible; it would then be retyped, and after four to six rewrites it might please him, and he would end the day saying, "I *will* teach myself to write—I WILL." In those early days his pen could not keep pace with the speed of his thoughts, and dictation seemed the only means by which he could capture them—so the struggle continued.[12]

The format of *The Mask* was governed by the size of the paper, which was hand-made, cheap, and came from near-by Fabriano. The typography was dependent on what founts of type the printers had to hand. The firm of Morandi was able to produce a small quantity of Elzivere, which pleased him immensely, so experimental pages were put in hand. The layout was based on an early copy of *Vitruvius* that he had picked up for a few lire.

He soon realized that he could not supply all the articles and editorial matter and engrave all the blocks as well, so he encouraged Ellen Tesleff, a promising young artist, to engrave. He could count on her for blocks in the future. He also set D. N. L. to work, in her spare time, translating from Italian books dealing with the theatre: these translations formed a reserve of material for occasions when original manuscript was short.

One day, he came upon T. de Marinis in his bookshop in the Via Vecchietti, and they became friends. When Craig found that De Marinis had a large store of the blocks which he had used to illustrate his wonderful catalogues of incunabula and early Italian literature, he struck a bargain with him: free advertising space in *The Mask* in exchange for the use of any of these old blocks for illustrations. They would make excellent "padding," and "Allen Carric"—another Craig *nom de plume*—could always write something about them.

A prospectus was printed, announcing that *The Mask* would be published in English, German, and Dutch, under the imprint of the Direktion Vereinigter Kunst,[13] and would sell at three shillings a copy. Craig imagined that Magnus would translate the German version and that the Dutch wife of his Californian friend, Michael Carr, would look after the Dutch version; but it soon became obvious that there was more than enough to contend with in bringing out an English version alone, for the Italian type-setters found it difficult enough to work from the English manuscripts, which Craig continually altered in order to make the pages look more attractive; so the grandiose prospectus was scrapped and the price was reduced to one shilling.

At the end of June 1907, Martin returned to England. Craig decided that he needed more space and more assistance to carry out all his different projects, so he moved from Loeser's villa to another that was larger and even more picturesque, named "Il Santuccio," No. 35 in the Via San Leonardo, only a little distance away. Here Craig was joined by the painter Michael Carr and his wife, the proposal being

that Carr, who was a very practical man, should help Craig to con-
struct and manipulate the model stages for his experiments, while his
wife looked after them both, and filled in time by translating from the
Dutch an enormous book on the history of the Javanese shadow theatre.
Opposite Il Santuccio were a couple of smaller villas, and in one of
these D. N. L. found rooms where she lived and typed, and tried to
keep pace with Craig's literary output.

Craig also discovered a genial postman called Gino Ducci, an amateur
printer who had his own small printing press. This postman was fired
by the spirit of adventure too, and he worshipped Craig; he installed
his press at the villa and used to work on the small jobs like letter-
headings, pamphlets, and book-plates, at all odd hours when he
wasn't delivering letters![14]

With Carr's help Craig set to work, trying to materialize his theories
about a moving scene. For this they built a model stage that filled the
end of one room; it was twelve feet high, twelve feet wide, and eight
feet deep; the proscenium opening was six feet wide and three feet
high, but was adjustable to other measurements. We have seen this
idea develop over the years in preceding chapters, but it is worth going
over the salient points once more in order to see why the model
turned out the way it did.[15]

The idea of using pure movement to express ideas first came to him
while he was producing *The Masque of Love*. During the two years
following this production, "abstract movement" became his main
preoccupation. At that time (to help him with the production of
Much Ado About Nothing for his mother), he had purchased a copy
of Serlio's *Five Books of Architecture*, in which his eye was caught by
a woodcut that fired his imagination. It showed a floor divided into
squares from which there seemed to emerge a simplified architectural
structure. In place of painted scenery, he visualized scenery made of
screens with two-way hinges, thus providing a plastic medium with
which scenes could be composed in any shape and of any size, limited
only by the size of the folds of the screens; and with the assistance of
electric lights and projectors, he would colour and decorate them
impressionistically.

With this in mind, he was about to start his first experimental school
in London, when chance took him to Berlin and to Meyer's bookshop,
where he found a copy of Semper's volume on theatre architecture: it

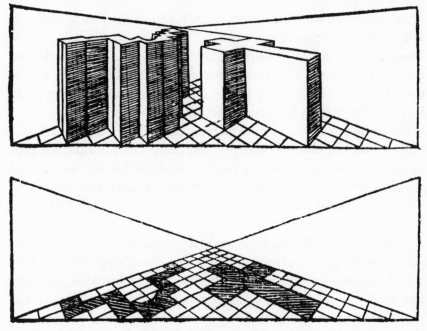

Two diagrams from Sebastiano Serlio.

was through this book that he first learnt about the Asphaleia System of hydraulic lifts, already installed in many German theatres. Returning to Serlio, it now occurred to him that, in place of screens, the whole stage could be divided into a number of sections which could rise at any point and produce the same effect.

Once again chance led him on, this time to one of Isadora Duncan's recitals, and as he watched her improvising the movements that she called her "dance," he began to realize that it might be possible for an audience to derive an emotional experience from the movement of plastic forms as well . . . from three-dimensional structures . . . He would use movement to express ideas in time and space. The flexibility of his scene would no longer be just a means to facilitate the change from one background to another, but like the rolling sea or storm driven clouds, his symphony of "movements" would be an emotional experience in itself.

He had vague ideas of a machine like an organ with which he could operate great cubes like he had once seen in Fingal's Cave, making them rise and fall at any speed. Through this "organ" he would also control the lighting that fell upon this ever-moving mass. As he saw Isadora continually improvising her movements against a background of music—no one performance being the same as another—so he saw his "scene" doing something similar. He had wanted to write about it, but didn't know how. He knew nothing about hydraulics and was fearful of asking, lest "the enemy"—that his suspicious mind saw lurking in every shadow—might take his idea and develop it before he did. He could only talk about it to Martin, who could follow it perfectly because, to him, it was a kind of visual music.

Then, in 1907, on February 9, following the clash with Duse in Nice and the parting with Isadora, he started to write about this idea for the first time. His scribbled notes appear in the back of his precious Serlio:[16]

. . . The squares on pages 19 and 20, Book 2, gave me the idea of a floor which, divided into squares, might be moveable—thereby obtaining at any time as many variations of the form of the floor, not only such as steps—platforms or seats etc., but such as deep wells —open spaces—raised squares of all sizes—raised walls—

So much for a floor—pliable yet firm, complicated yet simple in construction and effect—

But a pliable floor was not all I desired—I wanted a "*scene*" so mobile, which (within rules) might move in all directions—tempos— in all things under the control of the one who could dream how to move its parts to produce "*movements.*"

And shortly after this I found in the 3 and the 4 leaved screen (each leaf the width of each side of the floor squares) the solution of my question. . . .

To these I added a roof composed of the same shapes as the floor— suspended cubes, each cube exactly covering (and meeting when lowered) each square on the floor.

Thus

We have, therefore, a room or place moveable at all parts, and all ways, within certain laws and restrictions—That is to say we have the square and the right angle and the straight line. . . .

So far, then we have produced a place possible of all kinds of movement: straight—square or angular—So now—

Craig's first drawing for *Scene*, copied from the original and prepared for a wood engraving by the author, 1924.

we will give a hint of its use—Remember we are about to tell of the first steps of a new art—the art of movement—
and so. . . .

As I write it is not easy to refrain from singing—the moment is the most lovely the most hallowed in my life—For in a few minutes I shall have given birth to that which has for a long while been preparing—far back before I was born, and all during my life and now I am the one selected to this honour and am amongst the Creators—Yet I know how little truth there is in this, and how that all men are but the instruments chosen as per chance, by some unseen power which uses them, flatters them, and then destroys them at will.

Let us begin our new experience—
Let us witness and take part in a new (inspiration)

And now, even you—and you—and you ask for a rather clearer explanation. Not that you want to see the works—but you want to be able to imagine just what I have imagined—

Not an easy matter until I show you the thing itself—But take this example of which I have just given you a hint. Do you remember how the Oratorio by Bach, or the subject of the Passion (St. Matthew) commences? Does it not remind you of the rising of the sun—or of a tree growth?

Remember how imperceptibly it opens—how it proceeds—advancing in its severe order—its superb rigidity, without haste or delay—lawfully—how it relies on this, its compact and simple *form* to move us—how like a splendid tree it rears itself upwards—its thick basic trunk incessantly spreading upwards and outwards in innumerable branches and, lastly, how the joyful green leaves burst noiselessly into blossom, drinking in the moisture of the air—and how at last the sun beams touch the head of its endeavour rippling down and along its top most limbs.

> It is so that this Oratorio catches me—and it is some such progression that I would put before you in my "movement."
> It is some such laws I would discover (and think I am discovering), as are at the roots of music.

As he began to see the idea developing in his mind's eye he became more and more excited and, visualizing the performance of one of his "movements," he takes us to the theatre with him:

. . . The place is without form—One vast square of empty space is before us—all is still—no sound is heard—no movement is seen—On each side, a wall of grey reaches beyond our gaze; at the back . . . there seems to be no back—the floor seems to be an absence—the roof a void. *Nothing*—is before us—

And from that nothing shall come life—Even as we watch, in the very centre of that void a single atom seems to stir—to rise—it ascends like the awakening of a thought in a dream—

> no light plays round it, no angles are to be seen, no shadows are visible—only the slow deliberate inexorable ascension of a single form—near it, yet further back, a second and third atom seems to have come into a half existence. . . .

. . . and while they grow the first atom seems to be disappearing—a fourth, fifth, sixth and seventh, and yet, as we look, we are only conscious of four—Ah, birth of my love already you have multiplied four fold

—cease not until you will—

—continue to increase

But no eyes away from what is happening—Look there to the right—something seems to unfold—something to fold—what has unfolded—? slowly quickening, without haste, fold after fold loosens itself and clasps another, till that which was void has become palpable—some spirit seems to work there in the space, as in a gentle mind—A wind which blows open the void and calls it to life—

and now, to right and to left, one chain of life moves like a sea before us, while slowly breaking from atoms into pairs, slowly shapes, all alike, none less nor more than another, continue to arise in endless numbers—and to rise and rise while still the folds unfold and close—mounting one higher than another, others falling, until there stand before us vast columns of shapes, all single yet all united—none resting.

Until

    like a dew it settles—no more—enough.

    And may my love beginning, have no end.[17]

He rewrote a large part of this later in a kind of blank verse, but these first scribbled notes are the most inspired.

In order to clarify his idea he thought of making a number of designs which he would engrave upon wood and from which he would take prints at various stages as the engraving progressed; more and more cutting would reveal more and more light and the shape of the scene would slowly become apparent, exactly as would happen on a stage. He did one engraving,[18] then, at the Giubbe Rosse, he

Craig's first wood engraving showing his ideas for *Scene*.

showed a print to the artist Stephen Haweis. Haweis thought it a fine
piece of work, but told him that he would have found it much easier
had he used etching as his medium. Craig's first attempts at dry-point
had not pleased him, for, with his bad eyesight he could not easily see
what he was doing, but Haweis promised him that by using a waxed
plate he would find it easy. The next day, in his studio in the Via
Costa St. Georgio, Haweis showed him how to prepare a plate.

Two days later Craig had mastered the art, and between April and
May he made fifteen of his finest works, showing fifteen moments of
arrested motion during the development of "scene."

Having developed this beautiful idea so far, he could go no further
without seeking outside help, but this he would not do. Instead, he
talked mysteriously of an "instrument" that he had invented which
would do all he required . . . later!

So when it came to making the first model at Il Santuccio there were
no attempts at cubes rising and descending—the proscenium was not
even a tall rectangle, or a square, as in the etchings; instead he went
back to the proportions that he had used for *Dido and Aeneas* and
Bethlehem, with a long, low opening, twice as wide as it was high, and
in this he experimented with screens that were altered for each change
of scene.

It was while he was working on this model he discovered that, with
very sensitive manipulation, the screens could be imperceptibly moved
during the action of the play. Sometimes the opening of one large
fold of a screen would reveal a whole street, at other times a flat wall
would slowly develop an alcove, or a wall in shadow slowly opened,
and, as the shadow gave way to light, it revealed a great forest, which
was in no way realistic, but a vast projected silhouette. So he had come
back to the place from where he had started: making plastic scenery
for plays, but now they had added quality of mobility, which could
be developed continuously in front of the audience without bringing
down the curtain.

He soon found that he needed figures in order to give an idea of
scale to his scenes, and set to work, cutting them in bas-relief from
very thin planks of wood; he made them in two scales, one inch to
the foot and two inches to the foot—thus doubling or halving the
proportion of any setting in which they were placed. Although these
figures were extremely simple in form, some of them could be

manipulated to give very slight movements, such as the slow raising of a head or hand. Most of them were draped like ancient Greeks, for at that time the Greek tragedies interested him deeply, and it was the backgrounds to these tragedies that he was experimenting with. The figures were to move slowly, as the words were recited or sung by two or three singers and a chorus below the stage.[19]

One day, while he was making some prints from his ordinary boxwood blocks, he decided to ink the side of one of these figures, and he produced a print resembling a brass-rubbing from a church floor; this was so successful that he made prints from all the existing figures. These prints were christened "Black Figures," and were soon being exhibited, like the etchings, as samples of his graphic art.

Two of the figures used by Craig on his model stage, later to become the famous "Black Figures."

All these activities were going on at the same time, so his output in 1907 was prodigious. But with the approach of the winter, the future looked bleak, for money had been entirely overlooked.

Once, Isadora had suddenly appeared at Il Santuccio filled with enthusiasm by all that she saw in progress there, she had promised that the proceeds from her next two recitals would be sent straight to Florence to finance the new experiments. She went away and . . . forgot. Craig, who had banked on her keeping her promise, was deeply wounded, particularly when she did not even reply to his letters. He wrote to Magnus, telling him that he was no longer acting as Miss Duncan's impresario, and that the office in Berlin would no longer handle her business.[20] Although the percentage derived from the bookings arranged by Magnus was very small, it had been enough to keep the office going in Berlin and to cover a few of the expenses in Florence, where the cost of living was extremely low; Craig had become so used to this tiny trickle of income that it came as a shock when it ceased. Michael Carr and his wife were not paid for weeks, and Michael was so run down from overwork and undernourishment that they had to leave;[21] Ducci, the postman, sent letters pleading for arrears of wages, and D. N. L. only kept the printers working on *The Mask* by paying small sums "on account" from the private allowance that her family sent to her from England.

It was getting very cold on the hill, so Craig found warmer living quarters in a flat in the city, overlooking the river Arno and adjoining the famous Ponte Vecchio—the new address was No. 2 Lung' Arno Acciaioli; but he still kept Il Santuccio going, with an old carpenter coming in to help on sunny days.

During December, he turned all his efforts to producing the first number of *The Mask*, which he hoped to bring out in January of the following year, but he soon found that this would not be possible until he had gathered together sufficient material for the two or three numbers that were to follow, so he was forced to postpone the first issue until March. He also began to realize that there was a great difference between publishing *The Page*, a magazine that consisted of eighty-five per cent decorative illustrations and fifteen per cent irrelevant reading matter and a monthly magazine calling for revolutionary changes in the theatre, complete with up-to-date editorials, letters from correspondents, contemporary book-reviews, etc.[22]

He remembered that his father had, in 1874, written a number of articles on "The Architecture and Costume of Shakespeare's Plays": why not reprint them, illustrated for the first time with drawings that he knew to be in his mother's possession? He had always wanted to pay some kind of homage to his father's memory, and here, he felt, was a grand opportunity. The articles, which were concerned with the accuracy of the historical background to Shakespeare's plays, had originally appeared in *The Architect* while Edward and Ellen were still at their home in Taviton Street. Craig—always opposed to realism and archaeology in the theatre—did not write an introduction to the articles himself, nor was there any reference to the fact that Godwin was his father: instead, "John Semar" just wrote a few words, recalling that Beerbohm Tree had said that in Bancroft's version of *The Merchant of Venice* in 1875, to which Godwin had contributed so much, we had seen "the first production in which the modern spirit of Stage Management asserted itself"—Tree was referring to his own type of realism, but Craig preferred to read "modern" differently! There were twenty articles: the first appeared in numbers 3 and 4 of Volume I of *The Mask*, and the last in Volume VI. His mother lent him his father's original drawings, and sent him a cheque to help keep out the cold.[23]

It was at this time that he started using pseudonyms in a big way to cover his identity as the author of many of the articles and illustrations forming the bulk of each number of the magazine; these disguises also permitted him to have various opinions on the same subject! In *The Page* he had been "Oliver" and "James Bath," "Samuel Drayton," "Edward Arden," and he had used the initials, "S. D." for his first story, entitled "*The Sudden Death of Bobby Bridges and of Mr James Peel.*" The new masks behind which he sheltered were to number close on a hundred, including the various initials used in editorials, etc., but the first, and most important connected with this period was the name "John Semar," the editor of *The Mask*. (The name Semar came from Java, and Craig found it in Mrs Carr's translation of the book on the Javanese shadow plays; it seems that Semar was one of the merry characters well known to Javanese audiences.) Then came "John Balance," and "Allen Carric," "Julius Oliver," "Jan Klassen," and so on; "Adolf Furst" was the Berlin correspondent, "Jan van Holt" wrote from Holland, and others were invented daily. These were characters rather than names—for, having invented a name, he generally made a little note about the personality of its bearer, sometimes even inventing a special signature for him. Once, he cut out a number of little cardboard figures depicting these fabulous beings, and they stood about on his book-shelf to help him remember their different characteristics. At another time, he wrote John Semar's life, and engraved a portrait of him.[24]

These expeditions into the land of fantasy gave him a great deal of pleasure, and acted as a screen between him and the world of reality with its frustrations, jealousies, and expenses. Like Mr Micawber in *David Copperfield*, he knew that something would "turn up"—it was sure to, if only people would wait . . . and "then," as he would say, "we can all share in the fun." When he did not succeed in escaping from reality he would sink into the depths of despair, and would write such lines as: "I love what I am fighting for—the odds are 3 million to one, against me. I shall not give in but I shall certainly die—and soon."[25]

Although Florence is generally associated with blue skies and sunshine, it can be bitterly cold in the winter, when the winds blow in from the Apennines. Craig was not prepared for this and suffered terribly, for he still lived in his white linen clothes, and his flat was in an old house with tiled floors and, as in most Tuscan houses of the time, the only heating came from braziers. Shortage of money made life very dismal, and the only warm place in which he could work was the Café delle Giubbe Rosse, where he would sit and write, draw, or engrave.

Craig wanted to send a few of his etchings to The Society of Twelve, to be exhibited in the New Year at the Obach Galleries in London. This meant finding a copper-plate printer, and he found Signor Luigi Tassini, who produced the most wonderful proofs.

Tassini was a skilled craftsman of the old school, and by his unique handling of the plates, he was able to lend still greater emphasis to the lighting effects that Craig was trying to produce. Greatly encouraged, he began making more etchings, planning to issue them in portfolios similar to his *Isadora Mappe*, published by the Insel Verlag in Germany. He showed some of the prints to his friend, de Marinis, who was very impressed and allowed him to hold an exhibition in one of the rooms of his bookshop. This took place during the first three weeks of January, and at least brought in enough money to pay for food and lodgings for a while.[26]

A little sixteen-page catalogue was printed for these two exhibitions. Ten of the pages were given to a "foreword," in English and Italian, in which Craig again tried to explain the idea behind his etchings, but the explanation was so ambiguous that no one could understand it: he was still frightened lest his idea might be stolen, but he was also anxious that no one should realize that he did not know how to put the idea into practice.

The catalogue opened with the lines: "Of the twenty designs which I show here, fifteen are to be looked at as one of the main divisions of the Art of Revelation . . . they can but give the faintest shadow of my

intentions . . . ," but on page six he went so far as to say that these
fifteen designs "were studies for fifteen separate motions or moods of
movement as translated through an instrument." Then he added: "that
I should give an exact and laboured *description* of this instrument can
be no one's wish."[27] It was not until 1924 that he was able to see this
superb idea move before him in a three-dimensional model controlled
by just such an instrument.

By February 1908 he had managed to prepare the first four issues of
The Mask, and the first number came out in March. Five hundred
copies were printed, and a special "edition de-luxe," limited to sixteen
copies. The magazine, rejected by Foulis of Edinburgh and Maximilian
Schick of Berlin as being too expensive to print, had come out at last
in Florence on hand-made paper, having cost £10 to produce! Except
for a break, brought about by World War I, its publication was to
continue until 1929.[28]

The Mask proved in many ways to be one of Craig's most successful
and useful enterprises. It forced him to keep to a regular schedule of
work, it forced him to put his ideas down in black and white and,
because the magazine was limited in size, it also forced him to be as
concise as was possible when trying to give form to these new ideas.

As soon as *The Mask* was published it was sent to people all over the
world, and, being beautifully printed, was generally greeted with
respect at first sight. A copy reached Constantin Stanislavsky in
Moscow at a most critical moment in the development of his Moscow
Art Theatre's history; at a time when he, like some other artists, had
begun to see the uselessness of their attempts at realism on the stage,
unless, as he said, it was perhaps a "deeper, more refined and more
psychological realism."[29]

After Isadora and Craig had parted in Nice, she had gone to Moscow,
where Stanislavsky, seeing her for the first time, had become another
of her ardent admirers, and it was she who had first brought Craig's
ideas about the theatre to his notice; she had even given him a copy
of the German edition of *The Art of the Theatre*.

In his book, *My Life in Art*, Stanislavsky tells of his first impressions
of Isadora:

I watched her during her performances and her rehearsals, when
her developing emotion would first change the expression of her

face, and with shining eyes she would pass to the display of what was born in her soul. In remembering all our accidental discussion of art, and comparing what she did to what I was doing, it became clear to me that we were looking for one and the same thing in different branches of art. During our talks about art, Duncan continually mentioned the name of Gordon Craig, whom she considered a genius and one of the greatest men in the contemporary theatre.

"He belongs not only to his country, but to the whole world," she said, "and he must live where his genius will have the best chance to display itself, where working conditions and the general atmosphere will be best fitted to his needs. His place is in your Art Theatre."[30]

It was shortly after this meeting that Stanislavsky received the first number of *The Mask*, with Craig's article on "*The Artists of The Theatre of the Future*," and he then decided that Craig was the man best able to inspire them with new ideas or, as he put it, "give our art a new impetus forward and to pour more yeast into the dough." He persuaded Nemirovich-Danchenko and the rest of the management that it would be a wise move to invite him to Moscow, and so, at the beginning of May, they sent him a telegram asking him if he would be interested in discussing the production of a play.

The telegram arrived at a moment when Craig had just decided to work out the whole of *Hamlet*, as an exercise, on his model stage at Il Santuccio, and he immediately wrote to say that he was interested. Simultaneously, he heard from Magnus in Berlin that Reinhardt wanted him to produce *King Lear*, followed by *The Orestia*, and from Frederick Whelan in London that Beerbohm Tree was interested in an idea that he had put forward—that Craig design a production of *Macbeth*.[31]

Craig revelled in this sort of situation, for he liked to imagine he could act the clever businessman, when in fact it was a role that least suited his talents. He sent telegrams to all, saying that he had "important decisions to make about productions in Germany and Russia," or, "England and Germany," as the case might be, and "what offer were they prepared to make?" Tree was not in any hurry, and wrote saying he was willing to wait until Craig could come over for a discussion. Reinhardt telegraphed an agreement to pay 2,000 marks for the designs for *Lear*—if the sketches arrived by August 15—but Craig was not in a mood to be hurried and let time slip by as he played with the idea; eventually it was too late and the scheme came to nothing.[32]

He also realized that since he had started *The Mask*, it must go on—but who was to organize it if he was in Russia? D. N. L. had no experience as an editor, so he approached Magnus, who jumped at the suggestion, seeing great possibilities in it.

On August 22, Stanislavsky was at Westende les Bains, a small town on the sea-coast below Ostend (it seems that he found the North Sea air good for his health). Magnus, who was at The Hague trying to negotiate yet another production, hurried over to see him, and his subsequent report to Craig was as follows:

> . . . Stanislavsky makes the following proposition: that you come to Moscow October 1 (Russian style)—that is, about the 13th of October, stay there some weeks, speak to him, see the theatre, the work they are doing and have a talk. He says it is impossible to do things by letter as most of the time that brings confusion and mis-understanding, especially as he writes nothing but Russian and he would not have trusted any one to make a translation, so he did not write—He speaks French and German, but does not write it. He would like you (after you have seen the theatre and Moscow and feel you can stay there and work there) to become engaged to the theatre by the year—that is, they play seven months of the year—He feels it would only be in justice to you. He fears that if you came for only one production, the theatre would unconsciously or consciously have gained impressions from your work which they would not efface; and what they would benefit from that one production would be unjust to you if, after you were not there to also draw the benefit. In other words, that your ideas are subject to be taken advantage of, which he decidedly does not want. Besides, he says, if you did one production and you went away and came back again, it would mean starting afresh, as some might have forgotten what they learnt, and only *constant* training can bring forth the results desired. Now if you came and stayed, and found that the theatre had possibilities and the conditions were not too impossible and you could grow to love it, he would be very glad.

You would not have to be there the seven months at a stretch but could go off, of course, occasionally, when your part of the work was done, etc. They would not expect you to do more than about two productions this first season.

... Your trip there will be his *own* expense, and your preliminary stay. I told him you had no money and he would have to send you a thousand marks for the trip beforehand. This he agreed to do.

... It is the best proposition I have yet heard and certainly one which is more dignified than any other, for you deal with first class people.[33]

Stanislavsky was speaking, through Magnus, as one artist to another, and this pleased Craig; so did the thought of possessing 1,000 marks. Another important consideration was that he would not have to stay in Russia all the time, but could return to Florence and continue with his other work. Nemirovich-Danchenko was to settle the final terms.

Craig agreed, and at the same time he bargained with Magnus to buy *The Mask* from him, pay its bills, and take over the job as editor, while he remained the "Artistic Adviser." Craig was hoping for another lump sum, but Magnus said that he had not the necessary finance at hand and proposed coming to Florence with a Mr Holdert, who would be in partnership with him, then they would look into the whole matter and draw up a final agreement.[34]

Life in Florence was becoming increasingly difficult for Craig: apart from his financial troubles, he had become a well-known character, and his tall, handsome figure, with flowing locks and Ben Terry's features, attracted considerable attention, particularly from one or two Englishwomen there. Although admiring women were always a great source of gratification to him, at that critical moment he had no intention of getting involved. With brighter prospects on the horizon he was eager to have Elena and her children with him as soon as possible. Apart from wanting Elena's company, he needed her protection!

By September 22 he had managed to raise enough immediate cash to get to England, where he went first to see Tree at Her Majesty's Theatre. Tree was then fifty-five and Craig was thirty-six. As a young man Tree had known and greatly admired Godwin, with whom he had worked and with whom he had been in partnership in the formation of the Costume Society; he very much wanted to work with Godwin's son, whom he felt sure had inherited his father's as well as his mother's genius for the theatre. Their meeting was a happy one, and he agreed that Craig should take his time and make designs and models for a production of *Macbeth* and bring them over the following year. "Tree and all are being very kind to me," he wrote.[35]

That over, he went down to Elena, whom he hadn't seen for over a year. There, his excitement was intense, for the children were now aged three and four, running about and overjoyed to see him; Elena had spoken of him every day, so he seemed quite familiar to them.

He wrote to Martin telling him about the progress with Tree over *Macbeth*, and ended saying: "My boy at Southminster is a God—I am excited about that more than by 10 Macbeths."[36] As with everything else in his life, the slightest hint made him jump to conclusions, and he saw in this child who, like his mother, had no fear of him, a future assistant and collaborator . . . Coming back to earth, it was agreed that they should all return to Florence together. At last he was beginning to feel established; he had a family, and Elena, the only woman who really understood him. Later he tried to explain this to himself in one of his Day-books:

Again in Italy, with a good woman and two beautiful children. *Mine.* I have given life to many but to these I give love and will give all *my* life. Why these and not the others? why? . . . because of their mother. The story is a long one but some day I will tell it—it will tell of goodness and goodness and again goodness on her part—Elena's part. *That's* a story I shall enjoy to write.[37]

They arrived in Florence at the beginning of September, and no sooner had they found another flat in the Lung' Arno Acciauoli than he started to prepare for his Russian trip. But first of all he wanted Elena to see something special, and he took her to an old and disused open-air theatre in the Via dei Serragli. Built in the classical style in 1818, it was called the Arena Goldoni, and the whitewashed architecture looked beautiful in the sunlight with the blue sky above. He was negotiating the lease and it was here that he would at long last establish

his school—"Wasn't it lovely?" It wasn't his yet, but he called it
"My Theatre," and although at that time weeds grew in every corner
of the auditorium, which was open to the sunlight, and stout young
trees grew from a couple of cracks in the walls, he looked upon it as
though it were some great temple. The rent was 840 lire a year (about
£34) but, with the outlook so rosy he felt that would be easily found.
Elena sat in one of the boxes and he declaimed *Hamlet* to her from the
great covered stage. "What's Hecuba to him, or he to Hecuba, that
he should weep for her"—he loved Hamlet's soliloquy and would
often quote from it. Elena's applause echoed through the empty
theatre and happiness was everywhere.[38]

A few weeks later he was on his way to Moscow, travelling by way
of Berlin in order to make the last arrangements with Magnus regarding the take-over of *The Mask*. He arrived in Moscow, according to
his Day-Book, on October 16 and, luckily, there was no snow, for he
was still not dressed for it. Stanislavsky found him a great fur cloak and
some other heavy garments in the theatre wardrobe, and the warm
welcome he received from all of the actors made up for any discomfort[39]—he had never felt so welcome anywhere in his life. He
was taken to see Maeterlinck's *Blue Bird*, Ibsen's *An Enemy of the People*,
Griboyedov's *Gore ot Uma*, and Chekhov's *Cherry Orchard* and *Uncle
Vanya*, and he recorded that they were "lovely" . . . "masterly" . . .
and "beautifully acted."[40]

He was so excited about his reception that he even wrote to his
sister about it:

I arrived here at 4—manager called at hotel 5—I at theatre at 7 to
11. As 11 struck, 6 huge Russians seized on me and landed me in a
red and gold motor car—I was with them till 6 next morning—
during which small hours I heard and saw 2 specially engaged troupes
of Gypsy Russian singers and dancers who shrieked and wept and
leapt for me—and was transported to 3 different places of entertainment.[41]

The party consisted of Nicolai Tarasov, Nikita Baliev, Ivan Moskvin,
Leopold Sulerzhitsky, and Leonid Leonidov.

As they ate lobsters and drank champagne, he showed them photographs of his Arena Goldoni and told them about Florence. Next day,

when he "came to," he found the scribbles of three of his delighted hosts on the back of one of the photographs:

"You are a splendid man, that I have seen in my life." Nicolai Tarasov.

"And I too." L. Sulerzhitsky.

"You are Alfe et omega." N. Baliev.[42]

He stayed three weeks in Moscow, discussing with Stanislavsky in German, meeting the actors, and making photographs of the theatre; but although he enjoyed it all, he was lonely, and longed to be back in Italy.

He reached Florence on November 28 and entered in his Day-book:

Back in Florence . . . the place is a heaven—The Bridges—Palaces Shadows and Gold—Towers— . . .[43]

He tried to work out an agreement with the Moscow Art Theatre, but found that he was involved in trouble over *The Mask*. Miss Lees was not happy about the take-over, more particularly as Magnus had published a circular telling possible advertisers that the circulation was now ten thousand copies, while she knew it was well under one thousand; in addition Magnus refused to pay the bill that was being presented to him, which included all the expenses incurred by Craig, D. N. L., Ducci, and the Carrs over the last year! Magnus and Craig were once more playing at being smart businessmen, and were not doing it very well; they called in lawyers, but in the end it was agreed that existing contracts should be torn up, and Craig, to the great relief of D. N. L., again became the owner of the magazine.[44]

The agreement for the Arena Goldoni was at last signed, and the great covered stage became Craig's studio-workshop, *The Mask*'s offices, and the joy of his life.

He was experimenting with *Hamlet* when Stanislavsky first approached him, and he therefore decided that this would be the play of his choice for Moscow. He did not believe it was a good stage play, but he had always loved it, and it was a challenge.

Because he was so mentally involved in his one great idea of a new kind of kinetic theatre he thought he would, at least, try out his moving screens in *Hamlet*. This was a grave mistake, since he would be forced to compromise with the changes of scene required by the action of the play—and the screens were never intended for this purpose: they were only intended for abstract movement, but he would not see this.

He was due to return to the Moscow Art Theatre at the beginning of 1909, when he was to take along all his ideas for the play, and the whole production would be discussed; so, for the next three months he worked continuously on sketches of scenes and costumes and made profuse annotations of the play. In February he began to worry about who should play the part of Hamlet; he knew from experience that whoever it was carried the play. He felt that his only chance of success lay in persuading Stanislavsky to play it himself, and on February 13 he wrote a long letter to Maria Lilina, Mrs Stanislavsky, from which I extract these few paragraphs. He is describing Hamlet:

In appearance I see him as a large man with grand huge limbs and a heroic head of hair and large open eyes.

He is no ordinary man; his words and looks and actions are so extraordinary, so superfine, that men whisper (as they have always done) that he is mad. So was Dionysius mad, Christus mad: but they were gods: here, Hamlet is a man who is so full of the intoxication of love that no one can understand him, not his mother nor the critics, to this day. . . . I hope Stanislavsky is going to play Hamlet: he was born for it, and I see him as Hamlet and I hear him too.

I see him almost motionless, standing secure, firm like a snowcapped mountain, at whose base many small figures of mean men and thin women creep or scramble.

Do write to me. I rely on you as my real good friend to translate only what is sensible in this letter and to leave out what is dull.[45]

But Stanislavsky was not to be tempted, and in any case he was producing the play, while giving Craig all the freedom he needed as designer, co-producer, and inspirer of the company.

When Craig returned to Russia, it was to St. Petersburg, where the Moscow Art Theatre Company was then performing. Later, on the way back to Moscow, Craig asked Stanislavsky how they trained the actors in their parts. Stanislavsky replied, "here is the part"—he put an imaginary something in the palm of his right hand—"and here is the actor"—he placed another imaginary object on top of the first, and then, "Pam-pam-pam," he almost shouted, as he brought the clenched fist of his left hand into the palm of the right . . . the actor was being forced into the mould of the part! Craig was rather horrified, for although he did not look on actors as creative artists he had been an actor himself in the past—and after all, was not Stanislavsky an actor himself?[46]

One day Isadora turned up, and there was a rather tragic scene when she sought to rekindle Craig's affection by making him jealous. In the process she drank too much champagne and both Craig and Stanislavsky abandoned her rather than stay on to see her make a fool of herself.[47]

The discussions about the production of *Hamlet* now began in earnest, and they decided to take each character and each scene and analyse them in detail.

Then, to his dismay, Craig found that all that was being said, all his casual replies, were being recorded in note-books by two people— by Ursula Cox, in English and by Michael Lykiardopoulos, in Russian. (Michael was the secretary of the Moscow Art Theatre.) He found himself trying to be clever: when asked to describe the characters in the play, he did so, likening them to bears, toads, snakes, and tortoises! There were quite a number of passages in the play that he thought quite unnecessary, but instead of cutting them, he suggested that they rattle through them in the way that Italian comedians did when confronted with verbose parts, only giving full emphasis to those bits that developed the plot—a kind of tirade or bravura. When asked to show how, he realized that it could only be done with the Italian language, which he could never master. In trying to find a reason for every one of his flights of fancy, he only succeeded in further confusing his listeners; only when his two recorders were not about did he feel at ease and talk normally.[48]

They soon discovered that Craig only liked the characters of Hamlet, his father, Horatio, and the actors—these were "true," all the others were "false."

Far from being daunted by Craig's fantastic imaginings, Stanislavsky saw in them the most wonderful material, not only to be applied to the present production but to all future work in the theatre. Here was a man who was only theatre—who saw the whole of life through a proscenium arch; that which was not of use to the theatre, he did not see. "He is a fine poet and a wonderful artist—a producer of the most refined taste and knowledge," he wrote to Madame Gurevich, the critic and theatrical historian.

Meanwhile, Craig, overjoyed, was writing to Martin:

I have been here three weeks—Rehearsals have begun—in a most *orderly* fashion, and nice through and through owing to the really sweet nature of the manager—"Hamlet" the play—The entire company, taking their lead from the manager, do *everything* I say. It may be a dream, dear old chap, but my God, it's like Heaven after years of Hell. First and foremost, they take time, and nerves are not allowed . . . consideration for every second—every move— every idea—

Again (for it must fade, it can't be real), it may be all a dream. It is nearer those divine Purcell days than anything I have experienced, though I am a *guest* in this case, and receive a nice salary into the bargain.[49]

In July, however, Craig was glad to be back again with Elena and his children in Florence. He had given out so much that he was in a highly nervous condition; back with them, he began to relax. During the heat of the summer months they stayed for a while at Fiesole in the surrounding hills, returning to Florence in the autumn.

In October, a young man named Sam Hume turned up: he had been fascinated by Craig's writings in *The Mask* and had written to ask if he could be a pupil. Like Michael Carr, he had come all the way from California. Sam was a lovable type, except when he lost his temper, and that was generally because he could not understand Italian wines. One night, when he fought the entire gathering in an Italian café, whose numbers seemed multiplied by the many mirrors in which they were reflected, he had to be subdued by some Carabinieri who brought him to his senses by pumping cold water over him. Sam was immediately cured, but mortified by the method:[50] he would rather have been shot down by the sheriff! Craig set him to work making the models for *Hamlet*. Craig worked out his ideas with his screens on his large

model stage, and when he succeeded in getting what he wanted, Sam
was asked to make a model of it.

In December 1909, Craig went to England for a few weeks to see
his mother. He was so engrossed in the idea of his movable screens
that he could think of little else. He had already written a lot to her
about them, and about his experiments with the Moscow Art Theatre,
and she wanted to know more about them, particularly as she was again
playing with the idea of putting on another production with her son.
To encourage him, she ordered a whole set of screens to be made to
his specification, eighteen feet high, and her "Ted" demonstrated, on
a small model, how they could be used; he even planned the whole
of the *Merchant of Venice* for her, a play which she had in mind at the
time. But when he had gone she was persuaded, by some of her
"advisers," that the screens were cumbersome and unmanageable, so
they were put into store and were, later, broken up. This was probably
a good thing, for had he not supervised their movements as well as
the lighting they would indeed have been proved "useless" in the
hands of his enemies, and he was certainly too busy in Russia at the
time to be able to supervise the production.

While he was still in London he went to see Tree, taking some
designs and four models of scenes for *Macbeth*. Tree was immensely
impressed by them and, after Craig had left, he went into the problem
of costs, manœuvreability, and so on. The scene-painter, Joseph
Harker, was called in, and he, seeing a threat to the future of scene-
painting in Craig's three-dimensional scenes "painted with light,"
vigorously attacked them as being unpractical in every way. The
models were eventually confined to his care and some of them got
smashed.[51] This later led to a tragic misunderstanding between Craig
and Tree.

There was, however, one event that did make him very happy during
this visit, and that was meeting W. B. Yeats again. For Yeats, and his
poetic drama, the screens were an answer to a prayer. With a set of
them, in miniature, before him, Yeats felt that he could devise all the
backgrounds to his plays while he was writing them; he would play
with the screens until he found what he was looking for, then write
the play into them. His whole approach showed so much understanding of what Craig was trying to achieve that he gave Yeats a
model stage, complete with screens, and permission to use full-size

replicas at the Abbey Theatre in Dublin, free—so, in the end, Ireland and its poets were able to use his screens successfully and in a practical way, even before the Russians.

By February 1, 1910, Craig was back in Florence. His contract with Moscow had been renewed, and the 500 rubles a month were still rolling in, but what to do with them he just didn't know; he had never had so much regular money, and in those times, especially with the low cost of living in Italy, 500 rubles a month was a large sum of money. By February 28 he was back in Moscow again. Sitting in his magnificent hotel rooms he wrote in his Day-book:

How is economy learnt? I mean thrift . . . money . . . etc. Only by realizing that no one can have all the things they want,
    in fact that one can have only a few of the things one wants
                                and then,
by selecting from these something—two things—at most three—that one wants most of all.
    So—again a platitude—
But strange that until today I have only vaguely realised this.
That is not so clear as I can make it. I want to have enough money when I return to Italy in May, to take Nelly, Teddy and Nellie (Elena), the three who I love best in all the world . . . to the sea near Florence or to the mountains. . . . In order to do this I must live cheaply here . . . in rooms instead of a hotel, dine in not out, etc., etc.; then I shall be able to take back £50 for our holiday . . . perhaps! . . . I realize that my holiday with them is what I most long for. . . . It is I think the birth of thrift in the body of a spendthrift——Hurrah!
        . . . At present I have all the work I can manage.
    I have Hamlet to produce—"The Mask" to write for—Wood-
    blocks to engrave—A book on the way—
Irish and English work to think of and finish, & the problem to solve (of) how to pay my way—Nelly's way—the children's way—Ducci's wages—"The Mask's" way, and those connected with "The Mask"—
    It is easy in one way, for all these ways are my way—and that
    was never so before.
Everyone I have ever been working with, or living with, has

broken the progress by continually imagining that I admitted of any but one way—mine.

Now these who are with me are really with me and for me, and hey presto

in a moment the miracle happens—for I am for them.

It is to Nell that everything is due, for her support has been enormous—Millions of pounds could not give what she gives—nor the wisdom of Socrates—nor the power of Charlemagne—The wealth, wisdom and power of all these is contained in what she is.

She stands as an example of the grandest type of woman. . . . I was in love with her in Hampstead, 1901 and I am in love with her still—Moscow, March 5, 1910.[52]

This visit to Moscow was supposed to be the last, and would undoubtedly be the most strenuous. He was given a special room in the theatre, "with three windows," where an exact scale model of the stage and proscenium had been built by one of the carpenters. The scale was one inch to the foot, and he again reverted to a false proscenium, which gave him similar proportions to those he had used in Hampstead in 1901. He had brought with him the models made by Sam Hume, which were to show various arrangements of screens at specific points in the play, but he had also brought sets of screens, with folds of different widths, with which to demonstrate on the model of the Moscow stage how one scene developed into the next.

To help the actors see themselves within the scene, he made many little coloured cardboard figures of different characters.[53]He was now prepared to go through the whole production with each of the actors separately, then collectively, to explain the ideas he was trying to put over: the final rehearsals would be conducted by Stanislavsky himself. This was in fact the very same managerial arrangement proposed by Reinhardt and rejected by Craig in 1905, but the Russians had first created a feeling of friendship, so now he found the terms easy to accept.

Stanislavsky appointed his faithful friend and fellow worker, Sulerzhitsky (known to all as "Suler"), as Craig's helper in every sphere of the production. Suler was a midget in stature compared with Craig, and their appearance in public always caused amusement, which pleased them both. Suler was an ideal assistant for Craig because he was fearless and had a background full of adventure, rather similar to that of William Terriss. He had spent a period in a lunatic asylum for refusing to do military service, and after this had been sent to Siberia. Later, as Tolstoi's friend, he had undertaken a mission to Canada where he had learned some English, and this, together with German made it possible for him to converse with Craig on almost any subject. His was the sort of character that would obviously appeal to Craig:

A dear man, this Suler [he wrote], a rough diamond—full of intelligence and with natural talent for almost everything. He couldn't draw or paint—wrote a little, I believe—was not a composer of music and had never acted; but he seemed, by instinct, to understand all the essential things about the stage. He had also been a farmer, and he spoke very good English, A rare creature! Yes—and we all loved him. He talked of the actors to me—and probably to them—as a pack of stupids. *"They know nothing and they won't try and learn,"* he said.[54]

The question soon arose as to what the screens should be made of, and Craig's immediate reply was "metal," which produced laughter. They tried wood, and cork, and finally settled for the traditional canvas on wooden frames, similar to those built in London by his mother's scenic contractors. Craig, however, was instinctively right in saying metal, but, as with so many of his ideas, he was way ahead of the times. The manufacture of aluminium sections and sheeting as we know it today was unheard of then.

Having built the screens, the next thing was to move them. . . . Today, with electric dollys, the problem would be easily solved, but at that time it was a question of man-handling. The "imperceptible movements" required by Craig, and which he so easily demonstrated in a model, were almost impossible to carry out on the stage and, gradually, only the simplest manœuvres were attempted. As so often happens, advanced ideas were being bogged down by antiquated methods and the mental approach of timid traditionalists.

Craig's original idea was to have no curtains between acts and scenes; he wanted to develop from one scene to another in a series of continuous visible movements. Properties would be shifted by figures completely enveloped in dark grey garments who would also

I

illuminate the actors at certain moments with small lamps, similar to the Chinese tradition. The descriptions of the scenes written into a play did not concern him; they were *all* just places—

> When producing great drama [he once wrote], I have never been concerned in any attempt to show the spectators an exact view of some historical period in architecture. I always feel that all great plays have an order of architecture of their own an architecture which is more or less Theatrical, unreal as the play.[55]

All he was trying to create was a background to the dramatic action, a place that helped the actor and the action of the play, and above all, helped to create the mood suggested by the poetry of the words.

Because of an unfortunate incident just before the first performance, Craig was forced to agree to use the curtains between the scenes. While the scene-shifters were moving one of the screens, it fell and carried many others with it, and Stanislavsky therefore decided that the theory of continuous movement would have to be shelved in the interests of safety.[56] Craig was bitterly disappointed, but was unable to suggest any way of avoiding such a disaster occurring again. This accident was used by some of his detractors to prove how useless his screens were, as if, in the past, traditional settings had never fallen over accidentally!

Although Craig and Stanislavsky seemed to agree about most things, they argued continuously over the interpretation of the characters. This probably would not have happened with any other play, but Craig had a lot of very biased feelings about *Hamlet*: he saw in the Ghost his own father, Horatio was Martin, Hamlet was himself, and the actors . . . they were his familiars in the theatre, beautiful creatures from the land of his imagination. Ophelia was a mixture of all the foolish girls that he had known! He always became abstruse when anyone tried to pin him down; left to himself, his instinct as an artist generally led him to conclusions that were often startlingly original, but always of the theatre.

Realizing that Stanislavsky was connected with a firm that manufactured special materials containing metallic threads, he conceived an idea for the first Court Scene in which King Claudius and his queen would sit upon their golden throne at the back of the stage, surrounded by golden walls. From the King's shoulders would come an enormous cloak of golden material, which spread out towards the front, covering most of the stage. Through cuts in this enormous cloak appeared the heads and shoulders of the fawning courtiers; facing their King and with their backs to the audience, they were like so many grave stones in a golden graveyard. Down in front, silhouetted against this undulating background, the solitary black figure of Hamlet sat alone, part of a great shadow. This pleased Stanislavsky immensely, and proved to be one of the most memorable scenes in the production.[57]

One night towards the end of this visit, when there were no official recorders about, he started telling Craig about his "system," and Craig was so interested that he recorded it, under the date "March 6, 1910":

Tonight, after dinner, Stanislavsky and I spoke much about the theatre—and acting. He is writing a book upon his system of acting, in which he deals mainly, he says, with how to *"feel effectively."* (He tells me what follows):—"For instance, the aim of the actor is to be able at all times to call up the exact feeling which shall set in motion his brain and body. How? For example" (and Stanislavsky points to the first thirty lines in a play), "all these words are but so many words to me—I am not at all interested in them—what interests me is the men—there are two—I am one. I am entering, looking for him (the second)—I see him—that alone does not make me feel anything, unless I feared not to see him, or am surprised at seeing him—what makes me first feel is the first point at which we shall disagree.

"I run my fingers down the lines and there I have it—on the seventh line I find this feeling, wishes or acts clash with mine.

"First point of feeling.

"I go on in this manner for the rest of the scene, marking the different places where I shall be in disagreement with the others.

"So now I have found twenty different points. At each point the progression of my thought has met resistance—and at these points a fresh feeling will be aroused."

So speaks Stanislavsky. It is interesting—it is a theory of acting, arrived at through practising acting, and therefore demands respectful attention.[58]

By May, Craig was back in his beloved Florence with his family,
and was writing to Martin:

All went well in Moscow—I return in September. "*Hamlet*" November. I think I wrote you about it. But my work when I do it, and
when I see it appals me!! Only when I do *nothing*, then I am content
and see the value of what I am doing! But I expect I'm one of those
who have to do their damndest and let it be raved about as their
best—Those two years in Florence—they were taking me near to
something—dangerous and delicious. I think it was not entirely un-
connected with madness—One must not skip pages in the ancient
book—so I have gone back—yet I had half turned the leaf—had a
glimpse of the next . . .[59]

Craig found the change of climate and the peace and quiet of family
life in Florence rather enervating following so quickly in the wake of
the intense mental and physical activity in Moscow. Reaction set in
and he became quite run down. His doctor ordered him to the mountains where he went with Elena, leaving the children in the care of a
girl in Florence. He had to be well for the return to Russia in
September.

From the village of Faiedo in the Canton Ticino on August 11, he
wrote: "Nell (Elena) and I are seated in the village square and it is
evenfall, and on a cart, in the middle of the square, sit five musicians
who discourse sweeter music that any we have heard for a long
time—the dark line of the mountains at the back—the cool winds, the
trees in the square; all make it as happy as light things can make a
heavy world."[60]

A few days later they discovered the tiny village of Giornico, and
its unique twelfth-century church with an altar on a bridge over the
steps into the crypt. Craig saw it, at once, as a superb setting for
Religious drama. "The most beautiful, the most mystic, most human
theatre I have ever seen."[61] He made drawings of it, again letting his
thoughts turn to Bach's *St. Matthew Passion*—but now all his previous
ideas were replaced by an entirely new conception of the whole work,
and during the next four years he would be slowly working away as
another of his most loved projects—sparked off by the beauty of this
tiny church high in the mountains.[62]

While Craig was in the mountains news came to him that Stanislavsky was seriously ill with typhoid, and that *Hamlet* would have to be postponed. This was a great blow, but in some ways a great relief, for he was still unhappy about his work.

> I want time to study the Theatre [he wrote]. I do not want to waste time producing plays—for that is vanity—expensive—unsatisfying—*comic*. I know something about my art after twenty years study. I want to know more. I want to know enough to be of use to those who can *do* more. I want to leave behind me the seeds of the art—for it does not yet exist, and such seeds are not to be discovered in a moment. This HAMLET production for Russia is wasting my time. I seek to know. I do *not* seek a position or success—and this work in Moscow is old work. I have passed it all—gone on into places where I have really seen *something*—a glimpse of something wonderful. And now I have to return and work at this nothing—this "producing HAMLET."[63]

The delay gave him time to have second thoughts about *Hamlet* and he was glad to be able to give more time to *The Mask*. He also selected his best articles from past numbers, intending to re-issue *The Art of the Theatre* with this additional material. It developed, and became an entirely different book, which Heinemann published as *On the Art of the Theatre*, the first edition coming out on November 26. It was translated into French, Russian, and Japanese, and made his theories known throughout the world. No other book had such an impact on the contemporary theatre—or such far-reaching effects on the theatre of years to come. He also made seventeen more wood-engravings, and he spent a lot of time on further sketches for *Macbeth*.

During January and February he was encouraged to go to Paris by a Mrs Sturges, who led him to believe that there she could find all the money and support he needed for his school, as well as for a French edition of *The Mask*. He took rooms on the top floor of 226 Rue de Rivoli, next to the Hotel Maurice. This apartment had once been done up by a very important dignitary in government circles to accommodate a little lady friend, and the walls were covered with laurel-green silk embroidered with golden wreaths; the walls and ceilings of the bathroom and lavatory were lined with mirrors! This amused him enormously. He moved in and set up his model stage in the silk-covered room, and important people like Jacques Rouché, Antoine, Gabriel Astruc, and Edward Steichen all came to watch his moving screens. He had some stationery printed, using the address for *Le Masque* (for which he believed he would shortly have all the necessary capital), and at the same time, could not resist having visiting cards made for the new editor of the French edition—"Ivan Ireland"!

The artificiality of Paris and its amusements intrigued him for a while, then he grew sick of it all.

It's a smutty place [he wrote to Martin], it's occupied in exciting itself by tales of him or her—How she only loves girls—how he only seduces girls under age—how he only enjoys 'em when he's beating them—and this all seriously spoken of, and lightly—serious—The people who escape are those in Montmartre, and some in Montparnasse.

I was amongst some American women—friends of ID's, who seemed possessed by this sole passion for damning, easily and completely, their acquaintances—

I had three weeks of it—

The celebrated actors—dancers—singers and so forth do not refrain from the habit either—The whole thing revolves round a fallen edifice known by the Egyptians and symbolized by the obelisk on the Thames Embankment—

Not a lusty or virile word did I hear for three weeks in Paris—

All mamby pamby affectation of familiarity with vices too strong to do more than *mention*—ID is in such a circle—ends every evening under the table—

It is called being Pagan—it is in actuality being Parisian—

To conquer a vat of wine is my old idea of what Paganism accomplished but to be conquered by a couple of bottles of Mumm extra sec, is not even Hottentot.[64]

Disillusioned by the blather and by his failure to obtain the promised funds, and once more saddened by Isadora's behaviour in public, he left the great capital at the end of March and returned to Italy. There he found a letter from a poet friend of Stanislavsky, Dr Baltrushaitis, who was staying with his wife and little son on the Italian Riviera at the tiny village of Alassio—where a room and full board cost only five lire a day, children half price! On April 2, Craig, Elena, and the children were on their way to join them. In the peace of this remote seaside village he thought he might be able to work, and Baltrushaitis was nearby when he felt the need for stimulating conversation.

While Craig was in London, Tree had enthused over the designs and models for *Macbeth*, and had sent him a preliminary cheque for £100, but after Harker had implied that Craig's methods were unpracticable Tree had suggested alterations. What had seemed a very harmonious relationship had now become strained—no one ever quite knew why. Perhaps Tree's attitude seemed a bit too casual after the great welcome that he had received from Stanislavsky and the Moscow Art Theatre?—That was probably the trouble, for he wrote to Martin, saying:

> Today I feel free and fresh—because—don't jump—I've decided I cannot go on with Tree a day longer—and shall return him his £100 (when I can scrape it together) and withdraw my work from a vile theatre—
>
> If the theatre had proved even a decent place I would have gone through with it—but it's all squash and flob—so I feel better—[65]

He returned the £100; Tree was very hurt, and suggested that Craig keep it to cover his expenses. Then the whole situation suddenly took a nasty turn when Craig claimed damages after he heard that some of the models had been smashed: the matter was taken to court, but fortunately, common sense and a few real friends managed to prevent it from going any further and developing into a ridiculous display, terminated by a farthing's damages.

In Alassio, Craig now tried to see how he could make some use of the *Macbeth* models and designs. Together with a few more drawings, he thought that he might put together an exhibition; it was finally arranged with the Leicester Gallery, and he started to write notes for the catalogue in which he enjoyed making digs at "a London management."

Then one sunny day a letter came from his old friend, Sir William (then Professor) Rothenstein, telling Craig that some of his friends and admirers in England had formed themselves into a committee—the prime movers being himself, Martin Shaw, and the critic Charles Holliday—in order to arrange a dinner in his honour at the Café Royal. It was to be a tribute to him in recognition of all he had done for the theatre. Many important people, including special members of the press would be on hand. Amongst other members of the committee were Lady Gregory, Max Beerbohm, Laurence Binyon, Roger Fry, Augustus John, Haldane MacFall, Jimmy Pryde, H. G. Wells, and W. B. Yeats.

This demonstration of friendship from London, coming at a time when he was feeling bitter about the Tree affair, rather overpowered him—he was almost embarrassed. Then as he warmed to the idea and talked it over with Elena and Baltrushaitis, the importance of the event grew in his mind until he began to conceive of this simple gesture of friendship as a vast public mandate, calling for his return to England, and, by inference, granting at long last his request for an experimental theatre. In answering a letter from Martin about it he wrote:

> Oh my dear Martin, I didn't think it was in *England* you thought we should meet soon, or that I should be called over like that. . . . I'm struck all of a heap—I feel I want to do something to earn it. . . . It's overpowering . . . the letter came *yesterday*; I've been walking *ever since*.[66]

He visualized the whole ceremonial, picturing himself at the head of the great table with Elena . . . Then he realized that they were not officially married and started imagining all sorts of complicated issues, with the press making embarrassing use of the situation. In the past, he had twice planned a wedding, but something had always come along and prevented it taking place; Elena had become so much a part of his life that he had long forgotten the advisability of legalizing what was, to him, a well-established fact: now he felt he must do something about it at once so as to be safe from scandalmongers. He remembered an intoxicated Isadora the last time he was in Paris. Suspicion began to torment him and he fancied that "the enemy" would intervene bent on ruining the occasion. There was only one person to whom he could confide such fears; he wrote to Martin, asking his aid:

I want our marriage to be celebrated in *June* in England, some village—is it possible without a fuss???—It ought to be, because your kindness in July may kill me . . .

And then a warning about the other imaginary dangers:

. . . I don't want the purpose of this dinner to be changed by any *one* person who might take it into their heads to annex the whole affair. One person in particular is likely to make such an attempt— I.D. You will I'm sure prevent that. . . . I want the name kept out of it entirely. I'm sure I wish it were possible to be otherwise but the last few years have taught me clearly. Therefore, somehow or other you must prevent her from having a ticket.
There is *no one* else whose presence would be distasteful or disastrous. I can say this to no one else on earth, so please make sure about this for me and let me advise you to anticipate every accident. I was in Paris in February—and *six times* I was able to avoid seeing her— and only by a trick was I suddenly brought face to face before seven other people and all Paris is given to understand that we are married—and that etc etc etc—The Mask is supported by ID—that other *impossible things* ditto—"[67]

Martin, as usual, was calm and reassuring, and a few weeks later sent him a copy of the invitation that was being sent to interested supporters. It ran:

June, 1911

Dear Sir (or Madam),
 In 1900 Edward Gordon Craig began to stage operas and plays in a new and significant way. Such productions as Purcell's "Dido and Æneas" and "Masque of Love," Handel's "Acis and Galatea," Ibsen's "Vikings," Laurence Housman's "Bethlehem," and Shakespeare's "Much Ado about Nothing," gave a new direction to the Art of the Theatre.
 In this way, as well as through his writings, Gordon Craig held up an inspiring and dignified vision of the stage, and attempts to recover the canon of theatrical tradition led him to make experiments

in the direction of scenic representation, which have had a vital influence on the Theatre throughout Europe.

It is well known that the theatre in Germany, Austria, and Russia admits its debt to Craig's inspirations: his influence has, indeed, gone deeper than most people are aware of, and much that has been accomplished of late years owes its success to Craig's impulse.

It has been felt among many of those interested in the dignity of the Theatre in England, that it would be a fitting thing that some definite acknowledgement be made to Craig for his unfaltering devotion and high aims through almost insuperable difficulties.

It is, therefore, proposed to give a Dinner in his honour, which will take place on Sunday, the 16th July, in the Café Royal, Regent Street.[68]

On July 5, Craig, Elena, and the children were all in London. Martin and Will Rothenstein assured him that there would be no "scenes" at the dinner, so marriage was conveniently forgotten—much to his relief—for the idea of any official ceremony terrified him. London seemed remarkably quiet and empty. On July 16, the dinner took place, and apart from his mother and Elena there were 180 guests. Many of his old friends were there; Frank Harris was there too, so was Mrs Patrick Campbell, and J. L. Garvin, James Carew, Augustin Duncan, H. W. Nevinson, and Michael Lykiardopoulous from Moscow, who had the pleasure of saying that the Moscow Art Theatre was proud to be "the first European Stage on whose boards Gordon Craig was able to materialize his artistic vision . . . on the completest scale possible."[69]

He was excited at seeing so many of these English friends again: it was exhilarating being their guest of honour; but when it was all over, although the press reported it very fully, he had very little comment to make himself except:

so much has happened since July 16th I have not been able to keep a record of it. The Journals have an account of it, but they do not record the warm and generous welcome from my brother *Artists* nor the still icy reception given me by my brother *Actors* and stage fellows.[70]

Why, he wondered, had he allowed himself to get so worked up about it? As he often said in later years, "They gave me a high tea and then they all went home, feeling that they had done their bit" . . . But Elena had been presented to everyone and accepted as Mrs Gordon Craig, and that, he felt was a bridge crossed.

Part of August was spent at his mother's old farm at Smallhythe in the English countryside that he loved so much, where he was happy to see Elena, the children, and his mother together for the first time. They also paid a visit to Downshire Hill, where Elena was once more reunited with her family: they had not seen her for over ten years, and although Gaetano Meo never forgave Craig for having run off with his daughter, he was thrilled at her home-coming with two little children who could both speak to him fluently in his native tongue, which was more than any of his own children could do!

Craig took a house, No. 7 Smith Square, Westminster, and did a lot of entertaining. Bringing over his large model stage from Paris, he had it erected in a special room there, and demonstrated how his screens worked, hoping that this would awaken interest amongst actors and theatre managers. Among those who came were Nijinsky, Diaghilev, and Kessler—but when Diaghilev started chatting during a demonstration, Craig switched out the lights and refused to go on with the show![71]

On September 7 came the exhibition of his *Macbeth* designs and models at the Leicester Gallery and he sold quite a number of pictures— this enabled him to pay back the £100 loaned to him by his mother so that he could come to England for his "high tea." On November 26, *On the Art of the Theatre* was published. But the dates of both these events were unfavourably timed, for he could not take advantage of the great interest subsequently shown by the press because he was already on his way back to Moscow to be present at the final rehearsals of *Hamlet*, which was due to open on December 28 (Magarshack says December 23).

Craig arrived in Moscow only one week before the curtain went up. For some months Stanislavsky and Sulerzhitsky had been conducting rehearsals, based on all Craig's ideas and instructions. At rehearsals, a director not only guides the actors, but learns as he listens and watches all that goes on before him, making alterations to his general idea accordingly. This, of course, had happened with Stanislavsky, but when Craig saw the changes in the action, the costumes and, above all, in the lighting, he was furious and a row started. It centred around Suler, for of course Stanislavsky had been chiefly preoccupied with the actors. The costumes, Craig said, were badly executed and nothing like he had intended: he called for his designs; Suler said he had not left any; that led to another row, because Craig knew that he *had* left them with Suler—forty or fifty designs, on each of which was pasted a sample of the stuff that was to be used—he could only imagine that they were being withheld because they were lost, or for some petty personal reason. Then the lighting in certain scenes was not what he had asked for: why, when he had especially asked for the "Mouse-trap" scene to be played in semi-darkness, was he given the opposite effect? Just to help the actors find their way about the scene? Non-sense!—what a lot Suler cared for the actors, and so on . . . Craig just had not been there to see the production grow over the last six months, and now it was too late. He told Stanislavsky that he did not want Sulerzhitsky's name to appear on the programme—Suler walked out.

Stanislavsky was in an unenviable position. All the same, he stood by Craig and his ideas, and his methods of achieving them. David Magarshack quotes Stanislavsky's letter to Sulerzhitsky on December 22, part of which reveals Stanislavsky's attitude towards Craig:

> . . . Are you angry with Craig for the change of the lighting? I can't believe it. It is Craig, after all, who is responsible for the scenery and the whole idea of the production. Just as Peter Hansen, the translator of Ibsen, who thinks that Brand is his own play, is ridiculous, so should I have been ridiculous if I had claimed that the screens and the whole idea of the production of Hamlet were mine. There is nothing like success, and the "mousetrap" scene was highly successful yesterday. Besides you did not feel yesterday that Craig was right in deciding to play the scene in darkness and that in it (i.e. in the darkness) is our only hope of saving the performance? And, as a matter of fact, the darkness did conceal all the loose ends wonderfully. The last scene went off so well just because the darkness hid the operatic shoddiness of the costumes.[72]

From his reply the following day, we can also see the faithful Suler's side; he could not be the servant of two masters, and although he had been given the job to safeguard Craig's interests, he obviously owed his allegiance to Stanislavsky:

Craig is a great artist and will always remain so to me. That he is our guest I also know and, I think, I have proved during the two years of my work with him that I can put up with the rudeness, irritability and confusion of this man and, in spite of it all, be fond of him.

That Europe is watching him does not interest me in the least, for that will not alter my attitude to him or to anyone else. He can have any lighting he likes—he has a right to that—and I have nothing against it. I have helped him in the past, and today I shall work on the lighting in the bedroom scene, for there, as well as in the play as a whole, the screens are not everything. You and I and our theatre put a lot of work into it, and if something has to be changed, I will change it, if that is the wish of the chief producer of the play, I mean you. And, generally, so long as Hamlet is not finished, I am ready to carry out Craig's instructions, even if they do not coincide with my own views, so long as you find that Craig is right.[73]

With all his experience of men and the strange ways of the world, Suler had obviously never come across anyone so dedicated to his art as Craig, and he, like so many others before and after, could not stand the tempest that was let loose when anything came between this man and the ideas that he was trying to express through a medium which he loved, and for which he had more insight that most men of his time. Craig's rage was not with Suler personally, but with what he took to be a retrogressive movement in a theatre that should, instead, be advancing. The following day, all would have been forgotten, but Suler was hurt—particularly by Craig's demand that his name should be left off the programme.

All I can say [he wrote] is that after two years of hard work and endless sacrifice for Craig, who would never have completed his production without me, I certainly did not expect it. That's all. But I am not offended. Craig the artist I respect, but Craig the friend no longer exists for me. There can be nothing in common between him and me.[74]

Craig continued to look upon Suler as "a most lovable character," for he never realized what his own rages were like. (When I once gave him an impersonation of himself carried away by fury, he roared with laughter and told me that I exaggerated like a Sicilian actor—but I didn't!)

The first night came, and he recorded it in his diary under the date January 8, 1912, which, of course, was in accordance with the Russian calendar.

> First night of Hamlet
>> overwhelming success, and a fine performance, too, by the actors
>
> At sight of the play scene, audience burst with applause
> At the end of it I was called before the curtain.
> At the end of the play, called again with Stanislavsky and Kachalov, then on turning round, I find the stage packed—band and all—music strikes up and the company applaud me—
> The audience ask "what's on" and come and pull the curtains up and look.
> Stanislavsky and Nemirovich, on behalf of the Direction, are offering me a huge wreath . . . oh Lud!
> Nemirovich-Danchenko speaks—
> "All workers in the field of Art have one great happiness and one advantage over all other men: they realize on earth that brotherhood of which humanity only dreams. No political dispute, no geographical isolation, no racial difference can ever divide those who are joined by one common aspiration—the perfection of their art.
> "The manifestations of every true genius have always a national colouring, but the irresistible force of every genius lies in the fact that its single presence enslaves every nationality.
> "You, Mr Gordon Craig, came to us from England, from Shakespeare's native country, and you brought with you the production of one of the greatest dramatic works in the world—'Hamlet'—a play that for many decades is as dear and familiar to the Russian soul as it is to you Englishmen.

"You come with new methods for our art, and you have put in them all your poetical genius. We bow before you—thank you— and expect from you further work for the perfection of our art."[75]

Back at his hotel he wrote to Martin:

Dear old Martin. "Hamlet" was a success—I can't say anything else— though I would like you to have been here and seen and heard. It's a fine place this, all things on a big scale—[76]

To his sister, he wrote:

. . . I won't say it will equal the touch of "Masque of Love" or "Acis", but it will do its best under the disadvantage of having cost the management over £14,000.

Then follows an amusing sketch of himself jumping through Stanislavsky's hoop![77]

A sketch from Craig's letter to his sister about his production of *Hamlet* in Moscow.

Terence Philip, who represented *The Times* at the Moscow performance, seemed to appreciate a lot of what Craig had tried to put into
the production. He mentioned that:

> Mr Craig has the singular power of carrying the spiritual significance
> of words and dramatic situations beyond the actor to the scene in
> which he moves. By the simplest of means he is able in some
> mysterious way to evoke almost any sensation of time or space, the
> scenes even in themselves suggesting variations of human
> emotion. . . .
> . . . the production is a remarkable triumph for Mr Craig, and it is
> impossible to say how wide an effect such a completely realized
> success of his theories may have on the theatre of Europe . . .[78]

Over the two years during which he had worked intermittently on
the production, he had only received £1,500, plus expenses.

When all was over, Craig saw that he had made many mistakes.
He realized that he should never have attempted to use his screens for
the play at all—it was like trying to play a piece of music on an instrument for which it was not composed. The two scenes in which there
was hardly any evidence of screens were the most successful: the first
Court scene, with its King in a golden cloak under which the whole
Court sheltered, and the Play scene, which was similar, with the
throne at the back of the stage, but this time the courtiers were grouped
round it and facing the audience, while in the foreground the "Playactors" performed with their backs to the audience. Between the
"Playactors" and the Court, Craig had lowered the stage-floor so that
a deep trench was formed, with steps down into it from either side.
Kachalov, who played Hamlet, found it helped him enormously to
be divided from the King and Court in this way.

The arrival of the Players in Act II, Scene 2 dressed in their gay
colours, like so many birds flying in to bring joy to the young prince,
was another success. Craig always loved this scene and had hundreds
of ever changing ideas for it; their arrival always seemed to him like
lovely beings coming in from another world. In Paris, during the
previous year, he and Elena had gone to a music-hall where they had
seen some fine Chinese jugglers dressed in beautifully coloured silks,

who made their entrance, not from the side of the stage in the normal way, but by seeming to fly through the air; they were attached by their pigtails to a taut wire, down which they slid from the circle to the stage, accompanied by a strange sound of whistling, like hundreds of birds. He immediately saw this as the perfect entrance for the Players!—"I must do this in Moscow!" he shouted, as members of the audience stared at him, thinking that he was a bit "fou."[79]

Because of the screens, he had also been forced to compromise with his original ideas for Scene 1 in Act V, the Churchyard. In Florence, he had visualized this as the interior of some mysterious catacombs, dark and low-ceilinged, which grew lighter as the funeral procession arrived with torches, and in the model he had used screens half the height of those used for the rest of the production, and entirely covered by a ceiling. But the change-over from tall to small screens for this one scene would have involved a big delay and made continuity of movement impossible.

The duel scene at the end was to him, most unsatisfactory: once again the screens, accumulated from all the previous scenes, seemed to get in the way and it took a long time to clear the stage; there was also too much light and this showed up the costumes, which he considered to be badly made.

"Craig's *Hamlet*" became part of the repertoire and as the years went by, scenes, lighting, and action underwent various changes; photographs of the final scene that have been reproduced do not even show his own version with which he was so displeased. The only records of this revolutionary production are the vast note-books recording what Craig and Stanislavsky said, Craig's annotated version of the play, hundreds of sketches, and . . . the photographs of all the models and screen arrangements made in Moscow. As for the costumes, only a vague idea can be gained from one or two badly lit photographs of characters (some of which were issued as a set of postcards), and the painted cardboard figures, which were added to and used later in Kessler's superbly printed version of the play issued by the Cranach Press.

The year before, he had said: "This Hamlet production is wasting my time—I seek to know. . . . I want to study the theatre." Now he tackled Stanislavsky about financing his school, pointing out that the Moscow Art Theatre would derive all the benefit from the studies of such a school. But Stanislavsky already had a school of his own in mind, and a "system" to develop; and he must have realized that Craig, who had so little patience, could only teach those who already had some experience and were advanced enough to know how to learn from him.

Stanislavsky asked Craig what his system for teaching actors would be, and he replied:

> I shall teach them to *look* and to *see*. It is only when people *see* the beauty in things that they speak and move beautifully. It is only when they *see* that they understand—Thus, there is a flower—one asks, what is this? The idiot will giggle and gurgle and blurt out "A flower." The wise man will look at it—take it—smell it, possibly— and say in a simple voice "a flower". All his movements and words will have a grace born of understanding what he has seen. Thus the roughest people in the presence of beauty in nature speak and act beautifully.[80]

Here was an approach to art that could be more readily understood by an Eastern than a Western civilization.

Craig was soon to leave Moscow, but before he left he recorded the following significant event:

> This evening I dined with Prince Wolkonsky who was director of all the state theatres in Russia. Lykiardopoulos and P. W.'s nephew were there. Talked much about the theatre and its art—and dancing —Rhythm etc. . . . Wolkonsky spoke with enthusiasm about Dalcrose and his method of teaching the dance. Also of Appia. I said I understood Appia was dead and regretted it very much . . . was told he was alive. Wolkonsky then sent to his hotel for a dozen photographs of Appia's designs.
> They were noble things for the stage—If they are for the stage. For Opera I think.
> Wolkonsky spoke of him as a simple and delightful man. I must see him, for I feel that his work and mine are closely united.[81]

He had already heard about Appia in Berlin and again in Florence, and had seen two or three reproductions of his designs for Wagner's operas. He had written to a friend, Fritz Endel, asking how he could get in touch with Appia, who he thought might write something for *The Mask*, and Endel had replied that he understood Appia was dead. Now he had renewed hopes of meeting him. These two men were poles apart in their approach to the theatre: Craig, a volatile artist, inspired by Bach, saw abstract *Movement* as the theatre's art; Appia, with his architectural approach and mastery of sciagraphy, was inspired by Wagner and the great Swiss tradition of the Festspiel, and wanted to *build* something of lasting beauty as a background to it; but they were kindred spirits and when they did meet, two years later, it was as though two long-parted brothers had been united.

On January 30, Craig left Moscow, he also left Stanislavsky, Lilina, poor Suler, and a young actress with a broken heart, as well as many other good friends. From among them all, Eugene Vakhtangov stood out in Craig's mind as a budding man of genius; he followed his progress in succeeding years with joy, and a certain amount of pride, and mourned his death in 1922.

CHAPTER THIRTEEN

The School and Happiness—War
1912-1917

DURING HIS holiday in Alassio, Craig's thoughts were directed to one main project: the establishment of his school. The more he dwelt upon his experiences in Moscow, the more obvious it became to him that he could never realize any of his ambitions unless he had more time in which to experiment and develop his ideas so that there could be no mechanical difficulties when he next attempted to put them into practice.

His vision of "Scene" still remained undeveloped; there were notes and scribbled sketches but his lack of mechanical knowledge made further progress impossible. Nevertheless, he remained convinced that movement, not words, was the basis of the theatre's art:

> All great Drama moves in Silence—
> Events of the greatest magnitude and
> significance pass in silence . . .
> There were no words wasted in the creation of
> the Universe, neither can words create so much
> as an ant. All Nature is silent when it acts,
> and speech cannot take the place of action.[1]

He therefore developed his screens, incorporating in them the "continuity of movement" theory, as a more manageable alternative to his secret moving cubes.

Because of his upbringing in the traditional theatre, *Hamlet* had sprung to his mind as the subject with which to try out the possibilities of his new type of moving background; but had he not been experimenting with that particular play when Stanislavsky's first telegram arrived it is probable that he would never have chosen it for Moscow, or even attempted to use the screens there at all.

He spoke of his worries to Baltrushaitis—a dear friend, a philosopher and poet who spoke English perfectly, loved Shakespeare, and had a profound admiration for Craig's work. His advice was simple: Craig must sit down and plan his experimental school at once; he must not rest until he had made every effort to get support for it; he must also patent his idea for the screens. This sound advice and the quiet holiday by the sea had the desired effect and within a week Craig had filled a copy-book with a new scheme for the school, making a rough estimate of costs and detailing all the studies that would be undertaken—even the recreation periods were considered as time to be combined with study:

Wind instruments—Bars of long drawn out notes . . . at the same time, the treble wandering—speaking—crying—whispering—un-rhythmical.
These instruments after lunch and dinner—or in evening—an expression of feelings.[2]

He got a local carpenter to make him a new and portable model stage so that he could continue experimenting with his screens—a source of everlasting delight.

The invitation to London had raised his hopes; he had come to believe that it would lead to the establishment of his school. But he had found that no one there was interested in the experiment. Back in Moscow, the production of *Hamlet* had also proved to be a great disappointment to him personally; nevertheless, it had provoked an enormous amount of interest in the European press, which consequently, brought him widespread recognition, and this, he thought, might help him towards his goal. He decided to return to London and form a committee similar to the one that had promoted the "Dinner," and see if the necessary interest and finance could be raised that way. By February he was back with his family and they took a flat over Chick's Restaurant in Long Acre. But the London climate again made him ill. Then he heard from Kessler, who was in Paris and very much wanted to see him. He dashed over, intending to stay only a day or two—but the days extended into months.

Kessler was embarking on a new scheme: he proposed printing a monumental edition of *Hamlet* at his private press in Weimar. The translation into German would be made by Gerhardt Hauptmann, and Kessler wanted Craig to do the illustrations: having seen the prints that Craig had made from the little figures that were used on the models in Florence and Moscow, he thought they would make the most striking decorations when balanced with the right kind of type, which he intended to have specially designed and cut.[3]

Craig, who loved anything to do with typography, was immediately interested; he went a stage further and suggested engraving hundreds of little blocks with horizontal and vertical lines of different densities; with these he would "compose" the various scenes in the same way that the compositor sets type. Within a few days he had made some examples of what he had in mind. Kessler thought the idea brilliant, and that it would prove to be a revolution in typography. He offered to pay Craig £40 a month while he was working on the project. By March 27, 1912, Craig had cut between ten and fifteen new figures and had "composed" fourteen scenes from his movable blocks . . . The School was forgotten for the moment.

Kessler did everything he could to keep Craig's interest centred on the *Hamlet* book. He arranged for Elena and the children and a nurse to join him in Paris and they found a flat overlooking the Chamber of Deputies—they were doing things in a grand style! Kessler also introduced him to the great sculptor Aristide Maillol, and they became friends immediately. Maillol, at that time, lived at Marley le Roi, and here Craig and his little family used to foregather in the sculptor's studio, where they had picnic lunches and talked about art, or, with the sculptor's son, about the paper which he was going to make by hand for Kessler's book.

Everything was proceeding very happily until Kessler introduced Craig to the Countess Grehfühle, who had expressed a desire to meet him. She was a prominent figure in Paris society at the time; her house in the Rue d'Astorg was always filled with people of importance. Its vast salons, into which the sun filtered through two layers of heavy lace curtains, were banked with flowers, ferns and miniature palms; the setting was opulent and typically *fin de siècle*; when she entered, wearing one of her enormous hats, and usually preceded by two footmen . . . it was rather like an overdone theatrical performance.

None the less, she and all her splendour impressed Craig. They sat and talked and he told her of his various ideas, mentioning Bach's *Matthew Passion*, which would be done on an enormous scale. The grandeur of this scheme at once appealed to her and they discussed where such a lavish performance could take place in Paris; she suggested the Pantheon? . . . the Trocadero? . . . the Court Theatre at Versailles? . . . he had only to name the place and she would get it. They spent days looking at possible sites, at last visiting the Grand Palais; its vastness immediately attracted Craig. He now found his own rooms in the Rue de Rivoli too small for his work, so the Countess found him a disused church near by.

In Paris he also met old friends, like van de Velde, Yvette Guilbert and Edward Steichen, and new friends, such as Maillol, Chaliapin, and Rouché. Jacques Rouché, founder of the Théâtres des Arts, was a true admirer of Craig's work and, apart from buying a number of his drawings and etchings, wanted to collaborate with him on a production that would rival *Hamlet*, which he had seen in Moscow. But for the distraction offered by the Countess Grehfühle with her promises of support, this would probably have materialized. Instead, Craig, feeling that his position was safe enough for him to play "hard to get," suggested to Rouché that he turn his theatre into a school for five years, and so prepare enough students to be capable of doing something even better than Moscow: this, of course, only led to yet another story of how impossible Craig was to deal with.

He took on an assistant, one Adalbert Fastlich, a versatile young man from Vienna who could speak English and French and was blessed with a unique sense of humour. He was not in awe of the great Craig and was one of the few people who could joke with him, and, being a realist and very outspoken, soon pointed out that all this talk of producing Bach's *Passion* with the Countess was leading nowhere . . . What had happened about the Grand Palais . . . ? Nothing.

The talks suddenly took a new turn: the millionaire Paris Singer (who was then escorting and financing Isadora Duncan), came in on the scheme. Craig immediately sensed danger. He was aware that Singer was finding Isadora's personality rather overpowering, and

fancied that this was a skilful move on Singer's part to bring him and
Isadora together again. This situation brought Craig to his senses
and with his family he left Paris for London at once.

This time they took a delightful old house on the Chelsea Embankment which had once been an inn called The Good Intent, and was on
the corner of Cheyne Row and opposite Chelsea Old Church. Here,
with Fastlich as his secretary, he tried to bring his ship back on course.

He turned again to establishing his school. With the help of William
Rothenstein, Gilbert Cannan, and St. John Hutchinson, two committees
were formed: an International Committee which represented England,
France, Germany, Russia, Austria-Hungary, Italy, and Japan, and
included an impressive array of distinguished names, and an English
Advisory Committee, of which the chairman was William Rothen-
stein, and most of its members those who had promoted the dinner in
Craig's honour the year before. The executive office was given as
215 King's Road, Chelsea, which, unluckily, most people knew to be
Ellen Terry's home; however, subscriptions were to be addressed to
St. John Hutchinson at 18 Cheyne Row, Craig's own address.

In announcing the "aims of the School," William Rothenstein and
Gilbert Cannan tried to help Craig formulate some of his ideas in
black and white. The result was not very satisfactory—it did not read
well, was most involved, and unlikely to persuade anyone to part with
their money; there were such lines as:

> The School will aim at doing, and discovering the means of doing,
> what is left undone by the Modern Theatre. . . .
> . . . A body of picked men will take charge of the School when it is
> erected, and conduct researches into every aspect of the three
> elements—Sound, Light, and Movement—of which the Art of the
> Theatre is composed.
> . . . The School will, it is hoped, by the thoroughness of Art—with
> its economy of means and directness of purpose—combat and des-
> troy the expediency of commerce, with its vagueness and nullity
> of conception and its looseness in aim . . .[4]

Craig certainly did not compose the last paragraph, and it is doubtful
whether he even knew what was meant. His own words had been more
to the point when he had written:

I want to study the theatre—I do not want to waste time producing plays—for that is vanity—expensive—unsatisfying—*comic*. I know something about my art after twenty years study. I want to know more. I want to know enough to be of use to those who can *do* more. I want to leave behind me the seeds of the art—for it does not yet exist, and such seeds are not to be discovered in a moment.[5]

Attached to the prospectus was a little label which, it was hoped, would be filled in by interested supporters; it read:

I desire to contribute . . . . towards the Preliminary Expenses incurred in organizing this project, and enclose a cheque for the amount herewith.

But no one used it.

It was August and London was empty. The hot, damp atmosphere of the Chelsea Embankment was making him ill again.

He had arranged to have another exhibition at the Leicester Gallery, this time featuring many of his drawings and seven of the models made for the Moscow production of *Hamlet*. As usual, he had written many notes for the catalogue; the first note started:

There are at least twenty different ways of producing *Hamlet*, all of which are fairly bad, for *Hamlet* cannot be produced on the stage . . .

J. M. Dent had agreed to publish a fine quarto volume entitled *Towards a New Theatre*, in which Craig had assembled forty of his best designs, each accompanied by enlightening, witty and sarcastic remarks in much the same vein as those in the catalogue.[6]

He had prepared the October number of *The Mask*, and D. N. L. was seeing it through the press. Since 1910 there had not been much of his writing in the magazine, for he had less time to spare; instead he had made more use of reprints, translations and articles from contemporary writers. He had also simplified the format in order to make editorial work and printing easier. He was still working on Kessler's *Hamlet* in fits and starts, and being paid regularly.

Now he longed to get back to Florence and the Arena Goldoni, and was becoming increasingly impatient with the committee, which had been expected to produce his school as by magic. This frustration aggravated his state of nervous exhaustion, and his doctor advised him to get away from the humidity of London and into the mountains of Switzerland. Baltrushaitis and his wife were staying in Switzerland, near St. Moritz, so Craig and Elena joined them, leaving the children to enjoy the English countryside with their grandmother at Smallhythe.

After three weeks Craig was much better, and he and Elena returned to London where they looked for new offices. Elena found them at No. 7 John Street, Adelphi, which happened to be next to the old drawing offices that Godwin had occupied in 1874; Craig immediately took this to be a good omen.

Elena now assumed a big role in forwarding the whole scheme for establishing the School. She had found the new offices, she had been present at all the useless negotiations in Paris, she had attended all the committee meetings in London. After listening to various people making suggestions such as, "Why not approach so and so," and, "Couldn't we get help from . . ." and seeing clearly that nothing ever resulted from these suggestions she took it upon herself to see them through—and once she decided to do a thing she generally saw it to its conclusion.

With the most extraordinary courage, she started writing to various people that she thought had money or influence and, in many cases, visited them personally. The Irish playwright Lord Dunsany was the first to respond—he sent her a cheque for £100, with a note saying that "Enthusiasm was most nearly divine in man."

She lunched with Herbert Henry Asquith, who was then Prime Minister; he was sorry that he could do nothing himself, but—like so many others—was happy to give introductions, and so it went on. Sir Hall Caine was "much immersed in other interests"; J. M. Barrie found it impossible to help; Sir Edgar Speyer, the banker, was willing to give "moderate help," but added, "If the idea is that I should be one of the principal movers in such a cause, I'm afraid I would have to say No." Lasemby Liberty could only "trust that the venture will prove a great success and may initiate a new era in the world of art." The Flowers at Stratford-on-Avon were well-wishers too, but were only interested in the theatre as a local industry. Only Lord Howard de Walden, a simple and charming man, showed any real interest, and he found

Elena's enthusiasm contagious. He had tea on the office table at John Street and spoke about his love of opera; he was very impressed by Craig's etchings and drawings that he saw there; he wanted to know more; Elena sent him copies of *The Mask* and some of Craig's books—he seemed to be the only Englishman who was interested in the theatre as an art.[7]

Elena finally persuaded him to promise half the finance required by the School if she could find the other half, and he gave her letters of introduction to more rich people whom he thought might be interested, but there was apathy all round, the general opinion being why should anyone want to finance an experimental school *in Italy?* Most people were happy enough with Tree's grand realistic productions, or Granville Barker's "artistic" work; it was good entertainment; why change it?

In November, Craig's exhibition, which had been so successful in London, was added to, and transferred to the City of Manchester Art Gallery. There were public addresses by the Lord Mayor, Samuel Walter Royse; a fine catalogue was published, and great interest shown—but still no financial support was forthcoming.

Craig was getting utterly disheartened; then Elena suggested that perhaps he could start with half the money, hoping to find the rest later. This was, of course, the solution—particularly as the estimate for the School's financial requirements, which had been made in Alassio, was complete guess-work, compiled without any reference to current prices of materials or equipment; also included, were the expenses of publishing *The Mask* as the School's magazine.

On working over his estimate again, he realized that Elena was right; he *could* start the School. Lord Howard de Walden was brave enough to be the sole financier of the project, agreeing to give the school £5,000 to get it going, and £2,500 a year towards running costs for the two following years, while William Gable, the American lawyer and a good friend of Craig's, presented a full-size printing press.

From the depths of despair, Craig suddenly became wildly excited. The sun now seemed to shine upon the approaching year. He would be forty-one on January 16, and in the same month his newest and biggest book, *Towards a New Theatre*, would be published . . . and at last he would also be able to announce the establishment of his school. Then, remembering that his mother's birthday would fall on February

27, he reserved the happy announcement for that date as a gesture to her, when he wrote:

> Whatever I am, or may be, I owe to the inspiring influence of my mother; could anything be more appropriate than that I should join her name with the announcement of the project? . . . in other words I bring it to Her as a birthday offering, fully recognizing that I owe its fulfilment largely to her unwavering and helpful encouragement.

Then followed a passage that ran:

> The School will consist simply of a body of earnest and thorough workers, who, building upon the foundations of the work I have hitherto endeavoured to achieve, will strive, by means of experiences and research, to rediscover and re-create some of those magic and elemental principles of beauty, simplicity, and grace in that art-world from which, at present, they are conspicuously absent.[8]

But where was this "body of earnest and thorough workers" to come from? This, he had never stopped to consider! The announcement in the press brought a number of applications from all over England; most of them were, unluckily, from old stagers and stage-struck young women, but neither of these types was of any use to him. For some months, a young man from Manchester called Ernest Marriott had been helping him in London by remaking some of the models of the Moscow *Hamlet* and doing general secretarial work; he was a very practical, schoolmasterish young fellow who was fascinated by the theatre, and Craig decided that he should be the first of his student-assistants.

So Craig returned to Florence, taking with him Marriott and an accountant friend of his named Meadmore; they were to prepare the Arena Goldoni, while Elena stayed on in London to interview and report upon prospective pupil-teachers, for it had been decided to take on only those enthusiasts who were proficient at some art or craft so that "those who knew could teach those who didn't."

Back in Florence again life seemed perfect; he wrote in his day-book: "The wind drops and the sun comes out and all is calm—April

20th 1913."⁹ Five days later, the sun had gone, and all seemed black as he wrote: "Only I, in all the world, seem to have no heart—It could at least break, if I had one."¹⁰ The day before, on April 19, he had heard from Paris that Isadora's two children, Deirdre and Patrick, of whom he and Paris Singer were the fathers, had both been tragically drowned: "At the end of the Rue Chanveau [where Isadora lived], runs the Seine. The chauffeur set out at 9 o'clock to drive the children and their nurse to Versailles; he failed to take the bend, and dived straight into the Seine."¹¹

Poor Isadora was in agony, but Craig did not join her (she was in Singer's magnificent house); he kept in touch through Count Kessler and sent masses of flowers . . . he could only write. This unhappy woman who was so loving, yet always losing love, had now even lost a reason for living—"I died then," she said.¹²

Ellen, in London, could not understand why her Ted did not rush to the side of one who had borne him a child—perhaps he had never really loved her? She wrote to him, and in his reply to her we catch a glimpse of the extraordinary man that he was: an artist who conjures with the emotions, yet is incapable of coping with them in real life; a man whose whole life was dedicated to his work, who only had time for those who could fit themselves into the very brief moments of leisure when he allowed himself to return from his other world; a man who suffered continually when trying to give birth to his ideas, but who was acutely embarrassed by the sufferings of others. His letter, dated April 28, was written from James Gibbons Tower near Fiesole, where he was then staying:

But Mother dear, where have all the letters gone to that I wrote you. You write April 24th from the Farm as though I had not written to you.
Why should I go to Paris? Did I ask you? Well I soon made up my mind.
> Why should everyone weep?
> and why many things?
> Isadora herself does not weep—and everyone
> writes me she commands the situation—
Did I ask you in a letter whether I might write to her?
> I can't remember asking—

time seems to have altered—
gone quicker or slower
or something.

I am a dull thing at best—for I seem to have a work to do which has a regular beat -- -- -- -- -- --
but there are times when even my dullness
slips its cables—

And I do think one needs to be fairly dull to get a machine started— -- -- -- -- -- --

And so at 8 o'clock each morning I am at work and I end at 8 in evening and a little more work after supper—and this early to work used to be easy to me when I was alone once before in Florence—the time when all those etchings poured out rapidly—they were all done in about 8 exciting weeks—when I was alone—a few people called here or there
but no one near me.

And now a different work has begun—began before this tragedy— and the beat of the machine should not be broken. It had begun --
if it broke———
I don't know what would be.
So thoughts—tears—remembrance
longing to go—longing to fly
longing to break—to dive
—all the longings must be kind and sensible
to me and come and patiently move -- -- -- -- -- --

I have my quiet hours too—at night—the window open—the peace—space—looking like the place we call heaven—all asleep— work done—oceans of something trying to get loose and drown the city and this town—and also journeying through the space to Paris in an instant—to London—to many places and people—

So is it needful to say I wired to her at once? she to me—once twice three times—and I wrote and wrote—
—but travelled swifter than all wires
all letters, in person—or what we
know is US—
it is not needful for me to say anything
you must know that as your son I should
not forget *such*.

What I feel and see I cannot talk about—
even here.

I see many things—

I think I asked you if I should go—actually in person—to Paris—
but soon after I sent the letter (and one had no time to *think before*
sending) I made up my mind not to actually go.

To work!

I was there—that was enough and I know
now that Isadora knew.   Love, Ted[13]

To Martin he wrote:

No words can, or will, say my grief and pity for her. She has sent me
lovely telegrams. All suffering, or what I fancied to be such, is
wiped out; all misunderstandings too. I would not wish a man to
be free from grief . . .[14]

He could always feel more deeply when he was alone; and some
weeks later, when he watched a tiny procession on the hill at San
Domenico, I think little Deirdre was very much in his mind when he
recorded the following incident:

. . . I watched the approach of the banners, priests, and others—
then a hundred or two hundred children—little girls going to some
celebration—in white veils and little white dresses—and holding
candles.

Perhaps confirmation. Anyhow—of all these girls only one had
her candle alight—

And she walked on and on and turned her hand this way and that
to protect the flame. Her face showed anxiety—a small, pretty face.
She got to the Church with the flame still burning clearly.

Blessed little girl—I love you, and your dear little anxious face—
and your determination.

It is late—you're asleep now—Sleep well. As you passed me I
blessed you and prayed you would keep the flame of your life
burning . . .[15]

He plunged back into his work with unusual vigour. With the

School occupying the Arena Goldoni, new premises had to be arranged for *The Mask*; they found these on the opposite side of the road at 108 Via dei Serragli, but the actual printing would be done in a large, ground-floor room next to the Arena.

Although Craig had been working on projects for a school since 1904 he had never really settled down to decide how the "staff" should be composed—having taken it for granted that he personally would have time to do everything! There would, of course, be a special place kept for Martin later, if he could be persuaded to leave his beloved English lanes. Meantime, it seemed that the only sensible thing to do was to carry on with his own studies, helped by his new assistants, who, if they had any intelligence, would learn while they were helping.

It should have been called a workshop—not a school—for that is what it turned out to be. However, since it was called a school there would have to be some rules; these must be printed . . . suspicion crept in again: perhaps one of these assistants might steal the ideas and hand them over to the "enemy" . . .! He naïvely believed he could prevent such a thing happening by insisting that they each sign a statement saying: "I have read these rules, and accept them willingly, and will abide by them loyally." Amongst the rules appeared such paragraphs as:

. . . It is understood that every member of the School undertakes not to join any other school of a similar nature, no matter when or for what reason he should leave this one.

No member of the School, if he leaves it at any time, will be allowed to make use of the name of the School, or that of its Director, professionally. . . . No member of the School is to write to anyone outside the School news concerning it, or express his or her "opinion" of the work being done, or of other members.

"Opinions" are wanted neither inside nor outside the School.

Discretion, silence, and attention to work are expected.

When outside the School, rather than talk of its work, methods, personalities and results, the student should wear a mask of ignorance. . . .

"I do not know" is the one reply to make to the inquisitive, and for relations the best answer is, "When results are to be seen you shall be the first to see them."

No member of the School may write or convey any communication whatever to any Journal or Journalist without written permission from the Director.

Any student receiving any communication whatever, written, or otherwise, from persons connected with any Theatre, Institution or Journal—managers, actors, teachers, tradesmen, artists, journalists or other press men—in fact, from any person or persons outside the School, in which a proposal or suggestion is made that he should supply news of the School or its affairs, projects or experiments, or divulge any ideas or designs of the School, or its Director's methods and programme (or any part thereof), for any purpose or motive whatever, is expected to inform the Director without a moment's delay.

Whether the student be urged from high or low motives to give information, he is expected to refuse to comply . . .[16]

What was it that Craig wanted to study? First and foremost came MOVEMENT: "The movements of the Elements and Man." To help with this, he even thought to make use of films, because he had seen motion pictures showing the growth of plants and the formation of clouds which he had thought most beautiful. Connected with movement would be DANCE—ceremonials—posture, etc. Connected with dance would be MIME. Next on his list came LIGHT—the lighting of static objects with moving light such as reflections from moving waters, projected colours, and so on; then the effect of light on moving objects, as when figures emerge from shadows, exist briefly in the light, and disappear again into the darkness.

Connected with the above would be experimental work with his SCREENS. The use of gauzes, scene-painting, the study of optical mixtures as demonstrated by Seurat in order to get greater depth of colour and three-dimensional effects. Then there would be experiments with MARIONETTES of all kinds and sizes, in his ever-lasting quest for animated figures which could be controlled by an artist; connected with this, there would also be experiments with MASKS. All of which meant that the past must be studied too, for he had written, "Never copy the old but *never forget the old*—for there is always some good to be found in it." He considered therefore that it was most essential to establish a library and a museum in which would be preserved everything that they could find relating to the theatre's past history.[17]

K

It soon became evident that he would need a number of very good wood-carvers to make the necessary models and carve the marionettes, apart from carpenters to make the screens, build the shelves and cases for the museum, library, and so on. This problem was easily solved for Florence was full of craftsmen. The secretarial work connected with the school now developed to such proportions that it was impossible for D. N. L. to cope with it as well as looking after *The Mask*, so he engaged a young Englishwoman called Anna as his "private secretary."

Soon the selected pupils-*cum*-assistants began to arrive. One of the first was a brilliant man with a cockney sense of humour, an electrical engineer named Leslie Brown; he was also a capable photographer. His chief work was the building of special projectors and lighting equipment that Craig had sketched for the three large model stages.

Then there was Leigh Henry; he was a musician, not an inspired man like Martin Shaw, but capable of producing all the "effects" that Craig required, including the handling of many instruments from the East that Craig had bought. He could also teach the others about SOUND, one of the subjects that greatly interested Craig, who hoped to produce man-made sounds representing the sounds in nature, and even in those early days, thought of supplying them to the cinema.

There was Geoffrey Nelson, a competent young artist who was also capable of making plans and elevations, and was very useful when drawings of models or marionettes were required for the carpenters and carvers to work from.

Then came Richard Dennys; he had intended to become a doctor, but gave up the idea for love of the theatre. He and Marriott were the two most serious students—bent on learning everything. Dennys was a dreamer, Marriott was very practical; both wanted, eventually, to become producers, or what Craig called "Stage Directors."

There were three others, Clugson, Perkins, and Jones, but they have left no lasting impression: one of them, on realizing that the Arena Goldoni was an open-air theatre and not a "proper school" and that there were no "proper" masters, returned to England on the next train.

Lastly, there was Nino Meo, Elena's brother, the only one who spoke quite good Italian. He had a fine singing voice and unquenchable good spirits, and became Craig's personal assistant, living with him in a house with a tower in the Costa San Georgio overlooking Florence.

Only Nino could master the art of mime; he also had a natural bent for improvisation—which probably stemmed from the fact that his father was Italian.

The School had only been operating for a month when, one day, Craig came upon an excited crowd gathered round "something" near his house. He asked what they were looking at, and was told it was "un stetch" that had belonged to an "Inglese." The "stetch" proved to be an old stage-coach in black and yellow that was being offered for sale: the price—a few hundred lire! It was bought for the School, and four black horses were hired at week-ends so that they could all travel into the hills and valleys and out among the vineyards of Tuscany. This means of transport enabled them to get to festas in far-off villages and witness travelling actors performing in the open air, puppet-shows, religious processions, and travelling companies of acrobats. Wherever they went, the Tuscans were happy to receive them—one of the attractions being that the young Italian who blew the old coach-horn, knowing nothing about the old English traditional tunes, used to sound various Italian cavalry charges that delighted the old veterans, some of whom had served with Garibaldi.[18]

During one of these trips the coachman took them to San Gimignano; Craig sent a post-card to Martin with the words, "This makes my dream come true"—for there he saw the great clusters of mediaeval towers looking like the source of inspiration for his "Scene"! From that day he continually returned to this superb town where he liked to watch the effect of light on the towers at dawn and at sunset, when the stone changed from palest blue to yellow, to pink and then red, casting enormous shadows across the city.

They soon began to fill the School museum, and luck put them on the scent of one of the finest collections of eighteenth-century Javanese shadow-puppets, stored in the attic of an ancient palace on the Grand Canal in Venice. Marriott had also found some Burmese puppets at a sale in London. Florence, in those days, had some of the finest bookshops in Italy, and it was not long before the library was well stocked with books on perspective and records of the princely splendours of the Baroque and Rococo periods—at that time such treasures cost only a few shillings apiece.

There were four or five beautiful old theatres in the city: one was an opera house, one had become a music-hall, another a puppet theatre; there was also a dialect theatre where a good deal of improvisation was still practised—which gave all of them an opportunity to study a fast-dying art.

An experimental marionette, eight feet high, was made by the carvers, and attempts were made at manipulating it. Typical of the Italian craftsmen, on the day it was finished they hurriedly rigged it, suspending it from a platform twenty feet up and, as Craig arrived, the giant figure bowed, and with slow gestures, addressed him in Italian, wishing him good luck in all his enterprises.

Craig was happy at last, and his assistants seemed happy too. In such a city, with such a climate and at such a period in the world's history no student of the theatre should have been otherwise.

There was one subject that was never mentioned in the School—his vision of a moving "Scene." He had given the public a glimpse of its conception in his etchings made six years earlier, at the most inspired period of his life; now, he dared not take the risk of anyone shaking his belief in its realization, so he had to believe in it secretly, fearful that by any further intimation he might disclose too much. He cherished his dream of "Scene" above all else; did he not conclude his first writing on the subject with the words—"and may my love, beginning, have no end"?

With his school well established, he decided that he must celebrate the victory and publicize it. This he did by printing a special eighty-one-page brochure entitled *A Living Theatre*, containing articles about Florence, the Arena Goldoni, the school, the stage-coach, and *The Mask*, and including "Tributes to Gordon Craig" from all over the world.

He had the first copy of the first edition bound, and in it he wrote: "To Elena, who brought me my School in her hands"; this he presented to her. Elena was satisfied; she had been instrumental in getting for him the one thing that would make him really happy, and which, she hoped, would lead to the fruition of all his fondest ideas.[19]

By the end of the year, arrangements were made to annex the disused church next to the Arena as more space was needed that would provide some protection from the elements; an opening was made through to it, and at the beginning of 1914, Craig set the craftsmen to work building a great model for Bach's *St. Matthew Passion*, the project which he had been thinking about since 1900. He had recently wandered into many churches in and around Florence, staying on to listen to the services and watch the ceremonial. One evening he had sat quietly listening to Benediction in an old monastery at Fiesole; as the last candle was put out he was overwhelmed by the emotions that the service had evoked, and he walked for hours thinking how wonderful it would be to make his rendering of Bach's *Passion* as powerfully moving.[20]

In Zürich the biggest exhibition of Theatre Arts ever held in Euope was being organized and Craig was invited. His was the only English work represented, but it filled a whole room. In the next room was the work of Adolphe Appia. The exhibition opened on February 5, and eight days later these two artists met.

For Craig this was a great event; he wrote of Appia in his day-book, "he is a fine creature," and pages followed, describing their conversations. The meeting took place in a restaurant, where they were introduced by Mr Lamprecht. They embraced like long-lost brothers and, within minutes, were making drawings on the table-cloth to explain things to each other.[21]

Appia, who was Swiss, but distantly descended from Italian stock, was ten years older than Craig. Although he had published *Die Musik und die Inszenierung* in an obscure German translation in 1899, Craig had to admit that he had never seen it; (in any case, he found it very difficult to read anything theoretical in German or French). After seeing Appia's work, he no longer felt alone—here, at last, was a fellow artist travelling much the same road, and a friendship developed that was only surpassed by his love for his oldest friend and inspirer, Martin Shaw.

Craig wrote to Elena at St. Marmette on Lake Lugano, where she had taken the children after they had all seen the exhibition:

I get such good, true postcards from Appia. He is such a source of strong belief to me, that a postcard is as good as thirty visits from most people.

It has been a lucky day when we met, for indeed, in feeling, no two brothers could be nearer—

"To your delicious treasures, my smiles, and to their mother, equally, my hommage," he writes today. . . . Send him a picture of us and them. . . . Let them put their names—we'll leave ours out. Send a piece of paper to say "from EGC's babies to EGC's brother"— He'll love that, for he is so great in heart. God bless my treasures and their mother.[22]

Craig was staying at the Baur au Lac, the most expensive hotel in Zürich. There he met J. D. Rockefeller's daughter, Mrs McCormick, who, with all her wealth and a lovely little daughter, seemed so very sad. She found Craig fascinating to talk to, and was very interested in his work. She bought a number of his pictures and etchings, and asked him to keep in touch.

In May, Elena took the children back to England, where she was organizing an exhibition of Craig's work at 7 John Street, from which she hoped to raise more funds for the School. She had now succeeded in getting Godwin's old rooms at No. 6 and had turned them into a comfortable flat, from the back rooms of which one could look into the merry gatherings of the Savage Club.

In Florence, the Bach *Passion* model was finished, and Craig spent hours every day experimenting with the lighting.

On June 28, in not so distant Sarajevo, an archduke was murdered. Trouble was in the air . . . the newspapers began to fill with alarming news.

On August 4, Elena and the children, listening from the top-floor windows in John Street, Adelphi, could hear the murmuring of a vast crowd in Trafalgar Square growing into distant thunder; then it died down—someone was speaking. Then a terrifying shout went up; it grew nearer and nearer as a furious, howling mob stormed up the Strand, smashing any shop-front which seemed to bear a German name. England had declared war on Germany. Elena was in tears as she prayed. The children kept her company, wondering why she was so sad in the midst of so much excitement.

On August 5, the School closed. It was decided that *The Mask* had better hold up publication for at least six months . . .

The student-teachers, by then Craig's friends, had all left, and it would not be long before he heard that Ernest Marriott, Richard

Dennys, and Nino Meo had all been killed in action or had "died of wounds."[23]

Dazed by what was taking place in the world around him, Craig tried to work at this and that—at anything—but it was useless. The School had run out of funds and letters had been written to Lord Howard de Walden, but no reply came, for he had been caught up in the web of things military and political; his secretary, a certain Bellingham, had never favoured the School project, so it was conveniently forgotten under the stress of "more important" affairs. Then a letter arrived from Egypt:

Dear Craig, I am very sorry that I have not answered you before but we have been kept pretty hard at work preparing ourselves for the invasion of this country—which may, or may not take place. . . . I have sent to Bellingham to ask him to send you a cheque; if one can be spared from the very pressing needs in England. I have no money myself, being now in a position where little is needed.

I am afraid that all the arts must go short for a while now, as there is one long-neglected art to absorb everyone's energies.

I have no doubt all the others will flourish exceedingly after the war, when people's heads are clearer, and they appreciate life because they have been within reasonable distance of losing it.

I don't know whether you are still endeavouring to carry on the school during the frenzy, but I am afraid it will be a difficult business.

I will endeavour to do what I can to help you, but Heaven knows how destitute we shall be if this little trouble continues for some years.

Yours sincerely
H de W[24]

Craig felt that Howard de Walden was allowing the entire School project—the result of years of planning—to be thrown away for want of a few hundred pounds to keep it ticking over for a short while until the war was over. What were a few hundred pounds when the papers said that the war effort was costing one million pounds daily? He just could not understand. In a letter to Elena, one sees his innermost feelings on the subject:

> I never dreamed that a little war could add so to the numerous disturbances that one's work already *had* before it begun—and then later I realized that it *could* actually add to them—and then I determined it should not add to them—and it *takes time to carry that out.*
>
> For friends and foes alike bob around me (forgetful of one's own Theatre war), and do all they can by "kindness" and "cruelty" to dish all that one is slowly determined to do—dam it.
>
> I am amazed at *this*
>
> I think little else would amaze me—because people don't know what one is, and does, as a rule—but when they DO see, and *KNOW* that one is fighting for a cause that one will never relinquish—and when they do *know* that one is GOOD on this score, *then* it is that I am amazed, as I said, to think that for *this* itself and for *this*, in one, they will not get rid of all their *little*ness, and enlarge to the *larger* for the sake of the largest—
>
> YOU DO!
& God bless you[25]

Italy was not, at that time, involved in the war, and the English colony in Florence was basking in the sunshine, confident that it would all be over shortly. Craig began to meet this coterie and to go to some of their parties. He was introduced to "the people that matter"—and concluded that they did not matter at all.

However, he discovered amongst them one young woman in whose vivacious company he could forget the troubles of the world outside. She was an entirely new experience—"a hungry, savage young sensualist"—and he was fascinated; so much so that he began to fill a special note-book with records of their meetings, identifying her as KKK; at the same time, his Day-book contained more and more passages about women and their shortcomings!

He tried to design more Black Figures for *Hamlet*, then wondered what had happened to Kessler . . . Instead, he made a Black Figure of KKK, which he named "Beauty," and a companion figure called "The Beast."

To cut down expenses he tried living in the Arena, but it was damp and he became ill. He moved from one flat to another: even £3. 10s. a month for two rooms seemed far too costly.

His letters to Elena were full of news and projects. He wrote that he was "reading about the American Theatre" because he thought he might go to the United States; that he was "in correspondence with John Cournos of *The New York Times*"; that he "received many letters from Percy MacKaye." He also told her that Salvini had been to see him "several times"; that Professor Melville Anderson, an American, was a "lovely person"; that the Tesleffs were "the only nice people left in Florence"; that society in Florence was "rotten"—Florence was a village—he was going elsewhere, "perhaps to Samoa"; that he was preparing many new Black Figures "for an exhibition in London."[26]

On KKK, he only commented that she was "becoming a nuisance." Then he began to wonder if she was a beautiful spy, and became suspicious about letters addressed to her through *The Mask* offices. Shortly afterwards she turned up in London and pestered Elena with her company.

Soon 1915 came along. On his birthday he made the bitter comment:

A few days ago the terrible earthquake at Avezzano near Rome. Help is being sent to save life . . . at the same time help, to kill, is being sent in the other direction.[27]

In February, when his exhibition opened at the Dowdeswell Galleries in Bond Street, he expressed some of his feelings about civilization with a new Black Figure: this was a Punch-like puppet sitting on its haunches and thumbing its nose, and was called "Kultur, Culture, Cultura et Cie." There was also "Beauty and the Beast"—*The Westminster Gazette* remarked: "he is a beauty of a beast and she is rather a beast of a beauty." Twenty-four pounds from the proceeds of sales went to H.R.H. the Prince of Wales' National Relief Fund; the rest went to Dowdeswell's and the H. B. Irving Memorial Fund.

By May, Italy was in the war, and the censorship of letters between Italy and England made it very difficult for Craig to write to Elena in his usual outspoken way. All the same, he found it rather amusing referring to people under different names: for example, there was an agent called Peacock, who at that time was going to do "great things" for him; he appears in the correspondence as "Mr Dove," "Mr Pigeon," or "The Bird." This little game continued for the rest of his life, so that a book of reference is required by any student who wants to know the identity of "The Snake," "The Sponge," "Touch-not-yet-Cat," "Cow Eyes," "215," "ABC," "The Guinea Pig," "Moke," "Dead Pa," and hundreds more.

Florence and all its past associations no longer meant anything to him—it had become "a village full of petty intriguing foreigners." It was also dreadfully hot, so he went to a cheap little hotel at Marina di Pisa, by the sea—and found that he was missing Elena and the children. He made friends with Dante, a small boy who was the son of a local boat-builder, and spent hours with this boy and his family, enjoying the tranquillity of a simple home full of loving people.

One day, at near-by Livorno (Leghorn, to the English), he met the British Consul, Montgomery Carmichael, and the two men soon became fast friends; this new friendship helped him through the succeeding years. Carmichael told Craig that he could never hope for anything to happen if he remained in Florence, and suggested that he move to the capital—Rome: "Get to know people like the Ambassador, Sir Rennell Rodd—people that matter."[28]

Thinking there might be some sense in this, Craig wrote to Mrs McCormick, telling her that he was going to try to raise enough finance in Rome to start his school again—probably in the capital itself. By selling or pawning various items of school equipment, he put together enough money to travel south; then, just before he left, he received a letter of encouragement from Mrs McCormick, and a large cheque for a complete collection of his Black Figure prints, which this kind woman had just decided to buy.

Towards the end of November he arrived in Rome. He told himself that he would try not to be so difficult: to Elena he wrote, "My prime fault, I think, is a delight in antagonizing and not letting people down easily."[29] He *would* try to see "everyone that mattered." In the bar of the Hotel de Russe the first person he bumped into was Maurice Magnus.

Maurice, eager to "do something in the great struggle," had tried to join the Red Cross in Italy, France, Russia, and England, but no one seemed to want him because of his American passport, so, with a brave heart, he had joined the famous French Foreign Legion; this proved to be full of Germans, and as foul a hell as it was ever made out to be. He had deserted, and with great difficulty had made his way from Algiers, through France, into Italy, and had only just arrived in Rome.³⁰ He had no money but he knew everyone, and was just studying the social columns of the Rome newspapers when, to his delight, Craig walked in.

Magnus's first remark was, "My dear Craig, you can't live in a hotel—that's not the right background for you." Within a few days he had persuaded Prince Wolkonsky to lend Craig his vast studio flat in the Palazzo Lazzaroni in the Via dei Lucchesi. He had also had visiting-cards printed for him and got him an introduction to the King of Italy's tailor—to Magnus, the cards and the tailor were very important.³¹

Although Craig had always been a bit apprehensive of what "M.M." might do next, he still admired his ability to get things moving—even if these efforts did not always lead in the right direction. He decided that M.M. would be as good as any other agent and promised him fifty per cent commission on any deal he completed in relation to his work.

Within a month Craig had met and made friends with the very influential Mrs Strong of "The British School," and Mr Richardson of the American Embassy; he had also renewed his acquaintance with Prince Wolkonsky, Diaghilev, and Geoffrey Scott. These were all impressive names for M.M. to play with, but even better ones were in store, for Mrs Strong arranged special "occasions" so that Craig could meet Mr and Mrs Page, the American Ambassador, the Duke of Sutherland, the Contessa Lovatelli, Princess Bassiano, and many, many others. The Rennell Rodds were also most hospitable. Craig soon felt a very different person; this was grand company and could lead to grand things, he thought.³²

He next moved to Studio 18, 33 Via Margutta, near the Piazza del Popolo; this was the fashionable artists' quarter and was full of beautiful doe-eyed models. The studio was enormous, and he draped it with curtains. He sent to Florence for his favourite model stage (known as Model A), and all his screens, lights, masks, and marionettes. D. N. L. came down to help him furnish the place. He now had a studio that was quite unique, and Roman Society came to see him and the beautiful things that he did with coloured light and moving screens. On May 12, 1917, he wrote to Elena:

I sometimes don't *quite* know if it's dead I am, already, or alive . . .
they *do* nothing.
Have danced and still dancing to the old tune the cow died of . . .
the point is am I the cow . . . or are they?
I shall not stop . . . perhaps though I shall dance *better* . . . and that
may bring down the house—This week I have entertained 2 Princesses, 1 Prince, 1 Ambassador, 1 Ambassadoress and suite, 1 Legate
to the Pope, 3 Countesses, 1 Marquis, 8 Artists, 6 ordinaries, 1
Count—and a gentleman.

The Fare—"Teatrino simplice" [his model Theatre]. They will
do something to make honour to art and English art—but What
and when?
8 other appointments next 4 days settled—Chelsea is nothing to
it—and all single handed except for stray help here and there.
Thought you would like to know—and see my handwriting—it's
not shaky is it? Lord and Lady Gerald Wellesley just left. They
were most sympatico—and *I* flattered—but not to death. . . .
From Gordon Craig to Mrs Nellie Gordon Craig
& God bless her[33]

. . . but he did not tell her that Anna, his one-time secretary, had given
birth to a child and that he was the father.

Of the people in Rome only one made any particular impression
on him, the Contessa Piccolomini. She had "a pair of eyes indescribably
beautiful in shape—nose—chin—ears—hair beautiful—but with a
manner also beautiful." Once, when they were dining together in an
open-air restaurant on one of the hills of Rome, storm clouds
approached; they did not move; she just took off her hat and covered
it with a table napkin: "The drops began to come down on us, and
on her hair—and she went on talking of life—and the storm passed—
that's what is rather wonderful."[34] He felt that for the first time he
had met a beautiful woman who was also great and understanding.
This was no love affair. She was one of the few women to whom he
could talk about his loves and his failures and his hopes, and she could
advise him sympathetically.

Meantime, back in Florence things had gone from bad to worse
because there was so little money to spare. At Craig's request, D. N. L.
had asked the proprietors of the Arena Goldoni if, under the

circumstances, they would release him from his contract. They were kind enough to agree, saying that everything could be left until a new tenant was found. As it was very unlikely that anyone would want an open-air theatre in war-time, D. N. L. thought they would certainly be safe for the rest of the war, but the authorities suddenly discovered that it was not in use and requisitioned it for military purposes. Craig tried in vain to have this "take-over" stopped in view of the "valuable work of years that would be destroyed"; even Sir Rennell Rodd did his best to help. D. N. L., meanwhile, took the initiative and decided to clear the premises. Most of the museum and library had already gone to Rome, but the great Bach *Passion* model and a lot of equipment were still in the adjoining church. With the assistance of one of the old carvers who had helped to make it, the model was taken to pieces and, bit by bit, carried to a near-by frame-maker who let them have storage space behind his shop; everything else was piled into *The Mask* offices, until there was hardly space in which to move. The troops took over the Arena, but all the school equipment was safe. Craig came up from Rome to inspect the remains; D. N. L. had done a truly marvellous job.[35]

Then came more startling news: D. N. L. announced that she was expecting a child by him. As usual when confronted with such a situation, he felt quite lost, for he had been incapable of coping with emotional situations all his life. Without D. N. L.'s help *The Mask* could not have existed—for the last nine years she had dedicated her life to him and his work; she had even helped to finance *The Mask* during one or two difficult times. Now he would dearly like to help *her* but he was not in a position to do so—he had just written to Elena begging her to come over with the children, telling her of a wonderful scheme involving the use of marionettes that he wanted them all to work on, and it was all he could do to find enough money for their fares.

D. N. L. gave birth to a little boy on September 21 in Pisa; he was called David—or Davidino while still a child.[36] Later, he was to become an eminent photographer.

During his stay at Marina di Pisa, Craig had started to write some puppet plays, intending them for the amusement of his two children, whom he missed; but before long, characters resembling Bellingham,

D. H. Lawrence, Magnus, KKK, and various members of Florentine society and Roman aristocracy were gradually worked into a giant pattern where they rubbed shoulders with gods and goddesses from Greek and Roman mythology, and it soon became evident that these plays were really for adult consumption! He enjoyed writing them; the biting sarcasm with which they were freely laced helped him to get a good deal of rancour out of his system. He invented a lovable but vulgar character called "Cocki"—short for cockatrice—who figured in most of them. There were so many of these plays that eventually they filled three box-files; collectively, they were called *The Drama for Fools*, all written by "Tom Fool"—his latest pseudonym.[37]

He began to take a great interest in Signor Podrecca's marionette theatre in Rome, and also travelled to Turin and Milan to study the permanent puppet theatres there, and to meet the families that worked them. He was also in correspondence with Stanley Wilkinson, who had a delightful puppet theatre in England. Henry Furst, a clever and enthusiastic young man whom he had met in Florence, now turned up in Rome; he "wanted to help," so Craig put him on to translating from French and German everything available on the history of puppets. Craig was so impressed with the happy family life of the puppeteers in Milan and Turin that he conceived a mad idea of turning his giant Roman studio into a puppet theatre where everything would be worked by himself, Elena, and the children, and where his *Drama for Fools* could go on continuously.

Elena and the children were living with Ellen, to whom Elena was acting as companion-*cum*-secretary. The children, Teddy and Nelly, were busying themselves with a few erratic lessons in the three R's, and occasionally acting in charity performances to help the war effort or with Jean Sterling Mackinlay in her famous Children's Matinées. By this time, the war had brought them together with their two half-brothers, Bobby and Peter—May's children—of whom they felt very proud because they were both in uniform, and, of course, Rosie, whom everybody loved. Time went very slowly. Then suddenly a letter arrived from Rome saying that they must come over at once: they were going to work on puppet plays together, and they were going to publish a magazine called *The Marionnette*; the first number would be out at any moment.

To the children it was an exciting adventure, and they longed to be away from the Zeppelin raids. Elena longed to be with Ted again, but was worried about taking the children across the Channel because of the danger of meeting a U-boat; she believed all the ghastly propaganda about little boys having their right hands cut off by the "Huns" so that they couldn't fire guns when they grew up! However, after many tearful good-byes to Ellen and Elena's parents, they left one foggy morning, and five days later found themselves in the September sunshine of Rome. As they got off the train a great voice hailed them from the barrier, shouting, "Hurrah, hurrah!" and they were all united again.

Four years had elasped since they had all parted. Craig was now forty-five and needed a family around him. After the initial excitement of looking at Rome and being taken to meet Mrs Strong and all the counts, countesses, and princesses, they settled down to a plan of action. It then turned out that since the last letter all ideas of a puppet theatre had been given up! Instead, they were going to find a place with a warm climate and settle down there; and every effort would be concentrated on the new magazine called *The Marionnette*, and *The Mask*, which he intended to start again as a leaflet.

Guide-books were studied carefully and it was finally decided that the little fishing village of Rapallo, near Genoa, might prove to be a nice place to go to; it was even warmer than Alassio, and Max Beerbohm and his wife, who had lived there, had often said pleasant things about it. Everything was packed and stored and off they went, intending to stay in some hotel until they could find a little villa.

From this point in the story I shall sometimes be forced to refer to myself in the first person. Now, at the age of twelve, I was expected, as by some miracle, to develop suddenly and become my father's assistant.

From the day of my birth, my father had presumed that because I was Elena's son I would be supremely endowed "physically—morally—mentally," but I was shortly to prove that I was only tough, methodical, adventurous, and imaginative.

My sister was still more imaginative, but was less robust and therefore slower, and, like Father, she often got lost in a world of her own.

My mother was now thirty-nine, remarkably lively and energetic and full of unquenchable optimism; she still looked upon my father as a god. For the next ten years we were not to be separated except for brief periods when work took one or two of us elsewhere for its accomplishment.

CHAPTER FOURTEEN

Aftermath · "The Pretenders"

1917–1928

WE ARRIVED at Rapallo in November and found it bathed in sunshine, palm trees waving in the sea breeze, and the evergreen olives that covered the terraced hillsides giving an aspect of summer. We discovered, however, that we were in the "Zona di Guerra," or war zone, and had to carry special passes. All the big hotels were full of refugees or convalescing soldiers, but a small hotel just behind the Saracens Tower took us in, and our quest began. Father soon found out that I was more fluent in Italian than he was because I had picked it up as a child, whereas he, like many Englishmen of his generation, had never bothered to learn any foreign languages.

We went in search of the Villino Chiaro, where Max used to live—"just to have a look"—and found that the Villa Raggio, next door, was to be let: this consisted of three enormous rooms and five smaller ones, kitchen, etc., and a wistaria-covered terrace, under which was a huge wine cellar. There was a terraced garden with grape-vines, fruit trees of every kind, and many exotic plants. After much haggling it was agreed that we could have the place for eight hundred lire a year—which was not bad, since the rate of exchange soon went up to ninety, one hundred, then one hundred and five lire for the English pound. The sale of three woodcuts would take care of the rent for a year!

Craig returned to Rome via Florence, where he arranged for all the remaining school equipment and the pieces of the Bach *Passion* model to be sent to Rapallo; from Rome he sent up the contents of his studio there. Villa Raggio, Sant' Ambrogio, near Rapallo now became his headquarters. *The Mask* offices were given up as being too expensive and a post office box, number 444, was rented instead. D. N. L. agreed to do all the editorial work on the new magazine from her flat near the Ponte Vecchio in Florence. (Little Davidino stayed with friends near Pisa.)

Craig's main preoccupation during the past six months had been the preparation of his new little magazine, *The Marionnette*. This was a kind of sublimation of his original scheme, when he envisaged a marionette theatre in Rome. He planned to include in the magazine all the puppet plays he had written, and also to make use of the vast quantity of material on the history of marionettes, puppets, and shadow-figures that he had collected over the years, as well as the interesting translations made by Mrs Carr in 1907–8, and by Henry Furst during the last two years. He would not even call it a magazine; instead, it was to be "a performance . . . for Fools": the first page of the first number explains itself—

The editor was Tom Fool—that is to say, a court jester with a barbed tongue and special licence to trounce everyone, yet go unpunished.

Those who subscribed to *The Marionnette* would also get a copy of *The Mask*, now reduced to a leaflet of four pages—the first issue of which carried the old Scotsman's prayer as its motto:

GOD GRANT THAT WE MAY BE RIGHT, FOR THOU DOST KNOW THAT WE ARE DETERMINED NOT TO GIVE IN.

This motto seemed to set the pace, and the Villa Raggio became a hive of industry.

The first number of *The Marionnette* was dated April 1, the second number March 15—for the dates fooled about too—the last number being dated August 1918, although it was published in July 1919.

By then, what we later knew as the "First World War" had come to an end, and all the lights went on again in the little villages along the coast, which, after the wartime darkness, seemed positively ablaze. Europe was now like a garden which had been covered by the snows of a very severe winter; everyone waited to see what had survived, what would put out new shoots and grow again, and what had perished and would have to be uprooted.

THE MARIONNETTE

VOLUME ONE. NUMBER ONE. APRIL. I. 1918.

ADDRESS: BOX 444. FLORENCE. ITALY.

A PERFORMANCE FOR FOOLS. A DEMOCRATIC PERFORMANCE. A DIPLOMATIC PERFORMANCE A PERFORMANCE WHICH IS ARISTOCRATIC, — AUTOCRATIC—AND OLIGARCHIC: A DYNASTIC AND PASHAWLIC PERFORMANCE — A PERFORMANCE AS DEMOGOGIC AS IT IS OCHLOCRATIC; A DICTATO- RIC MOBOCRATIC BUREAUCRATIC PERFORMANCE.

PHR: " THE GRAY MARE THE BETTER HORSE ; "
" EVERY INCH A KING ".

See Roget: 1901. page 242. " Authority ".

ALL THE WORLD'S MAD BUT THEE AND ME, JOCK, AND SOMETIMES I THINK THEE'S A BIT QUEER.

BEFORE THE CURTAIN:
Ladies, Gentlemen, and Egoists.

HAVING lost our old offices owing to an unforeseen burst of enthusiasm on the part of nobody, we are reduced to a box: a private box ; Box 444. Easy to remember, ...and they still say artists are unpractical! ...Being reduced to a Box for an office, after the luxury of the tumble-down Arena Goldoni, (the coldest place on earth), it only remains to thank nobody for his burst of enthusiasm which caused us to skedaddle.

This pleasant duty executed, the Curtain may go up for all we care.

THE CURTAIN RISES.

The first page of *The Marionnette*.

Craig felt that he should do something to let people know he was still "alive and kicking," so he busied himself collecting together a number of essays in order to form a new book that he called *The Theatre Advancing*. It was published in America during October 1919 by Little, Brown & Company of Boston, and although it contained chiefly pre-war material it gave the critics plenty to write about. And the advance on royalties kept us all for the next twelve months.

The following year was an extremely busy one; it was also extremely frustrating, although in many ways very happy.

Florence Beerbohm returned to Villino Chiaro, followed shortly by Max. Ours were no longer a couple of lonely villas on the Riviera. They became more like a couple of well known cafés on the Paris boulevards where artists and intellectuals dropped in. Among them were Norman Douglas, Ezra Pound, Granville Barker, Gerhardt Hauptmann, Malipiero, and one day, a sad and disillusioned Isadora.

Beerbohm and Craig did not, as so many imagined, bask in the sun; they worked as hard as anyone in a city office. From the early hours Max might be seen, beautifully dressed as though for a boating party with his hat at a rakish tilt, pacing up and down the terraced top of his villino for hours as he "thought out" a chapter that he would later transcribe from beginning to end with hardly a blot; while at the neighbouring villa, Craig, in his white linen "tropicals," sitting in his shuttered room, would be writing and rewriting a chapter until the last version hardly resembled the first except in subject matter.

At this time, Craig observed that:

Max inherits a slight tendency to thank God that he is not as other men are—but being a sweet natured being, when someone holds up a looking glass to him, his face turns very young; it is covered with a confusion which is charming. . . .

He is nervous about people arriving—he needs 3 or 4 or more minutes notice of their arrival so as to provide for them what he considers the right atmosphere—the correct pose for their eyes to see. . . .

He is cynical and this goes deeply in him and he reckons its worth too highly.[1]

As a relief from creative writing, Craig started to collect material relating to the history of the theatres built in Italy between 1500 and 1800, and details of the lives of the Bibienas, the great family of architects and scene painters that flourished during the seventeenth and eighteenth centuries. As his interest in these two subjects increased, he began to fill two large vellum-bound note-books with all the material he could find in his library. He would also be busy struggling with magazine articles, or writing the prodigious number of letters with which he kept in touch with theatre people throughout the world. Meantime, I would either be making photographs of old prints or translating from Italian into English anything he could not understand in order to help with the historical work.

One day, Reggie Turner, an old friend of Max's turned up and stayed with him for a while. He had been a good friend to Oscar Wilde during his last, rather unhappy days in France, and his stories about Wilde were always interesting.

Once, when Craig was telling Turner of the difficulty he found in writing, Turner, to cheer him up, showed him a letter he had received from Max in 1916; in it was the following paragraph:

I have just been reading again Gordon Craig's *Art of the Theatre* and have come to the conclusion that he is, amongst other things, one of the three or four best living writers of English.

It is an amazingly beautiful "style" his—Really like a flower—and no "flowers" at all—Nothing of my kind, or Maurice Hewlett's.[2]

This comment on his work by such a severe critic as Max buoyed up Craig's morale at a time when he needed every encouragement, and led him to seriously consider giving much more of his time to writing; he toyed with the idea of composing a vast history of the theatre, as well as many other books.

In London, meanwhile, there was a sudden revival of interest in the art of wood-engraving, and Craig became a prominent exhibitor with the newly formed Society of Wood Engravers, in which Robert Gibbings was the prime mover. To Craig's surprise, prints from his old blocks made for *The Page* and *The Mask* sold very well indeed, and the following year Haldane MacFall wrote a special article on his work in *The Print Collectors Quarterly* in which he said: "He is a wise man who seeks for woodcuts by Gordon Craig, for they are amongst the supreme achievements of our time."

Letters asking for price lists came in from all over the world, and two were hurriedly printed, one for *Wood Engravings* (on boxwood), and one for *Black Figures*. Orders began to arrive, and I sometimes worked well into the night making prints so that they would be dry enough in the morning for him to sign; then I could send them off. Stimulated by this new interest in his woodcuts, Craig laid aside his pen, got out his tools, and started engraving again.

Up to 1921 he had designed and cut over 455 blocks on boxwood, plus about 120 book-plates; in addition, there were some 90 Black Figures. Many of the earlier boxwood blocks had been lost or destroyed, but we managed to collect together over 300. However, it was quite a job keeping the galleries and collectors supplied as well as compiling records of the editions and print numbers issued.[3]

Craig still corresponded with his friends in Rome, and at one time it seemed likely that a committee formed by Alfredo de Bosis and backed by many important names was going to bring about the re-establishment of his school. A special prospectus was published,[4] as well as *A Biographical Note* telling of his past achievements. He dashed down to Rome, full of hope, but it all came to nothing.

In Rome, he met Magnus again—now a very changed man. Recently, life seemed to have played him so many dirty tricks that he was contemplating retiring into a monastery. So many of the "names" with which he had conjured in the past were no more, or no longer meant anything. He could see no future for himself.

The following November, we all heard of his tragic end. He had written his *Memoirs of the Foreign Legion*, and was waiting to hear from the publisher. Always optimistic, he drew a cheque in anticipation of an advance on royalties; it bounced; (this was a period when banks could not afford to be philanthropic). He went to Malta, where he was visited by some plain clothes policemen. He did not know how to face such a disgrace and took poison.[5]

Four years later, Magnus's book appeared anonymously. D. H. Lawrence wrote a preface of eighty-three pages in which he did nothing but try to defame his onetime "friend." Only Mrs Ashby Macfadyen and Norman Douglas bothered to defend him in print.[6]

On returning from Rome, Craig went to London at the invitation of his friend and admirer, Lovat Fraser.

Lovat was one of those artists who could sit and talk on any subject while turning out hundreds of brilliant little pen-and-ink sketches that would later appear as book decorations. His style was somewhat reminiscent of Jack Yeats, brother of the famous poet. He had a special flare for reproducing the English eighteenth-century scene, and seemed to belong to those times himself. He was one of the few designers in the English theatre that Craig held in high esteem. Fraser, in turn, was always trying to help, and had arranged for the publication of *The Theatre Advancing* in England.

For this edition, published by Constable, Craig wrote a seventy-eight-page foreword. This foreword and his dedication of the book, "To the Enemy, with a prayer that they will be stronger, more malicious and, anyhow, funnier than they have been in the past," were saddening indications of his growing sense of persecution. During the war he had followed the political and military plots and counter-plots, and since the armistice, the bargaining by the great powers: all this intrigue had heightened his natural, rather theatrical suspiciousness, nurtured on Victorian melodrama and Dumas's novels, into near a phobia. He now saw the English theatre as a corporate body, doing everything in its power to break him. At one time he even imagined that "the Enemy" were actually spying on him and wished to do him bodily harm.

On his way back from London, he stopped in Paris, where the French edition of his book, *On the Art of the Theatre*, was just being published. It had been translated before the war by Geneviève Séligmann-Lui, with an introduction by J. J. Rouché, and a French edition had even been set up and printed in London, but the outbreak of hostilities had caused the publishers to put it aside. At last the *Nouvelle Revue Française* thought the time was ripe. The first printing was one thousand copies, and these were soon sold out.

The visit to England and France had resulted in nothing to Craig's material advantage. But seeing Lovat Fraser at work on his setting for *The Beggars' Opera* and accompanying him to rehearsals had diverted his attention from writing and engraving for a while, and reawakened his desire to express his ideas in three dimensions. As soon as he was home, we unpacked the large model stage (Model A), set it up with all its electrical apparatus and once again he began to experiment with his moving screens.

The Villa Raggio now became his school, or Theatre Workshop, and I became his one and only pupil-assistant. Life took on a more regular pattern.

For me, the morning usually started at 4.30 or 5 a.m., because if I wanted to follow my own pursuits, such as sketching, cycling, or fishing, or any of those amusements that appeal to a lad of sixteen— all of which my father considered "a waste of time"—I had to do so before breakfast. This, Mother generally prepared at about 7.30, and it consisted of a bowl of black coffee and freshly baked bread dipped in olive oil, pepper, and salt. Then I would go up to father's room, dust everything, pick up papers, put away books, and fill all his fountain pens. There were seven pens, and each had a different-sized nib, which, like different founts of type, he used to express different moods: the big fat pen was for all his best ideas and for happy thoughts, the fine pen was for historical work and proof-correcting, then there was a nasty medium pen that was only used for writing to certain people. After filling the pens I filled the pipes. Like the pens, the pipes were of different sizes and weights to fit different moods, and were filled with Craven A or John Cotton to suit the taste of the moment. The papers on the desk all had to be placed at right angles, in several piles . . . and one would be clever and foresee the sort of reference books he would require, and put them near by—that gained one points!

He would lie in bed elaborating his thoughts, then suddenly rise and go into his room to write or draw or engrave for hours. During this time no domestic sounds must interrupt him; the general sounds of nature, like the cicale or workmen in near-by buildings pleased him, but if he heard the daily woman arguing with mother he would fly into a temper and thunderbolts would be hurled in all directions. It was only after the sun had set that he chose to work with Model A. For hours he would experiment with an arrangement of screens and lights that he had been contemplating during the day; he would not go systematically through a play, but would pick on some sequence of scenes that had been suggested to him by something he had seen or read and would work forwards or backwards from there. These hours were the most exciting, for he seemed inspired and out of this world as he worked feverishly to capture an idea. When he had got what he wanted he would shout with joy like a small boy, and Mother would have to be brought and seated in the "audience" to watch the "movement."

Then would come my job of recording the whole process, making a plan of the scene and the various movements that developed it into another scene, the position and density of each of the lights, the colours of the gelatines, etc. When this was done, I had to show him the roughs before I copied the notes and diagrams into books which we kept for the purpose. As he looked at my technical notes and drawings, he would sometimes stroke his nose and hum—one knew at once that mischief was afoot—then he would suddenly alter some colour that

I had recorded as "green" to "yellow," or the name of the play for which the scene was intended from, say, *Romeo and Juliet* to *Othello*. When I protested that I was right and he was wrong, he would agree but, in a stage whisper, he would say that he had altered the Record to "confuse the enemy," adding, "dear boy, you and I would know at once that it was wrong . . . of course we would."

Sometimes, in the middle of work the tension would become so great that he would have to stop. Then he would either break into an old music-hall song, or I remember him once going out on to the landing and giving a marvellous imitation of an Italian street-singer screaming a moral ballad: Mother entered into the spirit of the moment and appeared on the landing above and threw him a coin. At other times, to relieve the tension, we would walk a few miles up the olive clad hills to San Pantaleo and buy a bottle of wine. But although he allowed himself this physical break, his mind would still be busy. On seeing an old peasant coming down the mountain road with an assortment of sacks strung round his neck, he would exclaim, "Look at him . . . there's old Gobbo . . ." We would then stop him and have a chat; then Father might ask this old Ligurian peasant, "Lei conosce Venezia?" to which the man would reply in dialect that he didn't know Venice, in fact, had never heard of it. This would be a disappointment: Father had hoped to question him about Signor Gratiano . . . Signor Bassanio —like a child, he could live all day in an imaginary world of Shakespeare's *Merchant of Venice*, or any other play he happened to be reading.

Nineteen twenty-one was a good year financially. Alfred Kreymborg, the American poet, dropped in on his way down to Rome where he was going to help edit "An International Magazine of the Arts published by Americans in Italy," which was to be called *Broom*: he had ample backing and was only too pleased to pay a fellow artist £90 for an article. Soon after this came a letter from Martin Hardie of the Victoria and Albert Museum in London, asking Craig what he would let him have for the Theatre Collection if the museum could find £250. Approached in this way, he became very generous and put together some particularly fine drawings, as well as models of two of his scenes from the Moscow *Hamlet*—these I had to make in plaster because, as he said, "if all the others, made of cardboard, get burnt, I want mine to survive."

Martin Hardie was happy, and the £250, translated into Italian lire, seemed a tremendous sum of money, so he decided we would all take a trip round certain towns in northern Italy and see what remained of some of the important old theatres in which he had become interested while compiling his records. He was worried about Elena's health too, and thought the trip would provide her with a welcome break from housekeeping.

The idea was that in each city we would photograph or make sketches of the theatre concerned, then nose about in book-shops and see if we could find any books on the subject.

When we reached Parma, which Father had visited before, I was so overwhelmed by the magnificence of the seventeenth-century Farnese Theatre that I was determined to find out more than the dull information to be found in books about it. Near the entrance to the theatre was a small door, and over it was written "Archivo di Stato"; I suggested that we might find some original documents there, but Father said archives were stuffy old places and dismissed the idea. While he was having his afternoon siesta I returned to the Archives and, to my delight, found hundreds of original drawings and manuscripts relating to the building of the theatre and to the performances given in it. Later, I persuaded him to come and look: he did so reluctantly, but when he saw the treasures, he took control immediately, and for days I was tracing and photographing while Mother, Father, and my sister copied page after page of the seventeenth-century manuscripts.

This discovery altered his whole attitude to the history of the theatre, which from now on took up more and more of his time. Books no longer satisfied him—we must get back to *the original documents*. I was very happy because I had introduced him to this new joy, and because I was often sent off on missions by myself with my old-fashioned full-plate camera, returning later with exciting photographs, having enjoyed a little taste of life away from home.

Towards the end of 1921 a letter came from H. T. Wijdeveld, the celebrated Dutch architect and stage designer, inviting Craig to exhibit at the International Theatre Exhibition that the "Kunst an het Volk" were organizing on a really large scale at the Stedelijk Museum in Amsterdam; it was to be opened in the first month of 1922 and would present the first opportunity since the outbreak of the war for artists of the theatre to get together. Craig entered into the scheme whole-heartedly and nothing else was thought of at the Villa Raggio until models had been made and crated, mounts cut, pictures mounted and lists made.

Finally, there was little time left, and we were still confronted with the problem of transport across Italy, Switzerland, and Germany on an almost non-existent transport system left over from the war. The Dutch Consul in Genoa said "leave it to me," and taking us down to the docks, introduced us to the captain of a cargo-ship that was just leaving for Holland. "There you are," he said, "my friend will look after everything for you."

The captain was a homely Dutchman who knew of Craig. He asked us to have a drink. Then he spoke some words down a tube, and a few minutes later, called us to the front of the wheelhouse and pointed down to the deck. There stood a strange group—the ship's Javanese crew. Two musicians started to play . . . Surrounded by a swarm of drab ships, these extraordinary little men, bare-footed, and on a deck covered with iron plates, rivets, rings, and bolts, performed a beautiful dance of welcome. When it was over they bowed and vanished below deck, while the crews of the near-by Italian vessels applauded and shouted. Craig was deeply moved.

The exhibition in Amsterdam was an enormous success. The first room was given exclusively to the works of Craig and Appia. Six other large rooms were shared by Europe and America. In one darkened room beautifully lit models from all over Europe were displayed.

Craig immediately wrote to Martin Hardie, telling him of the exhibition's importance, and arrangements were made for the whole thing to be transferred to the Victoria and Albert Museum in London, and later, to Manchester.

Because so many people at the Exhibition in Holland were interested in his etchings for *Scene*, Craig thought he would attempt a book on the subject, and while he was in London for the exhibition's official opening there, he met Gerard Hopkins of the Oxford University Press, who was very enthusiastic about the idea. On his return to Rapallo, Craig sat down and wrote the text in four weeks. John Masefield supplied a fine preface in verse.

Next came a trip to Milan, where Signor Scandiani of the Scala Theatre hoped to interest Craig in producing an opera. Here we enjoyed Toscanini's rehearsals of *Nerone* and the *Meistersingers*, visited the opera, went behind the stage and . . . fled to Venice. Craig had been terrified by what he saw of the stage machinery at the Scala— machinery which one might be *tempted* to use, which, in fact, the management would *want* one to use in order to show the world how up-to-date their theatre was—and he felt sure that any artist who worked there would eventually become subordinate to this machinery. A little later he heard from Appia; he had been tempted and was going there to design *Tristan and Isolde*. Time passed . . . then came a pathetic letter saying, "All is lost," and Craig knew that Appia had hit the very rocks that he had managed to avoid.

In September, Count Kessler suddenly arrived in Rapallo. He had already written to say he had every intention of continuing with his *Hamlet* project; now he came in person to encourage Craig to start again, and was delighted to see that some more figures had been cut during the war.

With far, far too many interesting things to do and far too many unformed projects, Craig's mind flitted from one thing to another; he was showing signs of exhaustion. The summer had been exceptionally hot; the supply of well water had got very low and was obviously contaminated. He suddenly developed typhoid fever—the only serious illness in his life.

Following the publication of *Scene* in the summer of 1923, I came to know for the first time what his etchings represented; until then, I, like so many others, had presumed that they were various scenes for an imaginary drama. As soon as I realized that each etching was a piece of arrested action within a great symphony of movement, I longed to see the progression of this movement in three dimensions. Father said, tersely, "We'll get to that one day . . . later."

In the carpenter's shop that I had established in the wine cellar, I experimented with a wooden model of *Scene*, and after some months, finally succeeded in perfecting a simple mechanism that made the cubes rise and fall by remote control. Overjoyed by my achievement, I rushed to fetch Father: his excitement was as intense as mine. As he worked my simple pulleys, the cubes, illuminated by two small lights, slowly began to ascend . . . he seemed to be in a trance and kept murmuring, "So it works . . . so it really works." For a moment he had glimpsed the materialization of his dreams. Again and again he came back to the carpenter's shop to handle my rough model as though it was the most precious thing in the world—all the time so remote, so deeply preoccupied with his thoughts that he was hardly aware of my presence.

I did not want him to lose heart about the practical development of this superb idea that I had grown to love as much as he did, so one day I said, "In a modern theatre, the mechanism required to make these cubes move could be quite easily installed." "How do you know that?" he asked. I told him I had discussed it with a young Italian friend who was studying hydraulics at the University of Genoa. His whole being changed; "How dare you!" he roared. "Who gave you permission to mention it outside these walls? You fool, you fool!" He shouted and raged, then collapsed, spent with emotion.

The whole incident had been too much for him. He had been a weak man since his illness and, as usual when he worked on something particularly dear to him, he had become apprehensive of the imagined "enemy," ready to steal and prostitute his ideas. In his already nervous state, he imagined that I had betrayed him . . . I had given his most treasured secret to the university. Later we discovered that his nervous condition was critical.

My model, which had given him so much joy followed by so much anguish, was hidden away in the back of the cellar, never to be seen again.

Since the end of the war, there had been a considerable demand for back numbers of *The Mask*, which had brought in a fair sum of money. This encouraged Father to contemplate issuing it again, and in 1923 it made its reappearance, but only as a single volume, its ninth. All but one article, by George Jean Nathan, were written by Craig under thirteen pseudonyms, and I was allowed to contribute six wood engravings under the name of "E. Carrick."

In 1924, two books were planned, the most important one being a semi-autobiographical work, published by J. M. Dent, which was called *Woodcuts and Some Words*—a title, incidentally, chosen by Max Beerbohm. It was illustrated with fifty-nine plates, and it certainly helped to boost the sale of his prints to collectors.

Meantime, I had been collecting together every known book-plate that he had designed or cut, and had made a careful check-list of them. It seemed an opportune moment to publish this too, so he added fifteen pages of text telling how he came to make book-plates in the first place, and Chatto and Windus published it under the title of *Nothing, or the Book-plate*, with many reproductions in colour. A pretty book, it was issued in two editions, one with twenty-five, the other with forty-five plates. I was also allowed credit for my work on this, under my new pseudonym.

While the above was in hand, the British Drama League suggested that Craig design and build them a model of one of his scenes as a show-piece for the famous British Empire Exhibition. His most popular woodcut at that time was "King Lear—the Storm," so he decided that this should be the subject, and gave me the job of making the model.[7]

An exciting feature of the model was the suggestion of driving rain—which he intended should be done on the actual stage by stretching lengths of wire diagonally across the stage in front of an indigo backcloth; the wire would respond to any slight movement and, together with thunder and lightening, would give a highly dramatic impression of a storm—but in the model I could not use wire because it would have been out of scale, so I painted a sheet of tin with midnight blue, scored it with a pin and got the same effect. Unluckily, an over-clever producer, on seeing it, remarked that Craig was being un-practical again—"imagine building a great backcloth of solid metal sheeting just to get that effect for a single scene." His detractors were still busy.

The First World War, as it came to be known, lasted from 1914 to 1918, but when the main fighting was over the years that followed were just as turbulent except that there was not quite so much blood-shed. There were the usual readjustments of frontiers, followed by revolutions, personal anguish, and shortage of supplies everywhere.

Craig was only forty-six in 1918 but he felt quite out of touch with the new world that was emerging around him. He jumped at any opportunity to make contact again; he needed to re-establish himself like so many other men of his generation, and, like other artists in particular, he found this difficult because in the intervening years there had been little to stimulate the imagination. There was also the immediate question of survival, which meant producing something, and all ways and means were considered. The sudden revival of interest in wood engraving had come as a godsend. He had also been lucky in finding publishers who were eager to print such books as *The Theatre Advancing* and *Scene*, which after all, were old works in new bindings. *Woodcuts and Some Words*, however, struck a new note; it was light-hearted and full of happy autobiographical anecdotes.

It was essential for *The Mask* to appear regularly again if he was to survive. But its contents were bound to be different, for he no longer had the same desire to write about the Theatre of the future; so many of his younger followers had been killed, or had lost touch—he felt very much alone; his interest turned instead to the theatre of the past, to selected aspects of theatrical history: Court theatres, stage machinery, the Bibiena family, and so on.

In January 1924 the first number of Volume X came out and the following numbers were being planned. They were full of the most interesting reproductions of little-known prints and drawings of old theatres, Baroque and Rococo scenery, and so on; the general tone of the articles also had more of a historical trend. Only here and there were flashes of the old fire evident, as some contemporary happening roused him to do battle.

Villa Raggio was proving too isolated, for Rapallo was still only a large village surrounded by hotels. It was one of my jobs to go into the post-office at least twice a day to collect and post the mail, as there was only one delivery to the house. Genoa, fifteen miles away, was the nearest town for supplies, and it was there, too, that most of the blocks were made for *The Mask*.

We started looking for a new home. At one time we even tried Venice but found it cold and depressing in the autumn. Finally, we found a lovely house on the outskirts of Genoa at San Martino d'Albaro, which was situated at the end of the tramline going east from the city and surrounded by orange trees and beautiful views.

During our stay in Venice, Father had developed an interest in John Evelyn's Diary. For the July issue of *The Mask*, he prepared the first part of an article on "John Evelyn and the Theatre in England, France and Italy," and he was happy enough with the result to publish it under his own name.

He gradually collected together other articles of a similar nature to form a book called *Books and Theatres*. J. M. Dent & Sons published it in 1925. In the preface he referred to himself as "an unemployed artist of the Theatre, who ventures for the first time to dip a finger into the icy waters of history." He managed to warm the icy waters, and the book was a great success. But it was not the success that he really wanted. He disliked doing research work on his own, and had no desire to be regarded as a historian: he just wanted to know more about the theatre of the past and to share his enjoyment with others.

The year 1926 found us in our fine new quarters, with central heating, a magnificent library, and a lovely garden—the most lavish home we had ever had. Elena and Nelly turned out exotic meals, and by now I was an able assistant, but Father was far from happy. His nerves were still upset and he began to think about death; the future seemed useless as the chances of his getting his experimental school or theatre grew more and more remote.

Another nervous breakdown followed, not as serious as the preceding one, but it took a curious form. He locked himself in a darkened room for a couple of weeks, convinced that people were trying to destroy him with spells . . . maybe even with poison. He would see no one except his immediate family. I had to knock in a special way before he would open his door and let me in. He was making himself worse, and Mother decided that I should go for help to Doctor Guelfi of Nervi, who had once saved my life. He returned with me and as I entered the darkened room, he slipped in too. He sat at the foot of the bed and in quite a normal voice asked, "Mister Craik . . . wich you tink de best English writer of comedy, Sheridan or Goldsmith?" Father, although furious at Guelfi's intrusion, couldn't help answering, "That's a silly question, because both Sheridan and Goldsmith were Irishmen." "Ah," said Guelfi, "you know all about de Teatro, you are right." Then, suddenly changing his tone of voice to that of a German drill-sergeant, he almost shouted, "But *I* know all about de Medicen. You are not ill. Get up!" He threw open the curtains and shutters and let in the blinding sun. There was a pause . . . Father sat up, then stood up and said, "I think you are right." "Good," said Dr Guelfi, "tonight I send you a marvellous tonic. Goodbye my friend," and he was gone. Guelfi's personality and the tonic did wonders.

A month later Father was a new man, and in the middle of August a long letter arrived from Johannes Poulsen in Denmark which completely revitalized him: here at last was a fellow worker in the theatre asking for his help in the production of a play!

Poulsen's letter, dated August 12, is too long to quote in its entirety but the relevant parts ran as follows:

On the 9th of November my brother Adam and I have our 25th anniversary as actors, and the Royal Danish Theatre will on that night play *The Pretenders*, by Henrik Ibsen. Adam is going to play the part of Earl Skule and I the part of Bishop Nicolas.

Now I am to ask you on behalf of the Chief for the Royal Theatre, William Norris, whether you would draw the decorations and the costumes for this performance. I myself am going to set the play up, but if you would come over here and set it up with me as interpreter, we shall be very pleased indeed. You have a free hand in every respect. You will have at your disposal a big theatre— bigger than His Majesty's Theatre in London—it holds 1,700 people, the footlights are 44 feet, and the depth of the stage is about 70 feet—a complete staff of actors and actresses, and besides an opera staff and an Orchestra, numbering 80 men, which is the best north of Berlin. . . .

. . . Furthermore we have a turning stage, round horizon, and one of the best and newest lighting systems in Europe.

. . . Finally every year the Crown pays the deficit, which amounts to about 50,000 English pounds.

This direct, warmhearted approach filled Craig with joy and a telegram went off in reply:

THANK YOU DEAR FRIEND. WILL CERTAINLY DO WHAT IS POSSIBLE. WRITING. G.C.

The letter that followed contained the following passages:

I sent you a telegram to say I would do all that is possible. By that I mean that in any case I will do something, so as to be one of the many to celebrate the 25th anniversary of the two famous brothers, Adam and Johannes Poulsen.

L

Whether I can come up to Copenhagen depends on what you want me to do.

Remember it is almost fifteen years since I did any work inside a theatre.

The experience in Moscow decided me to wait until I should possess my own theatre, which I believed the English would give me.

But your celebration is another thing—I must contribute towards that some little piece of work.

I will not disguise from you that my mind likes to concern itself very little with historical tragedy. It is Opera I think of most.

But I will willingly design you some scenes and costumes and help you set up the play—

Having agreed, he began to wonder if he could still cope with the amount of work that he generally put into a production, so he added a P.S.:

I won't come if you expect me to produce the play, for it's quite beyond my powers.[8]

It was agreed that he should go up to Copenhagen in October, and a suite of rooms was reserved for him at the Hotel Angleterre.

Meanwhile, at home, everything was put aside to make way for Ibsen's *Pretenders*, which he studied day and night. He made innumerable sketches for the scenes, some of which resembled those he had made for *The Vikings*, and because it was set against the same Nordic background many of the costumes and weapons were similar too.

When he arrived in Copenhagen he found that the stage was so large that to fill it with a sequence of colourful settings would result in something reminiscent of the Russian ballet, and the play would suffer. There was only a month for preparation, so he persuaded Poulsen to adopt an unusual idea—to make the utmost use of the theatre's marvellous system for projected backgrounds for all the large scenes suggesting the open air, and, for the smaller, interior scenes to revert to the Italian type of setting used in the Middle Ages, known as *luoghi deputati*. The paintings of Cimabue and Giotto give an idea of this type of background, and I received an urgent message to send him some photographs to show to Poulsen. At the same time he wanted Mother to note down the chimes of the old bells at San Pantaleo, and I was to send as much of Monteverdi's music as I could find.

As usual, the resident scenic artist was horrified at the suggested break with tradition; in fact, old Mr Pederson was so upset at the prospect of having so little to paint that he went on holiday, leaving his brilliant son to reap the glory of achieving every effect that Gordon Craig asked for.

The electrical engineer Neilson was years ahead of the rest of the theatre of his time and gloried in all Craig's requirements; his projected spiral snowstorm, used as a background to the Ghost of Bishop Nicolas, was a highly successful combination of Craig's imagination and his mechanical skill.

I did not go with him to Copenhagen as he needed someone in charge at Rapallo. Also, I think he was scared of taking me because I nearly died of double pneumonia when we went to Amsterdam together in 1922. However, he kept me informed of all that was happening and, on November 8, a letter arrived from him saying: "The scenes, today, surpassed my hopes . . . anyhow, all the Theatre tricks do . . ." He ended his letter with the news that he had found a servant to help at home: ". . . something rather special—22— daughter of peasant—but refined—smile nice—but very reserved." This was cheering news because good domestic help was almost unobtainable near Genoa, and Mother had been far from well for some time.

As the first night of *The Pretenders* approached and the tempo built up, Craig became more and more worried about all the details that he would have liked to change. When the curtain went up on November 14, he was nowhere to be found: he had wandered off into the dock area—"trying to forget"—and was drinking coffee in a small bistro with some Italian sailors.

As the minutes passed, curiosity drew him back to the theatre, where he paused at the stage-door to enquire from the doorkeeper how the play was going, but the man did not understand English. Then came the distant thunder of applause and he knew that at least the audience was pleased and that he had not let the Poulsens down. He walked to the back of the stage where he was swooped on by the actors who took him down to the footlights to share in the ovation. He was back on the stage of his beloved theatre, a happy man again.[9]

Before he left Copenhagen the artists of the Royal Danish Theatre all put their names to a delightful document, which they presented on November 17, paying homage to him as the "Ingenious creator and teacher," who, with his "clear mind and rich imagination . . . and sublime genius" had made it possible for them to perform *The Pretenders*.[10]

Prior to returning to Italy for Christmas he saw his friend Sir Eugene Millington Drake, then Chargé d'Affaires at the British Embassy, who told him there might be "a little surprise" in store for him in the coming year!

Over Christmas, we listened to all the stories about *The Pretenders*, and wondered what this surprise could be. Then, in the New Year, documents arrived from the Imperial Society of Knights Bachelor which suggested that Father had been knighted!

But there appeared to be some confusion—newspapers were reporting that "British Film Production has received an unexpected and significant recruit in Mr Gordon Craig, the famous son of Miss Ellen Terry"; the article was illustrated with a photograph of a person that none of us in the family had ever seen before; one paper listed some of the films that Gordon Craig had made, such as *Armageddon*, *Zeebrugge*, *Ypres*, and *Mons*; another referred to him as "The greatest film impressario that England has yet produced." The "surprise" was turning into an enormous practical joke until it suddenly became clear that the papers had confused Edward Gordon Craig with one Ernest Gordon Craig, who had made these documentary films, and for whom, it seems, the knighthood was intended.

The story did not end there, for in April Father received the following letter:

> 29, St. Georges Road,
> London, S.W.1.

Dear Sir,

It was with the utmost astonishment that I found my photograph in The Daily Express on March 29th with the name of Mr Gordon Craig attached to it. I should be much obliged if you would furnish me with an explanation by return of post.

There were only two prints of this photograph, one I have and the other I gave to my fiancee just before she left for Italy in the early part of the year.

Yours faithfully,
Robert Mothersole.

Enclosed with the letter was the newspaper photograph of the strange "Gordon Craig."[11]

A council of war was held immediately, Father saying that Mr Mothersole was apparently a sinister type of blackmailer of whom we should be most careful, but before putting the matter in the hands of the police, which might result in a lot of unpleasant publicity, we must find out more about this person. I was given a few hours in which to get ready, provided with a ticket and £5, and sent to London to "observe" 29 St. George's Road . . . and report.

I rather fancied this job and looked forward to being in London again. I stayed with my mother's sisters in Hampstead, going over to south-west London every day to watch 29 St. George's Road—where I discovered that a nice little man came out in the early morning and returned in the late evening. There was absolutely nothing that could be built into a "plot."

On the first Sunday after my arrival I lunched with Father's old school-friend, Paul Cooper, and his family at Westerham. I told them about the blackmailer and how I was watching his house, hoping that the story would impress them; they only smiled and nodded, but when I had finished, Mrs Cooper just had to laugh and the rest joined in. I then discovered that the whole thing was one of Paul Cooper's jokes, timed for April 1. Mothersole was the name of a butcher in Mrs Cooper's home-town and the address was that of one of Mr Cooper's assistants!

Through the Coopers, who were very kind to me, I met a young woman named Helen Godfrey, and we became engaged. I was then twenty-two, and longed for a life of my own. I wrote home, telling them of my decision to stay in England, find work, and get married.

When Father received my letter he was utterly bewildered, then he became furious, replying that I would be deserting him and the work and forbidding me to do anything so ridiculous.

Although I knew that I was his only assistant and that he counted on me for a great deal, I did not realize, at the time, that my leaving him could have such dire repercussions on so much of his work.

While I was trying to make him understand that my behaviour was absolutely normal, the little "servant" whom he had brought from Denmark announced that she was pregnant. Mother, who was ill, insisted that the girl must go back to her home; Father wanted to keep her on, and looked to Mother for her usual tolerance: there were tragic scenes, but the girl went.

Suddenly, from Nice, came the appalling news that Isadora had met her death in a car accident. Father could not bring himself to believe this tragedy . . . then he insisted that it must have been murder.[12]

Kessler was preparing to print the famous *Hamlet* in Weimar, and Father begged me to join him there to help Mr Gage Cole, the Master Printer: I was the only person who knew how to get the kind of impression required, showing the delicate side grain of the wood and at the same time producing the specially blackened details in certain blocks. While I was with him in Germany, he did his best to make my visit a memorable and happy occasion, and when my job was over he took me to Frankfurt, Berlin, and other places associated with his past. But when the time came to say "good-bye," he was almost in tears; he seemed a broken man.

Desolate and lonely, he returned to Genoa where further unhappy news awaited him—his "almost brother" in the theatre, Adolphe Appia, had just died.

Soon after my return to London I had to write telling him that I had been to see "Granny," as we all called his mother. She recognized me, but she seemed far away . . . I didn't think she had long to live. This was too much for him; he could not . . . would not believe it. Enid Rose, a faithful friend and admirer, went out to Genoa to see if there was anything she could do to help him with his work, but his state of mind was such that no one could help him—he was bordering on despair. He finally decided to come to England, and was shocked at the condition in which he found his mother. He stayed with Paul Cooper and his family. On July 17 his sister telephoned him to say, "Mother has had a stroke." I joined him, and we went to Smallhythe together.

The weather was oppressive. The prowling photographers and newspapermen disgusted us. But there were old friends too, who walked with us in the orchard, talking in undertones. It was wonderful to see Father and his sister Edy suddenly brought together again—children once more—but sad that they should be re-united by an impending tragedy. Their mother was hovering between life and death, and, on July 21, 1928, her great, loving heart could beat no more . . . Some years later Father wrote of her last moments in these words:

She died in the morning sun, which shone warm and yellow on to her. She sat up suddenly—opened her eyes—fell back and threw off fifty old years as she fell. She became twenty-five to look at—and in truth, she became once more Nelly Terry, back again at Harpenden with little Edy and little Teddy and the one she loved better than all the world.[13]

Edy and Teddy were now without that loving and powerful personality which had sustained them all their years, and the vacuum created by her going could never be filled.

CHAPTER FIFTEEN

Loneliness · the Collection · War

1928–1946

CRAIG NOW entered one of the most tragic periods of his life. Blow after blow seemed to have struck him down.

> And from now onward a new phase of life began for me. It *had* to begin—Teddy gone (March, 1927) and quickly other losses came—Isadora September 1927, Appia 1928, Mother July 1928. A new phase of life begins because the old way isn't the same.[1]

He left England and wandered back to Kessler in Weimar, where he pottered about the Cranach Press and advised on the printing of *Hamlet*. He wrote to his sister:

> Weimar for a few days . . . Then . . . not sure. Wandering—To me so many lost these months—Almost Teddy seems gone—more than almost—was closest.
> Not down, you know . . . but just . . . your know . . .[2]

Then he joined Elena in Genoa. She called in Dr Guelfi, with whose aid he managed to feel a little less depressed. He decided to take a mighty plunge and start this "new phase of life"—but he was fifty-six, and "life" began to have a nostalgic ring about it; the mere fact that he was conscious of "starting again" instead of carrying on, was not a good omen.

> I had got to know George Pearson—in those days, the only man

in the British film industry with vision. He had a great admiration for my father's work and they had once talked of making an idealized version of *Robinson Crusoe* together. He signed me up as the designer (or art director) to his film company and on the strength of this contract I decided to get married in October.

By then, Father had become resigned to my starting a life of my own and he came over with my mother and sister for the wedding, and for a short while he turned into an ordinary happy parent again.

He stayed on in London, meeting old friends, discussing schemes for productions with C. B. Cochran and others, all the time trying to plot his course for the future.

There was enough material prepared to enable him to keep *The Mask* going for a while, but he could not see how he would manage single-handed for more than a year, for although the valiant D. N. L. looked after the printing and the business side of the publication, its typographical layout, illustrations, and major editorial work were all done at home, where a great deal of the work had always fallen on my shoulders.

It became obvious to him that in the future he must depend entirely on his literary work to maintain himself. Unlike his sister Edy, and contrary to many people's belief, he did not inherit a lump sum of money by his mother's will; instead, the capital was invested and left in trust to my sister and myself; our parents, during their lifetime, would benefit from the dividends, which would bring each of them something like £350 a year. Ellen had been very wise; she knew that any lump sum given to her son would disappear in a flash without him even feeling the benefit, for he had no money sense whatever. Even now, he thought that £700 a year, between himself and Elena, would look after most of their normal requirements, and he started being gaily extravagant again.

He took a small flat in Bury Street, St. James's, and began to look for a secretary. He wanted to start his next book, which was to be about Henry Irving, and he felt that it would be easier to "talk" about his memories of the Lyceum, and get the book done that way. All the while, he was slowly getting into debt.

At that point, George Tyler, the American producer, got in touch with him to see if he would undertake "the designment" of a production of *Macbeth* in New York. For the first time in his life he

decided to compromise: he would make a pile of sketches and leave
them to do what they liked with them . . . all he wanted was the
money. When he signed his drawings "C.pb" he confidently imagined
that posterity would realize that this work was to be excused because
it was a "Craig-potboiler." He cribbed outrageously from his work
in Copenhagen, even using old drawings that he had discarded two
years earlier. Ian Jeffcott, a young unemployed architect, volunteered
to go back to Genoa with him to help with the stage layouts and the
whole job was over in no time at all. In one of his Day-books for 1928
he records the episode as follows:

Meantime, and running through this, there hovered Tyler of
America—proposing "*Macbeth*" to me—Harding, the actor—"a
dear fellow." Many talks—distracting and stupid it all seemed to
me—but some immediate money, so agreed to "design" things for
Tyler—but not to go over to U.S.A.

I returned then from London to Italy. A man called Ross came down
eighteen days later—and tried (*his* best, I suppose) to get my ideas—
but ideas are not *got* by such men, so he got none—and so all I
could do was to make designs.

Gave three weeks to it. . . . Got Jeffcott down. . . . My work on
"*Macbeth*" at Genoa had its delights as well as dis-delights. The first
six days at work alone on it I made in wood a single scene to stand
the entire play. I found it pretty good—far too good to show Ross—
so I put it away, and have it still.

Then I showed him other designs. He assured me he had never
read a line of my books—nor had he seen my designs—and was like
most of my fellow workers in the theatre of England—utterly
ignorant of what I had done these twenty years—

As he proved by his conversation. It was hopeless to give him
ideas—each one I gave him seemed to disappear and no response to
show he'd got it or half got it or missed it—

Like serving balls at tennis, which vanished—not one came back
over the net from Ross.[3]

To avoid press interviews about his "first American production" he
went to Heidelberg. He chose this town because it was full of nostalgic
memories of his youth and of a later period with Isadora. Here, he

thought, he'd find it easy to settle down and dictate, but the magic was gone from the place. He went on to Grenoble, then Lyons, and then to Paris. In each of these places he tried new secretaries who came out from England on the recommendation of various friends, but all proved useless: they were either "too timid" or "too business-like and uninspiring"; one he classified as a "lady-like whore."⁴

In Paris, he accidentally came across his eldest son, Bobby, whom he hopefully contemplated as his next assistant, but he was soon disillusioned. He started writing to Davidino, D. N. L.'s little boy, and pondered on bringing him up so that one day, perhaps, *he* could help. Realizing that he had neglected the boy, he was also trying to make up for it; one letter, signed "Papa," ends "Love me . . . I send a kiss into your heart . . ."⁵

In July 1929 he was back in London again, and his luck changed, for he found Daphne Woodward, a young woman whom he later described as "the best secretary I ever had": intelligent and quick, she spoke French fluently and was learning Italian; she also seemed to understand his loneliness and frustration. They started work on the Irving book, and encouraged by her interest in the stories of his past, his thoughts began to flow easily again; at last he felt all would be well.

Interruptions came, however, for he got involved in the proposed publication of the Shaw–Terry correspondence. Soon after his mother's death he had told his sister to do what she liked with these letters, but on reflection he had decided that their publication might be harmful to his mother's public image. A Shaw–Craig correspondence now started and the two men almost forgot what they were arguing about as their letters developed into parries and thrusts, each trying to wound the other's pride with strokes of the pen or a tap or two on the typewriter. Shaw's Irish devilment so irritated Craig that he carried the fight into his book on Irving, using every opportunity to take pot-shots at his adversary from its pages. As the book progressed, back in Genoa, he gradually assumed Irving's attitude to G.B.S., thinking less and less of him in every way.⁶

In October the last number of *The Mask* came out. It was the fifteenth volume and he felt wretched at being unable to cope with it any more.

By September 25, 1930, the Irving book appeared, and it was

received well by the press. His inspired description of Irving's acting in *The Bells* was a fine piece of writing, based on his original notes made in 1901. He was happy about the book himself, satisfied that at last he had paid homage to his old master, whose genius as an actor he had come to appreciate more and more through the filter of time; he made this quite clear in the prologue when he wrote:

> . . . Let me state at once, in the clearest terms, that I have never known of, or seen, or heard a greater actor than was Irving.
>
> This first crow as challenge, and as salute to the sun. I hear from all the hilltops, answers coming back from other reckless fellows who strut up and down their own runs, crying, "Cock-a-doodle-do! We too have seen the sun . . ."

About the same time, the English version of Kessler's Cranach Press *Hamlet* was announced. It was the most superb edition of a Shakespeare play to be printed in modern times and gave Craig a sense of great personal achievement, for although the work had been started in 1912 and a world war had intervened, he had managed to illustrate it with seventy-four woodcuts and "composed scenes" which were among his finest works as a graphic artist. The German edition had come out the previous year. Now they are both collectors' pieces.

Nineteen thirty also saw the publication by the Oxford University Press of an enormous folio volume in which there were fine colour reproductions of most of his drawings for *The Pretenders*. The ordinary edition cost seven guineas, the special edition ten guineas—a large sum in those days. Entitled *A Production—1926*, it was certainly on a par with those records of festivities published in the eighteenth century, including its dedication, "To His Majesty Christian X King of Denmark." King Christian graciously decorated Craig with the Order of the Knights of Dannebrog. He was very proud of this, his first honour, complimenting as it did his conception of the traditional relationship between artists and great princes.

Excited by the reception of *Henry Irving*, he started on a book about his mother, which he hoped to have ready for 1931. This was a particularly difficult task because he knew little or nothing about his father, who had played such an important part in her life, and he had no idea where to look for information. He came back to England, sought out family friends and tried to check on dates with them, but no one was able to help him . . . most of them were much older than he was, and had even worse memories.

He was still self-conscious about his illegitimacy. Considering his general attitude to life, this always seemed a bit ludicrous to me: that he was in the company of other eminent men and women like Leonardo da Vinci, Cézanne, Sarah Bernhardt, Ramsay MacDonald, and Lawrence of Arabia did not help him, for certain Victorian taboos were firmly established in his make-up; as a young man he had been aware of blushing and feeling awkward when his father's name was mentioned in company and he never got over this embarrassment.

His quest for information concerning his mother produced very little that had not already been published, so he decided to confine his book to an analysis of her character as an actress and a mother by trying to re-create her personality in these two roles through a series of intimate portraits and imaginary conversations. He called it *Ellen Terry and Her Secret Self.*

The result was brilliant, but it provoked a number of abusive letters from some of Ellen's female "admirers" who thought the book should have been written very differently, one of them putting venomous pen to paper as follows:

King of cads—Prince of Hypocrites—Lord of Cowardly Assassins, I salute you with a holy smack in that face which is now the mirror of a mean, spiteful, jealous soul! Your mother weeps in heaven at the spectacle of your degradation. To this can jealousy and vanity bring a man—the public traducing of his mother, the public slander of his sister.[8]

At one time he thought of using this extract in the advertising blurbs, printed next to the following letter that he had received from the editor of a newspaper:

I have not read anything for years that touched me so much. It is a beautiful book and one of the most perfect pieces of biography ever written.[9]

On the whole, he felt, the book had been a literary success, though Sampson Low, who published it, found sales very slow—probably because it clashed with the publication of the Shaw–Terry correspondence which many people may have bought thinking that they might come across some scandal. When Craig saw the "correspondence" in a sleazy Paris book-shop, displayed among some pornographic literature, he was horrified, and knew he had been right in trying to stop its publication.

In the same year, 1931, Sampson Low had also published a book entitled *Gordon Craig and the Theatre* by Enid Rose, a sketchy biography punctuated here and there with eulogies. The work of a most devoted admirer who saw Gordon Craig as a man who could do no wrong, it was too full of panegyrics to be of any use to serious students of the Theatre, did his reputation no good, and embarrassed him considerably.

In the very useful bibliography of Craig's work at the end of the volume, reference was made to *Among Tritons and Minnows* as being "in preparation," to be issued, it said, by the same publisher. In this new work, Craig planned to introduce many of his friends of high and low degree, ranging from artists like Chaliapin and Yeats (Tritons) to booksellers, cab-drivers, and theatrical producers (Minnows). Sidney Bernstein (now head of Granada Television) had lent Craig his London flat, and in these pleasant surroundings he was settling down to write this book when he was advised that a garnishee order had been issued in the High Court in favour of his first wife, May.

It seems that following his divorce in 1904–5, May had been awarded the custody of the children and considerable alimony, but Craig had been away in Germany at the time, and in any case, could not have paid it, so until her death his mother had settled it for him; when her payments had ceased, application had been made for the order to secure the money at source from all publishers in the United Kingdom paying him royalties.

Infuriated, he left the country vowing to publish no more books in England. As he had already received an advance on royalties from *Tritons and Minnows*, he decided that at any rate he would deliver the manuscript, which he did . . . in 1935. But it was never published— probably because during the years it had changed into a series of introspective notes in the form of an annotated diary, dotted with too many comments about his health, the weather, and so on.[10]

On leaving London he had gone first to Boulogne and then on to Paris, where Halcott Glover, of whom he was very fond, told him of a cheap little old-fashioned pension at St. Germain-en-Laye. Here he and Daphne found a couple of rooms and lodged *à la bohème*—a way of life that he despised.[11]

He had never suffered hardship in his youth; during his most difficult times in Florence, the Italians had been most generous to him because he was an artist, and in any case, living was very cheap in Italy: now, at the age of sixty, and for the first time, he was enduring all the privation that can sometimes be overlooked in youth, but which in later years can cause deep dejection. The £350, coming in irregular payments from his mother's estate, proved useless in his hands, although he was relieved to know that Elena and Nelly were managing better than he could. He was no longer able to pay Daphne any wages, but she stuck by him and tried to help with her own tiny income.

He had to have books, for they were always his chief companions. He found that he could get those he coveted the most by reviewing them for *The Architectural Review*, *The English Review*, and other magazines. He also got paid for these reviews, and thus he was able to supplement his income by £160 between April and December of 1932.

But this "extra" was soon dissipated at the Café de la Paix, where he liked the head-waiter, M. Alex; the surroundings also appealed to him and there he could hob-nob with friends passing through Paris. The artists' cafés of Montparnasse and Montmartre, which were cheaper, had never attracted him.

In 1933, he lost another friend, Paul Cooper, and to him this was "like the loss of an only brother."

According to the press, his old friend had left over £23,000. It occurred to Craig that he must do something about leaving some money too! He often recorded the sums left by people, adding comments such as "good for him," or "not much for such a celebrated man," or "well well!": to him, "leaving money" was nothing to do with providing for wife and family; it was just the show of cards at the end of the game ... "so he had the trumps all the time!"[12]

As he studied the Paris booksellers' catalogues he realized that all the books on the theatre that he had picked up in the past for a few lire or francs were now fetching what seemed like exaggerated prices. He began to see that although he had no investments, his collection back in Genoa must be worth thousands of pounds.

He also realized that he possessed an asset that could be a deciding factor in future negotiations concerning his school—whoever got him would get the collection! He started talks with a group of rich friends in Holland who had long shown a desire to help him; among them were Jacob Mees, the Rotterdam banker, who had the most complete collection of Gordon Craig woodcuts in Europe, and Franz Mijnssen of Amsterdam, whom Craig had known since 1906.

Meanwhile, he got in touch with Ifan Kyrle Fletcher, a young book-seller in England with whom he became very friendly, and discussed with him the possibility of a sale to the United States, should all fail in Holland. Kyrle Fletcher was writing a bibliography of Craig's work and hoped to visit Genoa in the coming year, 1934, to check on all his details. It occurred to Craig that this visit would present an ideal opportunity to find out what his things were worth. He would also put together a number of duplicate volumes and sell them to "I.K.F." for ready cash.

The idea that he might have a lot of hidden assets cheered him and he returned to Genoa, taking Daphne with him. There, he started parcelling up his books and manuscripts under various headings, gathering, sorting, and counting his wonderful collection of old prints and drawings. Kyrle Fletcher came over with his wife, Constance, in July, worked on the bibliography, bought duplicates to the extent of £130, and left him with the impression that "The Gordon Craig Collection" might even be worth something like £40,000.[13]

Back in Italy, Craig was content for a time: there was Elena and his daughter, Nelly, all his own familiar things, his dog Talma, his books, the smell of the place—why, it was home! But his restless spirit soon felt the need to be roaming, "searching." Before him flitted visions of this and that . . . "practise and keep attempting to record what you see in the mind's eye"—as he had written in his copy-book dated 1900: for over sixty years he had attempted to do just that, to the exclusion of everything else.

Exhilarated by the thought of £40,000 he could see visions of . . . But he could not see that his behaviour with his young secretary and her visible attempts to please him were breaking Elena's heart.[14]

One day, when it was too late, he came across the book in which he had first sung Elena's praise:

. . . she has brought me new life, new love, new trust . . . she is so beautiful always—so tender so strong and so true . . . the sun sees me, the earth hears me, shall I lie?

He read through his words again and added, "I read this in 1946—I who have failed her—I do not know what to do."[15] And that was the simple truth; he could see a vision in a cloud of smoke, but he was too shortsighted to see the tears in a loved one's eyes. Confronted by emotion, he just did "not know what to do."

In May, an important-looking letter came from Rome; signed by Pirandello and Marconi; it was an invitation to attend the Volta Congress, devoted to the theatre and drama,[16] to be held in October. The trip to the great capital, "all expenses paid," appealed to him and he went on the understanding that he only represented himself. There he met Marinetti, the futurist—"the most impressive of the Italians," Maeterlinck from France, Walter Gropius from Germany, Joseph Gregor from Austria, Haig Acterian from Roumania, Alexander Tairov from Russia, and his dear friend W. B. Yeats from Ireland.

He felt very low when he returned to Rapallo after "the lively, healthy time in Rome." His vibrant personality had affected many of the delegates and he soon had invitations from Russia and Austria, as well as more from Italy.

The first came from Count Ciano, who had arranged a meeting with Mussolini, and on November 20, Craig was back in Rome.

At 6 o'clock off to Palazzo Venezia—expected to see the Duce—but didn't—saw another man—the head of state. He sat at the end of a long room at a table—alone. A door opened—I went in—we talked then I came out—but hèlas! without seeing the Duce.[17]

Such was the entry made at the time. He had presented Mussolini with his two books, *Towards a New Theatre* and *A Production*, but nothing spectacular had happened. He was very disappointed. Mussolini had always appealed to him as a man of genius and a man of power combined, a man who controlled everything—rather as he himself imagined his "stage director" would do in the theatre; but after his brief visit he felt like a member of an audience who had been round to the back of the stage for the first time and discovered that the "Fairy Palace" was only canvas and battens.

Ten days later he heard from Amaglobeli, director of the State Academic Little Theatres in Moscow, that he was invited to go there in the spring with a view to undertaking a production. Again, all expenses were to be paid. He agreed to go.

Meantime, he finished his manuscript of *Tritons and Minnows* and managed to send it off to Sampson Low by the end of January 1935. Then he prepared his entire collection in readiness for its forthcoming sale. But to whom? Its purchase was being discussed at Harvard, in Vienna and London, and the city of Genoa had offered to place the lovely old Teatro Sant' Agostino (built in 1703), at his disposal if he could find the necessary finance to run his school there.

He was getting his personal things together in preparation for his trip to Moscow, via Vienna, when a telegram arrived on March 8 from de Pirro in Rome: a great production was being planned; he must return at once, "all expenses paid"! He just had time to dash down and see what it was about. He was introduced to a Professor Gallenga-Stewart, whose fantastic idea was to put on *Quo Vadis* in the ruins of the Colosseum, with Christians burning as human torches while Gigli sang the *Ave Maria*; the famous boxer Carnera was to wrestle with a bull . . . the lions of a well-known circus were already booked . . . there would also be a Bacchanalian orgy! De Steffani was writing the libretto; Tocci, the music. And Craig—who had just been received by Mussolini—was the very man to direct it! As Silvio d'Amico remarked at the time, "the whole thing was laughable."[18]

Returning to Genoa, he picked up his luggage and left for Moscow with Daphne, who was now pregnant. Stopping at Vienna to see Gregor, he heard that so far nothing had developed about the purchase of his collection there.

On March 2, 1935, he was once more in Moscow, where the welcome was most heartening. On the platform to greet him were Amaglobeli, Meyerhold, Tairov, and Podgorin, together with twenty or thirty actors and workers from the theatre, about fifteen photographers—and a band.

He was fêted everywhere. At all the theatres he was given a tremendous ovation, lime-lights were directed on him and the audience applauded; he felt happy, but also embarrassed.

He was taken to the Moscow State Jewish Theatre and saw *King*

Lear performed by S. Mikhoels and directed by Alexei Gravoski, which he found "touching—fine and original—all superb and perfect." He was so impressed by the whole production that he went to see it four times; never before had he been so carried away by the performance of a Shakespeare play.

He looked up his old friend Stanislavsky, who was bed-ridden. He found Baltrushaitis too, who had become the representative for Lithuania. Everyone seemed poorer than when he was last there in 1912, and he could not understand why Nemirovich-Danchenko should be obliged to open his own front door.

He was excited to meet men like Piscator, Brecht, and Litvanov, and interested to see youngsters like Herbert Marshall and Jo Losey ("the melancholy") trying to learn the Russian way. But it was Sergei Eisenstein who impressed him most of all, and he described him as "the best of the Moscovites."[19]

The discussions about a possible production developed and Craig was very keen to do *Macbeth*. His hosts were also very receptive to his idea of establishing an Experimental Workshop there. Then, from some chance remark, he learned that any money that he might earn could not be taken out of the country; this came as a great blow to him; he had always preferred to live in Italy and could not contemplate spending the rest of his days in Russia. His vision of a Gordon Craig Workshop in Moscow that he could visit for a number of months every year slowly faded; he was sad, for he had appreciated his warm welcome there and found Russian enthusiasm inspiring.

On May 6 he and Daphne left Moscow and returned to Vienna, where, on the morning of May 22, 1935, Daphne slipped off to see the doctor, saying she did not feel very well. Craig went to see Joseph Gregor, who still had high hopes of acquiring the Gordon Craig Collection for the National Bibliothek, and wanted to introduce him to various wealthy people who might provide financial support. At 1.30 in the afternoon, Craig received a message that Daphne had given birth to a little daughter. He went to see her in the evening . . . and suggested that they call their baby "Two Two," because of the date. Two weeks later, as Gregor's project seemed to be moving so slowly, they went on to Venice, then via Milano back to Genoa. Little "Two Two" had been left with a nurse in Vienna.[20]

Shortly after his return to Genoa, Italy became involved in the war with Abyssinia. Craig had no time for politics and could not under-stand what was going on. But the horrors of the war in Abyssinia gradually began to disturb him. Italy, the country that he had always looked upon as home, was changing—"I must go," he wrote, "I cannot stay and see and hear Italy turned from its serenity into this sort of thing."

The climate, the financial problems and the changed way of life in Russia did not appeal to him; he had already decided that he could not work under existing conditions in England: France seemed to be the only asylum. France meant Paris—that Sargasso Sea for middle-aged artists and intellectuals in search of eternal youth. However, it was an important centre, and he visualized that with the £40,000—which he still imagined he was going to get for his collection—he might even buy a chateau at Versailles or St. Denis, or any of those other places around the city, mentioned by Dumas: there, he would publish *The Mask*; there, he would have room for us all to live with our families. He wrote to me about it, and when I replied that I did not think the idea would really work, he said I was an "obstructionist."

All his hopes now hinged on the sale of the collection. Since he did not want to be involved in the negotiations himself, he delegated certain friends in various countries to push the transaction through for him. I was one of the delegates. He liked to believe that none of us knew about the others; each of us was cautioned to work in the utmost secrecy, and each continually received letters of instruction on exactly what to say and how to behave.

While waiting for results, he spent the early part of 1936 packing books in preparation for the great day. Running short of cash, he des-patched eight of the boxes to Kyrle Fletcher as security for the loan of £100.

Little Two Two was now being cared for by a friend of Daphne's, and, she quite naturally, was worried about the child.

Daphne's presence in the household at Genoa was causing Mother so much distress that Nelly at last voiced her feelings on the matter, and that precipitated events: Father left for France, taking a vast number of trunks, boxes, and portfolios, and, of course, Daphne.

By June they were back in Paris, where they started looking for cheap rooms and good bistros, being tempted all the while by the book-shops and the Café de la Paix. The quest was expensive and unsuccessful and finally, with the cold weather upon them, they retreated to the old pension at St. Germain-en-Laye.

Nineteen-thirty-seven came . . . and in the Café de la Paix, quite by chance, Craig saw Kessler, but so altered as to be almost unrecognizable: his life had disintegrated around him; his wonderful collection of paintings had gone; Weimar was only a memory for him. Craig could not understand the reason; it appeared to be bound up with politics. He was shocked when he heard a little later that Kessler had died in Lyons on December 7.

Nineteen thirty-seven went . . . and his day-book contains the comments: "What dull days—What dull pages."

As a result of this very dullness and loneliness he began to feel like a man lost on a desert island and sought comfort in one of his favourite books—one that he had first discovered in his lodgings when he was playing *Hamlet* in Rugby in 1894—*Robinson Crusoe*. Years later in Italy, he had made one or two wood engravings to illustrate it; at one time, he had discussed doing the book with Kessler, who had been very enthusiastic; now, this masterpiece loomed large in his life, and again the urge to take up the work came upon him as he read and reread passages he loved.

Soon, he began to identify himself with old Robinson, whom he visualized as gradually assuming the appearance of the bits of rock and driftwood with which he lived. His room, which had to serve as studio-*cum*-bedroom, he imagined to be his cave: he *was Robinson Crusoe*.

Daphne's little room was also her office, and there she tried to cope with an unending amount of typing. He set her to work copying page after page from his old diaries and day-books with the idea that he might write his autobiography—the early drafts of which bear some resemblance to Crusoe's diary. He was also writing about his trips to Rome and Moscow, and his continual revisions kept her very busy.

They now had little time or money for entertainment. Occasionally they went to the cinema, and he had to admit that he liked certain films such as John Ford's *Stage Coach* and some featuring Harry Baur. Most meals were followed by a game of patience, "Napoleon" being the favourite. He never went out without cards in his pocket and would say to himself as he played, "If I win this game, so and so is going to happen . . ."; thus, winning gave him hope, and he always played on until he had won.

His correspondence grew and became his lifeline with the outside world. Among those to whom he wrote and from whom he liked to hear were Laurence Irving, Percy MacKaye in America; Friedland and Meskin of the Habima Players in Tel Aviv; Paul Cooper's son, Francis; Gertrude Hildersheim; Max Beerbohm, and, of course, Martin Shaw: these were the people who helped to keep him alive.

He corresponded with Elena as though nothing *un*usual had happened in their relationship, and kept her informed of all that was going on and all his plans for the future. Meanwhile, she waited patiently, sure that, like all the other phases in his life, the present one would pass.

He had all sorts of schemes that he believed in completely, and when the rumblings of war grew louder towards the end of 1938 he seriously thought of joining the Habima Players in Tel Aviv.[22]

I still acted as his assistant and as chief of his "secret service" in London whenever time permitted, but this was not easy with a wife and family to keep.

One event that brightened the year for him was his appointment to the distinction of Royal Designers for Industry; coming at a time when he imagined that nobody in England remembered him, it seemed to him as important as a knighthood.

All the time, the threat of war grew daily, and he hoped that no rash political move would upset his plans for the sale of his collection to Harvard University, then the most promising customer. He wrote in his day-book:

I wish to see a law passed in every land which provides for peace this way—

Any two or more men who meet to secure a peace for their two or more countries will have to return from that meeting with the peace.

If not—if excuses are made—terms not arranged the two delegates, be they the Chamberlains and Hitlers of the day shall be shot with full military honours and two more delegates chosen to *do* what the dead two failed to do.

This would save the lives of some 6 or 8 million persons or more, save the destruction of thousands of large and small towns, works of architecture, paintings, libraries, etc., and allow the constructive world to continue at its task undisturbed. It is not an unusual proceeding—for if military men fail in their trust and endanger the lives of their whole regiment drastic punishment follows. If diplomats and ministers and heads of state had to subscribe to a like discipline, fewer idiots would get to the top of the diplomatic ladder and the world would be well served—

Then, a little further on, comes the fateful entry: "*War is declared after endless attempts to keep* this man Hitler peaceful."[23]

The whole tone of his diary changed as he started to record all that was going on around him, other people's reactions, intimate pictures of events: he realized for a while that he was just one among millions. He worried about Elena and Nelly, and wondered what had happened to his son Bobby, whom he believed to be somewhere in Paris.

He was still in touch with me, and although I did my best to persuade him to come over to England, he said he could not: he was held down by his "Collection." After he had left Genoa, Elena had slowly despatched to him the remaining boxes of books, all sixty or seventy of which were housed in various places at the pension: the collection, which he had seen as the solution of all his troubles only a few years before, now held him prisoner. He was still frantically hoping that a last-minute cable would clinch the deal and that all could be shipped to America: he would then travel to the south of France, and the sun.

Mother and Nelly had already stored their furniture and Father's model stage with friends in Genoa, and on May 20 they passed through Paris on their way to London. Father went to the station to meet them and they celebrated their brief reunion by dining at a restaurant. The next day Mother left to join her sisters and myself in England; she had hoped to persuade Father to come as well, but, like Mr Micawber, he told her that he felt sure something was going to "turn up," then we could all go south together.

Time was flashing by and the political situation was changing daily: still the cable from America didn't arrive.

Meanwhile, little Two Two joined Craig and Daphne at St. Germain —she was five years old and Father had not seen her for all those years. Although her presence was an extra burden at a difficult moment, her youthful indifference to the world around her brought a new sense of value into his life; for a period she became the centre of his attention, and he took a great deal of pleasure in inventing bedtime stories for her and drawing pictures of a family of bears—

All three brothers—without fathers or mothers—but with a grand-mother and grandfather—They all lived in a tree 3 to 4 storeys high— nicely furnished, very ordinary—as I noticed. When in a fix Browny had a ring which he twisted 1–2–3 and down came a geni—crash through whatever ceiling was above them. This made them jump, and then they all felt better—They said "Geni do so and so" and it was done.[24]

On June 1, a cable arrived from America: Harvard would be willing to *store* the collection if it could be transported there *in safety*; the purchase would be discussed later. Transport of any sort was now impossible; all vehicles of every kind, from early motor cars to even earlier ox carts were being put into use to take families to the south. The English banks had moved to Bordeaux. Air-raid warnings were continually sounding. How to get sixty cases of books from St. Germain-en-Laye to a main-line station was an insurmountable problem. Craig found himself surrounded by his priceless collection, helpless and without money. Stranded British civilians in Paris queued each week at the American Embassy for a small allowance which had been arranged through diplomatic channels.

Finally, the Germans arrived; all was quiet and very orderly, but everyone was apprehensive. Then suddenly, on December 30, Craig, Daphne and little Two Two with all remaining British subjects in Paris were gathered together and taken to

FRONT—STALAG 142

BESANÇON[25]

Besançon in the Comte, the birthplace of Victor Hugo and normally associated with winter sports, now seemed a little bit of Hell. The barracks into which they were crowded had recently been occupied by Senegalese troops. The place was verminous, damp and bitterly cold; the toilets were uncovered places in the courtyards; the huts were filled with bunks in four and five tiers. Craig was, of course, separated from Daphne and Two Two, and his despair was accentuated by the behaviour of some of the internees who found curses, swearing, and "all sorts of foul language" the only relief to their hopeless plight.²⁶

Craig, always prone to attacks of bronchitis, suffered pitifully; in a few days he grew thin and his hands began to shake; he was sixty-eight, and very ill.

Among those who came to Paris soon after the occupation was a young civilian lawyer from Munich who was attached to Hitler's headquarters. His job was to collect together all the literature that he could find on the history, architecture, and administration of theatres so that at the end of hostilities Germany would have a wealth of material to assist her in rebuilding and reorganizing her national theatres, then, still governed by rules and regulations that were mostly two hundred years behind the times.²⁷ This young man found his way quite accidentally to "Shakespeare and Company," Sylvia Beach's little American bookshop situated near the Odéon Theatre: here he found quite a number of books that he wanted, and, according to Sylvia:

> After an hour or two he pointed to several piles of theatrical works, including most of Gordon Craig's . . . with difficulty I finally made him understand that they were not for sale. . . . He was a very polite and discreet sort of person and before he left, with the help of gestures and sad expressions, I made him understand that this father of the modern stage was now interned. He seemed quite concerned. . . . The quiet gentleman noted this and asked me to send him details about the family. . . . In a few days he came back with another German, this one in uniform—They introduced themselves as Mr Heim and Mr Conrad—they told me with beaming smiles that Gordon Craig and his family would be back by Christmas.²⁸

And so it was that on January 5, eleven days before his sixty-ninth birthday, his two deliverers came to St. Germain to see him and introduced themselves. He recorded their names "Heinrich Heim and Bruno Conrad" and felt that he must add "and yet there are people who will ask me to hate the Germans"!²⁹

Through the disasters of war, and following the worst experience of his life, the sun shone upon him once more. Now, when it was impossible for him to ship the collection, his friend Percy MacKaye seemed to have persuaded Harvard University to send £100 as some kind of down-payment on it! This translated into 21,000 francs, and they danced for joy in their little rooms. A few days later, Heinrich Heim camé in and paid 10,000 francs for a set of *The Mask*, saying, "Deliver it at the end of the war."

Sylvia Beach, recognizing that Heim had saved Craig's life, wrote to thank him with the simple words: "It is indeed a miracle that you have performed."

Craig found that reading "thrillers" suited the mood of the moment and they became his favourite pastime. Otherwise, he worked on *Macbeth*; since the Tyler production and his last visit to Moscow, his interest in this play had grown and he now considered it to be the best that Shakespeare had written. Sometimes, he took up his engraving tools and worked on another block for *Robinson Crusoe*; at others, he added notes to the books and pamphlets in his Collection. He was still making detailed entries in his day-book and it never occurred to him that it was dangerous to write critical notes about the Gestapo or the other authorities.

In September, Joseph Gregor came to see him and again broached the question of the purchase of his collection by Vienna. Gregor also suggested that Craig should come with it, for he was sure his old friend would be happier there. They now discussed a more realistic sum, equivalent to £15,000.

In the meantime, Heinrich Heim had been working on Craig's behalf, and Dr Posse, director of the National Gallery of Dresden turned up with a firm offer of 2,389,000 francs and an immediate down-payment of 400,000 francs. This seemed too good to be true and he signed the contract on November 12. He was told, however, that the collection would eventually be housed in Linz.[30]

He could not disappoint his old friend Gregor, so he allowed him to take away between fifty and sixty drawings for the Vienna collection. Gregor was delighted and proposed reproducing them in a portfolio as part of the great publication known as "Monumenta Scenica" in which Craig had already shown considerable interest.[31]

With what seemed a "vast sum of money" at his disposal, Craig thought his whole future was safeguarded and was again wondering how to get to the south of France. In the meantime, he went round Paris happily paying off all the booksellers, proprietors of bistros and restaurants, and various tradesmen who had been kind enough to give him credit over the last two years: in a very few days he had paid out 34,000 francs—which says much for the goodwill of the Paris shop-keepers and restaurateurs.[32]

On account of his age and in recognition of his past work, the occupying authorities soon exempted him from all controls and asked nothing in return. He was one of the lucky ones. He began to meet old friends from Germany, including the Von Nostitz family whom he had first met in 1906, and new friends such as the young Frenchman Jean-Louis Barrault. Life became interesting again and the south was forgotten.

In June, he moved into a large studio at 85 Rue Ampère, near the Place Pereire in the 17th arrondissement. There, he took all his cases of books and prints, for it has been thought inadvisable to trans-port them to Linz while the roads were so crowded with military vehicles.

By the end of 1942 he was wholly engaged on his memoirs, which he had already decided to call *Index to the Story of My Days*. Totting up his expenses for the year, he found to his amazement that 102 meals at the Ritz had cost him 43,947 francs, and that for seldom more than two persons!

A hernia which had bothered him intermittently for the last ten years suddenly became troublesome again, but by 1943 he was "still living as fully as ever and in love with life."[33]

In 1943, Odette Lieutier re-published his *De l'Art du Théâtre*, with a new preface that he had written in 1924. For war-time, the publica-tion was extremely well done, and the wrapper announced that Jean-Louis Barrault referred to the book as his "Catéchisme" . . . "the true artists' guide to the Theatre," which he was "never without . . ." Craig received 180,000 francs, which soon went in his favourite book-shops, Dauthon, Jorel, Rivière, Saffroy, and so on, where he delighted in buying rare "opuscules" of theatrical interest.

In August a new name appears in his diary: "Elinor . . . the black-haired poetess." Gradually, Elinor takes up more and more space until she becomes his only interest. She, it seems, is young and works with the Red Cross; she comes from Germany. He throws off years and is twenty-five again. He writes to her daily (some letters are sixteen pages long): he feverishly awaits the replies. They meet and dine together, always looking for new and more secluded restaurants. They drive or walk in the summer evenings among the trees of the Bois de Boulogne or the Luxembourg Gardens. Their letters are full of tenderness and urgency; when shall they meet again? But it is leading nowhere, for she has her duty . . . and a husband back in Germany. After four months of alternate rapture and torment, his letters to her are found by her husband: Craig thinks it unkind of her to have let him discover them. When the time comes for them to say good-bye, they are heart-broken. It is November. On the rebound, he falls in love again, this time with an "adorable" young Spanish actress: "This is what beauty is," he writes . . . and he is tormented once more . . .

By December he had resumed work on his memoirs. Inspired by his recent passionate experiences, he turned to his early meetings with Isadora in Berlin and began to write of those days in a new romantic vein: a trip in a motor-car becomes a ride "in a carriage and pair." He tried to forget jealousy and criticism and began annotating his old note-books with new comments, chiding himself for having been so unkind in his earlier judgement on her intelligence and behaviour.[35] For six months romantic love had carried him away, rekindling his desire to live.

By 1944 he had despatched only a very small part of his collection to Germany: there had been demands for the boxes to be "packed in readiness to leave," then, "on account of air raids," transportation had been delayed and only fourteen of about sixty boxes had been sent.

He received his last payment of 400,000 francs and when that had almost gone he could no longer remain detached from this "politicians' war"; he had to give up eating in expensive restaurants and take his turn in endless food queues. The war was on his threshold, and when the Allies invaded France in June, he was actually interested in the news. In August the people of Paris erupted and revenge was showing itself in its ugliest form: shooting was going on down the road in the Place Pereire and in many other streets. Craig and Daphne were horrified, and very worried about little Two Two, but they were looking forward to the arrival of the Allies with excitement.

That year I was engaged on a special job that took me to France, and a few days after his seventy-third birthday we were together again. I came up from the south, bringing oranges for Two Two, whom I had never seen, and what I knew to be the treat of treats for him—a

really big tin of Benson & Hedges' pipe tobacco. They had been short
of fuel for some time and when I arrived they were burning parts of
an enormous ladder that served to adjust the skylight in the studio.
Father was so pleased to see me that he hardly knew what to say, but
later, he described our reunion in a letter to Mother:

> These days our Teddy has been here and I have been in bed two of
> the times but got up for the other time—when we had a festa—he
> bought some oysters (I'd seen none for years) and I opened one of
> my 2 last big bottles of Champagne.
> What talks we had! and what a lot of good and useful things he
> brought me—He'll tell you about all that—What he'll not be able
> to tell you about is the firm impression he made on me of having
> built himself up. He seems to have developed as a person and it gave
> me repeated pleasure to look at him and realize that.[36]

Four months later he wrote me a joyful letter saying all was well—
he had just sold the French rights to a de luxe edition of his illustrated
Robinson Crusoe "for enough money to keep us for six months." He
had also managed to get the release of certain funds that had accumulated at his bank in England; he sent me a cheque, telling me to cash
it and take the money to Mother as a "nice surprise," and, forgetting
that Paris was not the only place that suffered from rationing, he also
suggested that I buy a fine peach-fed ham and take that along too!

The period of reawakening that followed the Second World War
was much the same as in 1919, only this time the readjustment to peace
seemed more organized.

For Craig, there was the excitement of hearing again from Elena,
Nelly, and Martin. We, in turn, wanted to know what he needed most,
and to all of us came the same reply, "English Tobacco"; after such a
long deprivation he relished the thought of tobacco in the same way as
Ben Gunn relished the thought of toasted cheese in *Treasure Island*.
Of course, on his instructions, the tobacco must be sent "disguised,"
for fear the French postmen might notice it and smoke it! And then
there was the fun of secretly acknowledging its arrival as though it
were some contraband: having sent him two packets of "Old Judge,"

a pipe from Astley's, and some "Tudor Rose" to try, I received the
following note:

—the Judge came and had a smoke with me—and his brother came
later—so unlike both brothers their sister Rose Tudor—a really sweet
creature worthy of the stem from which she springs—I mean the
Astley Family of St. Germain—So confusing these mix-ups—I was
struck by Rose—her charm.[37]

Slowly, he began to meet more English people as they came to
Paris on various missions. In 1946 he had the pleasure of seeing Laurence
Olivier with the Old Vic Company:

I saw Olivier in "Lear" [he wrote], not a seat to be had: so I was
given a *tall* office chair in the orchestra—I could see well and was
not seen. The music was a trifle loud—but it was a rare experience.
Olivier was admirable—the others, all but *Cornwall* and *Edgar*, were
inaudible or couldn't act—if you know what I mean. But Olivier
actually *is* an actor.[38]

He met Janet Leeper too, and their friendship led to the publication
of her delightful little King Penguin book entitled *Edward Gordon
Craig, Designs for the Theatre*, in which she wrote about his life and
work. Then there was Peter Brook and his wife, Natasha: he admired
Peter and thought Natasha adorable. They brought him presents and
did their best to make his life happier.

One day, Wing Commander Douglas Cooper called in on his way
through Paris, and gave him some exciting news: he had heard that
dozens of cases of "Craig Archives" had been found in a salt-mine
near Munich. It seems that these "dozens of cases" must have included
the lorry-load of volumes and papers taken from Florence, because
only fourteen boxes had gone from Paris and the major part of his
collection was still with him in the Rue Ampère.

Advised by various friends, Daphne filled in forms which he signed,
claiming the return of the property—most of which he had not seen
since 1907! Since he did not know what material had been taken
from Florence, and had assumed that the fourteen cases from Paris had

probably been destroyed, he looked forward to the arrival of these boxes like a child awaiting a lot of delayed Christmas parcels.[39]

He was getting a certain amount of money from England, but it was not enough to cover his expenses. He had high hopes of starting *The Mask* again, also that I would rejoin him to do the printing; his friend, Rudolf Melander Holzapfel, found him a press, type, and paper, but the project fell through. The vast studio in the Rue Ampère was becoming a very expensive storehouse. Daphne was glad to find a well-paid job translating with UNESCO as she could then help with the rent, but Craig, thinking his work was being treated as of secondary importance, did not appreciate her "deserting" him for other duties.

Once, when travelling south of Paris to Fontainbleau, he had discovered the little town of Corbeil that had charmed him. He now decided to go there "to be away from it all," and stayed at Madame Bricard's Les Corteaux, where the food was prepared superbly. Corbeil was a happy choice, and from there he wrote to me in 1946, his old cheerful self again—

I am here in Corbeil which for several reasons seems to be a fairly good copy of Heaven—and I am recovering my brass trumpet and a sackful or two of banners— . . . There's a garden resembling a sort of Eden and a pond like a mirror—and a silence at night like swans' down—in fact if I hadn't signed up at a theatrical agency only last week, I'd go in for poetry—I wonder if there's money in poetry? I want money so much—so much money that I can pay off the theatrical agent's fees and get released again and go off to Aleppo, and give up art too—art seems to me to be full of regrets—whereas Aleppo is full of fleas: I'm assured of this—so on second thoughts I'll only go to Dijon . . . a circus was here one evening—3 children 3 men and 1 goat performed the entire thing—no tent—one lamp— on the river side—800 spectators on benches and soap boxes—a band i.e. 1 drum 1 bassoon—maybe you will not believe me when I tell you I never was present at such a perfect spectacle—never saw such a scene—nor heard such persuasive music—and left the ring in a state of enchantment.[40]

Paris was near enough if he was needed there. Meanwhile, in the peace and quiet of Corbeil, he was happier. One of his letters to Baliol Holloway, with whom he enjoyed a happy correspondence, shows the rejuvenating effect of the change:

I came away from Paris 15 days ago to rest—went to an attic in a French village—forgot I was 74—supposed I was 44—hated the attic—its rats—its bare boards and the rest of its damn sillyness— then discovering it was not the attic's fault but my own I was humbled and damned myself—and returned to Paris. Then after a pause of 2 days I returned to the countryside and its absurd attic—to discover if it was I who was the absurdity—it was.

So I went back after 4 more days of agony to Paris. Leapt into a Black Market Restaurant, spent my last 1,000 francs on a lunch and my last but one 1,000 fr. on lunch for a lady—and decided that the country was really the spot I loved best (BEING DOG TIRED after all these 6 years) So I came once more to the attic—spat on it—and went into the neighbouring chateau—and here I am and shall stay—absolute luxe de luxe—Strange—but when you reach 74, you too may get fancies into your head. Dismiss them now—never go to an attic.

About me, enough—now about you—I have a cutting sent me of your doings—in a play—as chorus—or something idiotic—Young men like you should stick to your guns—and to play skittles (not chorus) is your game. You will I am sure.

What about playing Hamlet (now listen) with a black patch over your right eye? *Why? because all LONDON would ask why*—and I want to hear all London asking that. I think of the several quiet bits of bye play you could make with that patch—and what a criticism it would be on all the critics—Why not risk it—without telling anyone in the company—It would be another success de scandal (and better) like Robert Macaire and the great Frederick. Don't tell me you "don't see your way"; how can one quite see one's way without one eye—and was not our dear Hamlet ½ blind—doesn't the bitterness of it lie just there—the sadness *and the sudden seeing* of the last scene—doesn't it all get explained by that patch?

So conscious of this defect (?) of his before Ophelia—head down half the time he speaks with her—maybe it was the only patch of mourning the proud soul would allow itself—but the consternation

of the court as it turns to see its prince enter in ordinary dress—but
with the one *spot*. Their faces!! his face too—
Oh that I might drill the crowd for you—but can't *you* do that?

Do you take me to be fooling?

I am not—

In one evening (and be sure to pack the house) you'd capture
all London.

In each soliloquy you brush it gently up—till it lodge on
your forehead—or sideways—or rapidly or muddlingly—*I tell you
that patch is an idea*!

. . . he has both eyes—he sees only too well—but the patch
is the armour. Who dare ask him . . . why? the patch . . . a temporary
pain in the right eye – – – only worn in court scenes: not in scenes
with ghost—yes worn *after* ghost goes end Act I, till he comes full
thrust toward H & M, Act II he has it—raises to the forehead when
with the actors, of course, and with Horatio—enter Osric, down
comes the patch—Too plain?—too obvious? you think?
I don't—all through the play it acts like a chorus in an old Greek
play—but being plain and obvious is no defect—provided the
manner of using the patch, the play with it, be delicate and fine.

To Corbeil came Elena, en route for war-scarred Genoa to see what
had happened to the things she had left behind. They spent some happy
days together talking about past adventures—such as avoiding bailiffs
in Hampstead or sitting up until 4 a.m., listening to Yeats telling a
story; they walked about the countryside—and when she left it was
as though he had been awakened from a dream.

M

CHAPTER SIXTEEN

A Journey to the South
1947–1966

ON MARCH 27, 1947, Edy Craig, who had not been well for some time, suddenly sat up in bed at her cottage in Smallhythe, exclaimed, "It's all black . . . who's put out the light?" and died.[1] Writing to me about her death, Father said:

> I don't grieve—but I shall grieve. Solemn things of that size quite astound me—I feel no emotion—it's only as the thing creeps later on into me . . . *then* do I begin to descend into sadness.
>
> A quiet or quick or slow going is, all the same, a going—into the darkness which she rightly said was black. We have no idea of black: Soot—night time—all such darkness is still not Black, but where there is nothing, that gulf-like shade of Black, can only be.
>
> But now—to us all it's dust—ashes—it seems idiotic—but there is the good God—and so, strange to say, all must be well—I have never been a church man—but I have experience that no church ever brought me—and it is good.
>
> . . . our friendship (E & I) was an ideal thing from year 1 to year 20 or so—then a large gap—and it became ideal again about 2 months ago—and we both looked forward to ending as we began—
>
> So I sit here puzzled at the loss of a young sister 20 years old and 2 months.[2]

Having got as far as Corbeil, he felt the temptation to wander further south towards the sun, to get the Alpes-Maritimes between himself and the north-east winds.

In 1948 he tried Le Cannet just above Cannes, but finding that it was too full of the kind of people he disliked, he moved higher up to Camassade, where he lived simply and happily in an old inn, until it was sold. In 1952 he went still further up to Tourrettes-sur-Loup which he loved, but after a while it seemed too remote and he finally settled in Vence—the little town on the rocks which he had visited in 1906, when he was formulating his ideas for *Scene*.[3]

Until he came across Al Young at Tourrettes and the beautiful Countess Károlyi at Vence, he had very few local friends and still depended on correspondence for his contact with the kind of people that made living worth while.

When Derek Hudson was preparing his book on Jimmy Pryde, Craig took great delight in writing to tell him of their early days together, and after publication, he liked this biography of his old friend so much that he hoped someone would write as good a book about him one day. Other correspondents were Richard Ainley and Richard (Bebb) Williams, both actors, and Paul Cooper's son, Francis—"it's so nice hearing from these youngsters."

Laurence Irving's letters pleased him most of all. Laurence, who was then working on his grandfather's biography, sought his advice, and Craig enjoyed helping him, regarding him as the rightful heir to the affection he felt for his old master.[4]

The queries from Derek Hudson and Laurence Irving led Craig to question the dates and details in his own memoirs. Again, he tried to check with various friends, including Gertrude Hildersheim and Martin Shaw, only to find them as vague as himself: he began to realize he had left his research work till far too late in life. Once, in an effort to help, I pointed out that he had made an incorrect statement concerning some event, and he shut me up with: "How do you know? You weren't even born"!

By 1952 "the collection," still at the Rue Ampère studio, was becoming a tremendous burden. The fourteen boxes had been returned from the salt-mines, together with an enormous quantity of material from *The Mask* offices, and the place was overcrowded. The rent, although comparatively low, was very much in arrears; Daphne was paying most of it, for she and Two Two were using part of the premises as a flat, sometimes letting a room to a friend. However, the owners wanted it vacated in order that they could do it up and ask a much higher rent. So once again, the question arose of getting rid of the contents.

+ here sit I in my deck-chair +
scribble or read or do nothing.
A cat has taken a fancy to come & sit
by me in the old straw hat / shown here ☺

Craig's sketch of himself and cat on the Côte d'Azur.

Far away from it all in the olive-clad hills of the Côte d'Azur, Craig could not see the urgency; he managed to get by with the little he had with him, and preferred not to think of Paris and the collection. Occasionally, he would write to Daphne, asking for certain books, and he liked to feel that he would have all his things around him again . . . one day . . . soon.

Rumours soon spread that the collection was once more for sale. Various bodies showed interest and made enquiries, including the University of Southern California, which first contacted me through my friend Albi Rosenthal of Oxford, and the Appia Foundation in Berne, which got in touch with Craig through Professor Edmund Stadler. Craig seemed to be interested for a while, then started to invent difficulties; he did not really want to get rid of his collection—any more than the old farmer wants to get rid of his faithful old sheepdog . . . he would rather someone else did it and told him afterwards, but a big transaction like this could not be conducted without him.

Negotiations went on for years, then M. Julien Cain, the Chief Administrator of the Bibliothèque Nationale, secured it for Paris: not because he offered the largest sum of money, but because of his sympathetic understanding in allowing Craig to retain various things he required for the second part of his memoirs, and other items which, for sentimental reasons, he felt he would like to have by him during the remaining years of his life. To Craig, parting with all his treasures to America or Switzerland seemed too final, whereas Paris was quite near and he felt sure the curator, André Veinstein, whom he liked, would treat his things with care and let him borrow a book if he wanted it. His collection, like many others, was a very personal thing; he knew every item in it, and even when his memory for new friends and faces became confused, he still knew exactly where to find a reference among the firm old friends on his shelves.

The sale was announced in the English papers on July 23, 1957; one mentioned the sum of £13,000 as the price paid. The deed was done. Craig had millions and millions of French francs which he put into the bank at Nice, thinking he would have enough money for all his needs were he to live for another fifty years!

The first part of his memoirs, covering the years 1872 to 1907, and called *Index to the Story of My Days*, was published by the Hulton Press in the same year as the sale. As with all his other books, he sent the first copy to Elena; it contained a note saying:

. . . only pages 212 and 236 worth while to read—the rest part rubbish, part incomplete—anyhow best I could do. Our life in Florence with our two, begins in Volume II; it will make some of 'em open their eyes.[5]

The passage that he had marked on page 212 was:

It was in 1900 I first met Elena Meo—and she is one of the few women I know, or know of, who knew what she was, wished, and where she was going, and what she had to do. She then did this with all her might.

. . . a durable fire in the mind ever burning
Never sick, never old, never dead, from itself never turning . .
(Sir Walter's lines)
We both undertook to do what we liked doing and could do.

There are many sensible men and women who seem to have no firm liking for doing any one thing—no capacity to up and do it (unless tempted all the time by rewards) and no capacity to enjoy the task they have set themselves. Elena had and I had that capacity, and we have it still. We enjoyed our tasks so much, we were easily able to do without most of the rewards which Fortune brings to most people . . . London's clubs—motor cars—a nice balance to one's credit at the bank—a London and country house—plenty of suits and dresses and hats and shoes and ribbons.

And on page 236 the passage marked was:

For although I have swayed in the wind for more than eighty years of life, by bending to the wind I have prevailed for fifty-two years with my dream for the Theatre. In my heart the dear Theatre as it is, in my soul the Theatre as it shall be.

It was with this last paragraph that he intended opening the second volume of his memoirs.

But he never wrote the second volume, for at the end of the year, Elena, who had been ill for some weeks at her thatched cottage in Buckinghamshire, died unexpectedly on the morning of December 24, and again he wrote—"I can't believe it." He had taken Elena so much for granted over fifty-eight years; she had always been the companion of his thoughts and without this company he was lost. He put his manuscript away; and, as far as he was concerned, the second part of his life was finished.

Nelly, who had lived with Mother at Long Crendon, received a letter from him saying he did not expect to live much longer. She rushed out to see what comfort she could bring him and found him in excellent health for his age, but suddenly aware that he too might die someday. Now, he really felt alone, and needed Nelly's company. She settled down to caring for him and became his cook, nurse, and companion.

In 1958 he was made a Companion of Honour. For a brief moment, he thought of going to London for the investiture, but his doctor would not allow it, so a little ceremony took place in Nice. Proud of this distinction, he would often say, "I was very honoured when our Queen made me . . . hmm . . . whatever it was," for he never could remember the title.

The following year, Martin Shaw, the closest of all his friends also departed this life . . . Max Beerbohm had gone two years before . . . Now, all the lights that illumined his youth had been put out, and only his own clear but flickering flame burnt on.

His family now consisted of Nelly, who looked after him, myself, with whom he corresponded weekly and to whom he confided all his troubles, Rosie, his eldest daughter who lived in South Africa, who always kept in touch with him and whom he still loved dearly, David Lees, who called in to see him whenever he was near, and Two Two, the youngest, who flitted in and out, as vague about life as he was (in her, he saw a picture of himself at the same age). His eldest son, Bobby, paid him one or two surprise visits. He never heard from any of his other children and did not even know if they were still alive.

There was a continual stream of visitors passing through Vence who wanted to see him; when he was in a good mood they amused him; otherwise, he was positively rude to them. He rather fancied himself in a new part which was a blend of two characters, Montaigne and Voltaire, with Voltaire predominating!

When the weather was sunny and a gentle breeze blew in from the sea he liked to stroll about Vence or Tourrette dressed in his Arab burnous, his eyes shaded from the glare of the sun by a local straw-hat with an enormous brim. He always carried Irving's walking-stick, which he waved aloft in salutation while shouting a very musical "Ha-ha-haa!" like three notes on a bell. He always took with him an old leather attaché-case containing paper, pens, and pencils . . . so that he was prepared, should any ideas come to him. Round his neck, suspended on a long plaited silk cord, hung his watch, together with a very fine scarab inscribed with the name of King Amassis which Elena had given to him—"This scarab has a magic property if anything has, it is a real Talisman," he wrote.

He had his favourite restaurants and cafés that suited different moods, and a strange assortment of friends with whom he liked to chat: the postman, the barber (who was Italian), various shopkeepers, as well as a mixture of foreign residents. He had no time for Matisse, but of Picasso he said, "Oh, he's a jolly fellow . . . twinkling eyes . . . we always wave to each other!"

Among those visitors whom he always welcomed were Sir Ashley Clarke, whom he had known since 1947, and Bernard Miles who, with an amused glint in his eye, used to join him in pulling the modern theatre apart and putting it together again . . . differently. Then there was Alfred Junge's youngest son, Evald, a fervent admirer who did everything he could to help him, from arranging exhibitions and broadcast talks to buying him books and tobacco.

Of all the young people around him in these last years, the one who impressed him the most was Ferruccio Marotti from Rome. Marotti, who was writing a book about him, to be published in Italian, had bothered to come to Vence and stay there for six months, weathering all his moods, in order to get first-hand information and consult original documents; he had also learned English in order to converse with him and translate his writings. Above all, "he only asked intelligent questions." Marotti, with his Italian sense of humour was amused, not frightened by Craig's sudden outbursts of fury which could be provoked by a cloudy day, indigestion, or the receipt of a silly letter. As Father wrote to me:

> Marotti is 21 but with the capacity of 35. . . . He makes up for the thirty-seven young hopefuls who have, in the last thirty-seven years, buzzed around me—
> and its proving very real—It is especially lucky for me, for I am feeling in need.[6]

When Marotti's book was published in October 1961, I read a lot of it aloud, translating as I went, while Father lay back in the shade of a tree murmuring—"clever boy, that." Later, when I told him that Marotti had come over to England and, in order to get information for his next book, had gone through thousands of documents in my collection, he said, "that's the way to do it . . . ," then he added, "how the hell do you manage to have all those documents about me?" I reminded him that I was on the way to being sixty myself, and had been collecting material about him for over thirty years, and that he and Edy had given me quite a lot of it . . . "Yes, I forgot," he said with a twinkle in his eye, "I always think of you as a boy."

In 1962 another book about him came out, this time in French, written by Denis Bablet who, with his wife, had also spent some time at Vence doing research. This book pleased him too, but he always called it "Bablet's *Thesis*."

His ninetieth-birthday celebrations brought him lots of pleasure and a new zest for life: it was a grand age to have reached and he told himself that he would now live to be a hundred.

He could not attend the opening of the great exhibition of his collection organized by the Bibliothèque Nationale in Paris, but was delighted with the well made catalogue listing all his treasures.

In London, Bernard Miles asked me to organize a special little commemorative exhibition in the foyer of the Mermaid Theatre, and the catalogue for this, although minute in comparison, pleased him even more.

Through Discurio, Evald Junge issued a limited edition of three double-sided twelve-inch recordings of Father's vivid talks about Irving, his mother, Isadora, and other celebrities, which he had made originally for the British Broadcasting Corporation between 1951 and 1953. The records were accompanied by a brochure containing some of the unpublished material formerly intended for *Tritons and Minnows*, and a recent photograph of him by my daughter, Helen, my son John having arranged the typographical layout. All these personal touches gave him great joy.

The French edition of his memoirs came out in the same year, and Heinemann reprinted his famous book, *On the Art of the Theatre*, with a note saying that since 1911 "it has been a source of inspiration, anger and delight to all who are interested in the drama." He was glad the word "anger" had been included, for as he said, "It's good for them to feel angry, it makes them do things."[7]

The following year Marotti helped to arrange for the Bibliothèque Nationale Exhibition to be transferred to Venice during the usual Biennale celebrations, where a most comprehensive exhibition of Appia's work, from Berne, was shown with it. I was invited to attend, and on the way back to England, stopped at Vence for a while to tell Father all about it. I brought him one of the impressive posters that advertised the exhibition: it covered the whole of his bedroom door and again he was overjoyed, sometimes turning on the light in the middle of the night to look at it, like a child with a Christmas stocking. He was particularly pleased to have his work under the same roof with Appia's again.

While I was there we talked happily about many things. He wanted me to finish engraving some of his designs for *Robinson Crusoe*; I was also to finish his books on "The Bibiena Family" and the one on "Italian Theatre from 1500 to 1800." In addition, I was to write his life—"and don't whitewash me . . . remember, the sky is not all stars." And so the list continued; the work he wanted me to complete would require another ten to twenty years I got the impression that he wanted to "clear his desk," to be assured that everything was being looked after.

Between my visits, my sister kept me informed of all that happened, writing the most amusing letters that brought every incident to life. One contained the following:

> One day after tea, when he was reading *Index*, he suddenly said "Nelly, can you tell me where I can find a sensible book . . .? This is just drivel—written for a lot of females to read and get excited about" . . . I gave him *On the Art of the Theatre* . . . you should have seen his face light up with pleasure—He sat and read it right through.[8]

But she began to worry because he would insist that he could still do everything for himself and this often resulted in fits of giddiness.

He took it into his head that Vence was a "dead and buried village," and he would go off on his own, night after night, to Nice in a taxi, which he would keep waiting until he felt like returning home.[9] In Nice he was looking for life—and hoping to make contact with the dead: "Somewhere along the Promenade des Anglais . . . who knows . . . I might find the spirit of I.D.," he told me in a whisper—for it was there that she had met her tragic death, garotted by her floating shawl caught in the wheel of the racing car in which she was being driven. Once more he went through his old note-books from his early days with Isadora, thinking of publishing an exquisite little book about her.[10]

After a while this thirst for "life" in Nice quietened down. Instead he and Nelly would sometimes drive to one of his favourite restaurants and sit long after their meal, reading *Macbeth* together; it became a kind of game, each testing the other's memory on stray lines here and there. Or he would read Shakespeare's Sonnets, which he loved more and more—and which he felt sure were addressed to a black cat!

On June 26 he wrote:

Dear old boy, Nelly tells me that I have not answered your recent letters—oh dear me—if you know how difficult it now is to write anything at all—but I dare say you do know. How little I have to say—my life is a day to day time of dullness. I get up late—I sit— I puzzle—I end by doing small nothings—and as you see, it's a struggle to take pen and write about nothings. I *smoke*, I play cards— Patience—daily. That quiets me—92, is that my age—? I think it is—well——

I read the newspapers daily—3 quarters *dull* stuff and the last quarter fairly dull. I enjoy the warm days . . . I dread the cold ones. Few visitors call—all the better—but one or two are enough. It's a queer age—92 is. My white pussy cat is a JOY. Never a harsh word— always loving—*looks* at me—[11]

He found it difficult to escape from this melancholy state of mind. I tried to help him by sending as many books as I could; one in particular, with reproductions of Hans Burgkmair's superb woodcuts of the Triumph of Maximilian I, succeeded in turning his mind away from the slow march of time; he wrote:

It seems to me I shall be unable to pass a day without giving hours to this marvel. WHEW! I feel a kind of wreckage, I mustn't pass the late evenings with these dangerous pages.[12]

Then one day I heard from my sister that Father was almost penniless: his bank had told him that the "millions of francs" which he had imagined to be more than enough for the rest of his life had all gone. Though angry with her for "bothering" me, he accepted a small cheque to bridge the immediate gap; "Things are not good," he wrote, "but . . . what a nice word BUT is."

The acute situation was eased when Bernard Miles, who was in Vence, bought some of Father's treasures. An English bookseller, passing through on holiday, was clever enough to call in, put down a bundle of notes, and say: "What can you give me for that, Mr Craig?";

he went away with a hoard worth twenty times the sum. His old pen-friend in America, Lee Freeson, helped him to sell one or two special items to some American collections for large sums, and those of us who had any money to spare found ways of getting him to take it. His cousin Sir John Gielgud, with whom he corresponded a lot and whose continuation of the Terry tradition he so admired, proved a marvellous friend in this time of need. He dreaded having to live in penury again, as he had done before in St. Germain-en-Laye.

In London, a little group of anonymous well-wishers formed them-selves into a society called "The Friends of Gordon Craig," and by subscribing generously to a fund, they were able to relieve him of all his worries about the future. This was a magnificent gesture.

By October 8 he was again wrestling with his melancholy thoughts.

. . . Oh Lord [he wrote] how old *old age* is. One doesn't (one *cannot*) conceive *how* old and awful old age is, till one is up to the eyes. *Then* . . . one says puff and blows it all out of the open empty windows.[14]

But often the "puff" didn't work.

The following month, Nelly, who was preparing some food, heard a crash, and ran into his room to find him collapsed on the tiled floor. She called the doctor and phoned or telegraphed any of the family whose addresses she had. I arrived by plane and found her with young Two Two—who, poor child, had lost her mother a few days before.

Father lay on his bed with closed eyes, his long arms moving in the air above his head, the first finger and thumb of his right hand con-tinually moving as though he was holding a needle and embroidering some complicated pattern in an imaginary tapestry, while with his other hand he seemed to be searching for something in the air. I stroked his head, but he did not appear to feel my touch; I grasped his hand tightly: "Who's that?" he asked. "It's Teddy." "Oh—oh—oh . . . for how long?" "Every day." "Fine-fine-fine." We took turns in being with him and trying to feed him with drops of water and grape juice, which the doctor said was all his system needed or could cope with.

He seemed to be getting further and further away; he became more and more unintelligible, and almost unrecognizable too. He still embroidered the air and uttered strange sounds. I noticed that words of comfort seemed to bewilder him: he was lost between a real and an imaginary world. One evening, he murmured something that sounded like "warefuzzy" . . . I thought perhaps his mind was back at the Lyceum . . . "*Where is Fussy?*"—Fussy was Irving's dog. There was no point in saying, "That's all right," or "There, there," because it wouldn't fit in with his picture, so I shouted, bold and loud, "He's up with the Govn'or!" His poor face became radiant as he murmured, "Good, good," and he patted the bed. Later, he asked if the world was still going round: I remembered him talking about the "end of the world" to an old peasant called Raggio, near Rapallo years before, so I shouted a reply in Italian. "Why, that's old Raggio—hurrah!" he cried. It was if he had suddenly penetrated some barrier, and, as I sat watching him slowly improve, I thought of J. B. Priestley's beautiful play *Johnson over Jordan*, for which I had once designed the scenes; I now seemed to be in just such a play myself and blessed Priestley for all the help he gave me.

Telegrams had followed David all over Europe and when he arrived Father was able to recognize him. Marotti arrived shortly afterwards; "Dear boy . . . have you come from Rome?"—he was so touched. His neighbour, Alfred Neuman, of whom he was very fond, but whom he insisted on calling "Billy," came in and they talked as though nothing had happened; only a few words, but he knew that his wanderings were over and he was back in Vence. His old doctor, who had shed tears when he left a few days before, just said, "C'est une miracle!" Father's terrific tenacity had carried him through. But I felt that another stroke, however small, would be his end.

Soon he was up again, but now life just ticked by. His beautiful calligraphy grew more and more undecipherable but he still *tried* to write and I replied with letters that evidently cheered him. The moments were helped past by Catherine Károlyi, Alfred Neuman, Mrs Wethered, and her sister, Miss Deans, all of whom came to sit and talk . . . sometimes just to sit and say nothing. But he knew.

The second stroke, which caused him to fall again, came in July. On the eleventh, the artist and writer C. Walter Hodges, who was passing through Vence, called hoping to see him and he wrote to tell me of the visit:

I went to see him and held his hand, and Nellie cossetted him and repeated to him who I was; but he did not look up, and it was impossible to know whether he did not hear or understand, or whether he simply wished to stay withdrawn. Perhaps it was a "bad day." Nellie asked me to report to you what I had seen, and I am sorry it has to be sad. But it was interesting and fascinating, if I may say so, to see coming back through the aged features of your father the lineaments of the very handsome young man one sees in his early photographs.[15]

On the morning of July 29, Nelly went into his room to see if he wanted anything . . . Only his outward form was there: his inner grace, and one of the most fertile imaginations of our age, had flown. His remains were accompanied to the Marseilles Crematorium on August 1 by his son David Lees and Ferruccio Marotti, then his ashes came back to the English countryside that he had loved so much.

Today, as I look through his sketches and manuscripts, I am caught by the excitement and the enthusiasm in the ideas that he has recorded— revelations of beauty, always a revelation, always a development of the art of the theatre. The fervour and devotion that he put into his work is enshrined within it, and as one follows his words or looks at a scribbled sketch . . . why, there he is again, and all the old excitement begins once more.

ENVOY

As I was writing this last chapter, I came across a note to "Dear Martin" which seemed to be a fitting end to the life of this wonderful man who lived and thought entirely in terms of the theatre—

A sudden notion has come to me to put at the end of my Memoirs the two words of Dido—"Remember me" . . . not the words, but the music of just that cry—It comes back to me . . .

NOTES
BIBLIOGRAPHY
AND
INDEX

NOTES

Among the sources quoted below will be found the following abbreviations: E.T. Personal, E.G.C. Personal, Edy Personal, and Elena Personal. These indicate first-hand memories passed on to the author by Ellen Terry, Gordon Craig, Edith Craig and Elena Gordon Craig.

CHAPTER ONE: 1872–1875

1 E.T. Personal.
2 E.T. Personal and the author's personal correspondence with C. R. Snow, Esq., grandson of Teddy's first nurse.
3 Dudley Harbron: *The Conscious Stone—The Life of Edward William Godwin* (London: Latimer House; 1949).
4 E.T. Personal.
5 Walter Calvert: *Souvenir of Miss Ellen Terry* (London: Henry Drane; 1897). Ellen was very fond of this little book on her life.
6 E.T. Personal.
7 Kathleen M. D. Barker: "The Terrys and Godwin in Bristol," typescript of Lecture given to the Society for Theatre Research, 1967.
8 Kathleen M. D. Barker, in a letter to the author.
9 E.T. Personal.
10 E.T. Personal.
11 E.T. Personal.
12 E.T. Personal.
13 E.T. Personal.
14 *Ellen Terry's Memoirs* (London: Victor Gollancz; 1933). This edition is more useful than the 1908 edition published by Hutchinson, because it includes additional biographical chapters by Edith Craig and Christopher St. John.
15 Harbron: *The Conscious Stone.*
16 E.T. Personal. The story of the Godwin–Terry romance told by Marguerite Steen in *A Pride of Terrys* (London: Longmans; 1962) seems to be derived, in part, from what David Loshak so rightly refers to as "questionable statements" ascribed to Ellen Terry by Lady Duff Gordon in *Discretions and Indiscretions* (New York, 1932), but I can find no evidence that Godwin was ever friendly with G. F. Watts, nor can I imagine such a relationship between two personalities whose conception of art and life was so diametrically opposed.
17 E.T. Personal, and a page from her Personal Note-book in which she recorded all the important dates in her early life. Author's Collection.
18 E.T. Personal.
19 E.T. Personal.
20 ET–EGC Correspondence. Author's Collection.
21 ET–EGC Correspondence. Author's Collection.
22 E.T. Personal.
23 Ellen Terry: *Ellen Terry's Memoirs.*
24 Harbron: *The Conscious Stone.*
25 Louise Jopling: *Twenty Years of My Life* (London: John Lane; 1925).
26 Ellen Terry's personal correspondence with Mr Wilson. Author's Collection.

27 *The Bancrofts. Recollections of Sixty Years* (London: John Murry; 1909); *Mr & Mrs Bancroft on and off the Stage 1889* (London: Richard Bentley; 1888)—these two very different editions are well worth comparing.

28 George Godwin, F.S.A. (1815–88), helped Charles Kean with the archaeological background to his plays. He was also an architect, he too worked in Bristol, and is often confused with Edward William Godwin, F.S.A. (1833–86), Gordon Craig's father.

CHAPTER TWO: 1875–1888

1 Ellen Terry's personal correspondence with Mr Wilson. Author's Collection.
2 Ibid.
3 G. F. Pardon: *Routledge's Popular Guide to London and its Suburbs* (London: Routledge; 1862).
4 Ellen Terry: *Ellen Terry's Memoirs*. Ellen also refers to Kelly's "tenderest voice" in a letter to Mrs Bancroft quoted in *The Bancrofts, Recollections of Sixty Years* (London: John Murry; 1909). The best account of Kelly's life is to be found in *The Dramatic List* edited by Charles Pascoe (London: David Bogue; 1880).
5 David Loshak: "G. F. Watts and Ellen Terry," in *The Burlington Magazine* (1963).
6 This photograph is in the Author's Collection.
7 Laurence Irving: *Henry Irving* (London: Faber and Faber; 1951). This fine book has been invaluable when checking the dates of various Lyceum productions and American tours.
8 Ibid.
9 E.T. Personal.
10 I record the story that my father told us more than once long before the version that appears in his book *Ellen Terry and Her Secret Self* (London: Sampson Low; 1931).
11 Edy Personal.
12 ET–EGC Correspondence. Author's Collection.
13 E.T. Personal.
14 My grandmother not only told me this story but took me through the same ordeal when I was a small boy.
15 W. R. Lethaby: *Form in Civilization* (London: Oxford University Press; 1922).
16 E.G.C. Personal.
17 E.T. Personal.
18 EGC–ET Correspondence. Author's Collection.
19 E.T. Personal.
20 (Stephen Coleridge): *The Heart of Ellen Terry* (London: Milles and Boon; 1938).
21 Laurence Irving: *Henry Irving: The Actor and his World* (London: Faber and Faber; 1951).
22 E.T. Personal.
23 Harbron: *The Conscious Stone*.
24 EGC–ET Correspondence, Heidelberg. Author's Collection.
25 Ibid.
26 ET–EGC Correspondence. Author's Collection.
27 ET–EGC Correspondence, Heidelberg. Author's Collection.
28 Ibid.
29 Ibid.
30 Ibid.
31 Ibid.

CHAPTER THREE: 1889–1892

1 ET–EGC Correspondence. Author's Collection.
2 Ibid.

3 Ibid.

4 Ibid.

5 E.G.C. Personal.

6 Ibid.

7 Personal recollections of Miss Maudie Gibson.

8 ET–EGC Correspondence. Author's Collection.

9 Ibid.

10 Ibid.

11 Ibid.

12 This little "handout" is printed on a folded sheet of paper, and as far as I know, is unique. Author's Collection.

13 E.G.C. Personal; also *Souvenir of Ravenswood presented at The Lyceum Theatre, 1890.*

14 E.G.C. Personal.

15 Terriss–Craig Correspondence. Author's Collection.

16 E.G.C. Personal; Tom Heslewood, the actor, who was one of the party told me the same story.

17 I am indebted to C. R. Snow, Esq., "Essie's" grandson, for the copy of this letter.

18 E.G.C. Personal. Also, W. L. Courtney: "Professor Hubert Herkomer R.A., His Life and Work," in the *Art Journal* (Christmas number, 1892).

CHAPTER FOUR: 1893–1896

1 Henry Irving's Correspondence with E.G.C. Author's Collection.

2 E.G.C. Personal.

3 ET–EGC Correspondence. Author's Collection.

4 E.G.C. Personal. When my father first showed me how to engrave he would recall all the happy hours spent with Jimmy and "The Kid" (Nicholson's nickname), and elaborated on their various methods for my benefit. I now have all my father's engraving tools. He gave most of his blocks to his youngest daughter, Daphne, now Mrs Padron.

5 Tom Heslewood, who was so helpful to Laurence Irving when he wrote his grandfather's life, told me many stories about this production. In 1928, I used to join Heslewood and Walter Collinson (Henry Irving's dresser), daily for lunch at a public house in Covent Garden and there I listened to them tell countless stories about the "Guv'nor," "Young Ted," and "Terriss," all of which have been useful.

6 This four-page announcement is extremely rare and I have only heard of one other copy apart from the one in my collection.

7 ET–EGC Correspondence. Author's Collection.

8 Ibid.

9 A copy of this poster is preserved in the Enthoven Collection at The Victoria and Albert Museum, South Kensington, London.

10 ET–EGC Correspondence. Author's Collection.

11 Ibid.

12 Ibid.

CHAPTER FIVE: 1896–1899

The EGC–May Craig and EGC–Jess Dorynne correspondence in my collection is of far too personal a character to quote from, but the information that I have been able to extract is embodied in this and the next chapter.

1 ET–ECG Correspondence. Author's Collection.

2 EGC–Jess Dorynne Correspondence. Author's Collection.

3 ET–EGC Correspondence.

4 David Cecil: *Max* (London: Constable; 1964).
5 E.G.C. Personal.
6 EGC–Edith Craig Correspondence. Author's Collection.
7 "Actors of the Past," by Charles Mathews in *The Era Almanac*, 1868, stuck in an 1898 scrap-book. Author's Collection.
8 Ellen Terry: *Ellen Terry's Memoirs*.
9 *Sunday Times* (London), August 19, 1923.
10 E.G.C. Personal.
11 ET–EGC Correspondence. Author's Collection.
12 Martin Shaw: *Up to Now* (London: Oxford University Press; 1929).
13 E.G.C. Personal.
14 Ibid.
15 I am indebted to Mr Stanley Watkins for the vivid description of the house, where he often stayed after Gordon Craig had left.
16 This tragic episode is recorded in letters kept in a Special File in the Author's Collection.
17 Edy Craig, who was very closely connected with her brother in the making of this book, gave me many details about its production. The original wood-blocks are now in the Special Collection of the University of California, Los Angeles.
18 The sketches in my collection, which were made by Craig during this period are remarkably free from the influence of James Pryde or anyone else.

CHAPTER SIX: 1899–1900

1 All the foregoing quotations are from Note-book T, which is double-sided. One side of this book bears the title "Designs" and the dates 1900 to 1912, and contains a list, description and history of over 350 of his drawings; the other side bears the title "Theatre," and the dates 1904.5.6. On page 105 in the centre of the book is a section dated 1900 which has the title "A List—To save waste of time and assist the moods": it is from this section that I have made the extracts.
2 I am greatly indebted to Mrs Joan Shaw, Martin Fallas Shaw's widow, for permission to use the great number of letters from Gordon Craig to her husband which are continually referred to in this volume as: EGC–MFS Correspondence.
3 My father frequently told me of this important episode in his life and showed me the sketches that he made at the time; some of these are at the Bibliothèque de l'Arsenal, Paris. The two later sketches were reproduced in Denis Bablet's *Edward Gordon Craig* (London: Heinemann; 1966).
4 *Prospectus of The Purcell Operatic Society*. Author's Collection.
5 EGC–MFS Correspondence.
6 Ibid.
7 EGC–Edith Craig Correspondence.
8 Ibid.
9 Ibid.
10 Shaw–Craig Correspondence. Author's Collection.
11 Apart from Martin Shaw's own recollections of *Dido and Aeneas* and those carefree times in his book *Up to Now* (London: Oxford University Press; 1929), my account is based on my father's reconstruction of this production on his model stage, which I recorded in 1920. At that time, he also reconstructed the settings for *Acis and Galatea*, *Bethlehem*, *The Vikings*, *Much Ado About Nothing*, and *Hamlet*, working each of them out in detail, with coloured light, gauzes, and figures. He started one day when I asked about *Dido and Aeneas*, and worked on the model continuously for over a month.

12 I have one of Craig's Note-Books entitled "Acis and Galatea 1901–1902" which also contains many of his notes made at an earlier date for *Dido and Aeneas* and *The Masque of Love*, and includes notes in another hand, showing the stage movements for both *Dido* and *Acis*.

13 E.G.C. Personal.

14 Purcell Operatic Society Account Sheet. Author's Collection.

15 E.G.C. Personal.

16 Letter heading in the Author's Collection.

17 ET–EGC Correspondence. Author's Collection.

18 EGC–MFS Correspondence.

CHAPTER SEVEN : 1900–1901

1 EGC–MFS Correspondence.

2 Note-book T. Author's Collection.

3 E.G.C. Personal.

4 EGC–MFS Correspondence.

5 ET–EGC Correspondence. Author's Collection.

6 Original letter in Author's Collection.

7 Prospectus for *The Masque of Love*. Author's Collection.

8 Martin Shaw: *Up to Now*.

9 Max Beerbohm: "Mr Craig's Experiment," article in *The Saturday Review*; reprinted in *Around Theatres* (London: Rupert Hart-Davis; 1953).

10 ET–EGC Correspondence. Author's Collection.

11 Craig, in his book *Index to the Story of My Days*, gives the receipts as £533. 6s. 4d. The box-office returns, which I possess, show them to be £938. 17s. 0d.

12 EGC–MFS Correspondence.

13 Ibid.

14 *The Artist* (December 1901).

15 This Note-book, entitled "Confessions 1901-2-3," contains all the quotations that I have used for the rest of this chapter. It is one of the most interesting and revealing manuscripts. Author's Collection.

CHAPTER EIGHT : 1901–1902

1 Note-Book "Confessions, 1901-2-3." Author's Collection.

2 ET–EGC Correspondence. Author's Collection.

3 Elena Personal and E.G.C. Personal.

4 E.G.C. Personal.

5 Note-book "Confessions, 1901-2-3." Author's Collection.

6 Ibid.

7 Ibid.

8 ET–EGC Correspondence. Author's Collection.

9 EGC–MFS Correspondence.

10 Ibid.

11 E.G.C. Personal and a very careful description related to me by Edith Craig.

12 EGC–MFS Correspondence.

13 ET–EGC Correspondence. Author's Collection.

14 Graham Robertson's preface to *The Art of the Theatre* (London: Foulis; 1905).

15 Note-book with the title "Acis and Galatea 1901-2." Author's Collection. This book also contains sketches, stage movements, and caricatures.

16 E.G.C. Personal.
17 Max Beerbohm: article in *Saturday Review*; reprinted in *Around Theatres*.
18 E.G.C. Personal.
19 MacFall–Craig Correspondence. Author's Collection.
20 Martin Shaw: *Up to Now*. The leading parts in this production were taken by Mr Anderson Nicol, Mr Robert Maitland and Miss Gertrude Woodhall.

CHAPTER NINE: 1902–1903

1 Elena Personal.
2 EGC–MFS Correspondence.
3 E.G.C. Personal.
4 EGC–MFS Correspondence.
5 Interesting correspondence between Craig and Housman on the subject of this production is to be found in the Special Collection of the University of California, Los Angeles.
6 Marguerite Steen: *A Pride of Terrys*.
7 ET–EGC Correspondence. Author's Collection.
8 Elena Personal.
9 Note-book T, which contains plans of the settings and a cast list. Author's Collection.
10 Ibid.
11 EGC–MFS Correspondence.
12 E.G.C. Personal.
13 Edy Personal.
14 Laurence Housman: *Bethlehem, A Nativity Play* (1902). My copy has copious notes by Mrs Dryhurst. I am also indebted to Mr Stanley Scott who has a lot of interesting material on this performance.
15 Edy Craig at one time possessed all the costumes and in 1929 we discussed it in detail. She had very vivid memories of this production and had enjoyed working on it with her brother, who had made use of a lot of her ideas.
16 *Rembrandt. 38 Radiorungen* (Berlin, n.d.). The copy in my collection has notes and sketches by Craig.
17 I am indebted to Mrs Maud Barfield (*née* Douie) for this information.
18 Copy in Author's Collection.
19 E.G.C. Personal.
20 ET–EGC Vikings Correspondence. Author's Collection.
21 Edy Personal.
22 EGC–MFS Correspondence.
23 James Huneker: *Iconoclasts. A Book of Dramatists*. (London: Scribner's; 1905).
24 ET–EGC Vikings Correspondence.
25 Ibid.
26 Ibid.
27 Count Harry Kessler was most impressed by this production and described the last scene to me very clearly. A good idea of the colour and movement in "Leonato's House" can be got from Byam Shaw's drawing of the scene reproduced in *Souvenir of the Ellen Terry Jubilee Commemoration, Theatre Royal, Drury Lane, 1906*.
28 *Ellen Terry and Bernard Shaw, A Correspondence* (London: Reinhardt; 1949).
29 EGC–MFS Correspondence.
30 Count Kessler told me about this period in great detail and I have based my account on his narrative.
31 ET–EGC Correspondence.

CHAPTER TEN: 1904–1905

For this chapter, apart from using the Craig–Otto Brahm Correspondence and the file of General Correspondence for the Years 1904–1905 in my collection, I was able to recall the long conversations on the subject of "Venice Preserved" between Craig and Kessler at Weimar in 1929 when I was helping with the Cranach Press *Hamlet*. Once again the Craig–Martin Shaw Correspondence has been invaluable—as well as the scattered notes among the personal letters between my father and mother, and the ET–EGC Correspondence.

1 File marked "School," Author's Collection. It is interesting to note that "Design" was not listed as a subject to be studied.

2 The reference to losing the "engagement of my life" is typical of Craig. Some one would suggest that it *might* be interesting to do such and such a production one day and Craig would write to his friends announcing, "I am about to produce ..." or, as in this case, because he had written to Kessler saying that he had no intention of being controlled by some archduke, he would take it for granted that all was over.

3 EGC–Otto Brahm Correspondence. Author's Collection. This correspondence is extremely interesting. It is obvious that many misunderstandings arose because Craig found it very difficult to understand German, particularly when written, and most of the letters have attached literal translations made by friends who seem hardly better equipped than Craig himself.

4 Janet Leeper, quoting from Craig's *"small note book crammed with information,"* suggests that Craig left for Germany in July 1903; Craig, in his *Index to the Story of My Days*, suggests that it was in June. Although during both these months he "thought" he might be going, he was, in fact, still at Trafalgar Studios, from where he was writing to Martin and Elena. Worried by his child's death, solicitors letters about rent, impending Divorce Court proceedings, lack of money, and dismal prospects, there is little wonder that, in retrospect, he was confused about dates.

5 EGC–MFS Correspondence. Author's Collection.

6 *Spemans Golden Buch des Theaters* (Berlin, 1902), and Herbert Henze's "Otto Brahm and Naturalist Directing," in *Theatre Workshop* (New York, 1937).

7 This volume, with Craig's notes, in the Author's Collection.

8 Craig–Otto Brahm Correspondence. Author's Collection.

9 Ibid.

10 Ibid.

11 Ibid.

12 An imperfect typescript of this letter does not give the date of publication and I do not know if it was published in full—Craig wrote to his mother saying that it was published "in all the papers." Denis Bablet in *Edward Gordon Craig* (London: Heinemann; 1966) gives an English translation from some German version. Ifan Kyrle Fletcher and Arnold Rood give the date as January 10.

13 Martin Shaw: *Up to Now*.

14 Isadora Duncan: *My Life* (London: Gollancz; 1928).

15 Ibid.

16 For the remainder of this chapter I have referred to Craig's correspondence with Martin Shaw and to Craig's Address Book for the years 1903–7, which also contains notes. But the main source of information comes from a small octavo Note-book with the title "EGC and I.D. 1904–1914. Book Topsy." This book of 114 pages contains Craig's contemporary records of the first and subsequent meetings with Isadora. It is written in great detail and is full of youthful exhilaration. In 1927, 1944, and 1954 he seems to have re-read these pages and added critical remarks.

17 Isadora Duncan: *My Life.*
18 Typescript for B.B.C. radio talk May 31, 1952.
19 Constantin Stanislavsky: *My Life in Art* (London: Geoffrey Bles; 1924).
20 According to Walter Terry's book, *Isadora Duncan, Her Life, Her Art, Her Legacy* (New York: Dodd, Mead; 1963). "Dora Angela Duncan was born in San Francisco on May 27, 1878, and was the fourth child of John Charles and Mary Doray (Gray) Duncan."
21 Although Craig, in old age, wrote about a coach and horses taking them to Potsdam, his note-books only refer to Dr Federn's motor car.
22 "EGC and I.D. 1904–1914. Book Topsy." Author's Collection.
23. Ibid.

CHAPTER ELEVEN: 1905–1906

1 This is an extract from a six-page note which was kept in Craig's Note-book "Confessions, 1901–2–3," Author's Collection. Marked *ID*, it starts with the words, *"Shall I confess to this piece of paper?"*. It is dated "March 3rd," when Isadora decided to go to Hanover on her own.
2 Isadora Duncan: *My Life.*
3 Ibid.
4 EGC–MFS Correspondence.
5 Ibid.
6 Ibid.
7 EGC–ET Correspondence. Author's Collection.
8 Reinhardt–Craig Correspondence. This file also contains letters from Kessler and Magnus, who did their best to promote an understanding between Craig and Reinhardt; these, together with the file of General Correspondence for 1905–1906 and a file of accounts for the same period, are all in the Author's Collection, and, together with the Craig–Martin Shaw Correspondence, have been my chief source of information for this chapter.
9 Reinhardt–Craig Correspondence. Author's Collection.
10 Craig was furious when, one day, he went round to Friedmann and Weber's Gallery and found two young artists making rough sketches of his designs. (EGC Personal.) Probably this silly little incident did more than anything else to estrange Craig from Reinhardt with whom he had been very friendly.
11 Files of Correspondence regarding The Mask 1906–7–8 and Letters from Mr Magnus 1904–5. Author's Collection. Two important publishers who turned down the idea were T. N. Foulis of Edinburgh and Maximilian Schick of Berlin.
12 File of correspondence marked "Berlin 1906–07" with the subheadings: "Insel Verlag," "White Fan," "Isadora Mappe," "Translations of Art of Theatre," "Stumpf," "Various Exhibitions," and "Isadora Tours." Author's Collection.
13 Craig–Duse Correspondence. Author's Collection.
14 EGC–ET Correspondence. Author's Collection.
15 Craig–Duse Correspondence. Author's Collection.
16 This design, reproduced as plate 4 in Janet Leeper's *Edward Gordon Craig* (London: King Penguin; 1948), is now in the Special Collection of the University of California, Los Angeles.
17 I met Maurice Magnus two or three times before his death in 1920, and later was lucky to acquire a lot of his office correspondence covering the period when he worked for Craig and Isadora in Berlin. There are many letters to and from him scattered through all the files of Craig's correspondence between the years 1905 and 1909 and other letters are bound in with my copy of his book *Memoirs of the*

Foreign Legion (London: Martin Secker; 1924). I also have a transcript of his un-published MS "Gordon Craig and His Art," which he wrote in 1907. I have made use of all this material in this chapter.

18 Note-Book "Confessions 1901–2–3." Author's Collection.

19 EGC–MFS Correspondence.

20 Ibid.

21 According to D. H. Lawrence in the preface to *Memoirs of the Foreign Legion*.

22 Craig Personal. Kessler also told me other stories of how Magnus delighted in impressing people. He also regarded him as Craig's "most faithful assistant."

23 The originals of these designs were in my mother's possession; for a while they hung in the Ellen Terry Memorial at Smallhythe until they were handed back to me.

24 EGC–MFS Correspondence.

25 Gordon Craig: *Index to the Story of My Days* (London: Hulton Press; 1957).

26 The manuscript for the original preface is to be found at the beginning of Note-book T. Author's Collection.

27 Gordon Craig: *The Art of the Theatre* (London: Foulis; 1905).

28 At the same time he started a new Note-book entitled "Theatre. Shows and Motions 1905–1908–9"; this is packed with ideas of all kinds for Masques, Motions, Scenes for *Hamlet*, and so on. Author's Collection.

29 These appear in his book *Towards a New Theatre* (London and Toronto: J. M. Dent & Sons; 1913) and in Denis Bablet's *Edward Gordon Craig* (London: Heine-mann; 1966).

30 Correspondence *re On the Art of the Theatre*—this file, in the Author's Collection also contains the publisher's sales returns.

31 EGC–MFS Correspondence.

32 Ibid.

33 Collected Note-books on Isadora. Author's Collection.

34 Isadora Duncan: *My Life*.

35 Martin Shaw, *Up to Now*, Oxford University Press, 1929. This most joyous book, full of biographical material relating to Craig and Isadora, gives an admirable impression of the Craig–Isadora–Shaw collaboration, though Shaw never bothered about dates.

36 Isadora Duncan: *My Life*.

37 Craig–Duse Correspondence. Author's Collection.

38 Years later when I travelled with my father over the same route he told me of the mounting joy that he experienced when he first entered Italy; he described it as a feeling that he was "coming home after a long period at school," and once again quoted whole passages from Goethe.

39 Craig Personal.

40 Enrico Corradini: "L'Arte della Scena" in *Vita d'Arte* (1908). Isadora Duncan also writes rather effusively about this period in her memoirs, *My Life*. I have made use of my father's personal recollections supported by various notes in his Address-book and an unpublished article entitled "Eleonora Duse" (Author's Collection). The original design for the scene seems to have been lost, but another is reproduced in Craig's book *Towards a New Theatre*. Ferruccio Marotti's extensive research on this subject, printed in his volume *Gordon Craig* (Bologna: Cappelli; 1961), has also been very useful.

41 From the leaflet in the Author's Collection.

42 EGC–MFS Correspondence.

43 Gordon Craig: *Index to the Story of My Days*.

44 EGC–MFS Correspondence.

45 Ibid.

46 EGC–Duse Correspondence. Author's Collection.

47 Ibid.
48 Isadora Duncan Correspondence. Author's Collection.
49 Marotti: *Gordon Craig*.
50 EGC–MFS Correspondence.
51 Duncan: *My Life*.
52 Collected Note-books on Isadora Duncan. Author's Collection.

CHAPTER TWELVE: 1906–1912

1 Collected Note-books on Isadora Duncan. Author's Collection.
2 Walter Terry quotes Ted Shawn as saying of Isadora: "She did not dance *to* music. She danced what music did to her . . . she was not particularly concerned with beat or form."
3 E.G.C. Personal.
4 This etching, which is very rare, is known by the title "Little Gate." Marius Bauer's work was always a source of inspiration to Craig, and when I was with him in Holland in 1922 he took me to the Rijks Museum and he spent hours showing me his wonderfully imaginative work.
5 EGC–MFS Correspondence.
6 Ibid.
7 Craig: *Index to the Story of My Days*.
8 Craig Personal.
9 Craig: *Index to the Story of My Days*.
10 Martin Shaw: *Up to Now*. Shaw's description of this episode is delightful but too long to include here.
11 Apart from the Craig–Martin Shaw Correspondence, my references for this part of Craig's life are the files of correspondence dated 1907–8, a file of correspondence marked "The Mask 1906–7–8," another marked "Maurice Magnus *re* The Mask," and a file of Confidential Letters from Dorothy Nevile Lees, part of a long correspondence with me over the five years preceding her sad death in 1966. Knowing that I was preparing a book on Craig, she also wrote me a closely typed 107 page MS account of her work with him during that period of her life which she devoted to helping him run *The Mask*; this file is marked "D.N.L. The Mask." All these files of correspondence are in the Author's Collection.
12 "D.N.L. The Mask." Author's Collection.
13 This prospectus is very rare—copy in Author's Collection.
14 "D.N.L. The Mask." Author's Collection.
15 EGC–MFS Correspondence.
16 This volume is now part of the Rondel Collection in the Bibliothèque de l'Arsenal, Paris. My quotations from his scribbled notes are from a transcription that I made years before.
17 Although Craig's detractors will have noticed that this whole "Movement" seems to take place in the dark, when we experimented with the model of this "scene" in later years the gradual appearance of light gave the effect that he shows us in his etchings.
18 This is reproduced in Janet Leeper's *Edward Gordon Craig, Designs for the Theatre* (Harmondsworth: Penguin Books; 1948), Plate 18. It first appeared in *The Mask* in April 1908 as the work of Julius Oliver!
19 Many of these figures were given by my father to his daughter Nelly, but quite a number are also in the Author's Collection.
20 Collected Note-books on Isadora Duncan. Author's Collection.

21 Craig–Carr Correspondence. Author's Collection.

22 "D.N.L. The Mask." Author's Collection.

23 ET–EGC Correspondence. Author's Collection.

24 An extremely competent master's thesis on "Gordon Craig's Theatre Magazine, The Mask" was prepared by Mrs Lorelei F. Guidry at Tufts University in 1963: in this work the author makes clear, for the first time, how much was written by Craig and how much by other authors.

25 EGC–ET Correspondence. Author's Collection.

26 "D.N.L. The Mask" and Confidential Letters from Dorothy Nevile Lees.

27 "Catalogue of Etchings being designs for Motions by Gordon Craig Florence 1908." Author's Collection.

28 "D.N.L. The Mask." Author's Collection.

29 Constantin Stanislavsky: *My Life in Art.*

30 Ibid.

31 Craig–Reinhardt Correspondence. Author's Collection.

32 Ibid. Had Craig combined forces with Reinhardt instead of with Stanislavsky, the theatre today would have had a richer heritage.

33 Craig–Stanislavsky Correspondence. Author's Collection.

34 "Maurice Magnus re The Mask." Author's Collection.

35 EGC–MFS Correspondence.

36 Ibid.

37 E.G.C.'s Day-book 1. 1908–1910. Author's Collection. This note was written when he was returning to Florence from Moscow in July 1909. When re-reading his Day-book in 1955, he realized that he overlooked his much loved daughter by his wife May, and since then he had grown to love his younger daughter by Daphne, so he added the words "—but I will not forget Rosie and 2.2."

38 Elena Personal and "Arena Goldoni Papers." Author's Collection.

39 EGC–MFS Correspondence.

40 These records appear in the first volume of Craig's Day-books which, from this, period become the receptacle for his daily thoughts on all subjects, as well as a record of the people he met, his projects and his achievements. The 12 volumes of closely written pages that cover the years 1908 to the end of 1943 are in the Author's Collection. My father gave these volumes to me some years before he died, with instructions that I should "censor" some of the comments that he had added after re-reading the books in later years. Apart from the enormous wealth of information contained in these volumes, the entries are often illustrated with little drawings and diagrams, as well as by photographs, theatre tickets, restaurant bills, and all the ephemera that helps to bring the past back to life.

41 EGC–Edith Craig Correspondence. Author's Collection (on the photograph the names are spelt differently and the date is given as "Oct 29 European time").

42 E.G.C. Day-book 1. 1908–10. Author's Collection.

43 Ibid.

44 In Janet Leeper's book *Edward Gordon Craig* there are references to *The Mask* being put "into the safe care of a Robber" . . . "Recovers *The Mask* from the Robber." The file of letters that I possess, entitled "Maurice Magnus and The Mask," does not show that Magnus was in any way "a robber"; he just outsmarted Craig and Craig never forgot it.

45 Craig–Stanislavsky Correspondence. Author's Collection.

46 My personal recollection of Craig's description of this incident when he was discussing *Hamlet* with Kessler in 1929.

47 Collected Note-books on Isadora Duncan. Author's Collection.

48 One set of these recorded conversations is preserved in the Rondel Collection in the Bibliothèque de l'Arsenal, Paris. The other set is in The Museum of the Moscow

Art Theatre, Moscow. Ferruccio Marotti made use of them in a wonderfully reconstructed talk between Craig, Stanislavsky, and others that was given on the Terzo
Programma of the Radiotelevisione Italiana and was published in 1964.
49 David Magarshack: *Stanislavsky. A Life* (London: MacGibbon & Kee; 1950).
Craig considered that this book contained the most accurate account of his attempt
to collaborate with Stanislavsky in Moscow.
50 E.G.C. Personal.
51 EGC–MFS Correspondence. The remaining models were exhibited later: at the
outbreak of World War II they were sold, together with a lot of furniture that had
been stored in a London warehouse for years. I was able to buy back some of this
material when the war ended and two of the models are now in the Special Collection of the University of California, Los Angeles.
52 E.G.C. Day-book 1. 1908–10. Author's Collection.
53 Later, he remade a number of these figures in wood. Many of the original coloured
cardboard figures are in the Special Collection of the University of California,
Los Angeles.
54 E.G.C. Day-book 2. 1910–11. Author's Collection.
55 Gordon Craig: *A Production 1926* (London: Oxford University Press; 1930).
56 Craig–Stanislavsky Correspondence. Author's Collection.
57 E.G.C. Personal. This and many of the other scenes for *Hamlet* I rebuilt for my
father on his model stage. I used photographs as a basis for their reconstruction and
he then lit them, at the same time he described details of the performance in Moscow.
58 E.G.C. Day-book 2. 1910–11. Author's Collection.
59 EGC–MFS Correspondence.
60 Ibid.
61 Ibid.
62 The drawing of this church is in the Author's Collection.
63 E.G.C. Day-book 2. 1910–11. Author's Collection.
64 EGC–MFS Correspondence.
65 Ibid.
66 Ibid.
67 Ibid.
68 Printed invitation in the Author's Collection.
69 E.G.C. Day-book 2. 1910–11. Author's Collection.
70 Ibid.
71 Ibid.
72 David Magarshack: *Stanislavsky: A Life*.
73 Ibid.
74 Ibid.
75 E.G.C. Day-book 2. 1910–11. Author's Collection.
76 EGC–MFS Correspondence.
77 EGC–Edith Craig Correspondence. Author's Collection.
78 Unsigned article in *The Times* (London), January 9, 1912.
79 Elena Personal.
80 E.G.C. Day-book 2. 1910–11. Author's Collection.
81 Ibid.

CHAPTER THIRTEEN: 1912–1917

1 E.G.C. Day-book 2. 1910–11. Author's Collection.
2 This copy-book, known as "The Alassio M.S. Book," has been damaged at some
period by water but is still legible. It forms part of a file with the title "School—
Arena Programme. Model A. E.G.C. 1911–14." Author's Collection.

3 E.G.C. Day-book 3. 1911–19. Author's Collection. This has been the source of information for most of this chapter.

4 This prospectus, together with all other printed matter relating to the School, are in a folder marked "School Printed Matter." Author's Collection.

5 E.G.C. Day-book 2. 1910–11. Author's Collection.

6 *Catalogue of an Exhibition of drawings and models for Hamlet and other plays*, etc., September 1912. Author's Collection.

7 All the information for this last paragraph, together with the quotations from the various letters, are in a file marked "Elena and School," in the Author's Collection. This file also contains some of the "Petty Cash Accounts" for the first year of the School.

8 Typescript of "Announcement to the Press," in the file "Elena and School." Author's Collection.

9 E.G.C. Day-book 3. 1911–19. Author's Collection.

10 EGC–MFS Correspondence.

11 From an account sent to Craig by Fernand Divoire. Among the Collected Notebooks on Isadora Duncan. Author's Collection.

12 William Bolitho: *Twelve against the Gods* (London: Heinemann; 1930).

13 Original letter from E.G.C. to his mother preserved among the Collected Notebooks on Isadora Duncan. Author's Collection.

14 EGC–MFS Correspondence.

15 E.G.C. Day-book 3. 1911–19. Author's Collection.

16 "School Rules," in the file "School, Printed Matter." Author's Collection.

17 The MS outlining the studies for the student-teachers at the School is in great detail and is accompanied by drawings, it is of extreme interest, and forms part of the file "School–Arena Programme—Model A—1911–14. Author's Collection.

18 E.G.C. Personal, and Dorothy Nevile Lees Confidential Correspondence. Author's Collection.

19 Elena's presentation copy of *A Living Theatre* is now in the Special Collection of the University of California, Los Angeles.

20 Author's personal recollections.

21 Ibid.

22 EGC–Elena Correspondence. Author's Collection.

23 E.G.C. Day-book 3. 1911–19. Author's Collection.

24 This abridged version of the letter was copied by Craig and sent to Elena. Author's Collection.

25 EGC–Elena Correspondence. Author's Collection.

26 Ibid.

27 E.G.C. Day-book 3. 1911–19. Author's Collection.

28 EGC–Elena Correspondence. Author's Collection.

29 Ibid.

30 (Maurice Magnus): *Memoirs of the Foreign Legion* (London: Martin Secker; 1924).

31 E.G.C. Personal.

32 E.G.C. Day-book 3. 1911–19. Author's Collection.

33 EGC–Elena Correspondence. Author's Collection.

34 E.G.C. Day-book 3. 1911–19. Author's Collection.

35 Dorothy Nevile Lees Confidential Correspondence. Author's Collection.

36 Correspondence with David Lees. Author's Collection.

37 Many MS notes for these puppet plays, together with some unfinished plays, fill a large folder marked "D for F" (*Drama for Fools*). Author's Collection.

CHAPTER FOURTEEN: 1917–1928

1 E.G.C. Day-book. 1920–29. Author's Collection. This Day-book also contains a number of very amusing photographs of Max, Florence Beerbohm and the Craig family. Apart from my own recollections this "1920–29" volume of E.G.C. Day-books is my chief source of information for this chapter.

2 Copied by Craig on to the first page of his Day-book. 1920–29. Author's Collection.

3 For the number of woodcuts and book-plates that Craig engraved see his two books: *Woodcuts and Some Words* (London and Toronto: J. M. Dent; 1924) and *Nothing—or The Bookplate* (London: Chatto and Windus; 1925).

4 This prospectus was published in French and English and is very rare. There is a copy of the English version in E.G.C. Day-book. 1920–29. Author's Collection.

5 D. H. Lawrence, preface to *Memoirs of The Foreign Legion*, by M. M. (Maurice Magnus) (London: Martin Secker; 1924). Dorothy Nevile Lees Confidential Correspondence in the Author's Collection.

6 In 1925 Norman Douglas published, privately, a booklet of 54 pages, entitled *D. H. Lawrence and Maurice Magnus: A Plea for Better Manners*, in which he referred to Lawrence's preface as "a spleenful hash." He also quotes Mrs Macfadyen's letter to the press.

7 Some years ago this model lay, a sad wreck, in the basement of the Drama League's offices in Fitzroy Square.

8 This correspondence was first published by Craig in his folio volume *A Production 1926* (London: Oxford University Press; 1930).

9 E.G.C. Personal. There is also a very interesting article on the subject of this production in Vol. VII, No. 3 (1966) of *Theatre Research* (published by International Federation of Theatre Research). The article is by Mogens Hyllested and is entitled "The Pretenders: Copenhagen 1926."

10 The copy of this document is in E.G.C. Day-book. 1920–29. Author's Collection.

11 These documents and press cuttings were kept by Craig in a special scrap-book, which he entitled "Sir E. Gordon Craig 1929. A miscarriage of Injustice." Author's Collection.

12 Eighteen pages on this subject are among the Collected Note-books on Isadora. Author's Collection.

13 Gordon Craig: *Ellen Terry and Her Secret Self* (London: Sampson Low, Marston & Co.; 1931).

CHAPTER FIFTEEN: 1928–1946

1 E.G.C. Day-book. 1920–29. Author's Collection.

2 EGC–Edy Craig Correspondence. Author's Collection.

3 E.G.C. Day-book. 1920–29. Author's Collection.

4 Ibid.

5 From the original letter in the Collection of David Lees.

6 In the Author's Collection, apart from the three typescript volumes of unabridged Ellen Terry–Bernard Shaw Correspondence, there is also a file of correspondence between Craig and his sister about the publication of the letters. The correspondence reveals on Craig's side a lot of misunderstanding and bitterness towards Shaw, and groundless fears that his mother's public image might be damaged, while his sister, one gathers, felt that to publish the letters was a businesslike thing to do; she also realized their immense historical interest.

7 The question of illegitimacy preoccupied him so much that he collected press cuttings and, at various times, made notes about his feelings on the subject which he kept in a special envelope now in the Author's Collection.

8 From the file of "Correspondence re: Ellen Terry and her Secret Self." Author's Collection.

9 Ibid.

10 Transcription of the original MS "Tritons and Minnows." Author's Collection.

11 File of Correspondence 1934–36. Author's Collection.

12 E.G.C. Day-book. 1931–33. Author's Collection.

13 Ibid.

14 Elena–EGC Correspondence. Author's Collection.

15 "Confessions 1901–2–3." Author's Collection.

16 Apart from the E.G.C. Day-book 1933–35, there are files of correspondence relating to this "Visit to Rome" and subsequent "Visit to Vienna and Moscow": I have made use of all these documents in this chapter. The files and Day-book, in the Author's Collection.

17 E.G.C. Day-book. 1933–35. Author's Collection. I also have his long and very amusing unpublished article about the meeting.

18 E.G.C. Day-book. 1933–35. Author's Collection.

19 E.G.C. Day-book. 1935. Author's Collection.

20 Ibid.

21 E.G.C. Day-book. 1936–37. Author's Collection.

22 EGC–Elena Correspondence. Author's Collection.

23 E.G.C. Day-book. 1938–39. Author's Collection.

24 From a letter to the Author in which he retold one of the stories.

25 E.G.C. Day-book. 1939–40 War. Author's Collection.

26 E.G.C. Personal.

27 Heinrich Heim Personal Correspondence with the Author.

28 I am grateful to Howard C. Rice for drawing my attention to this Sylvia Beach MS in Princeton University Library, and for allowing me to quote it.

29 E.G.C. Day-book. 1941–43. Author's Collection.

30 Ibid.

31 Ibid.

32 Ibid.

33 Ibid.

34 Ibid.

35 Collected Note-books on Isadora. Author's Collection.

36 EGC–Elena Correspondence. Author's Collection.

37 E.G.C. Correspondence with the Author.

38 Ibid.

39 For information regarding the history of the Gordon Craig Collection I have not only used the E.G.C. Day-books but also a large file entitled "The E.G.C. Collection." This not only contains the correspondence with various libraries and institutions but also details of the sale to Germany—its return to E.G.C. and final sale to the Bibliothèque Nationale. Author's Collection.

40 E.G.C. Correspondence with the Author.

41 Craig–Holloway Correspondence. Author's Collection.

CHAPTER SIXTEEN: 1947–1966

1 Clare Atwood, one of Edith Craig's closest friends, used these words when telling me of my aunt's death and I reported them to my father.

2 E.G.C.'s Correspondence with the Author. Author's Collection.

3 Ibid.

4 E.G.C. Personal.

5 This presentation copy, with inscription is in the Author's Collection.
6 E.G.C.'s Correspondence with the Author.
7 E.G.C. Personal.
8 Ellen Craig's Correspondence with the Author. Author's Collection.
9 Ibid.
10 E.G.C. Personal.
11 E.G.C.'s Correspondence with the Author. Author's Collection.
12 Ibid.
13 Ellen Craig's Correspondence with the Author. Author's Collection.
14 E.G.C.'s Correspondence with the Author. Author's Collection.
15 From C. Walter Hodges's Letter to the Author. Author's Collection.
16 EGC–MFS Correspondence.

GENERAL BIBLIOGRAPHY

In the last few years Ifan Kyrle Fletcher of London and Arnold Rood of New York have completed a bibliography of Gordon Craig's literary works which is so comprehensive that I am saved the task of attempting one here (which would, in any case, run to over a hundred pages): *Edward Gordon Craig, A Bibliography* is published by the Society for Theatre Research. Those who are interested will find in this work details of all the articles as well as the books that Craig wrote, there are also references to the great number of exhibitions of his drawings and wood-engravings held all over the world: I have only referred to a few of these, for so many of his exhibitions were unimportant factors in his life and, like the many magazine articles he wrote, were just a way of making money to keep us all alive. I have, of course, referred to most of his published books at different points in this book.

Apart from the unpublished material mentioned in my introductory note and the sources of reference given at the end of this volume, I would like to mention the following works that I have also consulted during the making of this book.

The Era Almanac, conducted by Edward Ledger, 1868–1900.

The Manual of Domestic Economy, by J. H. Walsh. Routledge. 1861.

The Hornet, a weekly magazine edited by Joseph Hatton, 1866 to 1876.

The Dramatic List, edited by Charles Pascoe. London: David Bogue; 1880.

Herbert's Guide to London. London: Henry Herbert; 1883.

A Dictionary of Drama, by Davenport Adams. London: Chatto and Windus; 1904.

London's Lost Theatres of the Nineteenth Century, by Errol Sherson. London: John Lane; 1925.

Life Was Worth Living—The Reminiscences of W. Graham Robertson. London and New York: Harpers; 1931.

William Nicholson, by Marguerite Steen. London: Collins; 1943.

Ellen Terry and Bernard Shaw—A Correspondence, edited by Christopher St. John. London: Max Reinhardt; 1949.

Edy. Recollections of Edith Craig, edited by Eleanor Adlard. London: F. Muller; 1949.

James Pryde 1866–1941, by Derek Hudson. London: Constable; 1949.

Gordon Craig et le Renouvellement du Théâtre, the catalogue of the Gordon Craig Collection at the Bibliothèque Nationale, Paris, 1962.

GRAMOPHONE RECORDS

Three twelve-inch Records of *"Radio Talks" by Gordon Craig*, issued by Discurio, 1962, consisting of:

"Reminiscences of Ellen Terry"

"On the Old School of Acting"

"Isadora Duncan"

"A note on Masks"

"Celebrities I have met"

"How I played Hamlet at Salford"

Dido and Aeneas, by Henry Purcell. E.M.I. recording of a performance conducted by Sir John Barbirolli, 1966.

Acis and Galatea, composed by Handel. Recording of a performance conducted by Sir Adrian Boult, Éditions de l'Oiseau-Lyre.

Both of the above are issued with librettos that are of great assistance to those trying to revisualize Craig's productions.

Index

In this index GC = Gordon Craig, and all plays, books, etc., with which he was concerned are listed under the entry for "Craig, Gordon"

A Note About the Author

Edward Anthony Craig

was born in London in 1905, the son of Gordon Craig and Elena Meo. He was brought up in the English countryside until the age of three, when he and his mother went to join his father in Italy. At the outbreak of World War I, he returned to England to live with his grandmother, the actress Ellen Terry, at her home in Kent. Under her supervision, he made his first and final appearances on the stage, acting with Ellen Terry in numerous charity matinees. In 1917 he rejoined his father in Rome and remained with him as his "chief assistant" until his own marriage in 1927. Following his marriage, he earned a precarious living in England by painting, wood engraving, and illustrating books; then he went into films as a designer, and also worked on many notable London theatrical productions (including Macbeth *at the Old Vic in 1932, which he designed and produced, and Emlyn Williams's* Night Must Fall, *for which he did the décor). In 1938 he founded the first film school in England, which came to an abrupt end at the outbreak of World War II. He then became art director to the Crown Film Unit (Ministry of Information) and helped to produce such documentaries as* Target for Tonight *and* Western Approaches. *After the war he entered the Rank Organization as supervising art director of the Pinewood Studios. He is now engaged in writing a history of Italian Baroque and Rococo theatre architecture, designing occasional film décors and lecturing on Gordon Craig and on film-making. Edward Craig is a Fellow of the Royal Society of Arts and a member of the Architectural Association. He lives in Buckinghamshire, has two children— Helen and John—and is married to Mary Timewell.*

A Note on the Type

The text of this book has been set on the Monotype in a type face named Bembo. The roman is a copy of a letter cut for the celebrated Venetian printer Aldus Manutius by Francesco Griffo, and first used in Cardinal Bembo's De Aetna of 1495—hence the name of the revival. Griffo's type is now generally recognized, thanks to the researches of Mr. Stanley Morison, to be the first of the old face group of types. The companion italic is an adaptation of a chancery script type designed by the Roman calligrapher and printer Lodovico degli Arrighi, called Vincentino, and used by him during the 1520's.

The book was printed by Universal Lithographers, Inc., Timonium, Maryland, and bound by The Haddon Craftsmen, Inc., Scranton, Pennsylvania.